TOOLS

OF THE

TRADE

TOOLS
OF THE
TRADE

METHODS, TECHNIQUES AND INNOVATIVE APPROACHES IN ARCHAEOLOGY

EDITED BY

JAYNE WILKINS & KIRSTEN ANDERSON

UNIVERSITY OF
CALGARY
PRESS

University of Calgary Press
2500 University Drive NW
Calgary, Alberta
Canada T2N 1N4
www.uofcpress.com

LIBRARY AND ARCHIVES CANADA CATALOGUING IN PUBLICATION

Tools of the trade : methods, techniques and innovative approaches in archaeology / edited by Jayne Wilkins & Kirsten Anderson.

Collection of papers presented at the 37th Chacmool Conference, Nov. 10-13, 2005.
Includes bibliographical references and index.
ISBN 978-1-55238-249-3

    1. Archaeology--Methodology.
I. Anderson, Kirsten, 1978- II. Wilkins, Jayne, 1981-

CC173.T66 2009   930.1028   C2009-900742-8

The University of Calgary Press acknowledges the support of the Alberta Foundation for the Arts for our publications. We acknowledge the financial support of the Government of Canada through the Book Publishing Industry Development Program (BPIDP) for our publishing activities. We acknowledge the financial support of the Canada Council for the Arts for our publishing program.

Cover design by Melina Cusano
Page design and typesetting by Melina Cusano

TABLE OF CONTENTS

tool (tu:l), *sb.*

1. a. 'Any instrument of manual operation' (J.), a mechanical implement for working upon something, as by cutting, striking,
rubbing, or other process, in any manual art or industry;
…

2. *fig.* a. Anything used in the manner of a tool; a thing (concrete or
abstract) with which some operation is performed; a means
of effecting something; an instrument.

(*The Oxford English Dictionary*, 2nd ed., 1989, Clarendon Press, Oxford)

INTRODUCTION

Jayne Wilkins and Kirsten Anderson

From the initial discovery of a site to its final interpretation, archaeologists use a variety of tools to perform each step of their research and analysis. An initial site survey in its most simple form involves pacing through a defined area and noting or collecting surface materials. However, technological advancements throughout the years have expanded the variety of survey tools available, most of which are time-efficient and minimally invasive. For example, remote sensing is a tool that provides archaeologists with the ability to quickly and accurately identify potential site locations using both aerial and ground imaging, often without stepping on the ground.

Once a site has been located, an entirely different suite of tools is required for the recording and collection of archaeological data. Site set up and excavation requires consideration of the type of information to be recorded, the goals of the project, and the research design. Therefore, it is important that the tools selected are both appropriate and effective, whether they are the most advanced or the original tried and true. From its initial establishment, the discipline of archaeology has seen consistent improvement in the accuracy and efficiency of methods of excavation and data-recording. Most recently, archaeologists have started to incorporate instruments such as total stations, global positioning systems, and digital photography (Hester et al. 1997); however, most continue to use traditional methods of paper, pencil, and line level. By combining these approaches, the quality of the information recovered improves and ultimately expands the kinds of research questions that can be investigated.

The analysis and interpretation of archaeological materials forms the final step in the research process. The most basic level of analysis involves identifying the attributes of individual artefacts. This may include, but is not limited to, colour, material, size, shape, and function. On their own, artefacts reveal evidence of their manufacture and use, and when studied together, a group of artefacts may provide information about culture, geographic location, or the associated environment. A complete collection of recovered artefacts can be analyzed at the site level, where it is possible to identify the function of various areas within a site, the spatial organization of activities and features, as well as the potential size and composition of the group that once lived there. Tools incorporated into a site-level interpretation often include spatial analysis, the identification of activity areas, and chronological reconstruction.

Finally, archaeological investigations at the regional level change the focus from individual sites or artefacts to consider the spatial distribution of sites across a defined area, as well as the economic or cultural motivations for their arrangement. Regional analyses generally involve environmental reconstruction, settlement pattern analysis, and/or site location modelling. In recent years, the introduction of computer technology effectively increased the number of regional studies, as accurate interpretations at this level require the manipulation of large amounts of data. Regardless of the level of analysis selected – artefact, site, or region – archaeologists must apply tools based on their suitability for investigating a particular research question.

When new tools are introduced, they are often initially well received but applied to research questions with a specific focus. As these tools continue to gain recognition, new ideas lead to the exploration of creative and innovative applications. It is during this stage that existing limitations emerge, resulting in a period of evaluation and necessary refinement. Geographic Information Systems (GIS) analysis is an excellent example of an archaeological tool that is currently undergoing a period of assessment. The initial success of this tool was followed by grim methodological and theoretical criticisms and accusations of environmental determinism. In response, many archaeologists now work to incorporate aspects of social significance and human agency into their models of settlement patterns, land use, and site location modelling. As new research questions continue to test the boundaries of potential applications, the methods must change to meet the demand. The discipline of archaeology is evolving, and so are the tools we use to learn about the past.

JAYNE WILKINS AND KIRSTEN ANDERSON

THE CONFERENCE

The Chacmool conference is an annual event organized mainly by undergraduate students in the department of archaeology at the University of Calgary, Alberta. The theme of the conference in 2005 was "Tools of the Trade: Methods, Techniques, and Innovative Approaches in Archaeology" and provided the inspiration for this volume. In late 2004, the conference committee solicited papers and symposia on topics related to two cognate themes (1) *tools of the past*, their manufacture, use, and cultural significance, and (2) the *tools of the present*, which are employed by archaeologists to understand the past. The conference organizers envisioned an event that would inspire the discussion of invention and the impact of technology on cultural development, including the origins of tool use, prehistoric technology, innovations in weaponry, agriculture, architecture, and transportation, and the role of trade, exchange, and diffusion in the spread of technological achievements. This element of the meetings was meant to serve as a self-reflexive exploration of technological development given that in recent years, archaeologists have been employing an increasing array of new tools to better interpret the archaeological record. This leads to the second component of the conference, which aimed to bring together scholars and students who wished to discuss the *tools of the present*, the innovative approaches to the analysis of archaeological materials and assemblages.

The conference organizers were surprised by the overwhelming response of archaeologists who wished to discuss archaeological method. It was clear that scholars had responded favourably to the opportunity to discuss the innovative ways in which they had approached the study of past peoples and their archaeological signatures. Thus, sessions at the conference were organized to fulfill the needs of researchers who focused on various geographical locations and cultural timeframes but employed similar methodological approaches. There were a significant number of papers addressing new field methods, experimental approaches, *chaîne opératoires*, stable isotope analysis, microbotanical residue analysis, climate modelling, ancient DNA analysis, space syntax, Geographic Information Systems (GIS), and remote sensing, and sessions were organized according to these topics. As planned, the resulting conference stimulated much conversation and debate regarding these and other archaeological methods and encouraged scholars to address the future role of these methods in the endeavour to understand the human condition via the archaeological record of the past.

With respect to *tools of the past*, the conference was well attended by pal-aeoanthropologists who study the origins and evolution of humanity. Discussions in the plenary session and the session entitled "From Stone to Cell-phone: The Origins and Evolution of Technology" addressed two main topics. First, researchers discussed the evidence for tool use among non-human primates and the implications for our traditional presumption that the use of tools defines humanity and distinguishes us from other animals. Second, researchers addressed the debate surrounding the origins of modern human behaviour and the archaeological signatures associated with it. As originally intended, the conference participants were exposed to a somewhat introspective and self-reflexive perspective on the origins of tool use, technological development, and the means by which we have become the only species to ask the questions: What is it to be us and how can we find out?

THE CONTRIBUTIONS

What follows is a sample of some of the most memorable presentations from the conference provided by a wide range of international archaeologists, senior professors, and students alike. The volume begins with a consideration of the earliest tools used by humans and presents examples of innovative tools used by archaeologists to interpret past human behaviour in regions and time periods as diverse as pre-Columbian Mesoamerica, Plio-Pleistocene Africa, and prehistoric North America. A broad range of interrelated topics and issues are touched upon in this volume:

1. Origins of tool use, culture, and modern human behaviour, primatological studies, cognitive psychology, and macro-evolutionary theory,

2. Analyses at the level of the artefact, technological analyses, experimental archaeology, and *chaînes opératoires,*

3. Qualitative vs. quantitative analyses, ceramic petrography, non-archaeometric and archaeometric approaches to ceramic analysis,

4. Analyses at the level of the molecule, stable isotope analysis and ancient DNA,

5. Archaeological visibility, the role of plants and archaeological 'non-sites',

6. Analysis at the level of the site and beyond, computers, digital mapping, Geographic Information System, and space syntax.

At first glance, the diversity of topics, regions, and time periods may seem vast, but the volume is meant to celebrate the variety inherent in archaeological analysis. It provides examples of innovative approaches that can be modified to address similar concerns in other regions and time periods. As the editors of this volume, we hope to encourage archaeologists to draw from outside fields in their interpretation of archaeological sites; to develop new methods in their consideration of old questions; to ask new questions about the areas in which they work; and to move beyond the established approaches and methods traditionally employed in their region and time period of study.

With respect to the question of tool use origins, two contributors to this volume consider the Oldowan period of African prehistory (2.5 mya–1.4 mya). The Oldowan traditionally represents the earliest-known occurrence of human tool use, the advent of which is usually seen as a massive achievement in human cognitive ability and cultural aptitude. However, primatological studies reveal that tool use and culture, where culture is defined as "socially transmitted innovation" (Van Schaik 2004:139), were probably inherited from a common ancestor before the divergence of the hominid line (McGrew 1992). In this volume, Amber E. MacKenzie reviews the evidence provided by primatological studies of chimpanzee, orangutan, and gorilla populations and raises many interesting questions regarding the perceived importance of tool use in understanding human origins; if tool use doesn't make us unique, then what does? Susan Cachel examines the relationship between the appearance of tool-using behaviour, Oldowan assemblages, and human intelligence. Many traditional explanations for the origins of intelligence in vertebrate animals, especially humans, emphasize the role that social dynamics plays in the development of cognitive complexity (Whiten and Byrne 1997). Cachel, however, argues that attentiveness to the natural and physical environment ('natural history intelligence') may be more pertinent for understanding the evolution of human intelligence. Interestingly, several aspects of Oldowan assemblages (2.5 mya–1.4 mya) exhibit characteristics suggestive of an intimate knowledge of the regional environment and the ability to track resource availability. Cachel suggests that some of these behaviours are consistent with those usually used to identify modern human behaviour in the archaeological record.

Questions regarding the origins of modern human behaviour have received considerable attention over the past decade (Bar-Yosef 2002; Henshilwood and Marean 2003; Marean and Assefa 2005; McBrearty and Brooks 2000, Willoughby 2007). Modern human behaviour is usually recognized in the archaeological record via the presence of incontrovertible art, structural features and elaborate hearths, fishing technology, carved bone and ivory, complex burial practices and other features consistent with contemporary hunter-gatherer groups. These traits appear coeval in the Upper Palaeolithic of Europe but exhibit considerable temporal and spatial variability in the African Stone Age. Pamela R. Willoughby examines the debate surrounding this issue in light of macro-evolutionary theory, posing several questions about the development of human culture: How do we define behavioural modernity? Was the development of behavioural modernity a biological or a cultural process? Was the change gradual or a punctuated event? Continued investigations into these questions and others regarding the origins of tool use, culture, and behavioural modernity are warranted.

As discussed above, archaeologists employ an increasing array of new tools to better interpret the archaeological record and address questions regarding human behaviour. Experimental archaeology is used to generate and test hypotheses and interpretations, based upon archaeological source material, like ancient structures and artefacts. It contributes to Binford's (1977) Middle Range Theory by providing linking arguments between the static archaeological record of the past and the dynamic record of present human behaviour, relationships, and organization. Various experimental approaches incorporate different aspects of artefact replication, performance testing, reverse engineering, and taphonomic effects. Three contributions to this volume use unique experimental approaches that contribute significantly to our understanding of past human behaviour and technology. First, Nick Waber employs experimental research to determine how variance in atlatl length affects throwing distance and accuracy. Performance testing demonstrates the benefits of atlatl use for dart propulsion and provides an adaptive explanation for atlatl length restraints. Eugene M. Gryba and Purple Kumai also employ an experimental approach in their consideration of Glass Buttes obsidian, heat treatment, and use wear, introducing an inventive means by which raw and heat-treated lithic material from the archaeological record might be distinguishable. Via replication, Jason Roe examines the morphological and technological characteristics of Embarras Bipoints from the Northern Plains, which has diagnostic qualities and can be used to further our understanding of culture-history in Alberta. He goes further to suggest that the study of the patterns and anomalies in both the archaeological and the replicative *chaînes opératoires* can help to illuminate the human process of making points. In addition to the use of experimental approaches, these three analyses share their level of analysis – the artefact. They attempt to identify the factors that conditioned human choice during artefact manufacture and address the questions: How did people construct these artefacts and why did they do it that way? They employ experimental archaeology – *the tool of the present* – to further understand the use and manufacture of various *tools of the past*, the atlatl, heat-treated obsidian, and the Embarras Bipoint.

Experimental studies that address the above questions regarding the production of material culture often contribute to *chaîne opératoire* studies. *Chaîne opératoire*, as part of a more general group of archaeological constructs generally described as "sequence models" (Bleed 2001), is used to understand and describe the technological actions and operations of past systems and more often than not, stone tool production. There have been three related but somewhat independent approaches employed by archaeologists in various regions of the world. In Japan, *gihō*, literally translated as "*technique*," focuses on identifying the sequence of linked technological actions, or the routine of stone tool production. This routine is culturally determined, and as such, exhibits variation across geographic space. In France, *chaîne opératoire*, or "chain of operations" describes the technological actions and human process involved in the raw material procurement, production, use, maintenance, and discard of material culture items, while emphasizing the underlying cognitive process or grammar (Bleed 2001; Inizan et al. 1999; Leroi-Gourhan 1943). In North America, the concept of *sequence modelling* usually involves the manipulation of morphological or typological categories from the archaeological record that relate to different production stages (i.e., blank, preform, finished product). The emphasis is breaking down the presupposition that the final form of all lithic remains represents the intended products of the toolmaker.

Stone tool reduction is a continuous and dynamic process, and consequently, a significant amount of variation in stone-tool size and form owes to reduction, use, and retouch. For example, Oldowan cobbles become discoids and then become scrapers (Sahnouni et al. 1997). But reduction is a continuous process, and as Michael J. Shott puts it, defining types among these tools can be "like slicing a piece of water from a flowing stream" (Shott, this volume). Here, Shott presents a means by which the degree of lithic reduction can be quantified on a continuous scale, and the effects of attrition and chance identified, using samples of Midwestern North American Palaeoindian bifaces and endscrapers. Reduction analysis explains variation at the level of the tool and the assemblage in terms of curation, or tool utility, rather than tool function. The quantification methods presented by Shott may one day become standard tools of the trade in sequence modelling or *chaîne opératoire* studies of stone tool production.

Another contributor considers the *chaîne opératoire* of material culture, but in this case the objects of study are ceramic. Meaghan M. Peuramaki-Brown uses ceramic petrography to understand the pot production in pre-Columbian Honduras. The presence of potstands, which are produced from old ceramic products and maintain on them the remains of wet pots, provide a unique opportunity for the analysis of pot manufacture at the site of Rancho del Rio. Petrographic analysis reveals that some materials not available in the immediate area were included in the ceramics manufactured on site, bringing up interesting questions regarding inter- and intra-valley trade of temper products and schist in pre-Columbian Honduras. Studies such as Peuramaki-Brown's demonstrate how *chaîne opératoire* studies can shed light on the socio-economic and cultural characteristics of past peoples.

The analytical tools used by ceramicists and all other archaeologists are continually changing. Established methods are often replaced by new technology that promises to revolutionize our way of thinking; however, most would caution against the complete abandonment of traditional methodology. In an evaluation of pottery manufacturing traditions of the Peten Postclassic Maya, Leslie Cecil argues for the importance of both archaeometric and non-archaeometric methods. Each approach offers specific advantages for the analysis and understanding of ceramics. The introduction of innovative approaches such as archaeometric analyses expands the variety of data that can be acquired, as demonstrated by Peuramaki-Brown's petrographic study of Honduran ceramics discussed above. Indeed, the true utility of an analytical tool is demonstrated by the ability to improve current knowledge. As Cecil suggests, success occurs when several approaches are combined, creating well-rounded conclusions and a more complete understanding of the past.

The introduction of advanced and highly specialized tools provides researchers with an opportunity to reach a new stage of analysis at the artefact level – the molecule. With these new tools, archaeologists have the potential to revisit past conclusions, often resulting in completely new and unexpected interpretations. The use of stable isotope analysis in archaeology has demonstrated continued utility, expanding beyond questions of diet and subsistence patterns. In an investigation of spire lopped *Olivella biplicata* beads, Tobin Bottman tests three models of trade routes associated with the northern Great Basin. Oxygen and carbon isotopes are analyzed to determine the probable coastal origin of shell beads found at sites within the interior. Surprisingly, the results support the model based on a trade network that was previously thought to involve only the southwestern portion of the Great Basin (Bennyhoff and Hughes 1987). The results of this study demonstrate both the potential significance of stable isotope analysis for this type of research, as well as the importance of applying innovative research tools to test and potentially redefine our current understandings.

The molecular analysis of ancient DNA has dramatically improved our understanding of the genetic relationships within prehistoric populations, migration patterns, animal and plant domestication, and the relationship between modern humans and our extinct ancestors (Stone 2000). As the methods of data collection and analysis continue to improve, research questions have begun to explore exciting and diversified topics. While the original focus of molecular ancient DNA analysis was the understanding of human populations, Maria Victoria Monsalve and her colleagues take ancient DNA analysis in an entirely different direction. In their paper, Monsalve et al. explore the utility of ancient DNA analysis for species and sub-species identification among the remains of butchered animals from a precontact kill site near the town site of Banff, Alberta, and Rocky Mountain House National Historic Site. Due to the fractured nature and poor preservation of faunal assemblages from kill sites, comparative methods of zooarchaeological analysis seldom identify fragments to species level. Molecular analysis successfully identified elk and moose, with elk being tentatively identified to the sub-species level. The benefits of this study move beyond traditional archaeological application, as the accurate identification of prehistoric animal populations may assist in understanding and managing modern ungulate populations.

As the methods archaeologists use to explore the past continue to improve the way research questions are analyzed, they also allow us to consider components of the archaeological record that may have been previously overlooked. One of the most important examples concerns the role of plants in the archaeological record. Previous research has tended to overlook plant materials in favour of more highly visible and well-preserved materials such as stone, ceramics, and fauna. However, the recent expansion of methods has begun to identify plant remains in various archaeological contexts. In a discussion of subarctic Athapaskan and northern Northwest Coast cultures, Leslie Main Johnson reviews the archaeological evidence associated with plant use, including the role of different species. Johnson's paper confirms the importance of plants to the resource base, while showcasing the variety of unique and unconventional ways in which plant use can be identified archaeologically.

Another example of visibility in the archaeological record focuses on the site or regional level of archaeological analysis. Sites are often identified as highly visible material concentrations, which can reveal substantial information about the use of a specific area throughout the period of occupation. However, difficulty arises when attempting to understand movement throughout a region using a small number of well-defined site locations. Alternatively, small artefact scatters, or *non-sites* (Brady, this volume) have the potential to reveal new information with respect to regional mobility and settlement patterns. Surface survey has been an invaluable tool for the identification of archaeological sites; however, it can also be utilized as a method for identifying small, less visible artefact scatters. Ryan T. Brady refines traditional surface survey to understand the distribution of stone artefacts associated with wetland habitats across the Great Basin. Previous research has suggested two models associated with the use of wetland habitat, both of which Brady argues are overly simplistic. The results of the non-site survey indicate variation in the intensity of use among freshwater, brackish, and saline wetlands, as well as differences associated with the types of activities performed at specific areas and elevations. It also highlights the importance of innovation in the attempt to increase and improve our understanding of regional settlements and subsistence patterns.

Settlement pattern analysis, along with many aspects of archaeological research, has been greatly facilitated by the introduction of computer technology. Computers have brought about one of the greatest revolutions in archaeology with respect to storing, sharing, and analyzing data. Not only have computers increased the quantity and quality of information that can be processed, they have also had a profound influence on the types of questions archaeologists are able to ask and answer.

In recent years, one of the areas of archaeology that has seen the greatest impact has been spatial analysis. Three main areas of research: (1) regional and intra-site spatial analysis, (2) site location modelling for cultural resource management, and (3) landscape archaeology have come to rely on computer technology to address questions associated with our understanding of the cultural landscape. Perhaps one of the greatest innovations driving the refinement and expansion of spatial analysis has been the introduction of Geographic Information Systems (GIS), which have completely changed the role of spatial data and cartographic display (Knoerl 1991). Specifically, GIS analysis is a powerful research tool for the input, mathematical manipulation, analysis, capture, retrieval, and display of spatially referenced real-world data (Fisher 1999; Kvamme 1989).

GIS analysis has demonstrated continued success and expanding utility for archaeological applications, but its rapid integration has often been criticized for resulting in an absence of critical evaluation. The sophisticated nature of the technology has the potential to dictate research and the questions asked of the data (Allen et al. 1990). Therefore, it is important to focus research questions on the archaeological record and avoid compromising data in favour of the method. Archaeologists must also consider the costs associated with equipment and technical training, the quality of data analysis, and the availability of existing digital data. While graphical representations provide an excellent medium for display, the results can lead to the creation of impressive, detailed images without true analytical value. Go Matsumoto discusses some of the difficulties associated with GIS and digital mapping at the archaeological site of Pachacamac on the Peruvian central coast. In his paper, Matsumoto highlights the problems encountered during the collection and manipulation of data, while offering a number of suggestions for the future improvement of data quality and access among archaeologists.

One of the most recent advances in spatial analysis has been the growing awareness of the cultural importance of landscape. Two computer applications, cost surface analysis (GIS) and space syntax (Hillier and Hanson 1984) have been used to address cultural perceptions of space at the site and regional levels of analysis. Previous studies of landscape tended to focus on the distribution of resources or sites from an environmental and ecological perspective without consideration of the underlying social motivations of human settlement and movement. For example, cost surface analysis creates a computerized model of the landscape and evaluates the costs of movement associated with any number of specified variables. Until recently, cost surface was restricted to the evaluation of movement associated with physical costs (vegetation, elevation, slope, etc.). However, social costs such as religion or social structure play an equally important role in the movement of people across the landscape. In an evaluation of trade and exchange systems in ancient Egypt, José Roberto Pellini incorporates both physical and cultural factors into a cost surface analysis of ceramic circulation maps. His study demonstrates the important role of social factors in his region of study and beyond.

Following the theories of Bourdieu (1977) and Giddens (1984), which discuss the role of social organization in everyday life, space syntax analysis operates under the assumption that all space is socially constructed. Space syntax examines the construction of buildings with respect to the types of spatial boundaries they create. Within buildings, this may include the degree of accessibility associated with particular rooms as dictated by the arrangement of doors and hallways, while the space outside buildings is determined by the arrangement of physical structures, resulting in differential accessibility and defined areas of private and public space. Following the principles of space syntax, Joshua Wells examines changes in the organization of space throughout the Dohack and Range phases of the Terminal Late Woodland. Changes in the arrangement of built and open space reveal evidence for changes in social organization. Specifically, Wells identifies distinct differences in the arrangement of private and communal space during each phase, with the later Range phase developing patterns similar to those of the succeeding Mississippian period. As Wells suggests, this type of research may have greater potential for understanding the development and spatial distribution of Mississippian culture and influence.

As outlined by the principles of space syntax, the interior organization of buildings has the potential to reveal important information regarding social interaction. A variation of space syntax, spatial string-matching, uses the arrangement and function of different rooms from known cases (e.g., a well-preserved building) as a comparative method for identifying similarities in unknown cases. This process has the potential to reveal information about the intended function or use of poorly preserved buildings. As a result, buildings that were previously ignored or excluded can contribute to the interpretation of social organization. Ciler Kirsan and Ruth Conroy Dalton use the process of spatial string-matching to examine vernacular houses from rural Cyprus. In cases where the function and/or layout of a particular room is unknown, Kirsan and Conroy Dalton employ spatial-string matching to make predictions based on the level of similarity to known cases.

The papers included in this volume are a sample of the variety of analytical tools currently being applied in archaeological analysis. Each demonstrates how innovative tools used today answer challenges of the past and raise new questions for the future. Archaeology as a discipline has undergone many transformations and will no doubt continue to advance. Therefore, it is with great anticipation that we wait to revisit this topic in the years to come.

Acknowledgments. The editors would like to thank all the conference participants and session chairs that responded so enthusiastically to the 2005 Chacmool theme, encouraging discussion and debates involving 'tools of the trade.' Thanks are also owed to all the members of the conference organizing committee, especially the undergraduate conference coordinator Jennifer Evans, the faculty advisors Gerald Oetelaar and Scott Raymond, department head Anne Katzenberg, department administrator Nicole Ethier, and the countless student volunteers. We would also like to thank all those involved in the publication of this volume, Gerald Oetelaar and Scott Raymond for their continued guidance and advice, Sonia Zarillo for her help with the project, the Chacmool Archaeological Association, the Department of Archaeology, the University of Calgary Press, and, of course, the contributors.

REFERENCES CITED

Allen, K.M.S, S.W. Green, and E.B.W. Zubrow

1990   Interpreting Space: GIS and Archaeology. Taylor and Francis, London.

Bar-Yosef, Ofer

2002   The Upper Paleolithic Revolution. Annual Review of Anthropology 31(1):363.

Bennyhoff, James A., and Richard E. Hughes

1987   Shell Bead and Ornament Exchange Networks between California and the Western Great Basin. Anthropological Papers, vol. 64, pt. 2. American Museum of Natural History, New York.

Binford, Lewis R. (editor)

1977   For Theory Building in Archaeology. Academic Press, New York.

Bleed, Peter

2001   Trees or Chains, Links or Branches: Conceptual Alternatives for Consideration of Stone Tool Production and Other Sequential Activities. Journal of Archaeological Method & Theory 8(1):101.

Bourdieu, Pierre

1977   Outline of a Theory of Practice. Cambridge University Press, Cambridge.

Fisher, Peter F.

1999   Geographic Information Systems: Today and Tomorrow? In Geographical Information Systems and Landscape Archaeology, edited by Matt Gillings, David Mattingly, and Jan van Dalen, pp. 5–11. Oxbow Books, New York.

Giddens, Anthony

1984   The Constitution of Society: Outline of the Theory of Structuration. Polity Press, Cambridge.

Henshilwood, Christopher S., and Curtis. W. Marean

2003   The Origin of Modern Human Behavior. Current Anthropology 44(5):627–651.

Hester, Thomas R., Harry J. Shafer, and Kenneth L. Feder

1997   Field Methods in Archaeology, 7th ed. Mayfield Publishing, London.

Hillier, Bill, and Julienne Hanson

1984   The Social Logic of Space. Cambridge University Press, Cambridge.

Inizan, Marie-Louise, Michèle Reduron-Ballinger, Hélène Roche, and Jacques Tixier

1999   Technology and Terminology of Knapped Stone. CREP, Nanterre.

Knoerl, John J.

1991   Mapping History using Geographic Information Systems. The Public Historian 13(3): 97–107.

Kvamme, Kenneth L.

1989   Geographic Information Systems in Regional Archaeological Research and Data Management. In Archaeological Method and Theory, vol. 1, edited by M.B. Schiffe, pp. 139–203. University of Arizona Press, Tucson.

Leroi-Gourhan, André

1943   Evolution and Techniques 1: L'homme et la matière. Albin Michel, Paris.

Marean, Curtis. W., and Zelalem Assefa

2005   The Middle and Upper Pleistocene African Record for the Biological and Behavioral Origins of Modern Humans. In African Archaeology: A Critical Introduction, edited by A. B. Stahl pp. 93–129. Blackwell Publishing, Malden, MA.

McBrearty, Sally, and Alison. S. Brooks

2000   The Revolution That Wasn't: A New Interpretation of the Origin of Modern Human Behavior. Journal of Human Evolution 39(5):453–563.

McGrew, William C.

1992   Chimpanzee Material Culture: Implications for Human Evolution. Cambridge University Press, New York.

Sahnouni, Mohamed, Kathy Schick, and Nicholas Toth

1997   An Experimental Investigation into the Nature of Faceted Limestone Spheroids in the Early Palaeolithic. Journal of Archaeological Science 24:701–713.

Stone, Anne C.

2000   Ancient DNA from Skeletal Remains. In Biological Anthropology of the Human Skeleton, edited by M. Anne Katzenberg, and Shelley R. Saunders, pp. 351–371. Wiley-Liss, New York.

Van Schaik, Carel

2004   Among Orangutans: Red Apes and the Rise of Human Culture. Harvard University Press, Cambridge, MA.

Whiten, Andrew, and Richard W. Byrne (editors)

1997   Machiavellian Intelligence II: Extensions and Evaluations. Cambridge University Press, Cambridge.

Willoughby, P. R.

2007   The Evolution of Modern Humans in Africa: A Comprehensive Guide. African Archaeology Series. AltaMira Press, Lanham, MD.

1

Great Ape Tool Use and the Oldowan

Amber E. MacKenzie

Abstract. The manufacture and utilization of tools have long been attributed to the hominin line and were often used as a means to differentiate between ourselves and the other primates. However, in recent decades, the discovery that other great apes engage in such innovation disrupted previous notions of what makes our phylogenetic line so unique. Not only do chimpanzees and orangutans make use of floral material for various functions, chimpanzees have additionally been found to utilize stone on stone methods for food extraction. This recent observation, whether derived or ancestrally predisposed, has provided an ethnological link to the Oldowan, the earliest known archaeological culture appearing approximately 2.5 Mya. This paper is a comparison of the form and function of the Oldowan and the 'tools' that are currently being manufactured by modern non-human great apes. The insights drawn from these comparisons may provide a means to further understand the motivations that plagued our ancestors 2.5 Mya and, furthermore, may help to clarify the characteristics that define us as distinct from the other primates.

INTRODUCTION

The advent of the Oldowan tool industry (2.5 mya–1.5 mya) has often been cited as an advancement in the mental complexity of the hominin line (Van Schaik 2004:183), that consequently cascaded our Pleistocene ancestors further into modernity. However, evidence emerging from more recent work in primatology is countering this claim. The evidence suggests that contemporary non-human great apes exhibit a mental capacity equivalent to Oldowan hominins in terms of tool[1] use and manufacture (Wynn and McGrew 1989:388), and thus that the Oldowan archaeological industry was merely an extension of a pre-existing primate mental template (Van Schaik 2004:154). These studies, which have emerged in recent decades, have focused on the capabilities of the non-human great apes to manufacture and use tools in captivity and in the wild, focusing in particular on the chimpanzee (*Pan troglodytes*) (Alp 1997; Celli et al. 2004; McGrew 1992; Mercader et al. 2002; Povinelli 2000; Van Lawick-Goodall 1967; Whiten and Boesch 2001; Wynn and McGrew 1989), orangutan (*Pongo pygmaeus*) (Van Schaik 2004), bonobo (*Pan paniscus*) (Hohmann and Fruth 2003), and more recently the gorilla (*Gorilla gorilla*) (Breuer et al. 2005). Although some researchers feel it is inappropriate to use modern non-human great apes to infer Oldowan hominin behaviour and mentality (Povinelli 2000:1–2; Marks 2002:179), there are many who regard this form of ethnology as a useful mechanism with the potential to reveal more about the human evolutionary path than ethnological research based solely on contemporary humans (Van Lawick-Goodall 1967:91; Wynn and McGrew 1989:384; Whiten and Boesch 2001:60).

According to Kimura (1999:807), the current model of Oldowan technology consists of a 'least-effort strategy,' controlled primarily by raw material access and abundance. Evidence for this model can be seen in certain Oldowan archaeological sites, including sites in Omo, Ethiopia, and Koobi Fora, Kenya, where the artefact assemblages consist primarily of local and hence easily attainable raw materials, such as quartz and lava, respectively (Kimura 1999:808). One would surmise that if the Oldowan hominins were indeed slaves to their environment, then the contemporary non-human great apes who potentially rival their Oldowan cousins technologically (at least in terms of mental capacity) (Wynn and McGrew 1989:388) would similarly be indebted to their environment for their technological prowess. On the contrary, this does not

AMBER E. MacKENZIE

seem to be the case. Evidence is mounting that culture[2] may prove as equally influential as environment in terms of primate tool use and manufacture, based on modern reports of chimpanzee (McGrew 1992; Alp 1997; Whiten and Boesch 2001), orangutan (Van Schaik 2004), and bonobo (Hohmann and Fruth 2003) cultural activity within a technological context. Our knowledge of the gorilla tool-kit (Breuer et al. 2005) is quickly rivalling the chimpanzee, although the influence of culture on the technology of wild gorillas has yet to be demonstrated conclusively. The cultural idiosyncrasies observable in modern great apes combined with the lack of evidence for a 'tool culture'[3] in the Oldowan archaeological industry suggest a paradox that must be examined in the light of recent primatological evidence. Thus, this paper examines the 'tool cultures' of various communities of chimpanzees, bonobos, and orangutans, in an attempt to determine the level of cultural influence on the tool-kit of the Oldowan hominins in the absence of archaeological evidence.

EVIDENCE FOR CHIMPANZEE TOOL CULTURE

According to Whiten and Boesch (2001:60), each community of chimpanzees exhibits its own culture to such a degree that one can distinguish where an individual chimpanzee comes from based solely on his or her behavioural tendencies. It seems as though every community of chimpanzees has developed its own unique method to accomplish the same functional objective (Whiten and Boesch 2001:60).

An excellent example of chimpanzee cultural variation is given by McGrew (1992:180). Populations of chimpanzees in Gombe, Tanzania, and another in Kasoje, Tanzania, share a common genotype, and a nearly identical habitat. Each group makes use of an extensive tool-kit that overlaps to a degree but also exhibits a significant amount of variation. There is enough variation between these two populations to warrant evidence for cultural influence on chimpanzee technology (McGrew 1992:180). According to McGrew (1992:180), the Gombe community of chimpanzees engages in the use of eleven different habitual patterns of tool use, while the Kasoje community engages in only eight separate habitual patterns. Five of the tool use patterns habitual to the Gombe chimpanzees are absent in the Kasoje community, including the ant-dip, honey-dip, leaf-sponge, leaf-napkin, and the self-tickle patterns (McGrew

1992:180). Furthermore, two new patterns of habitual tool use have emerged in the Kasoje community that are absent in the Gombe group, including the ant-fish, and the leaf-clip patterns (McGrew 1992:180). Hence, there exist two different groups of genetically related chimpanzees, inhabiting nearly identical niches, that developed two unique methods for subsistence and comfort (self-tickle and leaf-napkin) despite environmental similarity.

Another example of technological variation shaped by culture among the chimpanzees can be seen in Alp's (1997:45) observations of technological in-novation among the Tenkere chimpanzees of Sierra Leone. This particular community has developed two novel habitual tool forms. Alp (1997:45) refers to one of the novel tool forms as "stepping-sticks," which involves the use of loose sticks as foot protection against the thorny kapok trees while climbing and standing during foraging behaviour. The other, which Alp (1997:45) refers to as "seat-sticks," involves the use of sticks to protect the body from the thorns of the kapok tree while seated and subsisting. According to Alp (1997:45–46), chimpanzees subsist on the kapok tree in many locations, including Bossou, Guinea, and Mont Assirik, Senegal; however, there are no records of this form of technology in any of these localities. Thus, culture must be the agent respon-sible for the emergence of these novel variations in the tool-kit of these West African chimpanzees.

EVIDENCE FOR BONOBO TOOL CULTURE

Not surprisingly, the bonobo shares a similar tool-kit with the chimpanzee, while continuing to maintain their own species variations (Hohmann and Fruth 2003:564). Like the chimpanzee, bonobos exhibit a significant cultural influ-ence over their tool-kits. According to Hohmann and Fruth (2003:568–569), the Wamba community of bonobos in the Democratic Republic of the Congo make use of a leaf rain hat to protect themselves from the rain during the rainy season, while the Lomako bonobos of the same nationality do not. Both regions share a similar annual rainfall, temperature, and available vegetation. Alter-natively, Lomako bonobos cover their bodies with twigs and leaves at night to guard against the incessant rain (Hohmann and Fruth 2003:568). Thus, the Wamba and the Lomako populations of bonobos developed two very different tool strategies to achieve the same means in similar ecological conditions. Like the chimpanzee, this condition infers the influential presence of culture on the bonobo tool-kit.

Evidence for Orangutan Tool Culture

Unfortunately the orangutan has often been overlooked in the study of human evolution, possibly as a result of the seemingly low frequency of tool production by wild orangutans (Van Schaik 2004:137). It is only recently that technologically proficient orangutans have been discovered in the wild (Van Schaik 2004:137). Additionally, orangutans are now known to contribute to the great ape tool culture debate alongside the chimpanzee and bonobo.

According to Van Schaik (2004:138), nearly all of the orangutans that belong to the Suaq community on Sumatra utilize two forms of tools to extract insects and honey from trees and the seeds from the thorny cemengang fruit. However, not one orangutan from the Ketambe population of Sumatra engages in such tool use. Furthermore, Van Schaik (2004:145) discusses the Singkil, Sumatra, community of orangutans who use a peeled-stick tool to extract the seeds from the thorny cemengang fruit. This same kind of tool use is observed in orangutan populations on distant Borneo. However, directly across the river from the peeled-stick tool using Singkil population is the Batu-Batu community of orangutans that do not make use of tools to extract the seeds from the cemengang fruit. Instead the Batu-Batu orangutans rely on brute force to smash the fruit and extract the calorie-rich seeds. Van Schaik (2004:145) contends that only a cultural explanation could cede a logical conclusion in a situation where two communities of orangutans, one knowledgeable in the use of tools, and the other reliant on brute force tactics, could inhabit an identical environmental niche merely a few kilometres away from one another. The river in this case serves as a geological barrier between the two communities, blocking the diffusion of group innovation. In addition, the independent emergence of peeled-stick tool use in Borneo is highly suggestive of the innovative capabilities of the wild orangutan.

Significant evidence exists for the presence and affect of culture on the technology of most of the great apes. Evidence for the technological and cultural capacity of the gorilla is expected to increase in the near future as research increases in this area. The Gombe and Kasoje chimpanzees, along with the

Wamba and Lomako bonobos, and the Singkil and Batu-Batu orangutans, exhibit cultural variation where one would expect to see congruency if environment was the only influential factor. Thus, a sense of cultural significance is established with respect to the technological capabilities of the non-human great apes. The lack of evidence for this form of cultural influence on the Oldowan archaeological industry of our hominin forbearers is unexpected, given modern great ape potential and known capabilities, and therefore deserves further discussion.

THE OLDOWAN PARADOX

The earliest reliable estimates for the appearance of the Oldowan Industrial Complex are known from the Gona region of Ethiopia, dating as far back as 2.5–2.6 mya (Semaw 2000:1197). However, numerous Oldowan localities have been discovered in both eastern and southern Africa, spanning a chronological range of approximately one million years. Among the most notable of these localities are Olduvai Gorge in Tanzania, Koobi Fora, Kenya, and the Omo River Valley of Ethiopia. The production of Oldowan technology, consisting primarily of cores, flakes, hammerstones, and manuports, is most commonly attributed to *Homo habilis*. However, additional fossil humans contemporaneous with *H. habilis*, such as *Paranthropus robustus* and *Paranthropus boisei*, have also been found in association with Oldowan stone tools (Klein 1999:235–236). Regardless of which early human ancestor was responsible for the emergence and subsequent production of Oldowan technology, there remains a lack of archaeological evidence to support the presence of a tool culture equivalent to that observed among contemporary great apes.

According to Kimura (1999:808), the influence of raw material selection, and therefore environment, on the Oldowan cannot be exaggerated based on available archaeological evidence. For example, localities such as Omo, Senga (Kimura 1999:808), and the lower levels of Koobi Fora (Toth 1987:770) exhibit a 97 per cent frequency of localized raw materials in their artefact assemblages. De la Torre's (2004:439–465) re-examination of the Omo material (consisting primarily of angular fragments and flakes) further substantiates Kimura's (1999:808) earlier claims of the fundamental influence of the environment on Oldowan stone tool production. According to de la Torre (2004:453), the selec-

AMBER E. MACKENZIE

tion of raw material and knapping patterns observed at Omo 123 and Omo 57 suggest a sophisticated knowledge of tool production in response to environmental conditions. Furthermore, de la Torre (2004:454) describes the apparent 'technocultural homogeneity' of early Oldowan archaeological deposits, an attribute which would seem to contradict the evidence provided by recent primatological observations of great ape behaviour.

On the other hand, Kimura (1999:809) notes that Olduvai Gorge exhibits an alternative pattern of raw material procurement. Lava and quartz are the most frequently exploited materials at Olduvai, with chert following close behind (Kimura 1999:809). According to Kimura (1999:809), raw materials at Olduvai Gorge are not proportional to the artefact classes present in the assemblages. Kimura (1999:809) believes that these disproportionate representations suggest that certain raw materials were chosen for certain types of artefacts. Stout et al. (2005:373) observed a similarly disproportionate selection of raw materials at Gona, Ethiopia, suggesting that preferential selection of raw materials was present 2.5 mya, among the earliest makers of stone tools. Variable preference for raw materials may be related to cultural variation in tool production. However, the above evidence alone does not suggest a cultural model of Oldowan technology; in fact, it can just as equally suggest the opposite, that the raw material itself was selected for based on material characteristics relevant to the manufacture of stone tools (environmental factors), as was suggested by Stout et al. (2005:375).

Isotope analysis on more than 30,000 pieces of chert found in level MNK-FC (1.65–1.53 mya) of Olduvai Gorge, suggest that Oldowan hominins may have transported all of this chert from further south, even though chert was readily available within the gorge (Kimura 1999:811). Unfortunately, Kimura (1999:811) adds that isotope analysis on chert is often variable, and thus the large sample of chert may actually be from within the gorge. If on the other hand the isotope analysis is correct, the transportation of chert from outside of Olduvai Gorge may suggest a cultural influence on tool production during the Oldowan. In other words, it seems illogical for a community of hominins to import such a vast quantity of material into the gorge, when the same material was already easily available, unless there was some degree of cultural motivation involved.

It is impossible at this time to determine regional cultural variation in the Oldowan using the same method employed on the previously examined great apes because you cannot isolate an instance of time where two separate groups coexisted, due to the inaccuracy of the current dating methods. However, despite the lack of archaeological corroboration and support from researchers (e.g., de la Torre 2004:454), there remains strong phylogenetic evidence to support the existence of an Oldowan tool culture.

Based on a consensus tree of over one hundred hypotheses of primate phylogenetic relationships, Purvis (1995) arranges the great apes into clades, such that the orangutan is the first to diverge from the last common ancestor of all the great apes, followed by the gorilla, and then the chimpanzees (common chimpanzee and bonobo), with whom we share the most recent common ancestor. As was demonstrated above, the orangutan, the chimpanzee, and the bonobo exhibit a culturally varied repertoire of technological forms. In this instance, it is most parsimonious to assume that the common ancestor of these great apes also possessed this behaviour, as opposed to each of the apes developing these behavioural tendencies in parallel. It is therefore rational to conclude that Oldowan hominins, such as *H. habilis*, also retained this ancestral cultural behaviour and had the potential to produce a regionally diversified tool-kit 2.5 mya, independent of environmental influence.

The regional diversification of technology is commonly perceived as an archaeological landmark indicating behavioural modernity in early humans (McBrearty and Brooks 2000:492). However, the presence of this form of cultural behaviour among modern great apes suggests that its use as an indicator of modern human behaviour should be considered in the context of degree rather than kind. In addition, the phylogenetic evidence detailed above lends support to the model proposed by McBrearty and Brooks (2000:486) that envisions a gradual development in the complexity of human behaviour over a long period of time, in opposition to the more punctuated model of a human cultural 'revolution.' At the very least, there is strong evidence to suggest that the human cultural condition is merely an elaboration of an ancestral primate trait and not a uniquely derived human attribute as previously considered.

CONCLUSION

Chimpanzees, including those belonging to the Gombe and Kasoje populations (McGrew 1992:66–72) and the Tenkere community (Alp 1997:45), all readily demonstrate the presence and affect of culture on chimpanzee tool production. Likewise, the Wamba and Lomako bonobos (Hohmann and Fruth 2003:568–569) and the Singkil and Batu-Batu orangutans (Van Schaik 2004:145) also demonstrate the influence of culture on their respective tool-kits. The presence of this innovative behaviour in the majority of the great apes suggests most parsimoniously that this innovative condition was the ancestral behaviour of the great ape clade and thus that Oldowan hominins likely exhibited this same condition or at the very least had the potential to do so. Furthermore, although there is presently little evidence of cultural variation in gorilla tool use, the widely accepted phylogenetic position of the gorilla relative to the other great apes (e.g., Purvis 1995:411) suggests that the gorilla should be equally capable of manifesting this behaviour as well.

Unfortunately, due to the limitations of the Oldowan archaeological record, a proper comparison is unable to be made, and no conclusive evidence can be drawn as of yet to support the cultural model of tool production in the Oldowan. It may be that a single community of hominins founded the Oldowan archaeological industry, which could explain the incessant uniformity between Oldowan archaeological sites. Additionally, it is possible that evidence that could have supported this hypothesis decomposed long ago, as it is likely that our early hominin ancestors engaged in the use of perishable materials for tool production to supplement their well-documented stone tool technology. Another likely hypothesis is that the existence of tool culture could simply be determined by the presence versus the absence of a stone tool technology between hominin communities. However, it is not possible to conclusively prove the absence of stone tools from a given area due to taphonomic processes. Nevertheless, the cultural activity of contemporary non-human great apes pleads the case of cultural influence on early hominin technology, regardless of the lack of archaeological evidence.

Future research should focus on the continued effort to fill in the gaps of the archaeological record, while continuing to develop a better understanding of known archaeological data. Additional research on great ape cultural behaviours, especially the gorilla, will prove fruitful, if only to reinforce the behavioural capabilities of our hominin ancestors. Finally, the conservation of the great apes is quickly becoming a pertinent issue. Populations of chimpanzees, gorillas, and orangutans continue to decrease despite current efforts to save them. Our closest relatives stand to provide a significant amount of information about our evolutionary heritage, and therefore their conservation is paramount to the study of hominin evolution.

Acknowledgments: I would like to thank Dr. Pamela Willoughby for her guidance and support in the writing of this paper.

REFERENCES CITED

Alp, Rosalind

  1997 "Stepping-Sticks" and "Seat-Sticks": New Types of Tools Used by Wild Chimpanzees (*Pan Troglodytes*) in Sierra Leone. *American Journal of Primatology* 41:45–52.

Beck, Benjamin B.

  1980 *Animal Tool Behavior: The Use and Manufacture of Tools by Animals.* Garland Press, New York.

Breuer, Thomas, Mireille Ndoundou-Hockemba, and Vicki Fishlock

  2005 First Observation of Tool Use in Wild Gorillas. *PLoS Biology* 3(11):e380.

Celli, Maura L., Satoshi Hirata, and Masaki Tomonaga

  2004 Socioecological Influences on Tool Use in Captive Chimpanzees. *International Journal of Primatology* 25(6):1267–1281.

De la Torre, Ignacio

  2004 Omo Revisited: Evaluating the Technological Skills of Pliocene Hominids. *Current Anthropology* 45(4):439–465.

Hohmann, Gottfried, and Barbara Fruth

  2003 Culture in Bonobos? Between-Species and Within-Species Variation in Behavior. *Current Anthropology* 44(4):563–571.

Kimura, Yuki

  1999 Tool-Using Strategies by Early Hominids at Bed II, Olduvai Gorge, Tanzania. *Journal of Human Evolution* 37:807–831.

Klein, Richard G.

  1999 *The Human Career: Human Biological and Cultural Origins.* University of Chicago Press, Chicago.

Marks, Jonathan

  2002 *What It Means to Be 98% Chimpanzee: Apes, People, and Their Genes.* University of California Press, Los Angeles.

McBrearty, Sally, and Alison S. Brooks

2000   The Revolution That Wasn't: A New Interpretation of the Origin of Modern Human Behavior. *Journal of Human Evolution* 39:453–563.

McGrew, William C.

1992   *Chimpanzee Material Culture: Implications for Human Evolution*. Cambridge University Press, New York.

Mercader, Julio, Melissa Panger, and Christophe Boesch

2002   Excavation of a Chimpanzee Stone Tool Site in the African Rainforest. *Science* 296(5572):1452.

Povinelli, Daniel J.

2000   *Folk Physics for Apes: The Chimpanzee's Theory of How the World Works*. Oxford University Press, New York.

Purvis, Andy

1995   Composite Estimate of Primate Phylogeny. *Philosophical Transactions: Biological Sciences* 348(1326):405–421.

Semaw, Sileshi

2000   The World's Oldest Stone Artefacts from Gona, Ethiopia: Their Implications for Understanding Stone Technology and Patterns of Human Evolution between 2.6–1.5 Million Years Ago. *Journal of Archaeological Science* 27(12):1197–1214.

Stout, Dietrich, Jay Quade, Sileshi Semaw, Michael J. Rogers, and Naomi E. Levin

2005   Raw Material Selectivity of the Earliest Stone Toolmakers at Gona, Afar, Ethiopia. *Journal of Human Evolution* 48:365–380.

Toth, Nicholas

1987   Behavioral Inferences from Early Stone Artifact Assemblages: An Experimental Model. *Journal of Human Evolution* 16:763–787.

Van Lawick-Goodall, Jane

1967   *My Friends the Wild Chimpanzees*. National Geographic Society, Washington, D.C.

Van Schaik, Carel

2004   *Among Orangutans: Red Apes and the Rise of Human Culture*. Harvard University Press, Cambridge.

Whiten, Andrew, and Christophe Boesch

2001   The Cultures of Chimpanzees. *Scientific American* 284(1):60.

Wynn, Thomas, and William C. McGrew

1989   An Apes View of the Oldowan. *Man* 24(3):383–398.

Notes

1   Beck's definition of 'tool' as the "employment of an unattached environmental object to alter more efficiently the form, position, or condition of another object, another organism, or the user itself when the user holds or carries the tool during or just prior to use and is responsible for the proper and effective orientation of the tool" (Beck 1980:10).

2   Culture will be defined here based on Japanese primatologist Kinji Imanishi's perception of culture as a socially transmitted innovation (Van Schaik 2004:139).

3   In reference to tool use and manufacture as a result of cultural innovation and transmission via social learning.

AMBER E. MACKENZIE

2

NATURAL HISTORY INTELLIGENCE AND HOMINID TOOL BEHAVIOUR

Susan Cachel

Abstract. With the first appearance of an archaeological record 2.6–2.5 Mya, hominid behaviour falls outside the foraging and ranging behaviours of non-human primates. Stone tool technology, animal carcass acquisition and processing, and long-distance ranging and transport of resources demonstrate an attention to the physical and biological environment ("natural history intelligence") that is different from the intelligence of non-human primates. Complex social interactions in other primates may generate intelligence, but attention to conspecifics probably hinders the development of knowledge about the ecology and behaviour of other animals and the ability to foresee the abundance and predictability of fluctuating resources. Elements of behaviour now often associated with the origins of anatomically modern humans actually make their first appearance in the Oldowan. The first hominid tools may have been hammerstones, used to batter open bones.

COMPLEX BEHAVIOURS IN ANIMALS

I will emphasize two themes in this paper. The first theme is that many animals other than great apes – especially other mammals and birds – can be useful in examining selection pressures involved in the origins of complex behaviours like tool use and manufacture or food storage. The second theme is that the social cognition and social dynamics of non-human primates may hinder the appearance of tool behaviour, if it orients attention completely to the competitive social world.

Tools often form the interface between humans and their environment. It is natural, then, that the concept of a special relationship between tool behaviour and human uniqueness is very old. It can be traced back to Greco-Roman antiquity, and tools also act as a major catalyst in many scientific models of hominization. However, there is a 3.5-million-year gap between hominid origins at 6 mya and the appearance of an archaeological record, and the traditional link between tool behaviour and hominid origins is thus currently impossible to support.

Animal tool behaviour has been intensively investigated in a comparative fashion by many researchers. Tools are often used to obtain food, especially when an animal lacks natural structures to acquire or process food (Alcock 1972). There seems to be no necessary relationship between tool behaviour and the origin of intelligence (Beck 1980). Anthropologists and primatologists have devoted much attention to cataloguing and analyzing great ape (particularly chimpanzee) tool behaviour, as well as foraging behaviour, and nest construction. The implication is that phylogeny or genetic relatedness is the major determinant of these behaviours and that their existence in great apes reveals something about their origin in hominids. However, similar selection pressures can yield similar behaviour in animals that are remote in ancestry. Beck (1982:4) discusses the bias against recognizing the complex cognitive abilities of other animals as a form of "chimpocentrism." In fact, no wild non-human primate engages in complex cooperative foraging, food sharing, food caching, habitual tool use and modification, artefact creation, or landscape modification to the extent that hominids or other animals do.

Corvid birds, for example, exhibit habitual tool use and manufacture and intricate tool modification under novel circumstances. One such corvid species is the New Caledonian crow (*Corvus moneduloides*), which is famous for the manufacture and use of tools to probe for and extract otherwise inaccessible food items, such as wood-boring beetle larvae. This species also creates hook tools, a category of tool not observed in the archaeological record until the Upper Palaeolithic (Weir et al. 2002). Miniature video cameras have been mounted on the tails of wild New Caledonian crows, in order to investigate natural foraging behaviour in the wild (Rutz et al. 2007). Two adult males yielded hitherto unknown information about tool behaviour in this species. Multiple tools were used for probing leaf litter on the forest floor; a stick tool was used for a prolonged period of time and transported by flying between different ground sites; and crows made tools from dry grass stems, a raw material not previously known to be used by this species (Rutz et al. 2007).

After birds acquire food, it may be stored – another behaviour not recorded among non-human primates. This behaviour indicates recognition that future conditions might change and therefore implies the existence of forethought or planning. Corvid birds exhibit a variety of complex behaviours that are related to food storage. These include food caching, shifting strategies between competing birds that both store food and thieve it, complex recovery of cached and perishable food items in fluctuating temperatures, and re-caching of food items upon observation by potential thieves (Emery and Clayton 2004; Raby et al. 2007). This range of flexible, complex behaviours rivals or exceeds that seen among great apes and has been noted both in the wild and under captive, experimental conditions. Tool manufacturing occurs spontaneously in hand-reared naïve juvenile crows, demonstrating that the ability is hereditary. It does not need to be learned and is not dependent on cultural transmission. Furthermore, the routine food caching behaviour of corvids appears to exceed the ability of great apes to plan for the future. Many chimpanzee food items are highly perishable under tropical rainforest conditions, but nuts, which are a highly important seasonal component of chimpanzee diet, could be easily cached by chimpanzees while remaining edible for a fair length of time. Yet, nuts are not cached by chimpanzees. Mental abilities are subject to convergent evolution. Similar selection pressures operating on phylogenetically distant groups can create similar modes of cognition. Complex cognition in corvid birds is equivalent to that of apes but is based on completely different brain mechanisms. The nidopallium and mesopallium, brain areas analogous to the mammalian prefrontal cortex, are relatively enlarged in corvids. In fact, recent investigations of avian brain anatomy reveal that birds and mammals have independently evolved brain areas devoted to higher cognitive functions (Avian Brain Nomenclature Consortium 2005). Thus, convergent evolution can occur in mental abilities, in spite of very divergent neuroanatomical substrates.

Much consideration has been given to the existence of culture in great apes, especially in common chimpanzees. Many researchers argue that tool behaviour and other behaviours in common chimpanzees show a variability that exceeds that of any other non-human species. They also argue that this variability is probably the result of learned behaviour transmitted through social interaction – i.e., it is the result of cultural differences between chimpanzee communities. However, the list of other primate species unequivocally exhibiting cultural behaviour continues to grow. Some of the most well-known examples come from Japanese macaques, where cultural traditions such as stone collecting and sweet potato washing have been observed for nearly forty years in some troops. Yet, cultural traditions are found not only among Old World higher primates. Cultural behaviour has also been documented in New World monkeys, which are only remotely related to apes and humans (O'Malley and Fedigan 2005, Yépez et al. 2005). And cultural behaviour has been found in many non-primates. Dialect differences in birdsong that develop through social experience and practice are a well-known example of such behaviour (Alcock 2001:24–28). And songbirds seem to be capable of understanding novel patterns of birdsong, implying the existence of complex communication usually thought to be unique to humans (Gentner et al. 2006). It is possible that cultural traditions would be discovered in many social vertebrates, if they could attract the research attention that chimpanzees have received.

NATURAL HISTORY INTELLIGENCE

Archaeology is the record of hominid behaviour. Hominids exhibit complex, long-distance ranging to acquire food and lithic resources, habitual tool use and modification, artefact creation, and landscape modification. These behaviours extend deep into the past. Hominid behaviour as inferred from the archaeological record represents an abrupt break from that of other Old World higher primates, and this break can be identified with the first appearance of an archaeological record between 2.6 and 2.5 mya. Although it has been claimed that chimpanzees are capable of generating an archaeological record while nut-cracking (Mercader et al. 2002), most archaeologists remain skeptical of the purported evidence. The vast majority (78%) of the stone material at the one published chimpanzee "site" (Panda 100) represents microshatter caused by hammerstone pounding. There is no evidence of stone flaking. Furthermore, if one argues that chimpanzee nut-cracking is a specialized ape behaviour, one must then account for the persistent high degree of tool behaviour at multiple sites by tufted capuchin monkeys (*Cebus apella*), New World primates only remotely related to apes and humans (Moura and Lee 2004, Fragaszy et al. 2004). Tufted capuchins use stones for digging and hammering open food resources. Hammerstones are transported to anvils, and the weight of a hammerstone can be between 19 and 50 per cent of a capuchin's body weight (Fragaszy et al. 2004).

Archaeological localities dating back to 2.5–2.6 mya document unique hominid behaviours. What are the hominid behaviours that occur in a unique suite? Hominids select and transport raw materials for stone implements, manufacture and use stone artefacts, acquire vertebrate meat and marrow through hunting and/or scavenging (including confrontational scavenging), transport carcasses and partial carcasses, alter animal bones to obtain meat and marrow, interact with sympatric carnivore species, and leave behind spatially distinct patterns of bone and stone within a site. In the Koobi Fora region, east of Lake Turkana, Kenya, sites dating between 1.64 and 1.39 mya demonstrate alternative foraging strategies and complex foraging for dispersed resources. In areas where suitable raw material for stone tools is not available, hominids do not discard tools: tools are carefully retained or curated. Raw material for stone tool manufacture may have been a crucial resource for hominids, and the proximity of lithic raw material sources of a suitable clast size may have profoundly affected hominid ranging and foraging behaviour. Complex foraging for dispersed resources implies an intimate knowledge of the regional environment, and the ability to locate and predict the abundance of resources that fluctuate widely in space and time (Cachel 2004). A number of hominid species coexist during these time ranges in East Africa. While more than one species may have engaged in tool behaviour, the taxon *Homo erectus* was probably responsible for the archaeological evidence between 1.6 and 1.4 mya.

As documented by the site of Dmanisi, dated to 1.8 mya, *Homo erectus* was capable of dispersing to the Republic of Georgia, far distant from sub-Saharan Africa. Dmanisi hominids were associated with animals characteristic of West European assemblages – i.e., they had adapted to a novel ecosystem and were exploiting new species – and were manufacturing Oldowan tools. It is important to note that dispersion into new environments, meat-eating and hunting of new animal species, and Oldowan tool manufacture was occurring in hominids whose brain size was remarkably low, ranging from 600 to 775 cc (Lordkipanidze et al. 2007).

What type of behaviour or sociality leaves behind an archaeological record? These complex behaviours mandate an attention to natural history, which is documented at an ancient date. Hominid natural history intelligence is based on complex, symbolic representation of the non-social environment and its abstract manipulation. The ability to generalize about objects and events in the outside world, to recognize patterns through the use of metaphor, to generate rules and laws about processes in the physical and biological worlds (external to the social world), to predict events, and to plan behaviours that anticipate or control these events is predicated in natural history intelligence. This intelligence functions in cognitive problems that involve anticipating properties of objects outside the social world or being able to reason about cause and effect in the world outside the social group.

During early time ranges, inferences of hominid mental activity are made from degree of artefact symmetry, utility of the working edge of the artefact, prudent use of raw material, tailoring of specific raw material to specific uses, artefact retouching, and repeated use and transport (curation) of artefacts. Far later in time, beginning about 40,000 BP during the European Upper Palaeolithic, first portable and then parietal art documents the attention of its creators to fine details of the morphology and behaviour of contemporary non-human animals. By 12–13,000 BP, portable and parietal art even documents human awareness of individual variability and ontogenetic processes within other species, and an apparent symbolic manipulation of these properties. Animal and plant domestication would have been impossible without human attention to and manipulation of the external environment. With the advent of a written record of human thought, there is undeniable evidence of such attention and manipulation.

Although even the earliest stone tools and archaeological sites indicate the presence of a distinctive type of hominid intelligence, many researchers consider that such qualitative differences in behaviour and intelligence occur very late in time. These researchers associate such differences with humans who are anatomically modern, although there may be a significant lag in time between the first appearance of such humans and archaeological evidence of art or symbolic manipulation. Neanderthals, for example, who precede and coexist with modern humans in the late Pleistocene of Europe, are frequently considered to be cognitively and behaviourally more primitive than any normal living humans and lacking any capacity for planning or forethought. Yet, primatologists routinely credit chimpanzees with forethought and planning, thus implying that chimpanzees trump Neanderthals. Unlike Mithen (1996:148), I am not separating technical intelligence (modules for tool behaviour) and natural history intelligence (modules for understanding the biological or physical worlds). I subsume both of these under the rubric of "natural history intelligence" (Cachel 2006).

A more fundamental difference with Mithen (1996) is that I contend that complex interaction with the biological and physical worlds demands not merely behavioural flexibility but an integration of data from multiple senses and a reorganization of neuroanatomical pathways that organize attention. This complex interaction creates the ability to monitor, to predict, and to manipulate objects and events in the natural world. As a consequence, natural history intelligence by itself contributes to the formation of general or fluid intelligence by expanding attentiveness and awareness away from the tyranny of the social world that generates the social intelligence identifiable in non-human primates.

Natural history intelligence corresponds to general or fluid intelligence, highlighting the importance of planning, predicting, and manipulating items in the non-social environment. Because the constitution of awareness is a model of the world, an organism must be highly aware of the world outside of its social group and social relationships before it can model, create symbols for, predict, or manipulate the external environment. Pre-attentive neural mechanisms for processing sensory information are doubtless crucial to its functioning. These mechanisms can be subsumed under the cluster of mechanisms generally known as the "cognitive unconscious." An example of such a neural mechanism is visual attentiveness in humans. Humans have been shown to possess special visual attentiveness and monitoring bias towards animals, as opposed to inanimate objects (New et al. 2007). This bias exists independently of object size, intrinsic interest, or prior expertise. Although sample targets (human, elephant, and pigeon) were small and partly camouflaged, human subjects quickly detected the targets at a rate that was significantly higher than large, bright inanimate objects (farm silo, red truck, coffee mug). Humans thus exhibit unconscious preferential attention for animals and people. This differential attentiveness is thought to reflect the evolutionarily ancient importance of a category of objects (animals) that may have no function or value in the modern industrialized world (New et al. 2007).

Natural history intelligence probably exists in other vertebrate species, but it does not seem well-developed in Old World higher primates, whose intelligence has been most well-studied, and which provide the bulk of the evidence for Machiavellian intelligence. With the advent of an archaeological record at 2.6–2.5 mya that preserves hominid behaviour (and certainly with the advent of a dense archaeological record at 1.7–1.5 mya), it becomes clear that hominids are behaving differently from any other primate.

THE SOCIAL COGNITION MODEL

Thus, natural history intelligence is not well-developed in non-human primates, even if they are closely related to humans. But the current consensus opinion is that complex sociality itself selects for intelligence in vertebrate animals (Whiten and Byrne 1997). This is the social cognition hypothesis, which argues that social dynamics and complex cognition evolved in tandem. Striving for status within the group emphasizes social manipulation, and develops reasoning abilities. Many researchers stress the existence of Machiavellian intelligence: that intelligence in primates and other vertebrates evolves from the assessment of social relationships, as well as the prediction of behaviour, and the occurrence of deceit and manipulation within a social group. According to this model, primate intelligence arises in social cognition through individual competition for dominance and resources, tactical striving for status, and "political" manoeuvring.

Because it orients non-human primate attention and awareness to happenings in the social world, Machiavellian intelligence may militate against the development of natural history intelligence, rather than contributing to its appearance. Competitive social life may enhance social intelligence, but, unless awareness of and attention to the non-social world occurs, this social intelligence will not be transferred to the world outside the social group. Cognition is ordered at the neuroanatomical level to emphasize conspecifics and social dynamics. Competitive social life consumes attention, as animals constantly strive for status. This suggests that the origins of hominid tool behaviour are rooted in a different kind of sociality than that characteristic of other Old World higher primates.

Implicit in the Machiavellian intelligence theory is the idea that social intelligence is transferable to other spheres. It implies that the field of concentration is irrelevant. It assumes that striking abilities for innovation and imitation in the social realm reflect abilities for imitation and innovation in the realm outside. Yet, this is not the case for primate tool behaviour, which has been extensively investigated.

PROBLEMS WITH THE SOCIAL COGNITION MODEL

Criticisms of the social cognition model are not yet generally found in anthropology or primatology texts, but they do appear in cognitive psychology (Heyes 1993) and in European primatology (Kummer et al. 1990; Kummer 2002). Beck (1982) and Povinelli et al. (2000) direct specific arguments against the social cognition model when it relies largely or heavily on great apes, particularly chimpanzees. Consideration of emergent complexity or experiments with software and new directions in artificial intelligence also suggest problems with the social cognition model. And it is becoming clear that the competitive arena of primate social life limits attentiveness to other things. A major primatologist (Silk 2002) argues that high-ranking female monkeys launch unwarranted and randomly timed attacks against random subordinates merely to induce insecurity and stress in all subordinate animals. The dominant animals "practice random acts of aggression and senseless acts of intimidation" – the title of Silk's paper. Furthermore, in spite of the famed ability of chimpanzees to form coalitions and engage in cooperative behaviour, chimpanzees do not engage in behaviours that benefit familiar but unrelated individuals under experimental conditions (Silk et al. 2005). Self-interest rules actions, and competitive social life therefore hinders the appearance of complex sociality based on reciprocal altruism – i.e., the type of sociality characteristic of humans. However, common marmosets (*Callithrix jacchus*), New World monkeys phylogenetically remote from humans, have experimentally been shown spontaneously to provision other, unrelated animals with food, even if the other animals do not reciprocate the behaviour

(Burkart et al. 2007). Humans and marmosets are the only two primate taxa exhibiting such altruistic behaviour. Because both humans and marmosets possess communal rearing of the young, the authors infer that reciprocal altruism arises from this breeding system. I previously predicted that communal rearing of the young like that seen among marmosets would generate complex sociality in early hominids (Cachel 2006).

Several avenues of investigation raise doubt that Machiavellian social cognition in non-human primates is a necessary substrate for the origin of hominid intelligence (Cachel 2006). I will only discuss two of these here. The first line of evidence involves non-human primate behaviour, both in the field and in captivity. Vervet monkeys at the Amboseli Reserve, Kenya, are the subjects of an intensive study of non-human cognition (Cheney and Seyfarth 1990). Vervets are knowledgeable about interpersonal dynamics within their social group and are knowledgeable about vervets outside their social group. But vervets do not seem to be aware of the natural world. One intuitively expects that a species' predators would be the focus of intense scrutiny and attention. Leopard predation accounts for nearly half of vervet mortality at Amboseli in 1987. Yet, predation by leopards is not associated with vervet awareness of leopard natural history. Cheney and Seyfarth (1990) even deliberately placed a stuffed ungulate carcass in a tree, mimicking normal leopard behaviour, in order to elicit vervet response and alarm at the proximity of their most notable predator. There was no vervet reaction. And Cheney and Seyfarth document other examples of vervet unawareness of natural history (Cheney and Seyfarth 1990). Thus, despite possessing social intelligence, vervet monkeys appear to be unaware of much of their external environment and are peculiarly obtuse about making associations and predictions about the external world, sometimes despite intense positive selection pressure for them to do so. In fact, Treves and Pizzagalli (2002) conclude that predator vigilance in primates is compromised by intense vigilance directed at conspecifics. Animals spend so much time monitoring other conspecifics, trying to ascertain who is doing what to whom when, that there is no time left to monitor the environment for potential predators.

The second line of evidence concerns male-female differences in primate tool behaviour. Wild adult female chimpanzees at Taï National Park, Ivory Coast, are more proficient and persistent at opening coula and panda nuts with stone tools than males are. The argument is made that males, concerned with male-male relationships, constantly monitor the behaviour of other group members and move away from nut sites in response to other animals. Relatively non-social, individual females are not impeded by the social milieu (Boesch and Boesch 1984; Boesch and Boesch-Achermann 2000). Measurement of the energetics of nut-cracking by the Tai chimpanzees demonstrates a nine-fold energy gain. Natural selection should promote this tool behaviour in both chimpanzee sexes, if other factors were not operating against it. The male need for surveillance of other males outweighs even a nine-fold energetic benefit. At Gombe National Park, Tanzania, female chimpanzees engage in termite-fishing significantly more than males, and at a younger age (Lonsdorf et al. 2004). No active teaching occurs. Yet, young females spend more time observing their mothers and eventually employ their mothers' tool behaviour techniques. Mothers interact with both male and female offspring to an equal extent, but males play more at the termite mound with other males, observe their mothers less, and engage in less termite-fishing behaviour (Lonsdorf et al. 2004). Male observation and practice time is reduced by dominance interactions rooted in sexual selection.

What brain mechanisms underlie attention and attentiveness? The bifurcation between Machiavellian intelligence and natural history intelligence resembles the bifurcation between the "emotional" brain and the "executive" brain that is discussed in studies of primate cognition and genomic imprinting. In terms of this paper, the hormonally driven emotional brain underlies the Machiavellian intelligence that is expressed by dominance interactions and political manipulation. The executive brain underlies natural history intelligence, which is more flexible, relatively released from hormonal influences, and attentive to events outside the competitive arena of the social group.

In humans, brain activation caused by emotion does not interfere with cognitive activation in the same brain area – instead, cognitive activity is enhanced, indicating that emotion can adjust activity within the same area (Gray et al. 2002). Recent human tests using functional MRI in many subjects establish that cognition and emotion are separable in humans. However, cognition and emotion are integrated in the lateral prefrontal cortex, and the integrated signal influences thought and goal-directed behaviour (Gray et al. 2002). Human lateral prefrontal cortex activity selectively mirrors emotional loads or demands, in order to maintain goal-directed behaviour at a certain level (Gray et al. 2002).

IMPLICATIONS OF THE NATURAL HISTORY INTELLIGENCE MODEL

Many of the elements of behaviour now often associated with the origins of anatomically modern humans (McBrearty and Brooks 2000) actually appear very deep in the archaeological record. They make their first appearance during the Oldowan between 1.4 and 1.6 mya or earlier. These elements include increased human dispersal abilities, spatial organization of behaviour at archaeological sites, primary access to animal carcasses whether through hunting or confrontational scavenging, inter-site variability, artefact change through time, and planning, as evidenced by raw material transport and curation. Researchers interested in the origin of human intelligence have traditionally focused on non-human primate tool behaviour, foraging behaviour, and sociality. Non-human primate sociality is widely believed to be the necessary factor in the evolution of human intelligence. However, the "Machiavellian intelligence" recently emphasized as typical of non-human primates may not be a necessary step in the development of natural history intelligence. Because the content of awareness is a model of the world, Machiavellian intelligence may even militate against the development of natural history intelligence. The social intelligence seen in non-human primates and humans is partly convergent or non-homologous. Applying human social terminology to the description of non-human primate social behaviour (e.g., "politics," "political," "Machiavellian") thwarts appreciation of the fact that human and non-human primate intelligence related to social behaviour may have disparate sources.

WERE THE FIRST TOOLS HAMMERSTONES? WHAT WAS BEING HAMMERED?

Given the widespread use of hammerstones by animals, including primates, it is reasonable to suggest that hammerstones were the first hominid tools. If this is so, what was being hammered open? Unlike non-human primates that use hammerstones to break open hard nuts or palm nuts, early hominids may have been battering open animal bones to extract marrow. The advent of flaking – a behaviour not observed in the animal world – would allow hominids to use stone flakes to cut through skin, and sever tendons and ligaments. Hominid-modified bones from the earliest archaeological sites show that vertebrate meat and marrow were utilized (Dominguez-Rodrigo et al. 2005). Unequivocal dietary signatures can be obtained from the chemistry of prehistoric enamel. Stable carbon isotope and trace element analysis of enamel from South African Plio-Pleistocene hominid species demonstrate that all these species – australopithecines, as well as members of genus *Homo* – were omnivorous (Lee-Thorp and Sponheimer 2006). They incorporated meat from grass-eating vertebrates into their diets. It is important to note that modern common chimpanzees living in open, savanna environments do not consume C_4 resources (Sponheimer et al. 2006). Thus, the study of common chimpanzee diet and foraging behaviour in open habitats neither resembles nor illuminates the behavioural ecology of the earliest hominids. Could australopithecines have been eating dietary items other than vertebrate meat that could generate a pronounced C_4 signal? It has been suggested that either termites or sedges might yield a high C_4 signature. Termite eating, in particular, immediately invokes the termite-fishing behaviour of common chimpanzees. Yet, the suggestion that termites or sedges might create a high C_4 signature has been tested and found wanting. Ingestion of termites and sedges cannot account for the strong C_4 signal in australopithecines (Sponheimer et al. 2005). Stable carbon isotope evidence therefore vitiates the model of termite-fishing in the earliest hominids that is based directly on chimpanzee termiting behaviour. Thus, the first tools were used to obtain food resources otherwise unobtainable by hominids. And, given the strength of the C_4 signal, it is likely that vertebrate meat and marrow were not merely seasonally contingent or fall-back foods but were a normal and regular component of Plio-Pleistocene hominid diets. The presence of a strong C_4 signal in all of the South African hominid species supports this interpretation. This evidence vitiates the idea that hominid tool behaviour arose during periods of resource stress, when normal food items were temporarily unavailable. This idea is based directly on the seasonality of chimpanzee nut-cracking behaviour (Boesch and Boesch-Achermann 2000). Rather, hominid tool behaviour became habitual at an early date and signified an ability to exploit food resources hitherto unavailable to primates.

The lack of clear evidence for a proto-Oldowan lithic technology supports the abrupt and momentous benefit of stone tool behaviour. A major problem is to elucidate the origins of stone knapping technology because no comparative animal models yield insight into how this might have originated. Hammerstone pounding creates microshatter and no useable flakes. Attentiveness to the utility of the razor-like sharpness of micro-flakes might have generated deliberate attempts to create larger, useable flakes. This attentiveness, however, could only have come about through the operation of natural history intelligence.

REFERENCES CITED

Alcock, John

   1972   The Evolution of the Use of Tools by Feeding Animals. *Evolution* 26:464–473.

   2001   *Animal Behavior*, 7th ed. Sinauer Associates, Sunderland, MA.

The Avian Brain Nomenclature Consortium

   2005   Avian Brains and a New Understanding of Vertebrate Brain Evolution. *Nature Reviews Neuroscience* 6:151–159.

Beck, Benjamin B.

   1980   *Animal Tool Behavior*. Garland Press, New York.

   1982   Chimpocentrism: Bias in Cognitive Ethology. *Journal of Human Evolution* 11:3–17.

Boesch, Christophe, and Hedwige Boesch

   1984   Possible Causes of Sex Differences in the Use of Natural Hammers by Wild Chimpanzees. *Journal of Human Evolution* 13:415–448.

Boesch, Christophe, and Hedwige Boesch-Achermann

   2000   *The Chimpanzees of the Taï Forest: Behavioral Ecology and Evolution*. Oxford University Press, New York.

Burkart, Judith M., Ernst Fehr, Charles Efferson, and Carel P. van Schaik

   2007   Other-Regarding Preferences in a Non-Human Primate: Common Marmosets Provision Food Altruistically. *Proceedings of the National Academy of Sciences, U.S.A.* 104:19762–19766.

Cachel, Susan

   2004   The Paleobiology of *Homo erectus* and Early Hominid Dispersal. *Athena Review* 4(1):23–31.

   2006   *Primate and Human Evolution*. Cambridge University Press, Cambridge.

Cheney, Dorothy L., and Robert M. Seyfarth

1990   *How Monkeys See the World: Inside the Mind of Another Species.* University of Chicago Press, Chicago.

Dominguez-Rodrigo, Manuel, Thomas R. Pickering, Sileshi Semaw, and Michael J. Rogers

2005   Cutmarked Bones from Pliocene Archaeological Sites at Gona, Afar, Ethiopia: Implications for the Function of the World's Oldest Stone Tools. *Journal of Human Evolution* 48:109–121.

Emery, Nathan J., and Nicola S. Clayton

2004   The Mentality of Crows: Convergent Evolution of Intelligence in Corvids and Apes. *Science* 306:1903–1907.

Fragaszy, Dorothy, Patricia Izar, Elisabetta Visalberghi, Eduardo B. Ottoni, and Marino Gomes De Oliveira

2004   Wild Capuchin Monkeys (*Cebus libidinosus*) Use Anvils and Stone Pounding Tools. *American Journal of Primatology* 64:359–366.

Gentner, Timothy Q., Kimberly M. Fenn, Daniel Margoliash, and Howard C. Nusbaum

2006   Recursive Syntactic Pattern Learning by Songbirds. *Nature* 440:1204–1207.

Gray, J.R., T.S. Braver, and M.E. Raichle

2002   Integration of Emotion and Cognition in the Lateral Prefrontal Cortex. *Proceedings of the National Academy of Sciences, U.S.A.* 99(6):4115–4120.

Heyes, C.M.

1993   Anecdotes, Training, Trapping and Triangulating: Do Animals Attribute Mental States? *Animal Behavior* 46:177–188.

Kummer, Hans

2002   Topics Gained and Lost in Primate Social Behavior. *Evolutionary Anthropology* Supplement 1:73–74.

Kummer, Hans, V. Dasser, and P. Hoyningen-Huene

1990   Exploring Primate Social Cognition: Some Critical Remarks. *Behavior* 112:84–98.

Lee-Thorp, Julia, and Matt Sponheimer

2006   Contributions of Biogeochemistry to Understanding Hominin Dietary Ecology. *Yearbook of Physical Anthropology* 49:131–148.

Lonsdorf, Elizabeth V., Lynn E. Eberly, and Anne E. Pusey

2004   Sex Differences in Learning in Chimpanzees. *Nature* 428:715.

Lordkipanidze, David, Tea Jashashvili, Abesalom Vekua, Marcia S. Ponce de León, Christoph P.E. Zollikofer, G. Philip Rightmire, Herman Pontzer, Reid Ferring, Oriol Oms, Martha Tappen, Maia Bukhsianidze, Jordi Agustí, Ralf Kahlke, Gocha Kiladze, Bienvenido Martinez-Navarro, Alexander Mouskhelishvili, Medea Nioradze, and Lorenzo Rook

    2007   Postcranial Evidence from Early *Homo* from Dmanisi, Georgia. *Nature* 449:305–310. Supplementary Information linked to doi:10.1038/nature06134.

McBrearty, Sally, and Alison S. Brooks

    2000   The Revolution That Wasn't: A New Interpretation of the Origin of Modern Human Behavior. *Journal of Human Evolution* 39:453–563.

Mercader, Julio, Melissa Panger, and Christophe Boesch

    2002   Excavation of a Chimpanzee Stone Tool Site in the African Rainforest. *Science* 296:1452–1453.

Mithen, Steven

    1996   *The Prehistory of the Mind: The Cognitive Origins of Art, Religion and Science.* Thames and Hudson, London.

Moura, A.C. de A., and P.C. Lee

    2004   Capuchin Stone Tool Use in Caatinga Dry Forest. *Science* 306:1909.

New, Joshua, Leda Cosmides, and John Tooby

    2007   Category-Specific Attention for Animals Reflects Ancestral Priorities, Not Expertise. *Proceedings of the National Academy of Sciences, U.S.A.* 104:16598–16603.

O'Malley, Robert C., and Linda Fedigan

    2005   Variability in Food-Processing Behavior among White-Faced Capuchins (*Cebus capucinus*) in Santa Rosa National Park, Costa Rica. *American Journal of Physical Anthropology* 128:63–73.

Povinelli, Daniel J., James E. Reaux, Laura A. Theall, and Steve Giambrone

    2000   *Folk Physics for Apes: The Chimpanzee's Theory of How the World Works.* Oxford University Press, Oxford.

Raby, C.R., D.M. Alexis, A. Dickinson, and N.S. Clayton

    2007   Planning for the Future by Western Scrub-Jays. *Nature* 445:919–921.

Rutz, Christian, Lucas A. Bluff, Alex A.S. Weir, and Alex Kacelnik

    2007   Video Cameras on Wild Birds. *Science* 318:765. Supporting online material: www.sciencemag.org/cgi/content/full1146788/DC1.

Silk, Joan B.

    2002   Practice Random Acts of Aggression and Senseless Acts of Intimidation: The Logic of Status Contests in Social Groups. *Evolutionary Anthropology* 11:221–225.

Silk, Joan B., Sarah F. Brosnan, Jennifer Vonk, Joseph Henrich, Daniel J. Povinelli, Amanda S. Richardson, Susan P. Lambeth, Jenny Mascaro, and Stephen J. Schapiro

2005   Chimpanzees Are Indifferent to the Welfare of Unrelated Group Members. *Nature* 437:1357–1359.

Sponheimer, Matt, Julia Lee-Thorp, Darryl de Ruiter, Daryl Codron, Jacqui Codron, Alexander T. Baugh, and Francis Thackeray

2005   Hominins, Sedges, and Termites: New Carbon Isotope Data from the Sterkfontein Valley and Kruger National Park. *Journal of Human Evolution* 48:301–312.

Sponheimer, Matt, J.E. Loudon, Daryl Codron, M.E. Howells, J.D. Pruetz, Jacqui Codron, Darryl J. de Ruiter, and Julia A. Lee-Thorp

2006   Do "Savanna" Chimpanzees Consume C$_4$ Resources? *Journal of Human Evolution* 51:128–133.

Treves, Adrian, and Diego Pizzagalli

2002   Vigilance and Perception of Social Stimuli: Views from Ethology and Social Neuroscience. In *The Cognitive Animal: Empirical and Theoretical Perspectives on Animal Cognition*, edited by Marc Bekoff, Colin Allen, and Gordon M. Burghardt, pp. 463–469. M.I.T. Press, Cambridge, MA.

Weir, Alex A.S., Jackie Chappell, and Alex Kacelnik

2002   Shaping of Hooks in New Caledonian Crows. *Science* 297:981. Supporting online material: www.sciencemag.org/cgi/content/full/297/5583/981/.

Whiten, Andrew, and Richard W. Byrne (editors)

1997   *Machiavellian Intelligence II: Extensions and Evaluations*. Cambridge University Press, Cambridge.

Yépez, Pablo, Stella de la Torre, and Charles T. Snowdon

2005   Interpopulation Differences in Exudate Feeding of Pygmy Marmosets in Ecuadorian Amazonia. *American Journal of Primatology* 66:145–158.

3

Tempo and Mode in the Palaeolithic: How to Understand the Origins of Culture

Pamela R. Willoughby

Abstract. The Palaeolithic represents the period of the origins and early evolution of material culture in Eurasia and Africa. It extends from approximately 2.5 million years ago in Africa up until around 10,000 years ago. This timespan corresponds with global environmental cycling of the Pleistocene ice ages, as well as with the appearance and evolution of members of the genus *Homo*. There are a number of models of the timing (tempo) and nature (mode) of change over the course of the Palaeolithic. Most link the evolution of certain human species to single, key episodes of technological change. But this simple equation of biology and culture has been shaken by the growing realization that there was more than one human species associated with key Palaeolithic industries. This paper reviews the evidence for Palaeolithic change and how these models might contribute to the discussion of the origins of technology and material culture.

Introduction

I was invited to organize a session on the origins of culture for the 38th Chacmool conference on "Tools of the Trade." This conference was envisaged as a mix of papers on new technologies for archaeological research, as well as a review of key aspects of world prehistory and general cultural evolution. I decided to use this opportunity as a chance to return to macro-evolutionary questions that interested me as a graduate student, which continue to influence the theoretical framework of my current research on modern human origins and the cultural record of the Upper Pleistocene in Africa. The major question is the timing and pattern of technological and cultural changes in the Palaeolithic or Old Stone Age. In other words, what do we know about the tempo and mode of cultural evolution over the first 2.5 million years of our history? Partly because they deal with deep time, Palaeolithic archaeologists have drawn much of their inspiration and models from palaeontology. This paper reviews some of the issues relating to the pattern of Palaeolithic change, and how models from palaeontology and various social sciences were adapted in order to understand our remote origins.

Tempo and mode are famous concepts in palaeontology. They were first explicitly used in a 1944 theoretical work by the great vertebrate palaeontologist, George Gaylord Simpson (1984). Simpson was reacting to the emergence of the modern synthesis in biology, which linked the micro-evolutionary events that geneticists could observe in the laboratory with the macro-evolutionary ones he recorded in the fossil record. He was trying to see how the two were linked, and how palaeontology, with its immense record of organisms through time, could help explicate patterns and processes underlying the evolution of life. He used tempo to refer to timing, and mode to describe the patterns or processes of change. Effectively, he was addressing the questions of when, how, and why certain events happened in the past. A similar concern has framed the development of Stone Age evolutionary models.

But when transposed to the study of human cultural evolution, there are some new issues. Like many other theoretical debates in archaeology, the study of the tempo and mode of Palaeolithic technological evolution is more about how we perceive the origins of culture than what actually happened in the past. It involves an understanding of how ideas about the past are constructed and utilized, as well as how material things are interpreted. Like other historical sciences, Palaeolithic archaeology is limited by the fact that it studies events that happened in the remote past. We cannot reconstruct this past in a laboratory; we can only study the artefacts and sites that remain. Unless we have a time machine, we will never know for sure what happened in our early history. Not surprisingly, it turns out that Simpson might have also believed this himself. After his death, it was discovered that he had written his own time machine story, *The Dechronization of Sam Magruder* (Simpson 1996). Using the framework developed by H. G. Wells (1949), he imagined a man from the future transported back to the Cretaceous. He observes dinosaurs and small mammals and muses on what he could do to change the course of Mesozoic evolution. Being a scientist, he engraves his observations on stone tablets that are found by people millions of years in the future.

THE CONSTRUCTION OF THE PALAEOLITHIC

In order to understand the tempo and mode of cultural evolution in the Palaeolithic, one must begin with a brief history of our own discipline. Prehistoric archaeological research is commonly said to begin with Christian Jürgenson Thomsen (1788–1865). Thomsen was the curator of the National Museum in Denmark and developed one of the first methods of classification of things, what became known as the Three Age System. He sorted artefacts by their materials into categories such as stone, bronze, and iron. He also proposed that there was a Stone Age prior to the use of metals (Thomsen 1836). In order to determine the order in which types appeared, he focused on co-associations of artefacts, especially those from closed finds (burials and other features). His resulting sequence of Stone, Bronze and Iron Ages were confirmed through stratigraphic excavations by his colleague, Jens Worsaae. Thomsen saw the Three Ages as successive stages; changes between them were the product of invasions, rather than local cultural evolution. The first of his Ages was subdivided into two phases. In the Early Stone Age, there were only stone tools. In the subsequent Later Stone Age, the first metal objects appear, as well as burials in megalithic tombs along with "crude" pottery vessels with incised decorations (Trigger 1989:76–77). Since Denmark does not appear to have much of a Pleistocene archaeological record, modern archaeologists would now classify the former as Mesolithic, the latter as Neolithic.

British and French archaeologists, who were soon uncovering evidence of very early sites, proposed their own subdivisions of the Stone Age into a number of time-successive phases. Sir John Lubbock, later Lord Avebury (1834–1913), proposed the creation of a Palaeolithic or Old Stone Age and a Neolithic or New Stone Age. The former was described as the age of flaked stone tools; the latter was the age of polished stone tools (Lubbock 1865). Edouard Lartet (1801–1871) is most famous for his palaeontological research, such as the original definition of *Dryopithecus*, the Middle Miocene ape of Europe. But among archaeologists, his field research in the Dordogne River Valley, along with English banker Henry Christy (1810–1865), is much better known (Lartet and Christy 1865–75). Using the association of certain index mammal species with specific stone artefact types or cultures, he created an archaeological or culture-historical sequence for Palaeolithic sites. This initially had four stages. The aurochs or wild cattle layer was the youngest; then came the reindeer phase, then the mammoth and woolly rhinoceros phase. The fourth phase, associated with the cave bear, was the oldest (Trigger 1989:95). Eventually the third and fourth phases were combined, using the site of Le Moustier as the model.

Gabriel de Mortillet (1821–1898) was the Assistant Curator of the Museum of National Antiquities at Saint-Germain-en-Laye, outside of Paris, for seventeen years. Starting in 1876, he became the Professor of Prehistoric Anthropology, at the Université de Paris. Among other tasks, he organized the prehistory exhibits for the World's Fair (*Exposition Universelle*) held in Paris in 1867. These were organized into rooms and were perceived as a history of work. His guidebook, *Promenades préhistoriques à l'Exposition Universelle* (De Mortillet 1867) offered a classification of Palaeolithic and later prehistoric stages and focused on the evolution of culture. Artefacts characteristic of each period now acted as index fossils in the same way as Lartet's mammals had earlier. By the end of the nineteenth century, there were a series of Palaeolithic stages, beginning with the Eolithic or Dawn Stone Age, the Chellean, the Acheulean, the Mousterian, the Aurignacian, the Solutrean, and finally, the Magdalenian. Most were named for specific archaeological sites that yielded distinctive assemblages of artefacts and/or associated faunal remains.

Concepts of Cultural Evolution

In parallel with the discovery of human cultural evolution, the expansion of Europe led to speculation about the nature of human society. Explorers, conquerors, traders, missionaries, colonial officers, and others recorded information about the life ways of the people they encountered. These disparate accounts led to the development of anthropology as a discipline (Wolf 1982). Non-Western people were soon used as the model for the prehistoric stages that Europeans had already passed through in their move to global supremacy. For example, Sir John Lubbock's (1865) most famous book, *Prehistoric Times*, linked the archaeological record of Europe to the ethnographic record of aboriginal peoples worldwide; there was no distinction between archaeology and ethnology. Both were part of a universal or unilinear pattern of cultural development. This was seen as gradual and continuous, and directed towards progress and perfection. While modern Palaeolithic archaeologists would never express it in the same way, they share a perspective with the nineteenth-century founders of their field of study. Most accept the idea that changes in the archaeological record parallel stages in the evolution of our own genus *Homo*. It appears that when a new fossil hominid species appeared, the associated archaeological culture also changed (see, e.g., Foley 1987). On the other hand, there seems to be signs of regular change over time in technology. Production methods changed and could become more sophisticated. Prepared core methods such as the Levallois technique led to the manufacture of distinct, standardized tools. When prismatic blade tool methods were developed, the number of finished tools per piece of raw material increased significantly. This was generally explained in parallel to the evolution of the genus *Homo*. This was traditionally interpreted as reflecting a regular increase in human brain size over time, until it reached the modern range (Klein 1999; McHenry 1995). So it was not a surprise that archaeologists assumed that increasing brain size meant increasing technological sophistication in Palaeolithic people.

Similar concepts of gradual, continuous, evolutionary change were popular in biological circles at the same time. The most important of these was Charles Darwin's (1859) concept of phyletic gradualism. The only illustration in *The Origin of Species* shows a series of lineages splitting and diversifying in response to changes brought about through natural selection. What was new about Darwin's model of evolution was his theory of natural selection. Individuals had variations. Natural selection acted on theses variations to promote the survival of some individuals over others. Over long periods of time, the changes in frequency of these variations would gradually lead to new species. Darwin believed that the record of the diversity of life was a product of differential reproduction. He did point out that it was difficult to test these ideas with the fossil record, as gaps were more common that complete lineages of ancestors and descendants. But he argued that this was because the fossil record itself was spotty and incomplete, disturbed by geological processes such as erosion and uplift.

Not surprisingly, there were alternatives to these gradualistic models. Rather than promoting balance and equilibrium, other researchers offered a perspective of change through revolutionary processes. These models were expressed both in biological and social sciences. The most famous were promoted by Karl Marx (1964) and Friedrich Engels (1895, 1972). For the founders of communism, the various parts of a society, such as its social organization, religion, culture, and economics, were organized in different ways. The economic base was the most important aspect of society; this included how people made a living, how the means of production were socially organized, and the technology of production. Other aspects of culture were seen as epiphenomenal, including social organization and ideology. Marx and Engels promoted a model of cultural evolution that owes a lot to the nineteenth-century cultural evolutionists who founded the study of anthropology, such as Lubbock (1865), Edward Burnett Tylor (1871), and Lewis Henry Morgan (1877). Cultures evolved, they argued, through a series of socio-economic states or formations. These existed in balance or equilibrium but contained inherent internal flaws. For example, in the capitalist world in which they lived, there were two main social classes, those of workers and owners. These groups had different motives and goals and would come into conflict. The only way such a society would change, they argued, was through revolution. The product would be a new social formation, communism (or socialism), and ultimately the end of history.

Marx and Engels took this model of social stasis, then rapid change or punctuation, and used it to reconstruct a series of historical stages, each progressing towards the ultimate solution. For them, there were four stages of pre-class societies; these included the pre-clan, matriarchal clan, patriarchal clan, and terminal clan. Class societies emerged in classical times and continued into more recent history. The three stages of class societies included slave, feudal, and capitalist modes of production. Engels (1895; Woolfson 1982) himself wrote about human evolution in an essay titled "The part played by labour in the transition from ape to man." He took evidence from contemporary ethnographic and archaeological sources and, like de Mortillet, stressed that tools and technology were responsible for the evolution of culture and society.

This brief review shows that nineteenth-century biologists and social theorists who supported ideas about evolution were split about its timing and general nature. When applied to the study of human history, evolutionary ideas became even more complicated. Twelve years after *The Origin of Species* was published, Darwin (1871) applied his methods of natural selection to the study of human evolution and suggested that people could also be explained as the products of natural selection. If this was taken further, it meant that people were not anything really special and had no claim to world dominance. Since all observed human groups worldwide had tools, technology, culture, and intelligence, could their biological and cultural history be explained in similar ways to that of Darwin's fellow Europeans?

TEMPO AND MODE IN PALAEONTOLOGY

Palaeontology, the study of the evolution of life using the fossil record, has addressed similar questions. One of the first to look at issues of what happened and why in evolution was George Gaylord Simpson (1902–1984). His book, *Tempo and Mode in Evolution* (Simpson 1984 [1944]), was aimed at the supporters of the modern synthesis in biology. This included Julian Huxley (1943), Ernst Mayr (1942), and Theodosius Dobzhansky (1937). Together with Simpson, their research in genetics and living organisms linked micro-evolutionary and macro-evolutionary patterns and processes. Mayr focused on the systematics of evolution and was responsible for one of the key models of how speciation could occur. Dobzhansky studied the genetics of organisms such as fruit flies, whose generations lasted only days. Among other things, Huxley concentrated on evolutionary models. Simpson was worried that most of the attention in early modern biology was on microevolution; it seemed that geneticists would be able to solve all problems in the history of life. According to Gould (1995:12), he wanted to show that palaeontology still had a role to play. It was not contradictory to genetics and could help to offer a synthesis of the two disciplines

(Simpson 1984:xxii, xxvii). They were merely operating at different levels; both could help explain tempo and mode, the how and why of evolution (Simpson 1984:xxx, 74). Simpson and his successors, Eldredge and Gould (1972), continued to stress that palaeontology had time, the most important focus if one was answering questions of the rates of evolution (Fitch and Ayala 1995:iii; Gould 1995:130). For Simpson, new taxonomic groups were the products of major ecological or environmental changes; as such, they had to differ significantly from their ancestors (Simpson 1984:110). They appeared due to one of three modes of evolution: speciation, phyletic evolution, and quantum evolution (Simpson 1984:198). Speciation occurred when there was local differentiation of two or more groups within a more widespread population (Simpson 1984:199). In phyletic evolution, there was a change of population as a whole; this was most likely linear and directional (Simpson 1984:202). Quantum evolution is what Eldredge and Gould (1972; Gould and Eldredge 1977) would later call "punctuated equilibria." For Simpson (1984:206), this is "the most controversial and hypothetical" aspect of his presentation. It represents "the relatively rapid shift of a biotic population in disequilibrium to an equilibrium distinctly unlike an ancestral condition" (Simpson 1984:206). He saw rates of evolutionary change occurring along a continuum or bell curve, from the one extreme of low rates (brachytelic) through average rates (horotelic), to the opposite extreme of rapid rates (tachytelic) (Fitch and Ayala 1995:v; Simpson 1984).

Almost thirty years later, Eldredge and Gould (1972; Gould and Eldredge 1977) used Ernst Mayr's concept of allopatric or geographic speciation to present their own discussion of rates of evolutionary change. Mayr (1942) suggested that populations at the edge of the range of a known species could become isolated by some natural event such as mountain building or the formation of a new river. Cut off from the range of the larger group, they would be subject to new pressures, so might change quicker. Eventually, genetic drift produces so many differences that they would effectively become a new species, incapable of breeding with their ancestors. Eldredge and Gould proposed that this kind of evolutionary change would involve fits and starts, rapid change with stasis in between. They labelled this model of change "punctuated equilibria" and argued that it explained most of what could be seen in the geological record. Unlike Darwin, they proposed that the geological record was a good indicator of what had happened in evolution. The breaks in the fossil record were not the product of bad preservation but represented discontinuous modes or processes

PAMELA R. WILLOUGHBY

of evolution. Punctuated equilibria brought renewed attention on Simpson's ideas of change, which were also recognized by a conference held by the National Academy of Sciences in 1994 (Fitch and Ayala 1995). By then, cladistics or phylogenetic systematics (Hennig 1966) had become the most common framework for evolutionary research. In cladistics, biological groups are linked by descent from a common ancestor. Using shared derived anatomical traits or synapomorphies, a single innovation can be responsible for the appearance of a new lineage or clade. Cladistics emphasizes splitting and cladogenesis and forces researchers to see evolution within a framework of alternating change and stasis, much as Simpson, Eldredge and Gould originally proposed.

These methods have taken evolutionary researchers in different directions. On one hand, Szathmary and Maynard Smith (1995:228) believe that the history of all life on Earth is composed of seven or eight major evolutionary transitions. The last, and arguably the most important, of these is the transformation of primate societies into human ones, through the innovation of language. Many groups developed social groups, but only humans made the final transition. They see the emergence of proto-language occurring as early as *Homo erectus*, a fossil human species that existed between 1.6 million and around 500,000 years ago. But for them, it is only with anatomically modern *Homo sapiens* that true language developed, as marked by universal grammar and semantic representation (Szathmary and Maynard Smith 1995:231). It is not clear if they see this as a rapid or gradual transformation. Whatever it was, it created something new, modern humans. An alternative perspective was taken by Edward O. Wilson in *Sociobiology* (1976). He saw this as the final step in the modern biological synthesis. Social behaviour would now be understood within biological terms; successful social formations were the product of natural selection, just like physical features. His goal was to break down the barrier between human evolution and the evolution of other organisms. As was the case for Darwin, there was no middle ground. People were subject to evolutionary forces, just like other organisms. This approach led to a new specialization in biology, and also in anthropology. There is now a whole theoretical school of evolutionary or Darwinian anthropology and archaeology.

A CASE STUDY:
AFRICA AND THE ORIGINS OF MODERN HUMANS

How do any of these arguments fit into a study of Palaeolithic change? The archaeological record shows that the first tools were produced around 2.5 million years ago, when the first members of the genus *Homo, Homo habilis*, existed. Most archaeologists and palaeontologists link the two, seeing key innovations in technology when new species of *Homo* developed (Foley 1987; Klein 1992, 1999). The appearance of the Acheulean around 1.5 million years ago is associated with *Homo erectus*, while the start of prepared core technologies are associated with archaic *Homo sapiens*, also known as *Homo heidelbergensis*. Middle Palaeolithic industries began between 200,000 and 300,000 years ago and are eventually associated with Neanderthals in Europe and the Near East and with anatomically modern *Homo sapiens* in Africa (Ambrose 2001; Willoughby 2005). When anatomically modern people appear in Eurasia, around 40,000 years ago, they are associated with Upper Palaeolithic blade tools, as well as a wide range of innovations in material culture (Mellars 1991, 2005). This pattern still generally fits the evidence, but it does not tell us whether change between industries was gradual or rapid. Also, the recent return to multiple coeval species of humans begs the question of which are responsible for what kind of technology.

The biggest change has been in the understanding of the role of Africa in the emergence of anatomically modern humans (Klein 1992; Stringer 2002; Willoughby 2001a, 2005, 2007). Studies of variation in mitochondrial DNA (Cann et al. 1987) and Y chromosomes (Hammer and Zegura 2002) reveal a recent common origin in Africa for all people, somewhere between 50,000 and 200,000 years ago. Descendants of these founders left Africa sometime around 40,000 years ago and replaced all other humans in Eurasia (Stringer 2002; Willoughby 2007). Most recent genetic research also supports the conclusion that there is little evidence of biologically significant variation in people worldwide. Plotting the distribution of human blood group types over space, Richard Lewontin's (1972) argued the same thing over thirty years ago. Along with the explosion of genetic studies came new chronometric ("time measure") dating techniques such as electron spin resonance and optically stimulated luminescence (Wintle 1996). These confirmed the association of anatomically modern *Homo sapiens* skeletal remains in Africa with Middle Palaeolithic or

Middle Stone Age artefacts; both could be between 30,000 and 200,000 years old. They could even be older, as some late Acheulean industries are virtually identical to Middle Palaeolithic/Middle Stone Age ones. All of this is quite remarkable, since, with the exception of the Mugharet es Skūhl and Jebel Qafzeh in the Levant, modern humans only appear elsewhere after 40,000 years ago.

Independently, the innovations in human genetics and archaeological dating created a new problem. The earliest modern Africans, while anatomically like us today, did not have the kind of technology that Palaeolithic archaeologists normally associated with behavioural modernity. Their ideas were still retained from the study of the archaeological sites in the Dordogne and Vézère river valleys of southern France that were first examined by researchers like Lartet and Christy. Lartet himself had investigated L'Aurignac, where a number of human burials were associated with artefacts that became part of the Aurignacian culture. This is now known to represent the beginnings of the Upper Palaeolithic, the period associated with the first anatomically modern people in Europe (Davies 2001). Lartet's own son, Louis, was responsible for the excavation of the Abri Cro-Magnon, the site in the village of Les-Eyzies that in 1868 yielded some of the first fossil remains of *Homo sapiens* and became the eponym for "anatomically modern human." The concept of behavioural modernity Palaeolithic archaeologists still employ today is based on European data where the appearance of anatomically modern *Homo sapiens* is accompanied by significant evidence of technological change. It was quite natural to expect some sort of quantum change with the onset of the Upper Palaeolithic, since Cro-Magnons were basically humans like us. Their association with new technologies was expected and helped to confirm that they were different from all other fossil hominid (or human) species.

The cultural differences between Cro-Magnons and other hominids are usually expressed in a trait list of behaviours and technologies that are supposed to have their beginnings in this Upper Palaeolithic, starting around 40,000 years ago. These include (1) blade or bladelet technology; (2) more evidence of curation of tools, saving them for repeated and future use; (3) the first organic artefacts, in bone, ivory, and antler; (4) composite and hafted tools; (5) evidence of personal adornment or jewellery; (6) portable art such as Venus and animal figurines; (7) cave painting or engraving; (8) long-distance transport of raw materials and finished tools; (9) enhanced trade, exchange, and information networks; (10) regional variation in stone tool assemblages, reflecting stylistic or ethnic patterns; (11) specialization in hunting one or two species; (12) first use of fish or shellfish; (13) increasing size of residential groups; (14) more structured settlements; (15) collector/radiating rather than forager/circulating pattern of mobility; (16) the first burial sites with grave goods, or burials become more complex; (17) expansion into new territories. Finally, they are (18) associated with the skeletal remains of anatomically modern *Homo sapiens* (Mellars 1991, 2005).

In the last two decades, the discovery that African Middle Stone Age people were anatomically modern has led to a series of new questions. If these people were skeletally like us today, then why was their technology more similar to that of the coeval Neanderthals than to the Upper Palaeolithic Cro-Magnons of Europe? Just what makes someone a modern human anyway? Is it a biological process or a cultural one? Does behavioural modernity only begin with the Upper Palaeolithic? If so, what caused the change, and can it tell us anything about tempo and mode of technological evolution? Some researchers argue for a gradual appearance of modern behavioural traits but an increasing tempo during the Upper Palaeolithic (Gamble 1994). Others, see a gradual, but Middle Stone Age, appearance of "modern" behavioural traits in Africa, something that would parallel the appearance of anatomically modern people (Henshilwood and Marean 2003; McBrearty and Brooks 2000; Willoughby 2001a, 2007). Francesco D'Errico (2003) takes this a step further, and argues that Neanderthals of Middle Palaeolithic Europe were also developing new technologies at the same time as their African cousins. If so, then anatomical modernity is not a factor in the creative revolution that is supposed to explain the innovations of the Upper Palaeolithic. If not, what other reasons could there be for the beginnings of these new technologies, as well as for the great "Out of Africa II" human migration?

Richard Klein (1992) suggests that there was a sudden change in African human behaviour around 50,000 or 40,000 years ago. This was the onset of true language, symbolically based language and culture. He proposes that African Middle Stone Age people were incapable of being truly modern in their behaviour. The beginnings of the subsequent Later Stone Age mark the appearance of true modernity and also enabled the Out of Africa migration. He sees these people as carrying their new technologies and ways of life into Eurasia, supplanting the indigenous populations who had lived there for centuries. While Klein's idea is quite extreme, there is some genetic evidence for a transformation around this time. Studies of the FOXP2 gene (Enard et al. 2002) had shown that it underwent significant mutation either with the appearance of *Homo sapiens* around 200,000 years ago or even as recently as 50,000 years ago. More recent deleterious mutations in this gene are associated with specific language impairment, a disease where people are incapable of complex grammar or speech. However, it does not affect general intelligence. FOXP2 remains the first identified gene associated with language ability. Another research team has identified a gene, *Microcephalin* or MCPH1 (Evans et al. 2005), which maintains the large size of the human brain. It too seems to have taken on a new role with the emergence of modern people. Studies of coding areas and genes are at the frontier of modern genetic studies and may still reveal much about recent human evolution.

When examining the record from Africa, things are quite murky. The Middle to Later Stone Age transition is said to be the equivalent of the Middle to Upper Palaeolithic shift in Europe. But unlike Europe, it did not involve the replacement of one kind of human by another. The problem is that this period is marked by the absence of archaeological sites in most parts of Africa. It is associated with the onset of one or more glacial advances. Lakes and rivers disappeared, and deserts expanded. Regions that have dense Middle Stone Age or Middle Palaeolithic occupations include the modern coast of South Africa, the Nile Valley, and the Sahara. They have little or no sign of a human presence between around 40,000 and 18,000 years ago. In South Africa, coastal peoples might have moved south onto the continental shelf as it was exposed at the height of the last glacial. But it appears that the expansion of the Sahara led to local population extinctions. There could also be other reasons for the drop in signs of a human presence. Ambrose (1998) proposes that the explosion of Mount Toba in Indonesia around 70,000 years ago led to global cooling and a nuclear winter scenario. Whether or not glacial advances or volcanic activity was responsible, it is clear that African populations went through some sort of bottleneck near the end of the Middle Stone Age. It is more likely that they had to recover from this event before an Out of Africa migration could be initiated.

How do all of these questions relate to my own field work (Willoughby 2001b; Willoughby and Sipe 2002)? In 1990, I initiated a field project examining Middle and Later Stone Age technology in Mbeya Region in southwestern Tanzania. I have recorded about one hundred open-air and rockshelter sites, which contain artefacts from these two periods. Fieldwork has now expanded into the adjacent region around Iringa City, best known for the Acheulean site of Isimila, which was investigated in the 1950s (Howell 1961). In the summer of 2005, I observed hundreds of large granite boulder outcrops, many of which appear to have been used as rockshelters during both the Stone Age and subsequent Iron Age periods. This seems to be a good place to test Klein's (1992) hypothesis for the late emergence of behavioural modernity. Some of the Iringa sites appear to include Middle Stone Age and all later periods of human occupation, including the Middle to Later Stone Age transition. If so, this was to be a region where it might have been possible to weather the environmental shifts associated with the end of the Middle Stone Age. It is close to the highland regions of central Africa, which might have served as refugia during the driest, coolest, phases of the last glacial (Hamilton 1982). In East Africa, the effects of Upper Pleistocene glaciation may not have been severe enough to cause local extinction of human populations. If we wish to study African adaptations throughout the last glacial, this is where we should look, something Klein (1992:12, 1999:492) himself supports. But it is necessary to have transitional sites in order to test models of tempo and mode of Palaeolithic change at this critical period in human history. Our 2006 test excavations in Iringa have demonstrated that this region will allow us to determine the tempo and mode of the emergence of behavioural modernity. At one rockshelter, Mlambalasi (7°35.458'S, 35°30.142'E), we uncovered a relatively complete sequence, which includes the historic period and the Iron Age; the latter represents the last 3,000 or so years and is associated with the appearance in the region of farmers, with pottery, metal tools, and the first domesticated animals and plants. Under this is a microlithic white quartz Later Stone Age, which dates to the Holocene, then human remains, representing possible Later Stone Age burials. Below the burials is a macrolithic or late Pleistocene Later Stone Age, and what appears to be a terminal Middle Stone Age deposit. In all levels, organic material (bone and shell) is preserved. At the second rockshelter site, Magubike (7°45.790'S, 35°28.399'E), one test pit produced a sequence of Iron Age, some kind of Stone Age material, then an extensive Middle Stone deposit. A second test pit included the Iron Age and then, with no gap in the depositional sequence, up to 1.6 metres of Middle Stone Age artefacts and fossil bones. The Later Stone Age seems to be completely missing in this test pit, and there is no hiatus in deposition where it should be present. The Middle Stone

Age tools are in a wide variety of volcanic rocks (everything except obsidian) and crypto-crystalline silica. Quartz is present, but only in small percentages. Most of these lithic raw materials are not found in the vicinity of the sites. As in Mbeya, Middle Stone Age people transported stone raw materials over long distances or must have had some sort of organized system of exchange. This is in direct contrast to the activities of Holocene Later Stone Age people, who made use of local resources, mainly small quartz pebbles. Our future field work will involve the determination of lithic raw material sources, as well as more extensive excavations to confirm what sort of activities were being carried out at the sites. It is also necessary to expand the culture historical information for this region, so we plan to carry out a survey for other archaeological sites. However, our preliminary results show that it is highly likely that the Iringa region was occupied by people for much of the Upper Pleistocene. Therefore, it offers real potential for the study of the trajectory of cultural change from the Middle to the Later Stone Age. It presents a good case study for the examination of the tempo and mode of cultural change at this critical period of human history.

Acknowledgments: Thanks to the organizers of the Tools of the Trade Chacmool conference for inviting me to organize a session on the origins of culture. I would also like to thank my two PhD students, Katie Biittner and Pastory Bushozi, who assisted in the test excavations of the Iringa rockshelters that are described at the end of this paper.

REFERENCES CITED

Ambrose, Stanley H.

1998   Late Pleistocene Human Population Bottlenecks, Volcanic Winter, and Differentiation of Modern Humans. *Journal of Human Evolution* 34(6):623–651.

2001   Paleolithic Technology and Human Evolution. *Science* 291(5509):1748–1753.

Cann, Rebecca L., Mark Stoneking, and Allan C. Wilson

1987   Mitochondrial DNA and Human Evolution. *Nature* 325(6099):31–36.

Darwin, Charles R.

1859   *The Origin of Species by Means of Natural Selection, or, the Preservation of Favoured Races in the Struggle for Existence.* John Murray, London.

1871   *The Descent of Man, or Selection in Relation to Sex.* John Murray, London.

Davies, William

2001   A Very Model of a Modern Human Industry: New Perspectives on the Origins and Spread of the Aurignacian in Europe. *Proceedings of the Prehistoric Society* 67:195–217.

De Mortillet, Gabriel

1867   *Promenades préhistoriques à l'Exposition Universelle*. C. Reinwald, Paris.

D'Errico, Francesco

2003   The Invisible Frontier: A Multiple Species Model for the Origin of Behavioral Modernity. *Evolutionary Anthropology* 12(4):188–202.

Dobzhansky, Theodosius

1937   *Genetics and the Origin of Species*. Columbia University Press, New York.

Eldredge, Niles, and Stephen Jay Gould

1972   Punctuated Equilibria: An Alternative to Phyletic Gradualism. In Thomas J. M. Schopf, editor, *Models in Paleobiology*. Freeman, Cooper, pp. 82–115.

Enard, Wolfgang, Molly Przeworski, Simon E. Fisher, Cecialia S. L. Lai, Victor Wiebe, Takashi Kitano, Anthony P. Monaco, and Svante Pääbo

2002   Molecular Evolution of FOXP2, a Gene Involved in Speech and Language. *Nature* 418(6900):869–872.

Engels, Friedrich

1895   The Part Played by Labour in the Transition from Ape to Man. *Neue Zeit* 14:23–38.

1972   *The Origin of the Family, Private Property, and the State*. Pathfinder Press, New York, first in 1884.

Evans, Patrick D., Sandra L. Gilbert, Nitzan Mekel-Bobrov, Eric J. Vallender, Jeffrey R. Anderson, Leila M. Vaez-Azizi, Sarah A. Tishkoff, Richard R. Hudson, and Bruce T. Lahn

2005   *Microcephalin*, a gene regulating brain size, continues to evolve adaptively in humans. *Science* 309(5741):1717–1720.

Fitch, William M., and Francisco J. Ayala, editors

1995   *Tempo and Mode in Evolution: Genetics and Palaeontology 50 years after Simpson*. National Academy of Sciences, Washington.

Foley, Robert

1987   Hominid Species and Stone-Tool Assemblages: How are they related? *Antiquity* 61(233):380–392.

Gamble, Clive

1994   *Timewalkers: The Prehistory of Global Colonization*. Harvard University Press, Cambridge.

Gould, Stephen Jay

1995   Tempo and Mode in the Macroevolutionary Reconstruction of Darwinism. In *Tempo and Mode in Evolution: Genetics and Palaeontology 50 years after Simpson*, edited by William M. Fitch and Francisco J. Ayala, pp. 125–144. National Academy of Sciences, Washington.

Gould, Stephen Jay, and Niles Eldredge

1977   Punctuated Equilibria: The Tempo and Mode of Evolution Reconsidered. *Paleobiology* 3:115–151.

Hamilton, Alan Charles

1982   *Environmental History of East Africa: A Study of the Quaternary*. Academic Press, London.

Hammer, M. F., and S. L. Zegura

2002   The Human Y Chromosome Haplogroup Tree: Nomenclature and Phylogeography of Its Major Divisions. *Annual Review of Anthropology* 31:303–321.

Hennig, Willi

1966   *Phylogenetic Systematics*. University of Illinois Press, Urbana.

Henshilwood, Christopher S., and Curtis W. Marean

2003   The Origin of Modern Human Behavior: Critique of the Models and Their Test Implications. *Current Anthropology* 44(5):627–651.

Howell, Francis Clark

1961   Isimila – A Palaeolithic Site in Africa. *Scientific American* 205(4):118–129.

Huxley, Julian

1943   *Evolution: The Modern Synthesis*. John Wiley and Sons, New York.

Klein, Richard G.

1992   The Archaeology of Modern Human Origins. *Evolutionary Anthropology* 1(1):5–14.

1999   *The Human Career*. University of Chicago Press, Chicago, 2nd ed.

Lartet, Edouard, and Henry Christy

1865–75 *Reliquiae Aquitanicae, being contributions to the archaeology and palaeontology of Perigord and the adjoining provinces of Southern France*. Williams and Norgate, London.

Lewontin, Richard

1972   The Apportionment of Human Diversity. *Evolutionary Biology* 6:381–398.

Lubbock, John

1865   *Pre-historic Times: As illustrated by ancient remains, and the manner and customs of modern savages.* Williams and Norgate, London.

Marx, Karl

1964   *Pre-Capitalist Economic Formations.* International Publishers, New York.

Mayr, Ernst

1942   *Systematics and the Origin of Species from the Viewpoint of a Zoologist.* Columbia University Press, New York.

McBrearty, Sally, and Alison S. Brooks

2000   The Revolution That Wasn't: A New Interpretation of the Origin of Modern Human Behavior. *Journal of Human Evolution* 39(5):453–563.

McHenry, Henry

1995   Tempo and Mode in Human Evolution. In *Tempo and Mode in Evolution: Genetics and Palaeontology 50 years after Simpson*, edited by William M. Fitch and Francisco J. Ayala, pp. 169–186. National Academy of Sciences, Washington.

Mellars, Paul

1991   Cognitive Changes and the Emergence of Modern Humans. *Cambridge Archaeological Journal* 1(1):63–76.

2005   The Impossible Coincidence. a Single-Species Model for the Origins of Modern Human Behavior in Europe. *Evolutionary Anthropology* 14(1):12–27.

Morgan, Lewis Henry

1877   *Ancient Society.* Holt, New York.

Simpson, George Gaylord

1984 [1944] *Tempo and Mode in Evolution.* Columbia University Press, New York.

1996   *The Dechronization of Sam Magruder.* St. Martin's Press, New York.

Stringer, Christopher B.

2002   Modern Human Origins: Progress and Prospects. *Philosophical Transactions of the Royal Society of London* 357(1420)B:563–579.

Szathmary, Eörs, and John Maynard Smith

1995   The Major Evolutionary Transitions. *Nature* 374(6519):227–232.

Thomsen, Christian Jürgenson

1836   Kortfattet udsigt over mindesmærker og oldsager fra nordens oldtid. In C.C.
        Rafn (ed.), *Ledetraad til Nordisk Oldkyndighed*, pp. 27–90. Copenhagen: Kgl.
        Nordisk Oldskriftselskab.

Trigger, Bruce G.

1989   *A History of Archaeological Thought*. Cambridge University Press, Cambridge.

Tylor, Edward Burnett

1871   *Primitive Culture*. London: John Murray.

Wells, Herbert G.

1949   *The Time Machine: An Invention*. Heinemann, London.

Wilson, Edward O.

1976   *Sociobiology: The New Synthesis*. Belknap Press, Cambridge.

Willoughby, Pamela R.

2001a   Recognizing Ethnic Identity in the Upper Pleistocene: The Case of the African
        Middle Stone Age/Middle Palaeolithic. In *Archaeology, Language and History:
        Essays on Culture and Ethnicity*, edited by John Terrell, pp.125–152. Bergin and
        Garvey, Westport.

2001b   Middle and Later Stone Age Technology from the Lake Rukwa Rift, South-
        western Tanzania. *South African Archaeological Bulletin* 56(174/175):34–45.

2005   Palaeoanthropology and the Evolutionary Place of Humans in Nature. *Interna-
        tional Journal of Comparative Psychology* 18(1):60–90.

2007   *The Evolution of Modern Humans in Africa: A Comprehensive Guide*. AltaMira
        Press, Lanham.

Willoughby, P. R., and C. Sipe

2002   Stone Age Prehistory of the Songwe River Valley, Lake Rukwa basin, South-
        western Tanzania. *African Archaeological Review* 19(4):203–221.

Wintle, Ann G.

1996   Archaeologically-Relevant Dating Techniques for the Next Century: Small,
        Hot and Identified by Acronyms. *Journal of Archaeological Science* 23(1):123–138.

Wolf, Eric

1982   *Europe and the People without History*. University of California Press, Berkeley.

Woolfson, Charles

1982   *The Labour Theory of Culture: A Re-examination of Engels's Theory of Human Ori-
        gins*. Routledge and Kegan Paul, London.

4

A Game of Inches: An Experimental Approach to Understanding How Atlatl Length Affects Performance

Nicholas Waber

Abstract. The atlatl, with over 9,000 years use in North America, is among the oldest and best-known tools in the prehistoric hunter's toolkit. The fundamental principles of the atlatl, that it is a lever that increases the length of the thrower's arm, thereby increasing the thrust imparted to a thrown spear or dart, are equally well known. However, several details regarding the atlatl's form and function have been largely ignored. For example, virtually every atlatl found in Western North America is between 54 cm and 66 cm long, but no one appears to have examined why. Based on the principles of leverage, a longer atlatl should throw a dart much further, yet prehistoric hunters sacrificed this potential range for some unknown reason. I decided to find this reason. To do this, I carried out an experiment: I built three atlatls of varying lengths and threw with them, measuring both distance and accuracy. By comparing the results, I found strong evidence indicating that atlatls outside the ideal size range represented by the archaeological examples forfeit accuracy to such a degree that any increased range is useless.

INTRODUCTION

The atlatl, or throwing stick, is among the earliest composite tools used by humans. It first appears in the French Magdalenian period (18,000–12,000 BP) and is known to have existed in North America for at least 9,000 years (Kellar 1955:285; Mildner 1974:7). At first glance, the atlatl appears to be quite simple: a hooked shaft used to increase the thrust of one's arm in order to propel a dart or spear with greater velocity. However, the efficiency and accuracy of performance is influenced by several factors. Previous studies (Butler and Osborne 1959; Howard 1974; Kellar 1955; Palter 1976; Peets 1960; Perkins 1989) have examined differences associated with variation in the flexibility or rigidity of the spear or atlatl as well as the use and placement of atlatl weights (bannerstones); however, variation in atlatl length has been largely ignored. Since the atlatl acts as an extension of the arm, the length of an atlatl should have a profound effect on both its distance and accuracy. Based on principles of leverage, a greater extension should result in a greater effect. If so, why is the average atlatl found in Western North America "between 21 and 26 inches [long] with an average of something less than 2 feet" (Kellar 1955:303)? Why are the atlatls not any longer? At what point might accuracy be compromised for an increase in range (and vice versa)? To address these questions, three atlatls of varying length were constructed and used to compare changes in distance and accuracy. An experimental approach was selected, as it provides an opportunity to experience the use of an atlatl firsthand, including the advantages and limitations associated with each weapon in the experiment. Furthermore, by placing strict controls on various factors of the experiment, atlatl length variation could be isolated as the primary variable, to determine if and how it influences performance. This paper will effectively demonstrate how variance in atlatl length affects both throwing distance and accuracy. Based on the results of this study, it is argued that limitations in length (as seen in North American weapons) are directly linked to the associated level of control. Longer atlatls have greater distance capabilities; however, they suffer from increased inaccuracy, making them difficult to use effectively.

THE EXPERIMENT

To test how atlatl length affects performance three atlatls of different lengths and six identical darts were constructed. As length was the only factor being considered, the atlatls were built using ¾-inch hardwood dowels to eliminate any flexure. The handles were wrapped in duct tape to provide grip and a short screw was bound to the tip of each atlatl to act as a spur. The atlatls were measured and cut to 45.72 cm (18 inches), 60.96 cm (24 inches) and 76.2 cm (30 inches). These dimensions were selected because the shortest and longest are just outside the average size of North American atlatls, while the medium length is midway between shortest and longest measurements (Kellar 1955:303). If an increase in throwing range is directly proportional to an increase in atlatl length, it should be visible in the data.

Atlatl darts were constructed out of 183 cm (72 inch) long and 0.95 cm thick (3/8 inch) hardwood dowels rather than by hand to achieve uniform flexibility, while facilitating the replacement of broken darts. The length of the darts was chosen because the dowels were already 183 cm long and also because they are comparable to those used by Howard in his 1974 experiments. The darts were fletched with two duct tape "feathers" on either side of the shaft. These materials were selected to guarantee uniformity (Baugh 1998). Further, both access to tail feathers and fletching experience was limited. Initial construction plans also included the addition of a small weight (steel nut) to the dart point; however, it was determined that steel nuts weighed twice as much as stone points of appropriate size (about 3 grams) (Browne 1940:210). Therefore, it was determined that the construction and addition of stone points was unnecessary, based on their negligible weight. An attempt to limit the effects of weather variation was made by throwing with all three atlatls every time data was collected.

The three throwers were selected on the basis of athletic competence and logistical availability. It was determined that every thrower should have a background in throwing-intensive sports such as baseball, lacrosse, or football so that they would have already developed the appropriate musculature and coordination to effectively throw with an atlatl even though none of them had any atlatl-specific experience. Also, by selecting a set of highly competitive young men (ages 18–24), it was ensured that they would do their utmost to outperform their fellow throwers, rather than perhaps corrupt the data by not putting in a hundred per cent effort. Apart from the experimenter, the throwers were not aware of the hypothesis. All of the throwers practised throwing with an atlatl for between 60 and 90 minutes during a separate session before testing began.

DISTANCE

To determine how atlatl length affected its range, each atlatl was thrown fifteen times from a set point on a level field. Distance, measured in feet, was recorded from this point to where the dart penetrated the ground. To speed the process, markers were placed at 100, 150, 200, and 250 feet. Uniformity in dart trajectory was attempted during each throw.

Observations: As predicted, longer atlatls achieved greater distances (Figure 4.1). However, it appears that the benefits taper off as length increases. As demonstrated in Figure 4.1, there are substantial differences between the short and medium atlatl and between the short and long atlatl; however, the difference between the medium and long atlatl is considerably less. This is likely due to increased resistance associated with wielding a longer, heavier atlatl as well as the weight of the dart shifting the centre of balance away from the thrower's hand. At some point, further lengthening of the atlatl no longer increases throwing range. Moreover, each of the throwers remarked on the "clumsiness" and "awkwardness" of the longer atlatl, as well as increased muscle fatigue when using this weapon.

Interestingly, the short atlatl had similar effects on the throwers. The comparably light weight of the small atlatl resulted in the throwers exerting too much force with comparatively little resistance. This was especially true when a thrower used the short atlatl after using the longer one. The individual would attempt to throw the dart with as much force as required for the longer atlatl and would become frustrated by the relative impotence of the short atlatl. In subsequent attempts, he would try to throw the dart even harder with disappointing results. This was likely not a factor that affected prehistoric hunters, as it is presumed that they would not switch between different weapons when hunting.

The medium atlatl reached distances comparable to those of the longest one, without awkwardness or exhaustion. It was the easiest to use and felt well balanced with the 183 cm dart when held back in preparation for the throw.

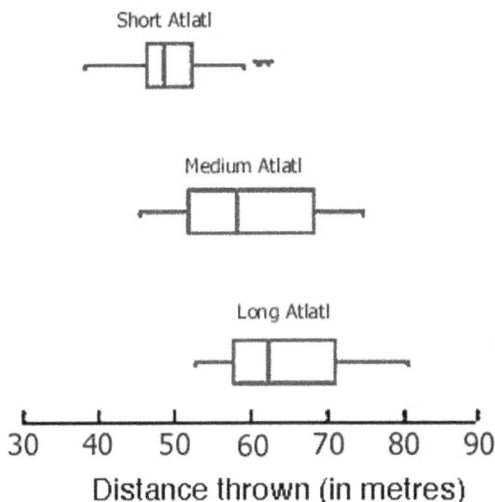

Figure 4.1. Long, medium, and short atlatl distance measurements in metres. Note the substantial difference between the short and medium atlatls, and the significantly less substantial difference between the medium and long.

ACCURACY

To examine the effects of atlatl length on throwing accuracy, darts were thrown at a target, 100 cm high and 60 cm wide, from a distance of thirty metres. The lateral and longitudinal distance between the target and where the dart entered the ground was measured and recorded.

Observations: As expected, the long atlatl was the least accurate, while the shortest was consistently the most accurate. The medium atlatl scored the most hits; however, it also showed the greatest inconsistency and broadest range of misses (see Figure 4.2).

When trying to hit the target, the most difficult factor was trying to determine the force necessary to throw the dart thirty metres. Keeping the dart on a straight path towards the target was relatively easy, but overthrowing was common. Of 90 throws (84 misses), 54 missed within 2 metres of the target side-to-side, while only 27 were within 2 metres of the distance.

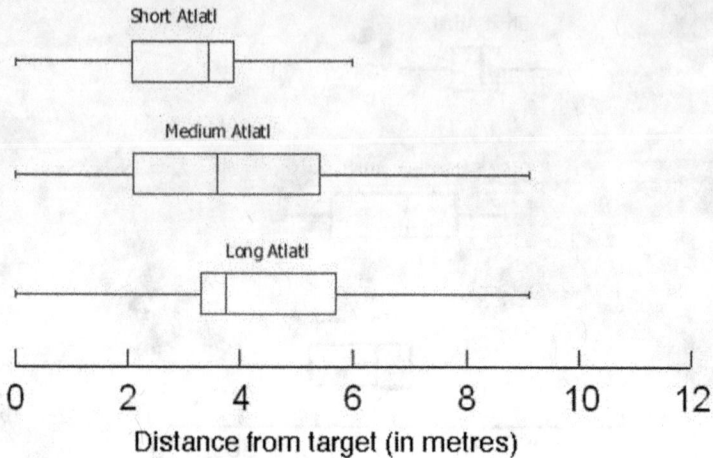

Figure 4.2. Long, medium, and short atlatl accuracy measurements, representing the distance the target was missed by in metres. The lower the number, the closer the spear landed to the target.

As discussed previously, the long atlatl is unwieldy. This difficulty becomes apparent when attempting to hit such a small target. The dart must be aimed near to the ground so as not to overshoot the target. Unfortunately, the high degree of force necessary to throw with the long atlatl makes precision aiming and consistent throwing extremely difficult. The short atlatl suffers from a similar problem. While it is the most consistent, it is likely due to the range of thirty metres rather than any beneficial aspect of the short atlatl. One must exert nearly as much force to throw the dart thirty metres on a relatively straight, flat trajectory as one must exert to throw it on a higher, arcing trajectory for maximum range. Therefore, with nearly every throw, the thrower is required to use full force. As demonstrated with the long atlatl, aim becomes extremely difficult when exerting a great deal of force. The high consistency in the short atlatl's performance is a direct result of the limited velocity associated with the flatly-thrown darts, which could not carry them far past the target. Using the medium atlatl, with comfortable balance, handling and the potential to throw twice the distance to the target, we found that we were frequently overthrowing, then overcompensating on subsequent throws. This resulted in the wide range of misses observed.

DISCUSSION

The variable factors contributing to atlatl performance are by no means a new topic of research in the archaeological community. Numerous studies have been carried out in the past, providing us with a variety of theories regarding the mechanisms behind atlatl function. Bob Perkins (a.k.a. "Atlatl Bob") has put forward a theory regarding flex as thrust in atlatl systems (Perkins 1989). As outlined by the theory, the energy stored in the flexed dart is used to push the projectile away from the launching platform, providing the dart with the necessary velocity. The atlatl is simply a means of accelerating the base end of the dart in order to achieve the desired flexure (Perkins 1989). While dart flexure is important, it has more to do with maintaining trajectory than increasing thrust potential. The oscillation of the dart in flight, like a conventional arrow, serves to keep the projectile flying point-on, rather than turning upwards or downwards. Flexibility is key, however, as even with a flexible dart atlatls of differing lengths will perform differently.

Perkins also suggests that the bow and atlatl are essentially the same type of weapon in terms of physicality and mathematics (Perkins 1989). The only difference is that the bow accelerates the flexible shaft in a straight path, while the atlatl accelerates it in an arc (Perkins 1989). This is not true, as both the bow and the atlatl accelerate the shaft in a straight path. The atlatl is not used as a catapulting device; instead, it is dragged behind the throwing hand and flipped forward as the thrower's arm extends. An arcing path would not only deprive the dart of most of its power but would also decrease its accuracy a great deal. The main result that comes from throwing with an arcing motion is that the dart is not forced to flex and, as a result, "stalls" soon after release; that is, it sweeps upwards, quickly losing momentum and falls to the ground with no more force than if it had been thrown by hand. Other atlatl experiments (Howard 1974:102) have found similar results when an arcing motion was used rather than a level throwing motion.

Finally, Perkins mentions that the atlatl itself is generally flexible and can be fine-tuned by adjusting the position of the bannerstone and the atlatl's flexure to match that of the dart (Perkins 2001, personal communication). Perkins uses the analogy of a diver and diving board to explain this theory, in that the inertia resulting from the mass of a projectile point causes the dart to flex, storing "spring energy," which is released, pushing the dart away during the throw. However, there are many factors to consider: unless a projectile point is significantly oversized (which would negatively affect the entire balance of the atlatl/dart system), the distal end of the dart does not produce enough inertia to mimic a bouncing, bending diver (the centre of gravity for an atlatl dart generally being quite close to the proximal end), the diving board flexes to a much higher degree than an atlatl and perhaps most importantly, the entire diving board and platform are not being flung in an overhand motion, releasing the diver well before the board would have the opportunity to unflex. While dart flexibility is an important factor in atlatl performance, it may not be as crucial as Perkins implies.

Calvin Howard (1974) put forth a theory that throwing spears or darts with an atlatl is more effective than throwing by hand because the atlatl provides a firmer grip on the dart while increasing the duration of contact between the thrower and the dart. As a result, the thrower may exert force on the dart for a longer period of time (Mason 1885 in Howard 1974:102). The results of the current study suggest that these attributes are false. First, it is not difficult to grip the shaft of a 183-cm-long, 0.95-cm-thick dart by hand, nor is it difficult to throw. The difficulty comes in throwing hard enough to propel the dart a greater distance. It is not possible to propel the atlatl fast enough to give the light-weight dart the thrust necessary to carry it further than a few metres.

Finally, the duration of contact between the thrower and the dart is virtually identical whether the dart is thrown by hand or with an atlatl. This is what makes the atlatl effective; it causes the dart to move further in the same amount of time (and therefore accelerate more rapidly) than when it is thrown by hand. The atlatl adds its effective length (the distance from the thrower's hand to the hook at the distal end, not the distance from the proximal end to the distal end) to the thrower's arm, and thus increases the distance the hook travels during a throw (see Figure 4.3). In the current study, the difference between the hand when reaching back to throw and at the point of release is approximately 90 cm. When holding a 60.96 cm (24 inch) atlatl (50.8 cm effective length) the distance becomes 140.8 cm. The duration of contact during the throw is approximately 0.3 seconds. Thus, the 60.96 cm atlatl increases the thrust behind the dart by approximately 1.69 metres per second (4.69 m/s, rather than 3 m/s). If this is true, then the length of the atlatl should be directly proportional to the velocity increase at the point of contact with the dart. It should be noted that with a regular overhand throw, the dart is generally released in an arcing

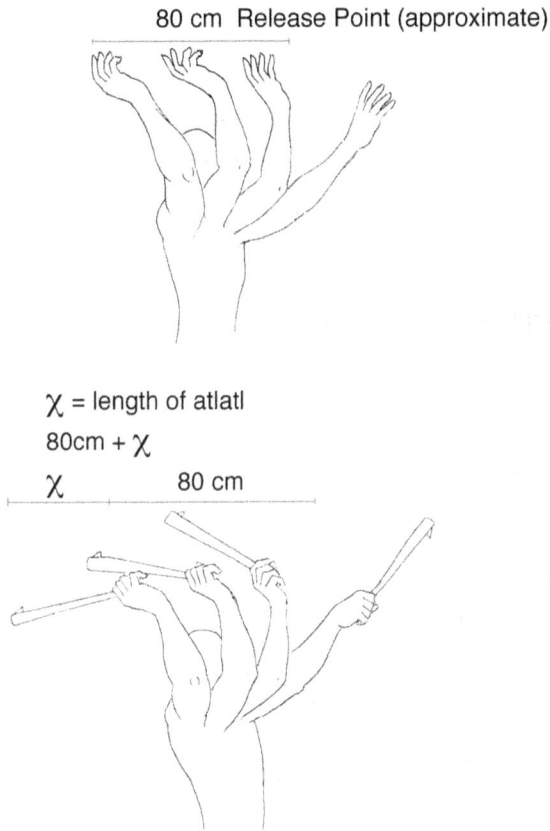

80 cm Release Point (approximate)

χ = length of atlatl

80cm + χ

χ 80 cm

Figure 4.3. The atlatl as an extension of the thrower's arm.

motion before the arm follows through. This is also the case when the atlatl is used; the dart is released just as the atlatl begins its follow-through.

It is important to examine the difference between an arcing motion and a straight trajectory more closely in order to understand why a catapulting motion would under-power a dart. At first glance, applying the above formula would suggest that the arc would actually produce a higher velocity than a straight trajectory. In order to move the tip of the atlatl from the ready to throw position to the release point 140.8 cm away, the tip would arc along a path roughly 221 cm long. This calculation is reached by viewing 140.8 cm as the diameter of a circle (which the arcing atlatl tip would travel if it kept going) and applying the formula for determining the circumference of a circle ($c = \pi d$) and dividing it in half, as the tip of the atlatl would only travel through 180 degrees of the arc. Unfortunately for proponents of the arc-motion theory, this throwing action would result in the dart being plunged into the ground directly in front of the thrower. For the arcing atlatl to effectively catapult the dart, the thrower would have to abruptly stop the atlatl roughly perpendicular to the desired trajectory. This would result in the atlatl tip travelling through 90 degrees (or less) of the arc. Thus, at best, an arcing motion could move the dart 110.5 cm, resulting in roughly a 22-per-cent decrease in potential velocity from a straight trajectory launch.

CONCLUSIONS

The atlatl is among the oldest and best-known weapons in the prehistoric hunter's toolkit. While the fundamental principles of this weapon system are well-known, there are several attributes, such as the importance of atlatl length, which have not received consideration. As suggested by the principles of leverage, increased length should result in an increase in range. From the experiments above, it is clear that throwing range increases with atlatl length. However, the benefit of increased range is not directly proportional to length, as this decreases beyond a certain limit. As the length of the atlatl increases beyond the ideal range, so does the inaccuracy of the dart. Specifically, a longer, heavier atlatl is difficult to use, rendering it less efficient than a smaller one, regardless of the fact that it can launch a dart farther.

Smaller atlatls are equally inefficient. They do not exhibit the range or power of the longer varieties and their short range accuracy is largely due to an inability to overshoot the target. Therefore, an atlatl of medium length provides both greater range and increased accuracy. The lengths of archaeological examples of North American atlatls range between 53 cm and 66 cm long, which correspond with the medium length atlatl used in this study. This would provide hunters with maximum range and increased accuracy. Medium length atlatls would also be comfortable to use and would not exhaust the thrower should the situation call for an extended period of use.

The importance of the atlatl to prehistoric subsistence is demonstrated by its widespread and continued use for over 9,000 years. Numerous studies have been conducted in an effort to develop a clear understanding of the form and function of this effective tool. To date, researchers have addressed factors such as the importance of dart and atlatl flexure and bannerstone placement (Perkins 1989; Perkins 2001, personal communication), while others have attempted to understand the atlatl mechanics through technological comparison (Howard 1974). Based on the results of the present study, it is clear that tool length is an integral factor in atlatl dynamics. The importance of range and accuracy suggests that prehistoric hunters had an established understanding of the length necessary to create the most effective hunting tool. While the atlatl follows the principles of leverage, it is clear that human experience (trial and error) plays an equally important role in technological innovation. Therefore this study demonstrates the importance of firsthand observation and the utility of experimental archaeology for understanding the past.

Acknowledgments: I would like to thank Alex Waber and Bryce Hamade for throwing spears so enthusiastically, and Dr. Sue Rowley for encouraging me to submit my paper to the 2005 Chacmool Conference.

References Cited

Baugh, Richard A.

  1998   Jiffy Fletching Using Duct Tape, http://www.primitiveways.com/pt_qikfltch.html

Browne, Jim

  1940   Projectile Points. *American Antiquity* 5(3):209–213.

Butler, Robert B., and Douglas Osborne

  1959   Archaeological Evidence for the Use of Atlatl Weights in the Northwest. *American Antiquity* 25(2):215–224.

Howard, Calvin D.

  1974   The Atlatl: Function and Performance. *American Antiquity* 39(1):102–104.

Kellar, James H.

  1955   *The Atlatl in North America* Indiana Historical Society, Indianapolis, IN.

Mason, Otis T.

1885   Throwing Sticks in the National Museum. *Smithsonian Institution Annual Report for 1884*, part 2, pp. 279–290, plates 1–16. Government Printing Office, Washington.

Mildner, Michael P.

1974   Descriptive and Distributional Notes on Atlatls and Atlatl Weights in the Great Basin. In *Great Basin Atlatl Studies*, edited by T.R. Hester, M.P. Mildner, and L. Spencer pp. 7-27, Ballena Press, Ramona, CA.

Palter, John L.

1976   A New Approach to the Significance of the "Weighted Spear Thrower" *American Antiquity* 41(4):500–510.

Peets, Orville

1960   Experiments in the Use of Atlatl Weights. *American Antiquity* 26(1):108–110.

Perkins, William R., and Paul Leininger

1989   The Weighted Atlatl and Dart: A Deceptively Complicated Mechanical System. *The Atlatl* 2(2):1–3; 2(3):1–4; 3(1):1–3.

5

Microscopic and Use-Wear Studies Plus Microblade Replication: Experiments with Raw and Heat-Treated Glass Buttes Obsidian

Eugene M. Gryba and Purple Kumai

Abstract. Experiments undertaken on different materials with raw and heat-treated Glass Buttes, Oregon, semi-translucent obsidian revealed significant differences in resulting patterns of use-wear. Microblade replication results are used to show how prehistoric knappers could have greatly benefited by utilizing heat-treated rather than raw obsidian in the manufacture of certain types of artefacts. It is suggested that the general results of both these studies be considered in the interpretation of obsidian artefacts recovered from archaeological contexts.

INTRODUCTION

This paper describes the results of microscopic examinations, use-wear experiments and microblade replications conducted on raw and heat-treated semi-translucent obsidian from Glass Buttes, Oregon. The project was initiated as an undergraduate term paper by Kumai. Her objectives were to investigate, through microscopic examinations and use-wear experiments, if there were recognizable similarities or differences between raw and heated obsidian and to identify the attributes that would distinguish the two samples from one another. Gryba heat-treated the samples. He chose replication of microblades as a way to demonstrate to Kumai how prehistoric knappers could have benefited by using heat-treated rather than raw obsidian for the manufacture of certain tools.

Because it involved obsidian from only one bedrock source, the results of this study must be considered preliminary. In addition, the findings have yet to be applied to the analysis and interpretation of obsidian artefacts recovered from archaeological context.

HEAT-TREATING OBSIDIAN

In previous knapping trials, Gryba discovered that heat treatment significantly improved the ease with which the semi-translucent variety of obsidian from Glass Buttes was flaked by direct hand pressure. This observation lends support to ethnographic accounts of North American aborigines applying heat treatment to obsidian. These include General J. W. Powell's observation of Plateau Shoshone, Voegelin's account of the Western Shasta, Foothills Nisenan, and Valley Maidu of northern California, as well as Grinnell's record of an unspecified Northern Plains tribe located north of the Crow (Hester 1972:63–64). Neither Gryba nor Kumai are aware of any published archaeological reports in which it was determined that heat-treated obsidian had been used for the manufacture of microblades. There is, however, widespread evidence from sites in Siberia and North America where microblade manufacturers had applied heat treatment to improve the workability of chert or other lithic types. It includes three Late Palaeolithic microblade-bearing sites in the Aldan River region of east-central Siberia (Flenniken 1987:121), the 10–12,000 BP Ustinovka I site north of Vladivostok (Kononenko et al. 1998), and possibly the Campus site at Fairbanks (Mobley 1991:25). In addition, microblades of Beaver River Sandstone, recovered from undated sites in the Fort MacKay area of northeastern Alberta, display unmistakable signs of having being made from stone that had been deliberately heat-treated (Gryba 2002). Given the broad temporal and spatial occurrences of microblade technologies throughout the volcanic belts that border the North Pacific (e.g., Fladmark 1985; Giddings 1964; Kobayashi 1970; Kuzmin et al. 2002), what would have prevented prehistoric knappers there from applying heat treatment to improve the workability of obsidian?

Samples of Glass Buttes obsidian were heated in an electric kiln. Optimum pressure flaking quality was attained when the stone was heated to around 750–800° F (ca. 325–350° C). This is a temperature range within which Gryba had successfully heat-treated Swan River Chert, Cat Head Chert, and Beaver River Sandstone. Only samples of raw obsidian and those that had been heat-treated to their optimum flaking quality were selected for this project.

MICROSCOPIC STUDIES AND USE-WEAR EXPERIMENTS

Kumai prepared thin sections at the University of Calgary geology lab and examined them under a low-powered microscope. Cutting, scraping and sawing experiments were carried out with 3–5 cm large unmodified flakes of both raw and heat-treated obsidian. Materials used for the experiments included a soft fibrous material (rutabaga), lilac wood, and bone. Each flake was used for approximately 1,000 strokes. In the sawing experiments, a back and forth motion was considered a single stroke while in cutting and scraping trials the motion was directed only toward the body.

Resulting use-wear patterns were prepared for microscopic examination by applying a thin layer of latex to the used edge or surface of the flake. The latex was then peeled off with film, mounted on a slide, and examined under a microscope. Photographs were taken of each prepared slide using Tungsten ASA 64 slide film.

Results of Microscopic Studies and Use-Wear Experiments

The general findings of the microscopic studies and use-wear experiments are summarized in Table 5.1. An examination by microscope and the unaided eye showed no visible changes in crystal structure or colour between raw and heat-treated samples of obsidian. New flake scars on heated obsidian exhibited fewer ripple marks and fewer and smaller fracture fissures, and they were slightly more lustrous than those on raw obsidian.

Table 5.1: General observations between raw and heat-treated Glass Buttes obsidian.

RAW	HEAT-TREATED
Easy to flake by percussion	Easy to flake by percussion
Can be pressure-flaked	Much easier to pressure-flake
Pronounced compression rings	Less pronounced compression rings
Many fracture fissures	Fracture fissures smaller and further apart
Shiny	More lustrous (under low light)
Smooth to touch	Smooth and waxy to touch
Less "cohesive," breaks easy	More cohesive or durable
Tiny shatter produced during flaking	Less shatter produced during flaking
Micro-chipping produced during use	Very little micro-chipping from use

In use-wear experiments, flakes struck from raw obsidian and used for sawing rutabaga, or in cutting or scraping wood and bone, displayed extensive micro-shattering. Much of the damage occurred at the base of fracture fissures. This trait was not usually observed on flakes of heat-treated material utilized in the same manner and suggests that heat treatment makes obsidian tougher and more resistant to breakage (Figures 5.1 to 5.4).

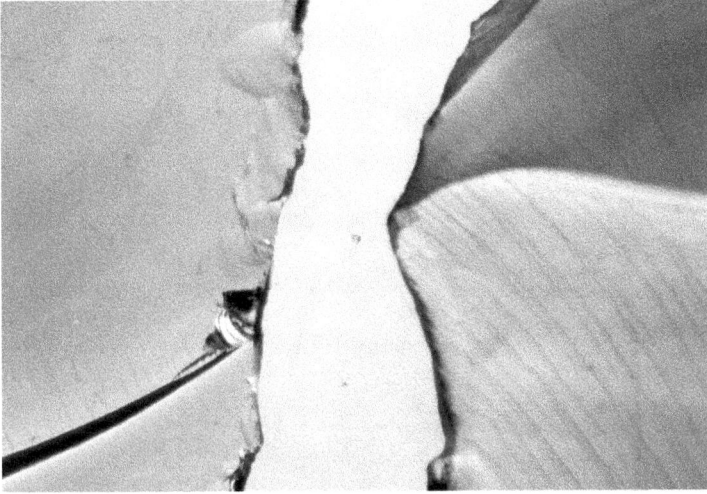

Figure 5.1. Comparison of use-wear damage on raw obsidian (left) and heat treated obsidian (right) that resulted from sawing a rutabaga.

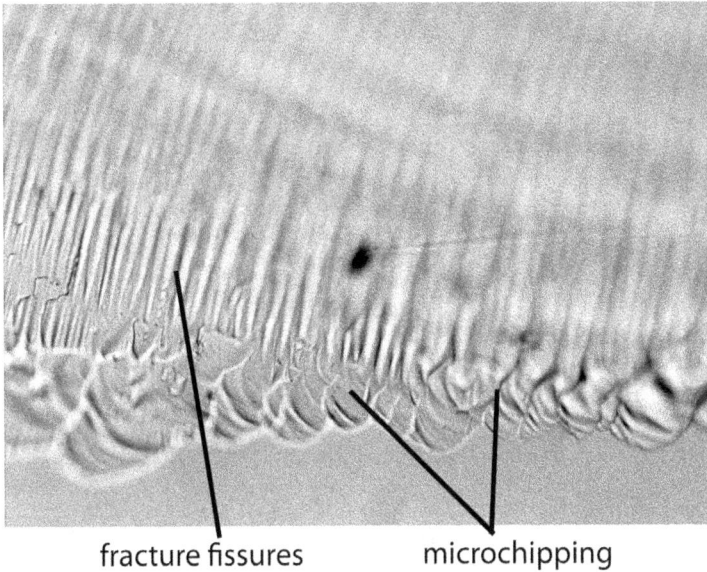

fracture fissures   microchipping

Figure 5.2. Type of use-wear damage created along the flake edge of raw obsidian used to scrape wood.

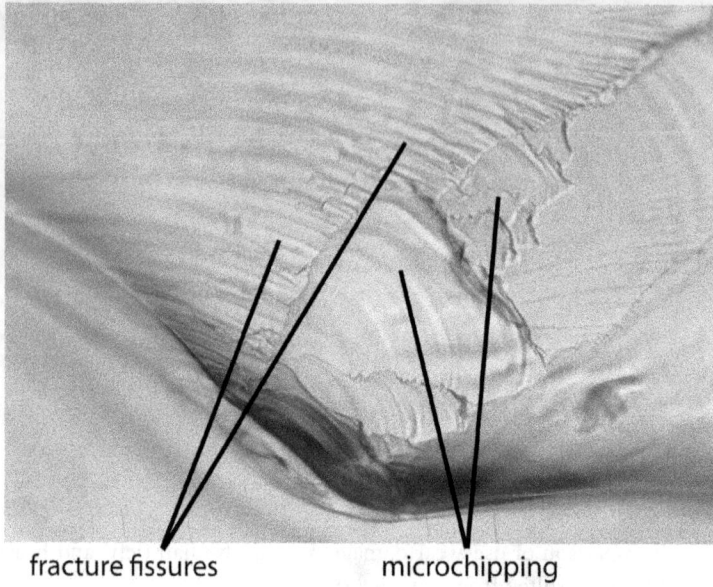

fracture fissures   microchipping

Figure 5.3. Type of use-wear damage created along the flake edge of raw obsidian used to saw bone.

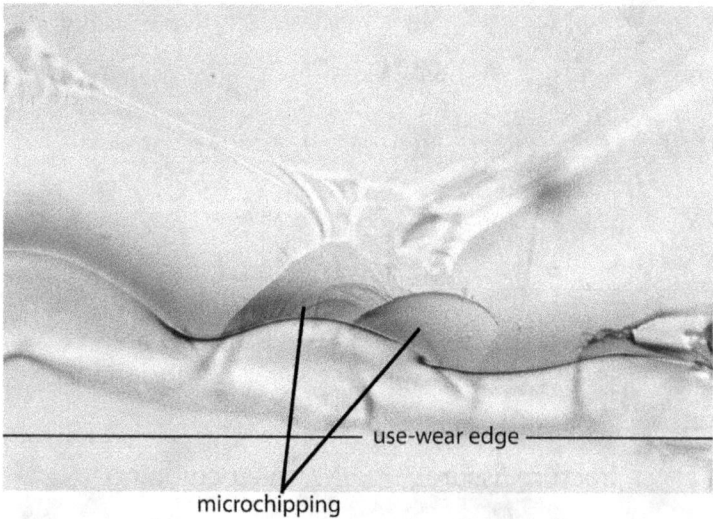

use-wear edge

microchipping

Figure 5.4. Type of use-wear damage created along the flake edge of heat treated obsidian used to saw bone.

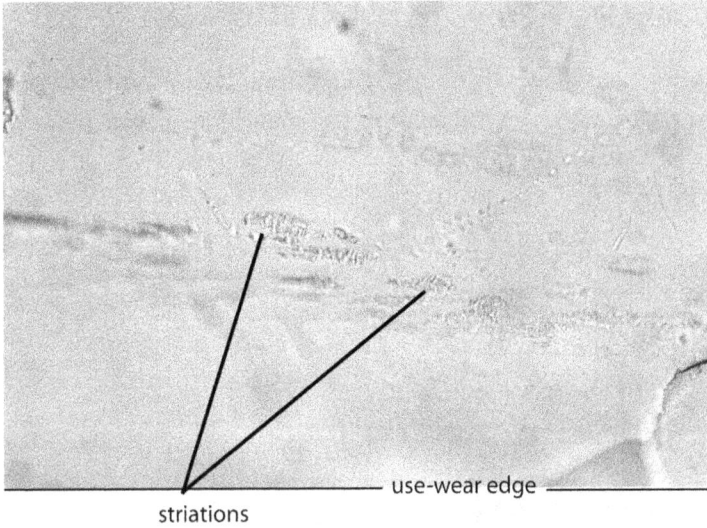

striations   use-wear edge

Figure 5.5. A series of parallel striations formed on a flake of heat treated obsidian used for sawing bone.

On a flake of heat-treated obsidian that was used to saw bone, some striations formed parallel to the utilized edge. These small grooves (Figure 5.5) may have been caused by grit, which had adhered to the flake, or by bits of obsidian that had become detached during the sawing process. In a similar experiment, a raw flake used exhibited extensive micro-shatter along the edge, but no striations (Figure 5.4). Polish was not noticed on any utilized flakes of raw obsidian but was observed on a heat-treated flake used to saw a lilac branch.

MICROBLADE REPLICATION EXPERIMENT RESULTS

Microblades were produced from raw and optimally heat-treated samples of obsidian by a simple free-hand pressure technique that entailed use of ca. 5–7.5 cm long antler flakers (Figures 5.6 and 5.7).

Figure 5.6. A core and microblades replicated from raw Glass Buttes obsidian.

Figure 5.7. A core and microblades replicated from heat treated Glass Buttes obsidian.

EUGENE M. GRYBA AND PURPLE KUMAI

A summary of the results is presented in Table 5.2. Heat-treated Glass Buttes obsidian proved much easier to work by direct hand pressure than did the raw material. As a result, larger pressure flakes and microblades could be detached from heat-treated obsidian than from raw samples. Also, because heated obsidian tended to be more durable; microblades did not usually break during detachment. Blades pressed off from heat-treated obsidian, when compared to those made from raw obsidian, exhibited a smoother fracture (i.e., displayed less rippling), showed less platform crushing, had a smaller and generally shallow bulb of percussion, hinged short less frequently, and were straighter in longitudinal profile. Because less force had to be exerted during detachment, microblades from heat-treated obsidian did not usually break during "pressure follow-through" as was frequently the case where raw material was used. In addition, considerably less micro-shatter was produced during microblade manufacture from heat-treated obsidian than was the case where raw material was used.

Table 5.2: Similarities and differences between microblades and cores replicated from raw and from heat-treated Glass Buttes obsidian.

RAW	HEAT-TREATED
Require more pressure to detach	Much easier to press off
Shows some platform crushing	Very little platform crushing
Some crushing of negative bulb	Less crushing of negative bulb
Bulb of percussion may be pronounced	Bulb less pronounced (i.e., less "overhang")
Blades may break with hinge fracture	Fewer blades broke with hinge fracture
Blades tend to break during removal due to pressure follow-through	Blades tend to remain intact; many just "pop off"
Blades may have a curved longitudinal profile	Blades are straighter in longitudinal profile
Cores develop curved fluted face	Fluted face tends to remain straight
Fluted face may show hinge fractures	Few hinge fractures on fluted face

When the microblade core is considered, these replication experiments demonstrate that there were obvious advantages for prehistoric knappers to have used heat-treated rather than raw obsidian. Because most microblades pressed from heat-treated obsidian tended to be complete and straighter, there was less need to reshape the fluted face to correct the core for hinge fractures or excessive curvature. If a blade broke short with a hinge fracture, there was always the risk that, if one of the lateral ridges created by a failed blade was utilized to guide the next blades, then there was greater chance that they, too, would hinge short. Correcting the fluted surface for hinge fractures or excessive curvature would have involved a significant amount of time as well as loss of material. In a worse case scenario, a misdirected blow could even have resulted in damage to the core to the point where it would have had to be discarded.

It is acknowledged that variations in metric dimensions, longitudinal curvature, or blades terminating in a hinge fracture may be due to variables such as the skill of the knapper, initial size or configuration of the core, flaws in the stone, type of flaker used, and so on, instead of whether the obsidian had or had not been heat-treated. Even microblades Gryba produces from heat-treated or raw obsidian can display a wide variability in size, shape, or completeness. But, by using heat-treated rather than raw obsidian, he discovered that he can greatly lower the incidence of blades hinging or shattering and reduce their longitudinal curvature.

SUMMARY AND CONCLUSIONS

Studies by Gryba and Kumai demonstrated that heat treatment significantly improved the workability of Glass Buttes semi-translucent obsidian, and that use-wear and replicative experiments can be very useful interpretive tools for distinguishing raw from heat-treated obsidian. Whether all varieties of obsidian respond as positively to heat treatment as does the semi-translucent Glass Buttes variety, how extensively in time and space was heat treatment actually applied by prehistoric knappers, and what types of artefacts were manufactured from raw or from heated-treated obsidian are issues that remain to be researched. It is suggested that before researchers can even start speculating on the manufacture or function of certain obsidian artefacts, they should first establish if the stone the tools were made from had or had not been heat-treated, as this likely determined the type of flaking technology employed in their manufacture, or their function or functions and the types of use-wear patterns created on them.

After this project was largely completed, Gryba conducted heat-treatment experiments on Hoodoo Mountain, Yukon, obsidian. Preliminary results of microblade replication and general pressure flaking trials tentatively suggest that heat treatment does not improve Hoodoo Mountain obsidian to the degree that it does Glass Buttes obsidian. Use-wear experiments on Hoodoo Mountain obsidian remain to be undertaken and reported.

REFERENCES CITED

Fladmark, Knut R.

    1985   Glass and Ice: The Archaeology of Mt. Edziza. Department of Archaeology, Simon Fraser University Publication No. 14. Burnaby, BC.

Flenniken, J. Jeffrey

    1987   The Paleolithic Dyuktai Pressure Blade Technique of Siberia. *Arctic Anthropology* 24 (2):117–132.

Giddings, J. L.

    1964   *The Archaeology of Cape Denbigh*. Brown University Press, Providence, RI.

Gryba, Eugene M.

    2002   Lithic Types Available to Prehistoric Knappers at the Fort Hills Oil Sands Lease near Ft. Mackay, in Northeastern Alberta. *Alberta Archaeological Review* 36:21–27.

Hester, Thomas Roy

    1972   Ethnographic Evidence of Thermal Alteration of Siliceous Stone. *Tebiwa* 15:63–65.

Kobayashi, Tatsuo

    1970   Microblade Industries in the Japanese Archipelago. *Arctic Anthropology* VII (2):38–58.

Kononenko, Alekesy V., Nina A. Kononenko, and Hiroshi Kajiwara

    1998   Implications of Heat Treatment Experiments on Lithic Materials from the Zerkalnaya River Basin in the Russian Far East. *Proceeding of the Society for California Archaeology* 11:19–25. Fresno, CA.

Kuzmin, Y. V., V. K. Popov, M. D. Glascock, and M. S. Shackley

  2002   Sources of Archaeological Volcanic Glass in the Primorye (Maritime) Province, Russian Far East. *Archaeometry* 44 (4):505–515.

Mobley, Charles M.

  1991   *The Campus Site: A Prehistoric Camp at Fairbanks, Alaska.* University of Alaska Press.

6

MAKING AND UNDERSTANDING EMBARRAS BIPOINTS: THE REPLICATION AND OPERATIONAL SEQUENCING OF A NEWLY DEFINED DIAGNOSTIC STONE TOOL FROM THE EASTERN SLOPES OF ALBERTA

Jason Roe

Abstract. During archaeological reconnaissance in the west-central foothills of Alberta, and during the excavation of site FgQf-16, a newly defined stone tool has emerged. The Embarras Bipoint is associated with the Mummy Cave Complex of the Early Middle Period. Through replicative studies and creation of *chaînes opératoires* of their manufacture, I will demonstrate that this new stone tool type has diagnostic qualities, which can be used to further our understanding of the Eastern Slopes culture history of Alberta.

INTRODUCTION

From the archaeological reconnaissance in west central Alberta and the excavation of sites such as FgQf-16, FgQe-16, and FgQf-62 a new stone tool has been defined. The Embarras Bipoint dates to the Early Middle Period, which is between 7,500 and 5,000 years before present. To date I have been able to identify over fifty Embarras Bipoints (for examples, see Anderson and Reeves 1975; Calder and Reeves 1977; Calder and Reeves 1978; Hunt 1982; McCullough 1982; Meyer et al. 2002; Meyer 2003; Meyer et al. 2007; Meyer and Roe 2007; and Van Dyke and Stewart 1985). These fifty plus stone tools are remarkable in that they share a unique technological patterning as well as an overall morphology that distinguish them from other stone tools. This paper is a condensed overview of the ongoing research I have been doing with Embarras Bipoints for my master's thesis at the University of Saskatchewan. As such I will provide a brief overview of the geographical and temporal distribution of Embarras Bipoints. This will be followed by a discussion on the replicative experiments being conducted and a synopsis of *chaîne opératoire* as the theoretical approach relates to the analysis of Embarras Bipoints. Last, there will be a sampling of some of the areas I have and will be studying involving Embarras Bipoint technology. This will demonstrate that Embarras Bipoints are stone tools with diagnostic qualities, which can be used to better understand the culture history of the Eastern Slopes of Alberta as well as some of the lithic technological practices of the Early Middle Period.

Thus far, Embarras Bipoints have been found in association with Mummy Cave Complex diagnostic artefacts of the Early Middle Period. As anyone familiar with this time period can attest, there is a wide range of projectile point forms. One has only to review the Gowen Site report (Walker 1992) or the literature on the Mummy Cave Site (i.e., Husted and Edgar 2002; McCraken et al. 1977) to appreciate the diversity of projectile point forms. One interesting observation that has come to light during discussions with Dr. E. Walker (personal communication, 2007) and that will be explored in Roe (n.d.) is the possibility that Embarras Bipoints and other temporally affiliated tools may date to the transition period between Mummy Cave and Oxbow complexes. A number of Oxbow-like projectile points, for example, have been recovered in direct association with Mummy Cave projectile points (see Meyer and Roe

JASON ROE

2007:33; Cyr 2006:12). A more exact temporal link will hopefully emerge as research continues.

In order to do a technological analysis of Embarras Bipoint manufacturing practices, there had to be an archaeological dataset that encompassed the entire reduction sequence. This was one of the reasons for excavating site FgQf-16. Situated south of the hamlet of Robb, the Upper Lovett Campsite, or FgQf-16, is located on a south-facing ten-to-fifteen-metre terrace, at the confluence of the Lovett River and Ronaghan Creek. The excavation, headed by Dr. Daniel Meyer, started in the summer of 2005 and finished in the summer of 2006. The excavation was done on a volunteer basis with financial support from the Alberta Historic Resources Foundation, Lifeways of Canada Limited, and Hinton Wood Products. A total of fifty-four one by one metre units was excavated producing 18,762 artefacts, which included a number of diagnostic projectile points, a suite of other interesting stone tools, and most importantly Embarras Bipoints. These data are supplemented by excavated materials from FgQe-14 and 16 (Calder and Reeves 1977), FgQf-10 (Hunt 1982), and FhQg-2 (Calder and Reeves 1978), as well as over a dozen isolated finds along the Eastern Slopes (Meyer 2003; Meyer and Roe n.d). The number of Embarras Bipoints increases when sites away from the Eastern Slopes such as EgPm-179 (Van Dyke and Stewart 1985) are included. This clearly demonstrates not only that there is a significant archaeological dataset to conduct a technological analysis of Embarras Bipoints but that this artefact type also has a wide geographical distribution across the landscape. Thus far, the geographical extent of Embarras Bipoints appears to be focused mostly in and along the Eastern Slopes, but predictably these stone tools have been or will be found along major waterways outside my main study area.

ATTRIBUTES OF EMBARRAS BIPOINTS

What is an Embarras Bipoint and why are these stone tools unique? There are three key morphological attributes and one technological features that make Embarras Bipoints unique; they include shape, size, material type, and flaking pattern (Figure 6.1). Other attributes such as transverse cross-section, lateral edge shape, and overall symmetry are important characteristics, but the following discussion will focus on the four main features.

Figure 6.1. Examples of Embarras Bipoints found along the eastern slopes of Alberta (figure from Meyer 2003).

The planview shape of an Embarras Bipoint is, obviously, bipointed. Other features associated with the overall shape include sinuous, excurvate lateral edges and a bi-convex to plano-convex transverse cross-section. In some cases the shape can range from oval to lanceolate, the symmetry can be skewed and the 'points' can be relatively rounded, but there is always a bipointed appearance (Figure 6.1: FgQf-16-1). As a matter of fact, since D. Meyer first named these tools in 2003, there have been numerous discussions of whether the term 'bipoint' could be slightly misleading (D. Meyer; personal communication). Nonetheless, even if an Embarras Bipoint does not have a 'classic' bipointed appearance (Figure 6.1: FgQe-16-289), one should have no difficulty identifying these stone tools by their bipointed shape.

Size is another distinguishing trait of Embarras Bipoints. Comparably they are larger than most stone tools, excluding large choppers, mauls, and hammerstones. Their size is directly related to their use as a hand-held tool (which I will briefly discuss later in the paper). The average length of an Embarras Bipoint

JASON ROE

is 11 cm with the largest example being 15.3 cm and the smallest measuring 7 cm. The average width is 5.5 cm with the largest width being 8.6 cm and the shortest width being 3.4 cm. The average thickness ranges from 0.6 cm to 2.7 cm with the average being 1.3 cm. This clearly demonstrates that Embarras Bipoints are large stone tools, even when compared to other characteristically large stone tools, such as expedient choppers or large projectile points.

The toolstone used to manufacture the Embarras Bipoint is significant because all of the examples have been manufactured from locally derived sources. The lithic material used for the majority of the known examples has been very fine-grained quartzite with a lesser number being made from Nordegg Member Silicified Siltstone, Glacier Pass Silicified Mudstone, crystalline siltstone, and possibly Banff Silicified Siltstone. The decision to use local raw materials is not only interesting but supports the general notion that Early Middle Period peoples had a preference for locally derived resources.

The use of quartzite as the main toolstone for making Embarras Bipoints is also interesting from a functional perspective. As a tool that appears to have been used in a multitude of tasks from cutting to scraping and gouging to drilling, a durable material works best. Quartzite is often referred to as an inferior raw material when compared to cherts, agates, and chalcedonies. However, as my thesis work will hopefully show, and I will only mention here, this is not necessarily true. The idea that to create a sharp edge requires a cryptocrystalline material, ideally obsidian, is erroneous and completely overlooks the fact that the sharpness of the working edge is not the only attribute of importance. Based on my personal experience, the edge of a quartzite flake may not be as sharp as that on an obsidian flake, but it is still sharp enough to perform most, if not all, of the same tasks. Perhaps then, the other benefit of using quartzite over most other toolstones is that this raw material is far more durable.

The last point to be made about the use of locally derived lithic materials, more specifically quartzite, is the higher than normal amount of very high quality lithic materials in the Hinton region in comparison to other areas of Alberta. One of the reasons Early Middle Period groups, and other earlier and later groups, remained in or frequently returned to this area could have been the availability of good knappable quartzite. So along with all of the other available resources, people would have been attracted to the area by the availability of high-quality toolstone for the production of the Early Middle Period tools, such as Embarras Bipoints or Reverse Unifaces.

The most informative technological and morphological characteristic of Embarras Bipoints is the noticeable consistency in the reduction sequence resulting in a similar tertiary stage flake patterning. For example, all of the known Embarras Bipoints have large, random, comedial, soft hammer percussion flake scars. Also, the sinuous edge, common to them all, is the result of removing flakes with edge bite striking platforms. A flake with an edge bite platform is created by soft hammer percussion where the fracture initiates well in from the lateral edge because the energy required to initiate a fracture at the edge is too great creating a exaggerated planview concavity on the edge (Whittaker 1994:189–190, 194). This characteristic, although very common with Embarras Bipoints, is more likely a result of the toolstone than the inferred behaviour of the maker.

More specifically, the most diagnostic technological trait on all the Embarras Bipoints is the more complex scar patterning on the dorsal surface as compared to the ventral surface. As such, Embarras Bipoints are stone tools that are predominantly worked on the dorsal side with accessory shaping and thinning on the ventral side. In other words, a large portion of the flake scarring on the ventral surface involves shaping, the removal of the bulb of percussion, or platform preparation for removing flakes from the dorsal surface. There are a number of avenues that can be explored because of this technological trend. For example, during the quarrying and/or the primary stages of production, were spalls requiring the least amount of modification to get the most common transverse cross-section (i.e., plano-convex and/or bi-convex) consciously selected or were spalls extensively modified to obtain this type of cross-section? Will the ratio of flake scarring on the dorsal surface versus the ventral surface be diagnostic of Embarras Bipoints? How do these operational sequences vary from those used for the other stone tools associated with the Early Middle Period? What about the *chaîne opératoire* for stone tools from other periods of time and other places?

Before continuing I will quickly address one of the most pressing questions about Embarras Bipoints and that is their function. The one solid interpretation I have of their use is definitely not as projectile points. The overall size of the tool is much too large to be used as part of a projectile system. Thus far, there has been no evidence for hafting, such as edge-grinding. Third, evidence of use-wear is generally consistent with tasks such as cutting, scraping, and chopping. This is why I believe Embarras Bipoints were used as a hand-held multi-purpose tool, possibly as a core tool where flakes removed from the dorsal surface were used in an expedient fashion. To fully address this question requires more work and so will be left to future research.

APPROACHES TO THE STUDY OF EMBARRAS BIPOINTS

There are a numerous ways to study lithic artefacts. This paper will explore two approaches, one methodological and the other theoretical, that I believe are the most appropriate for studying Embarras Bipoints. The first approach is through replicative studies. I have been an avid flintknapper for over a decade and from this experience I have learned two principles. One, there is an emic perspective to modern flintknapping referred to as "a community of practice" by Whittaker (2004:113–114). This may not be the same emic perspective flintknappers had in the past, but dealing with a flaw in the stone or a snapped biface are obstacles, which have to be addressed both in the present and the past. The second principle is that modern flintknappers can have an intimate understanding of technological behaviour(s). Having the ability to visualize and know how a piece needs to be held and the type of swing necessary to produce a long, wide, soft hammer percussion flake has greater interpretive potential than knowing a billet hitting a stone produces a flake. Arguably these principles of studying lithic reduction come with many biases, but, then again, any theoretical or methodological approach comes with inherent biases. How these biases are addressed in any study becomes the hallmark of good research.

As mentioned earlier, one of the telltale characteristics of Embarras Bipoints is the technological similarity visible on finished tools. This is why the *chaîne opératoire* approach is the best theoretical perspective for understanding these stone tools. A *chaîne opératoire* can be used to study the operations or actions an object goes through from a raw state to a finished product (Bleed 2001; Lemonnier 1992, 1993). The Embarras Bipoint is a complex stone tool so the *chaîne opératoire* will be complex. Nevertheless, making a stone tool involves a series of repetitive operations; that is, during the course of manufacturing Embarras Bipoints there are actions, which are repeated more than once. In many ways the hermeneutics of replication and *chaîne opératoire* take this complex sequence of actions and breaks it down into a smaller series or individual actions. Even though complex, the *chaîne opératoire* of Embarras Bipoints is

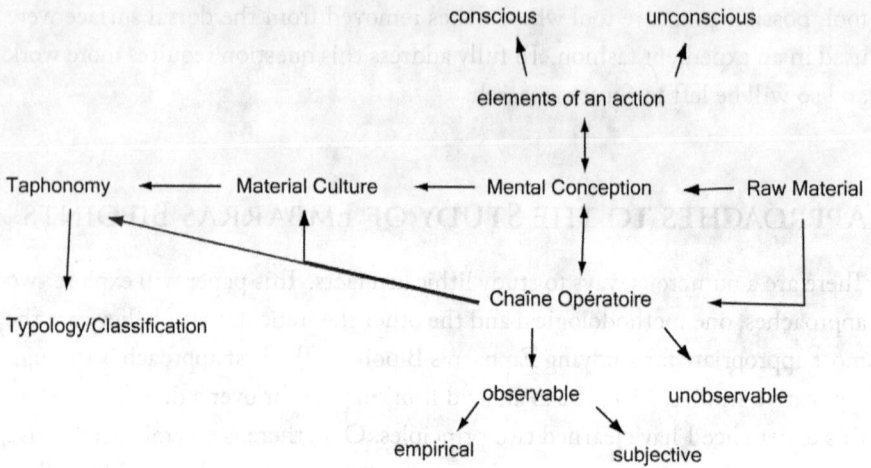

Figure 6.2. An example of a hypothetical *chaîne opératoire*.

consistent and, more importantly, transferable from bipoint to bipoint, suggesting that the reduction sequence was a controlled, learned behaviour, allowing us to explore such concepts as agency and/or other aspects of life during the Early Middle Period.

I will now briefly outline the *chaîne opératoire* of an Embarras Bipoint. To facilitate this discussion I have provided a generalized *chaîne opératoire*, and the following discussion will be in direct reference to the process as seen in Figure 6.2.

The first step in producing an object is to acquire the appropriate raw material. In this case, the acquisition of raw material does not include the cognitive, social, or political variables influencing the decision to quarry, access to the material, travel considerations, or intended purpose. Especially in the case of Embarras Bipoints, these aspects of agency are outside the realm of understanding for any operational sequence unless there are physical manifestations that could be linked to the *chaîne opératoire*. In other words, raw material, in this case quartzite, cannot be considered part of a *chaîne opératoire* until the material has been physically, chemically, or otherwise modified in some fashion by an individual.

JASON ROE

For simplicity's sake, the term *'chaîne opératoire'* is used for the entire sequence of actions relating to the Embarras Bipoints. Depending on the goal(s) of the analyst, this stage of the formula can be scaled to either a micro or macro level. The *chaîne opératoire* can be the entire operational sequence of an Embarras Bipoint from a raw state all the way to a discarded state, including the tools used, intended purpose, and so forth. Or, the *chaîne opératoire* can be a segment of a chain such as the shaping of one end on an Embarras Bipoint. And lastly, the *chaîne opératoire* can be the investigation of a single action such as the splitting of a cobble using bipolar percussion. Because of the potential range in scale(s), the formula requires fluidity and the generalized term *chaîne opératoire* works for this purpose.

An important guideline and the most obvious aspect of studying an operational sequence in its entirety, as a segment, or as a single action is that all of the properties have to be observable. The actions must be observable as either quantitative or qualitative features. This means the more inference one uses to make interpretations of data, the greater the chances the inference will not be valid. However, I do believe the more comfort or better understanding one has of the materials involved, the greater potential to use inference. But for the present study, each element of an action or set of actions will be treated as significant, be it empirical or subjective, as long as the features are observable. My early stage replicative studies will serve as an example to better illustrate the *chaîne opératoire*. The objective was to split quartzite cobbles in an attempt to produce suitable spalls that could be worked into an Embarras Bipoint. A number of different knapping techniques were used to determine which worked well on quartzite and which did not. The projected goal of the early stage experiments was to produce spalls that had minimal flaws, were large enough to be reduced to a finished form, and had an appropriate plano-convex or bi-convex transverse cross-section. Of the different techniques used, bipolar percussion produced the most consistent results. For many of the cobbles tested, the desired outcome could be accomplished in as few as one action. However, because quartzite is a challenging toolstone to work an average of five actions were required to produce a result.

Initially, my *chaîne opératoire* included the concept of a mental template. A mental template can be defined as "conscious ideas and ideals of the artifact makers, so that their identification is equivalent to recognition of cognitive or emic types which are those that would be distinguished by the artisan" (White et. al. 1977:380). A more in-depth discussion of the idea and definition of a mental template can be found in Peter J. White and others' 1977 paper, *Group Definitions and Mental Templates: An Ethnographic Experiment*. After some consideration, a more appropriate idea of the mental template is as a "flexible, mental conception" (Hassan 1988:287). Whereas the concept of a mental template is fairly rigid, the mental conception is more flexible or a more fluid concept of a prototype or design.

There are a number of elements that influence the flexible mental conception. I have adopted Lemonnier's (1986:152) four elements of an action. These elements can be further divided into those that can be cognitively manipulated (conscious) and those of which we may not be aware (unconscious). Again drawing from the early stage experimentation, one can visualize a quartzite cobble (raw material), an anvil and hammerstone (tools used), bipolar percussion (action), and my skills (specific knowledge). These are all physical manifestations or conscious decisions that can be used to make inferences about the unconscious or learned behaviour of the resultant action. The question that could then be asked is how was this conscious action influenced by previous actions and how will this action influence future actions? These questions involving conscious and unconscious elements of an action fit nicely with the flexible mental conception. This approach recognizes that the maker has a cognitive prototype of the finished product but also has the flexibility to alter and change strategies throughout the manufacturing process or *chaîne opératoire*. Understanding or being able to visualize the elements that influence the flexible mental conception provides a glimpse into the thought process behind making Embarras Bipoints. For example, quartzite, as a challenging toolstone, requires an average of five attempts to split a cobble by bipolar percussion using a sizable anvil and hammerstone. This type of physical action then becomes a learned behaviour that influences similar actions (i.e., splitting more cobbles) or determines the next best action (i.e., secondary and tertiary reduction) to produce a finished piece.

Further, the use-life of a piece is linked to both the *chaîne opératoire* and the mental conception, as the process of making an object is wholly influenced by its intended purpose. In other words, the object would not be manufactured unless there was a purpose. Thus the operational sequence of making an Embarras Bipoint is directly tied to the intended use and later use-life of the object. For some people, the *chaîne opératoire* terminates at the point when the object is discarded, lost, or otherwise enters into the archaeological record. I

JASON ROE

would argue that the *chaîne opératoire* continues until the item is collected and analyzed by the archaeologist. For this reason, the *chaîne opératoire* depicted in Figure 6.2, is directly linked to the taphonomic stage. The manufacturing residue from the production of an Embarras Bipoint can be discarded, thus entering the archaeological record directly, or the debitage can be used for some other purpose, in which case it re-enters into the material culture process.

As mentioned earlier, some may consider the *chaîne opératoire* of an object complete when the object enters the archaeological record. I include taphonomy because, even though the culturally intended purpose of an object has ended, there may be natural transforms which obliterate, smear, or otherwise affect the object. In other words, even the natural transforms are part of an ongoing life history of the artefact. The study of the various taphonomic forces that affect Embarras Bipoints between the time of their discard and eventual discovery by archaeologists would be a fascinating topic of study but will have to be left for future consideration.

The last stage in Figure 6.2 represents what we as archaeologists do with an artefact once it has been recovered from the archaeological record. Our biases will influence our interpretations of the object and, by extension, our reconstruction of the *chaîne opératoire*. A prime example of such archaeological biases would be the style versus function debate of the 1980s (see Sackett 1977, 1982, 1984, 1985, 1986, 1990; Wiessner 1983, 1984, 1985, 1989; Wobst 1977). As noted by Christopher Tilley (1989), absolute and complete objectivity is unattainable, but we still need to be aware of the various influences and biases that may affect our interpretations and make appropriate accommodations.

Thus far, I have only briefly discussed some of the results of my ongoing research with Embarras Bipoints. Some avenues of future exploration include the possible identification of Embarras Bipoint sub-types, a more in-depth analysis of the dorsal to ventral flaking ratio and its potential, and more tertiary stage replicative studies. I will also analyze and interpret the patterning in the *chaîne opératoire*, seeking out and explaining any anomalies in the making of Embarras Bipoints, such as the reasons for and effects of flakes with edge bite striking platforms on the overall reduction sequence. Finally, I will explore the idea that Embarras Bipoints were manufactured following the simple principle of maximum results using the minimum amount of effort.

CONCLUSION

In this paper I hoped to demonstrate that by studying the technological behaviour in the manufacturing process of Embarras Bipoints, there is the potential to better understand the stone tool practices of the people living during the Early Middle Period. To this end, I introduced Embarras Bipoints, provided some cursory data to elucidate the diagnostic potential of the Embarras Bipoint by looking at some of its more unique morphological attributes, and provided two analytical approaches that will best work to study them. This paper stems from the more in-depth work I am doing with Embarras Bipoints from a number of archaeological sites in and around the Eastern Slopes of Alberta.

REFERENCES CITED

Anderson, Ross, and Brian Reeves

1975   *Jasper National Park Archaeological Inventory*. Manuscript Report Series 158, Parks Canada, Ottawa.

Bleed, Peter

2001   Trees or Chains, Links or Branches: Conceptual Alternatives for Consideration of Stone Tool Production and Other Sequential Activities. *Journal of Archaeological Method and Theory* 8(1):101–127.

Calder, E. Marie, and Brian Reeves

1977   *Archaeological Investigations Luscar Sterco Coal Valley Project Prehistoric Sites FgQe-14, 16 and 18*. ASA Permit 76-62. Archaeological Survey of Alberta, Edmonton.

1978   *Archaeological Investigations, Site FhQg-2, Highway 40 – Robb Area*. ASA Permit 77-19. Archaeological Survey of Alberta, Edmonton.

Cyr, Talina

2006   *The Dog Child Site (FbNp-24): A 5,500 Year-Old Multicomponent Site on the Northern Plains*. Master's thesis, Department of Archaeology, University of Saskatchewan, Saskatoon.

Hassan, Fekri

1988   Prolegomena to a Grammatical Theory of Lithic Artifacts. *World Archaeology* 19(30):281–95.

Husted, Wilfred M., and Robert Edgar

2002   *The Archaeology of Mummy Cave, Wyoming: An Introduction to Shoshonean Prehistory*. Midwest Archaeological Center, Special Report No. 4 and Southeast Archaeological Center, Technical Report Series No. 9. National Park Service, Lincoln, Nebraska.

Hunt, Jennifer

1982   *Heritage Resource Impact Mitigation of Six Sites Near Robb, Alberta*. ASA Permit 81-147. Archaeological Survey of Alberta, Edmonton.

Lemonnier, Pierre

1986   The Study of Material Culture Today: Toward Anthropology of Technical Systems. *Journal of Anthropological Archaeology* 5:147–186.

1992   From Field to Files: Description and Analysis of Technical Phenomena. In *Elements for Anthropology of Technology*. Anthropological Papers Museum of Anthropology, University of Michigan No. 88, Ann Arbor.

1993   The Eel and the Ankave-Anga of Papua New Guinea: Material and Symbolic Aspects of Trapping. In *Tropical Forests, People and Food: Biocultural Interactions to Development*, edited by C.M. Hladik, A. Hladik, O.F. Linares, H. Pagezy, A. Semple, and M. Hadley, Vol. 13, chap. 57, UNESCO and the Parthenon Publishing Group, Man and the Biosphere Series, Paris.

McCraken, Harold, Waldo Wedel, Robert Edgar, John Moss, H Wright Jr., Wilfred Husted, and William Mulloy

1977   *The Mummy Cave Project in Northwestern Wyoming*. The Buffalo Bill Historical Center, Cody, Wyoming.

McCullough, Edward

1982   *Historical Resources Impact Assessment, Esso Minerals Canada Limited, Hinton East Coal Properties, Test Pit Target Areas*. ASA Permit 82-126. Archaeological Survey of Alberta, Edmonton.

Meyer, Daniel

2003   *Historical Resources Impact Assessment, Weldwood of Canada Limited, Hinton Division, Weldwood FMA 2002 Developments, Final Report*. ASA Permit 02-132. Archaeological Survey of Alberta, Edmonton.

Meyer Daniel, and Jason Roe

2007   Archaeology Along Canada's Rocky Mountain Eastern Slopes: Excavations at the Upper Lovett Campsite, Alberta. *Expedition* 49(2):28–35.

n.d.   FgQf-16: The Upper Lovett Campsite near Robb, Alberta. Unpublished in-term report.

Meyer, Daniel, Brian Reeves, and Murray Lobb

2002 Historical Resources Impact Assessment and Mitigation, Weldwood of Canada Limited, Hinton Division, Embarras 12 Forestry Unit, Haul Roads, Cut Blocks, and Gravel Source, Final Report, Permit 01-296. Archaeological Survey of Alberta, Edmonton.

Meyer, Daniel, Nancy Saxberg, Bradley Somer, Jason Roe, and Carmen Olson

2007 *Historical Resources Impact Mitigation Elk Valley Coal Corporation Cardinal River Operations Cheviot Mine 2005 Mitigation Excavations, Final Report.* ASA Permit 2005-396, Archaeological Survey of Alberta, Edmonton.

Roe, Jason

n.d. Embarras Bipoints: A Diagnostic Stone Tool of the Early Middle Period. Master's thesis (in progress), Department of Archaeology, University of Saskatchewan, Saskatoon.

Sackett, John

1977 The Meaning of Style in Archaeology: A General Model. *American Antiquity* 42(3):369–380.

1982 Approaches to Style in Lithic Archaeology. *Journal of Anthropological Archaeology* 1:59–112.

1984 *Style, Ethnicity, and Stone Tools.* Paper presented at the 16th Annual Chacmool Conference, University of Calgary, Calgary.

1985 Style and Ethnicity in the Kalahari: A Reply to Wiessner. *American Antiquity* 50(1):154–167.

1986 Style, Function, and Assemblage Variability: A Reply to Binford. *American Antiquity* 51(3):628–634.

1990 Style and Ethnicity in Archaeology: The Case of Isochrestism. In *The Uses of Style in Archaeology*, edited by M. Conkey and C. Hastorf, pp. 32–43. Cambridge University Press, Cambridge.

Tilley, Christopher

1989 Archaeology as Socio-Political Action in the Present. In *Critical Traditions in Contemporary Archaeology: Essays in the Philosophy, History and Socio-Politics of Archaeology*, edited by V. Pinsky and A. Wylie, 104–115. Cambridge University Press, Cambridge.

Van Dyke, Stanley, and Sally Stewart

1985 *Hawkwood Site (EgPm-179): A Multicomponent Prehistoric Campsite on Nose Hill.* Archaeological Survey of Alberta, Manuscript Series No. 7, Edmonton.

Walker, Ernest

1992   *The Gowen Sites: Cultural Responses to Climatic Warming on the Northern Plains (7500–5000 B.P.).* Archaeological Survey of Canada Mercury Series Paper 145, Canadian Museum of Civilization, Hull.

White, J. Peter, Nicholas Modjeska, and Irari Hipuya

1977   Group Definitions and Mental Template: An Ethnographic Experiment. In *Stone Tools as Cultural Markers: Change, Evolution and Complexity*, edited by R.V.S. Wright, pp. 380–390. Prehistory and Material Culture Series No. 12. Humanities Press, Atlantic Highlands, New Jersey.

Whittaker, John

1994   *Flintknapping: Making and Understanding Stone Tools.* University of Texas Press, Austin.

2004   *American Flintknappers: Stone Age Art in the Age of Computers.* University of Texas Press, Austin.

Wiessner, Polly

1983   Style and Social Information in Kalahari San Projectile Points. *American Antiquity* 48:253–76.

1984   Reconsidering the Behavioral Basis of Style: A Case Study among the Kalahari San. *Journal of Anthropological Archaeology* 3:190–234.

1985   Style or Isochrestic Variation? A Reply to Sackett. *American Antiquity* 50:160–166.

1989   Style and Changing Relations between the Individual and Society. In *The Meanings of Things: Material Culture and Symbolic Expression*, edited by Ian Hodder, pp. 56–63. Unwin Hyman, London.

Wobst, H. Martin

1977   Stylistic Behavior and Information Exchange. In *Papers for the Director: Research Essays in Honour of James B. Griffin*, edited by C. Cleland, pp. 317–342. Anthropological Paper No. 61, Museum of Anthropology, University of Michigan, Ann Arbor.

7

Systematic Properties of Stone Tool Reduction: Curation Analysis of Palaeoindian Bifaces and Unifaces

Michael J. Shott

Abstract. Like people, stone tools age. Like people, their attributes change with age. Many tools age by reduction during use, which varies by context in degree and pattern. Reduction possesses systematic properties. Yet analytical treatment, when attempted, is anecdotal. This isn't good enough. Reduction alters the size and form of tools. It is a continuous process whose treatment requires continuous methods. Each tool is reduced to some particular degree, sets of tools to varying degrees expressed as *reduction distributions*. I fit distributions of Palaeoindian points, New Guinea flake tools, and experimental scrapers to mathematical models like Weibull and Gompertz-Makeham, not to demonstrate (dubious) virtuosity, but for efficient description and to identify causes like chance and attrition. Reduction analysis is not a new tool, just the thoughtful use of simple measurements and mathematical models to make better sense of how the record formed.

There are only so many ways to design a wrench. Form, after all, often follows function. Owing to their nature or circumstances of use, tools like wrenches change little in size and form during use. Such empirical generalizations imply that the size and form of tools are related to their intended use and that their condition at discovery is determined by intended original use, not history or extent of use.

No matter how true these generalizations often are, they are demonstrably untrue of stone tools, perhaps the most abundant and therefore informative archaeological material. No one ever doubted that stone tools were reduced as they were fashioned, but until recently few archaeologists assimilated the corollary that many stone tools continued to be reduced during use, systematically changing their original size and form. Tools change, as a function of time and use.

TYPES AS ESSENCES, TYPES AS POPULATIONS

Traditional archaeological views of tool types resemble essential, not material, concepts of biological species. Into the Enlightenment, natural scientists imagined "well-defined species, presumably (since the Platonic dualism of realms of being was also still influential) corresponding to the distinctness of the Eternal Ideas" (Lovejoy 1936:227). This is a fancy way of saying that biologists considered species to be fixed, unchanging essences. Internally, species exhibited only trivial variation. Externally, the divisions between species were clear differences of kind.

Applied to lithic analysis, this view has two corollaries. First, tool types as Platonic essences possess integrity as joint morphological and functional kinds. Accordingly, there is no continuity, metrically or otherwise, between Middle Palaeolithic single, double and convergent scrapers, Australian steep-edge scrapers and flat scrapers, or North American Pickwick and Elora points. Second, the size and form in which archaeologists find tools are the size and form in which they were used (excepting fracture and other distortions).

Species are fundamental biological units of higher-order evolutionary theory. In the living world, species are defined in part by reproductive boundaries. Palaeobiologists cannot observe reproduction, so rely mostly upon anatomical differences to distinguish fossil species. Unable to observe living organisms, palaeobiologists must order fossil specimens into units like species but must not confuse taxonomy with other sources of variation (e.g., polymorphism, growth from birth to maturity).

To pursue the palaeobiological analogy, archaeologists define types from the great variation expressed in stone tools. But they cannot observe in use the tools that they classify and know that some stone tools were only parts of larger wholes, not integral wholes themselves. Like palaeontologists, archaeologists must accommodate systematic variation that occurs within, not between, taxa. Reduction is an archaeological analogue of biological growth that works in the opposite direction.

Reduction itself occurs flake by flake. Nominally, it is discrete but it is better understood as a continuous process, both because the incremental units – retouch flakes – ordinarily are very small relative to the tool and because reduction is measured by continuous variables or dimensions like length and width. If reduction is continuous, then tools vary in continuous terms (Hiscock and Attenbrow 2003), so cannot approximate Platonic essences. Any types formed among the complex variation in stone-tool size and form are empirical tendencies; they are populations, not essential types. This is not to deny the validity of typological concepts nor the reality of many stone-tool types. Even empirical tendencies sometimes are discretely different from one another. It is, however, to deny the necessity of essential types and to acknowledge that much variation in stone-tool size and form owes to continuous reduction combined with modes of use and retouch.

This is the reduction thesis, which had independent Old World and New World origins and far-reaching implications for ontological fundamentals like the nature and identity of types and how tool assemblages form. In biology, species possess at least a measure of integrity; lions never become giraffes. But in evolutionary time, species evolve into descendants by various modes, so typological integrity is breached over long spans or at higher taxonomic levels than species. In different ways, lithic reduction compromises the integrity of tool types. Lions never become giraffes but Oldowan cobbles become discoids become scrapers (Sahnouni et al. 1997) and Pickwick points become Eloras (Hoffman 1985:580).

Reduction and its effects on tool size and form – and therefore on typology – register clearly in Palaeolithic tools (Dibble 1987), North American stemmed bifaces (Hoffman 1985) and Palaeoindian hidescrapers (Shott 1995), Australian flake tools (Hiscock and Attenbrow 2003), and in Ethiopian hidescrapers

(Shott and Weedman 2007; Weedman 2002). Reduction effects are recognized in many tool types of many ages from many parts of the world. Types defined in these reduction trajectories lack integrity (but may retain descriptive validity); defining types among these tools is like slicing a piece of water from a flowing stream.

REDUCTION AND CURATION

Besides its typological implications, reduction engages the theoretical question of curation. This quantity is the relationship between realized and maximum utility of tools, i.e., how used up tools become (Shott 1996). So defined, curation itself engages the further concept of utility. "Utility" has several meanings (e.g., Shott 1996:269–271); for practical purposes, it signifies the amount of use that a tool can supply.

Practically, maximum utility is approximated as the greatest amount or degree of reduction that a tool can undergo, realized utility as the reduction (less than or equal to maximum utility) that it actually experiences. Size and form at discard gives the latter quantity. Nothing directly gives the former, but it is approximated by original mass, size, or volume. However utility is defined, therefore, its estimation requires knowing original size of specimens. Curation is not use life, which is simply the longevity of tools in time, number of uses or other units; specimens in a type can be highly curated even if the type's mean use life is short or, conversely, curated at low rates even though the type's mean use life is high (Shott and Sillitoe 2005).

Like use life or, for that matter, height or weight, curation can be measured by central tendency (e.g., mean, median) (Schiffer 1976:54). Unless all specimens had identical histories, however, the distribution of curation values is as important as central tendency (Shott and Sillitoe 2004), just as the distribution of height is as important as its mean in any population. Two artefact categories can be equal in mean curation but very different in their distributions, one showing little variation around the mean, the other a great deal. Consider an analogy to pencils. Two sets of discarded pencils both average, say, 50 per cent reduction of original length. In one, all pencils are reduced to that figure. In the other, pencils are discarded in equal proportions from slight reduction of 1 per cent to practically complete reduction to stubs at 99 per cent. In this deliberately exaggerated example, identity in mean disguises great variation in distribution that demands explanation.

At the assemblage level, degree or amount of curation is distributed across specimens to form curation distributions or curves. Curation distributions may seem esoteric but influence how the archaeological record formed (Shott and Sillitoe 2005), and so they are important to know. They remain practically unknown in lithic analysis, yet precedents elsewhere attest to their value. Faunal analysts and palaeodemographers routinely estimate age-at-death in their subjects. No faunal analysis is complete before determining death-age curves, whose form and scale distinguish hunting from attritional causes. No osteological analysis is complete before determining age-specific mortality because mortality distributions implicate diet, social complexity, density-dependent disease incidence or other cultural factors. In short, faunal analysis and palaeodemography are incomplete without regard for the scale and form of mortality distributions. Lithic analysis is incomplete without regard for curation distributions.

Curation curves can be compared between assemblages, but they also can be analyzed. Depending on their forms and the distribution of values that comprise them, curves fitted to the Weibull and other theoretical models may implicate the effects of chance versus attrition in tool failure. For instance, North American Palaeoindian fluted bifaces and endscrapers had different characteristic cumulative-survivorship curves and failure distributions (Shott and Sillitoe 2004:350–352). Biface discard was governed by chance, which is no surprise considering that bifaces ("points") are thin for their size and are subjected to myriad physical stresses from striking objects at high speeds. Endscraper discard was governed by attrition, again no surprise considering that scrapers are thicker and more robust for their size and in use are subjected to fewer and less variable stresses.

MEASURING REDUCTION

As important as it is for typology and curation analysis, reduction has proven difficult to measure. Until accurate and precise indices were devised, tool reduction could only be approximated qualitatively. For instance, Dibble's (1987) Middle Palaeolithic reduction thesis equated reduction stage with typological status (i.e., if a flake tool was reduced so much, it became a Type A tool, if so much more a Type B tool, and so on). Essentially, reduction approximated this way is a nominal variable, a necessary status in the absence of reduction measures. But only reduction indices grounded in estimates of tools' original size can measure reduction and curation as ratio-scale, continuous variables. This point is much more than academic because continuous measurement of reduction is faithful to the continuous nature of the reduction process (e.g., Larson and Finley 2004). Ratio-scale reduction can be analyzed in ways that nominal- or ordinal-scale reduction cannot be. So measuring reduction requires comparing the end result – the tool as discarded to enter the archaeological record and thus found by archaeologists – to its original size and form.

Archaeologists have devised and tested several reduction measures based on form, geometry, retouch characteristics, the allometry of original size and form, and archaeological context (e.g., Andrefsky 2006; Andrefsky 2008; Clarkson 2002; Hiscock and Attenbrow 2003; Shott and Ballenger 2007; Shott and Weedman 2007). All are useful, but their value might vary by tool type, industry, toolstone, context, or other factors. All are inherently limited, but in different respects; no biface-reduction measure, for instance, can be grounded in the cross-section geometry of flakes or in platform allometry because bifaces lack these features. Even some flake tools like endscrapers are modified extensively before use by trimming or removing features like their platforms. But several indices can be measured on the same specimens, so there are opportunities to compare them.

Comparisons will be complicated because measures do not scale identically. A geometric index commonly applied to Australian flake tools (Hiscock and Attenbrow 2003), for instance, is a ratio that varies between 0 and 1 and measures reduction in two-dimensional cross-section form of three-dimensional objects. Clarkson's (2002) invasiveness index varies over the same range but measures reduction by the sum of interval scores of retouch extent. Flake allometry measures (Shott and Ballenger 2007) also are ratios, often between two-dimensional measures (platform area and surface area). Depending on the allometric measure, values can range from 0 to well above 1.

No matter their differences in scale, reduction measures must be compared in controlled experiments and empirical data. But reduction is best measured using all means available, and no single estimator is likely to be best for all purposes or in all tool types. Several estimators are apt to correlate differently with one another. Measures' suitability for particular tool types and purposes are matters for further research. My purpose here is merely to demonstrate the use and implications of several simple reduction measures applied to Midwestern North American Palaeoindian tool types.

REDUCTION AND MODEL-FITTING

Shott and Sillitoe's (2004) earlier analysis involved small samples of Midwestern North American Palaeoindian tools. Here, I use much larger samples, especially of bifaces, and expand analysis by fitting reduction distributions to the Weibull and Gompertz-Makeham two-parameter models. Weibull α is a scale (i.e., use life) parameter, β a shape parameter that implicates different causes of failure or discard (Shott and Sillitoe 2004). If $\beta = 1$, failure is by chance; if $\beta > 1$, failure is by attrition. Significant departure from 1 was gauged by maximum likelihood estimation (Shott and Sillitoe 2004:344). Gompertz-Makeham a also is a scale parameter, b a shape parameter that measures failure rate as a function of time. Gompertz-Makeham b can be interpreted as curation rate, higher values indicating greater curation (Shott and Sillitoe 2005). Weibull and Gompertz-Makeham parameters do not scale identically; the same data can yield different estimates for parameters of the two models.

I compare bifaces and unifaces from occupational sites from two successive Palaeoindian phases, Gainey (ca. 11,500–10,900 RCYBP) and Parkhill (ca. 10,900–10,500 RCYBP). Shott (2004) described the phases and samples. I studied about 380 Clovis-Gainey bifaces and about 80 Barnes bifaces of Parkhill affinity from assemblages in the American Midwest. Endscrapers are common in Midwestern Palaeoindian assemblages, but data on metric dimensions suitable for estimating reduction are not. I used all available sources: two Gainey-affinity and two Parkhill-affinity assemblages from the Great Lakes.

Biface Reduction. A tool's size at discard is a simple matter of measurement. But knowing how much it was reduced in use requires knowing original size. For fluted bifaces, I estimated original size from dimensions of Gainey and Barnes specimens found in Midwestern or nearby caches. Cache bifaces were longer than analyzed specimens found at occupational sites, but not consistently longer in other dimensions of blade or haft. Accordingly, I estimated reduction as the ratio of each specimen's length to the mean length of cache bifaces; the

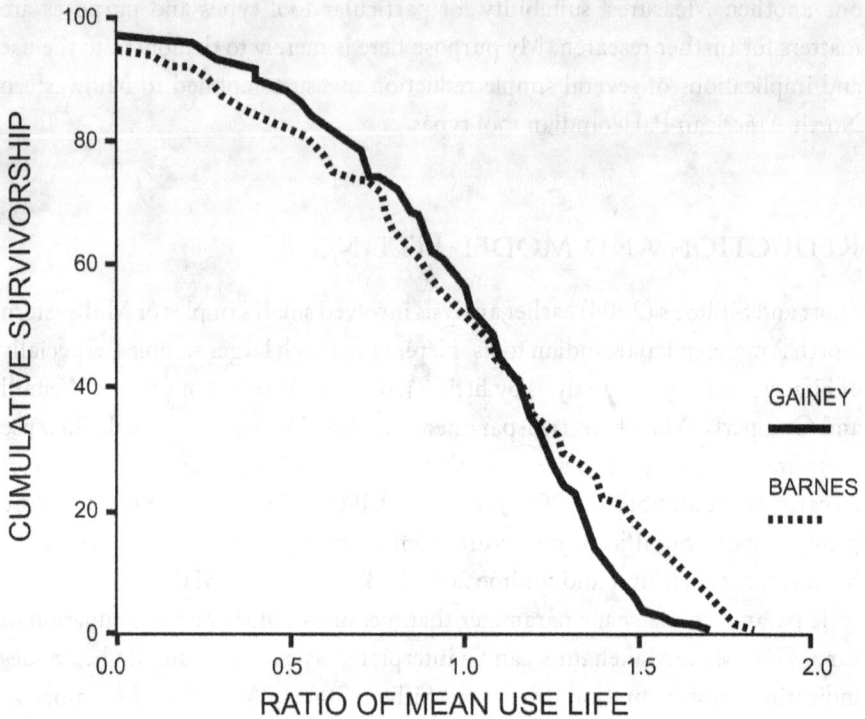

Figure 7.1. Cumulative Survivorship in Gainey and Barnes Bifaces.

resulting index varies between 0 and 1. Then I subtracted the result from 1 so that more reduced specimens have higher values.

Figure 7.1 shows each type's cumulative survivorship curve with the abscissa rescaled, for reasons discussed by Shott and Sillitoe (2004, 2005), to relative reduction, accomplished by dividing each specimen's reduction value by the mean for its type. Gompertz-Makeham estimates differ little between the types (Table 7.1) and confidence ranges overlap greatly. Gainey and Barnes bifaces differ little in model parameters.

Table 7.1. Fit of Gainey and Barnes fluted bifaces to the Weibull and Gompertz-Makeham models. (Parentheses following Weibull β values indicate similarity to or difference from a value of 1.)

	WEIBULL		GOMPERTZ-MAKEHAM	
	α	β	*a*	*b*
Gainey	.55	1.98 (> 1)	.12	7.39
Barnes	.48	1.64 (> 1)	.18	6.96

For both phases, Weibull β significantly exceeds 1, implicating attrition in the failure and discard of fluted bifaces. These tools wore out; they did not fail by accident. This result may surprise, both because fluted bifaces commonly are thought to have been lost in use and therefore scattered across the landscape as what many archaeologists call "isolated finds," and because attrition suggests use as knives or general-purpose tools at least as much as weapon tips.

Reduction or curation analysis is valuable for what it suggests about tool use and the formation of tool assemblages. In experimental points used as darts, failure typically is by chance (Shott 2002). Not so in Midwestern Palaeoindian bifaces, at least in the reduction measures used here.

Endscraper Reduction. Lacking caches of unreduced unifaces, original size must be estimated differently. In actualistic experiments, flake surface area (length * width) was expressed as a function of platform area (Shott et al. 2000: Table 4). I call this RED1, as follows:

RED1 = Area / 4.36 + .52 * (platform width*platform thickness).

RED1 estimates original size as flake area. In controlled experiments, Pelcin (1996:Table 11) expressed flake weight as a function of platform thickness. I call this size estimate RED2, as follows:

RED2 = Observed Weight / $(.011 *$ platform thickness$)^3 - (.63*$platform thickness$)^2 + (2.819 *$ platform thickness$).$

This expression estimates amount of weight reduction experienced by a tool. There are other uniface-reduction measures (e.g., Clarkson 2002; Hiscock and

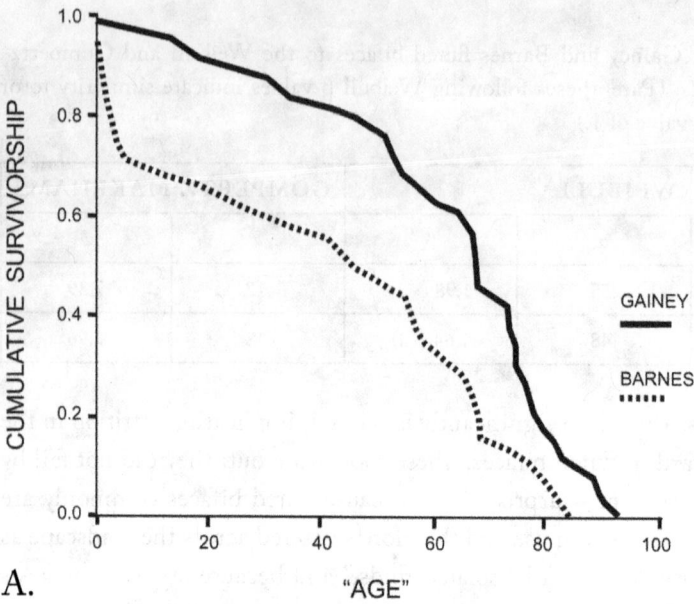

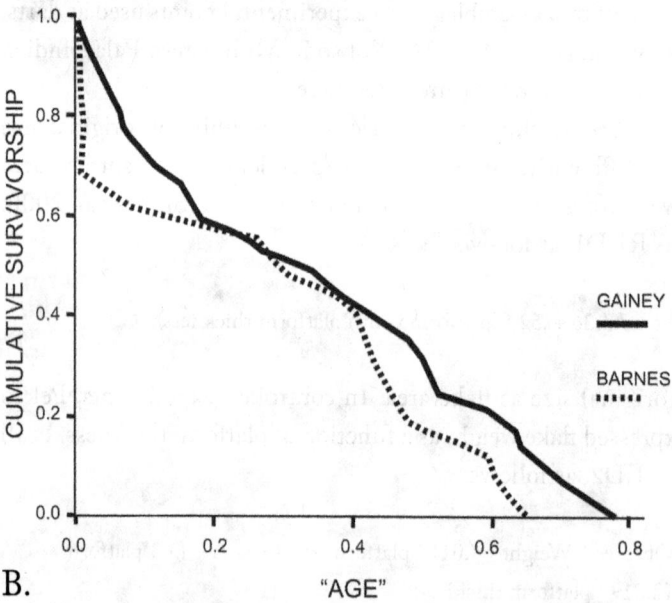

Figure 7.2. Cumulative Survivorship in Gainey and Parkhill Unifaces: A. Using RED1. B. Using RED2.

MICHAEL J. SHOTT

Table 7.2. Fit of Gainey and "Barnes" unifaces to the Weibull and Gompertz-Makeham models. (Parentheses following Weibull β values indicate similarity to or difference from a value of 1.)

	WEIBULL		GOMPERTZ-MAKEHAM	
	α	β	a	b
RED1 MEASURE				
Gainey	73.1	2.32 (> 1)	.015	.018
Barnes	60.0	1.01 ($\approx$ 1)	.003	.029
RED2 MEASURE				
Gainey	.42	1.36 ($\approx$ 1)	.002	.044
Barnes	.51	0.82 ($\approx$ 1)	.001	.045

Attenbrow 2003; Shott and Weedman 2007), but I use RED1 and RED2 as allometric reduction estimates. As with bifaces, I converted measures such that higher values signify greater reduction.

Strictly, the "Barnes" type pertains only to bifaces, which are diagnostic of the Parkhill Phase. For consistency only, I refer to Parkhill Phase unifaces as "Barnes." Gainey and Barnes endscrapers differ in mean of RED1, based on linear dimensions, but not of RED2, based on weight. In both cases, Gainey Phase specimens have higher values and therefore are more extensively reduced. Using RED1, there is considerably lower survivorship in Barnes specimens (Figure 7.2a). Accordingly, the Barnes β is lower, indicating chance, Gainey β higher, indicating attrition (Table 7.2). Gompertz-Makeham b values also differ. In RED2, distributions are more similar (Figure 7.2b); despite Gainey's higher value neither β significantly exceeds 1. (Figure 7.2a,b uses absolute, not relative, reduction ["age"] to emphasize differences between distributions.) Gompertz-Makeham b values are nearly identical. Measures differ in results. On balance, however, Gainey endscrapers are somewhat more reduced and therefore better curated.

Whatever reduction or curation measures imply about tool use, they more directly suggest how assemblages formed. Attrited tools do not fail at unpredictable times and places. Therefore, attrited tools should accumulate at places in numbers sufficient for their assemblages to be identified as large "sites." Attrited tools have more predictable life histories and longevity. Their size and composition in assemblages register the joint effects of rate of activity performance and difference in use life. Therefore, their assemblages should show correlation between size and composition. Tools that fail by chance do so without regard to time or place, so they might be more dispersed across the landscape. They should accumulate in more but smaller assemblages and at rates independent of activity performance.

Conclusion

The above are mere examples of reduction analysis and fitting distributions to mathematical models. As research continues, we must consider challenges and problems. There always is the empirical problem of more data, which bears no more than passing mention here. More significant are methodological problems.

We must learn more about the consistency of different reduction measures and the distributions that result from them. If the same tools yield significantly different distributions using different reduction measures, then we must determine the most valid measures. There is also the question of measurement scale of input data. Weibull arose in industrial settings. There it often is applied to very small data sets in which each tested specimen's time-to-failure can be input. But stone-tool assemblages, like human and other populations, often are large enough that input data on reduction must be pooled. The number and width of intervals chosen may influence results, especially in fitting to Gompertz-Makeham. Again, we need more study of possible effects before this approach to reduction analysis becomes standardized.

Besides the validity of measures, we must consider additional mathematical models. Weibull is common in engineering, Gompertz-Makeham in human demography. But general models like the exponential, and more complex models also should be considered. The steep decline in Barnes scraper survivorship at low "age" (Figure 7.2a,b), for instance, resembles high infant mortality, which might fit Siler's (1979) model.

Demographic models were designed for common patterns of mortality in human and animal populations. Animals and stone tools do not survive for

Michael J. Shott

the same lengths of time, so of course their mortality or curation distributions differ in scale. Scale parameters control for such differences. (Various reduction measures also may differ in range and scale; presumably, scale parameters can measure and thereby control for this variation.) More significant are differences in the shape or form of distributions. Demographic models assume low mortality either from birth or inception or after an initial period of relatively high risk, until late stages of life. Accordingly, a typical hazard distribution for humans and other animals is roughly U-shaped. There is no reason to assume that the distribution of risk of failure is similar in stone tools or other archaeological objects. Other models may be more suitable.

Besides its obvious implications for lithic typology and curation, the reduction thesis has a deceptively profound implication for the meaning to attach to tool assemblages. The traditional archaeological view identifies tool size and form with templates and thereby constructs types. It associates types with activities, whether broad ("scraper") or narrow ("dry-hide scraper"). Traditional premises are that variation in tool size and form is essential (i.e., forming sets of discrete formal types) and that types bear some relationship to activity or function. The view accepts a measure of uncertainty; some types are more distinct, have more formal integrity than others, and some types might be more multifunctional than others. Substantially, though, premises are qualitative. Traditional lithic classification identifies kinds of activities or uses. The presence of a cleaver in an assemblage indicates butchering, the presence of a scraper scraping.

The reduction thesis has different premises. It views variation in tool size and form as continuous, i.e., forming complex patterns of variable association and distribution but not discrete, essential types. It does not so much reject as moot the traditional view's form-function identities. However tools were used, much of their size-form variation owes to amount of use and pattern of retouch. The reduction thesis has more quantitative than qualitative, premises. In its view, the presence in an assemblage of, say, a tula slug is not evidence of a kind of activity, unless that activity is defined broadly as scraping-planing-cutting. Instead, its presence registers an amount of reduction that attended some kind and amount of tool use. That is, a type's presence in an assemblage no longer means "Kind of Tool or Activity X" but instead "Amount of Reduction Y."

The reduction thesis has profound implications for how assemblages form and what they mean. Methodological challenges remain before reduction analysis becomes a standard tool of the trade in lithic analysis. But there is no reason to ignore the challenges or the potential that reduction analysis holds to broaden the scope of cultural inference from sparse archaeological remains.

Acknowledgments: Work on this paper began while I held a fellowship from the Institute for Advanced Study at La Trobe University, Melbourne, Australia. My thanks go to Dr. Gilah Leder, Director of the Institute, and Dr. David Frankel of the Department of Archaeology for their kindness and support.

REFERENCES CITED

Andrefsky, William

2006   Experimental and Archaeological Verification of an Index of Retouch for Hafted Bifaces. *American Antiquity* 71:743–757.

Andrefsky, William (editor)

2008   *Artifact Life-Cycle and the Organization of Lithic Technologies*, Cambridge University Press, Cambridge.

Clarkson, Chris

2002   An Index of Invasiveness for the Measurement of Unifacial and Bifacial Retouch: A Theoretical, Experimental and Archaeological Verification. *Journal of Archaeological Science* 29:65–75.

Dibble, Harold L.

1987   The Interpretation of Middle Paleolithic Scraper Morphology. *American Antiquity* 52:109–117.

Hiscock, Peter, and Val Attenbrow

2003   Early Australian Implement Variation: A Reduction Model. *Journal of Archaeological Science* 30:239–249.

Hoffman, C. Marshall

1985   Projectile Point Maintenance and Typology: Assessment with Factor Analysis and Canonical Correlation. In *For Concordance in Archaeological Analysis: Bridging Data Structure, Quantitative Technique, and Theory*, edited by C. Carr, pp. 566–612. Westport Press, Kansas City, MO.

Larson, Mary Lou, and Judson B. Finley

2004   Seeing the Trees but Missing the Forest: Production Sequences and Multiple Linear Regression. In *Aggregate Analysis in Chipped Stone*, edited by C. Hall and M.L. Larson, pp. 95–111. University of Utah Press, Salt Lake City.

Lovejoy, Arthur O.

1936 *The Great Chain of Being: A Study of the History of an Idea.* Harvard University Press, Cambridge, MA.

Pelcin, Andrew W.

1996 Controlled Experiments in the Production of Flake Attributes. PhD dissertation, Department of Anthropology, University of Pennsylvania, Philadelphia.

Sahnouni, Mohamed, Kathy Schick, and Nicholas Toth

1997 An Experimental Investigation into the Nature of Faceted Limestone "Spheroids" in the Early Palaeolithic. *Journal of Archaeological Science* 24:701–713.

Schiffer, Michael B.

1976 *Behavioral Archeology.* Academic Press, New York.

Shott, Michael J.

1995 How Much Is a Scraper? Curation, Use Rates and the Formation of Scraper Assemblages. *Lithic Technology* 20:53–72.

1996 An Exegesis of the Curation Concept. *Journal of Anthropological Research* 52:259–280.

2002 Weibull Estimation of Use-Life Distribution in Experimental Spear-Point Data. *Lithic Technology* 27:93–109.

2004 Midwestern Paleoindian Archaeology. Unpublished ms. on file, Dept. of Classical Studies, Anthropology and Archaeology, University of Akron, Akron, OH.

Shott, Michael J., and Jesse Ballenger

2007 Biface Reduction and the Measurement of Dalton Curation: A Southeastern Case Study. *American Antiquity*, 72:153–175.

Shott, Michael J., and Paul Sillitoe

2004 Modeling Use-Life Distributions in Archaeology Using New Guinea Wola Ethnographic Data. *American Antiquity* 69:336–352.

2005 Use Life and Curation in New Guinea Experimental Used Flakes. *Journal of Archaeological Science* 32:653–663.

Shott, Michael J., and Kathryn J. Weedman

2007 Measuring Reduction in Stone Tools: An Ethnoarchaeological Study of Gamo Hidescraper Blades from Ethiopia. *Journal of Archaeological Science* 34:1016–1035.

Shott, Michael J., Andrew P. Bradbury, Philip J. Carr, and George H. Odell

2000 Flake Size from Platform Attributes: Predictive and Empirical Approaches. *Journal of Archaeological Science* 27:877–894.

Siler, William

1979   A Competing-risk Model for Animal Mortality. *Ecology* 60:750–757.

Weedman, Kathryn J.

2002   On the Spur of the Moment: Effects of Age and Experience on Hafted Stone Scraper Morphology. *American Antiquity* 67:731–744.

8

THE *CHAÎNE OPÉRATOIRE* OF CERAMIC MANUFACTURE AND CERAMIC PETROGRAPHY: A CASE STUDY FROM RANCHO DEL RIO, NORTHWESTERN HONDURAS

Meaghan M. Peuramaki-Brown

Abstract. This paper is a report of preliminary petrographic analysis of ceramic samples from the site of Rancho del Rio, Valle de Cacaulapa, Northwestern Honduras. The analysis involved three stages: 1) preliminary petrographic examination of sherds as a means of adding microscopic data to the current type-variety-mode typology used in the valley in order to investigate the *chaîne opératoire* of ceramic manufacture and production; 2) comparison of identified petrofabrics with clay 'globules' found on potsherds from the site; and 3) an attempt to located the actual source and/or environment of the clays used in pre-Columbian vessel manufacture. Five petrofabrics were identified in total and petrographically matched to some of the potstands studied.

Introduction

The macroscopic analysis of pottery as a means of understanding social concepts, political and economic 'boundaries,' and daily activities is a common aspect of pre-Columbian Mesoamerican studies. However, research questions addressing how and where pottery was manufactured seem less prevalent. Key reasons for ignoring these questions include:

- poor preservation of features;

- an inability to efficiently recognize manufacture locations and remains;

- the absence of questions posed regarding the *chaîne opératoire* of ceramic manufacture;

- the focus of excavations on major site epicentres and civic-ceremonial structures and less concentration on lower strata residential areas and large open areas (such as courtyards) where much activity was likely to have occurred;

- the belief that archaeological typologies based on macroscopic characteristics can supply significant and abundant information regarding the finished vessels (Wardle 1992:11);

- the lack of communication among material analysts, archaeologists, ethnoarchaeologists, and anthropologists as to the value of inquiries based in archaeometry and geology.

According to Arnold (1991), there are three classes of data that can potentially serve to identify ceramic manufacture locations in the archaeological record: 1) tools and facilities, 2) mistakes, production residues, etc., and 3) finished products (Arnold 1991:87; see Rice 1996 for similar classes). This third class can provide important information concerning patterns of distribution, characteristics of consumer population, and, most importantly, information on the physical manufacture of the items. Any analysis of these three stages can provide important data towards the reconstruction of the *chaîne opératoire* of ceramic manufacture: the "series of operations which brings a primary material

[clay] from its natural state to a fabricated state [final vessel]" (Cresswell 1976:6; brackets are author's examples). Understanding such operations and choices allows archaeologists a closer view of individual agency and shared ideas within given social groups of the prehistoric past (Lemonnier 1992).

THIN SECTION PETROGRAPHY: USE IN ARCHAEOLOGICAL INVESTIGATION

In order to study the manufacturing process of ceramic vessels it is necessary to employ techniques that provide greater insight into the physical materials than is provided by traditional macroscopic type-variety systems. Thin section petrographic analysis is a geological technique used to systematically describe, classify, and identify minerals and rocks (Barclay 2001:9; Bishop et al. 1982:285; Gribble and Hall 1992:6; Rice 1987:376; Rye 1981:51–52; Shepard 1965:139; Tite 1999:195; Vince 2003). When dealing with ceramics, petrographic analysis may also lead to the identification of intentionally added materials (temper) (Barclay 2001:10); thus, shedding light on such issues as potting choices, raw material access, paste recipes, etc. The recognition of such characteristics as sorting, shape, roundness and sphericity, and particle density, in addition to mineral types, can also aid in geographically or geologically locating raw material sources or manufacturing centres.

ARCHAEOLOGICAL SETTING: THE VALLE DE CACAULAPA AND RANCHO DEL RIO

During the summer of 2004, I was invited to join archaeological excavations at the pre-Columbian site of Rancho del Rio, located in the Valley of Cacaulapa in the Santa Barbara District of Northwestern Honduras (Figure 8.1). My work with excavations and the ceramics from the site strived to create a preliminary base from which the Rancho del Rio investigations into the *chaîne opératoire* of ceramic manufacture and resultant questions concerning production could be launched (Peuramaki-Brown 2004).

The Valley of Cacaulapa, in which Rancho del Rio is situated, is a narrow valley of the Rio Chamelecón and its tributary, the Rio Cacaulapa. The river

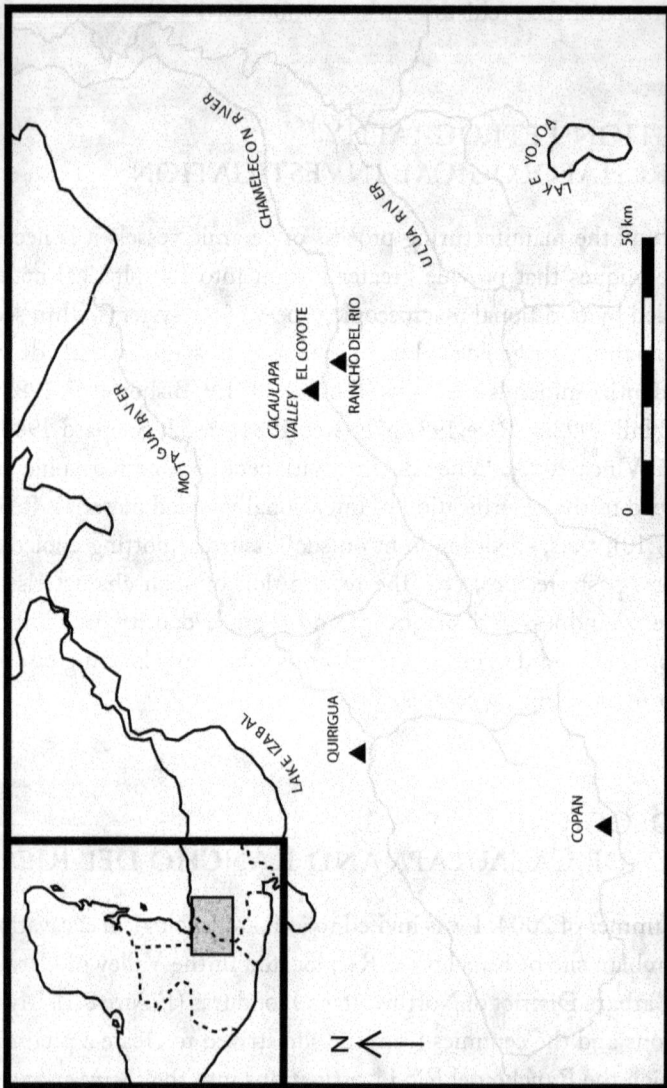

Figure 8.1. Map of Northwestern Honduras with location of Rancho del Rio (Redrawn from Small and Shugar 2004).

MEAGHAN M. PEURAMAKI-BROWN

originates in the igneous and metamorphic highlands to the south and carries water year-round. The valley is situated at the nexus of three geological zones: the Atima limestone formation (southeast of the valley), igneous rock intrusions and flows (to the south), and an area of sand- and siltstone. This unique position provided numerous resources for the pre-Columbian populations of the valley. The largest site in the valley, El Coyote, in the lower part of the valley, covers approximately 6 km^2 and encompasses a minimum of 360 platform structures. The strongest period of valley occupation occurs during the Late Classic (650–900 C.E.) and Early Postclassic (900–1100 C.E.) periods (Small and Shugar 2004).

Excavations at the site of Rancho del Rio centre on understanding rural economies, especially the production and exchange of rural produced goods. During a 1997 survey, Rancho del Rio was identified and recognized as comprising eight structures. Previous and ongoing excavations were aimed at determining the extent of site occupation (geographically and temporally) and opening the inner courtyard and revealing its relationship to the structures (Small and Peuramaki-Brown 2004).

To date, excavations have suggested that the ancient inhabitants of Rancho del Rio were possibly engaged in pottery production. Large middens consisting primarily of ceramic debris were encountered during courtyard testing and excavations (Small and Peuramaki-Brown 2004; Small and Shugar 2004). These included possible ceramic tools: broken sherds used as scrapers, shapers, and smoothers to make pottery, similar to those found at the site of K'axob in Northern Belize (Varela et al. 2001:186–187), vitrified ceramic (occasionally labelled as ceramic 'slag'), pieces of clay 'waste,' crushing implements (manos and metates), countless broken sherds of the four paste groups examined in this research, possible temper blocks of a low-grade schist, which I will discuss later, and 'potstands': modified jar rims used to support vessels during manufacture (Figure 8.2). The potstands hold tell-tale signs of pottery manufacture, consisting of large pieces of wet clay that fell off the wet pots as they were being shaped and dried onto these stands and, in some instances, were eventually baked or fired with the pot (how or why this was done is not known). Similar potstands have been recovered at the nearby site of Las Canoas and elsewhere in the valley (Stockett 2005:388). These stands can provide a potential direct link in the *chaîne opératoire*, from the raw material through the forming technology to the finished object, since they supply a possible identifiable local fabric.

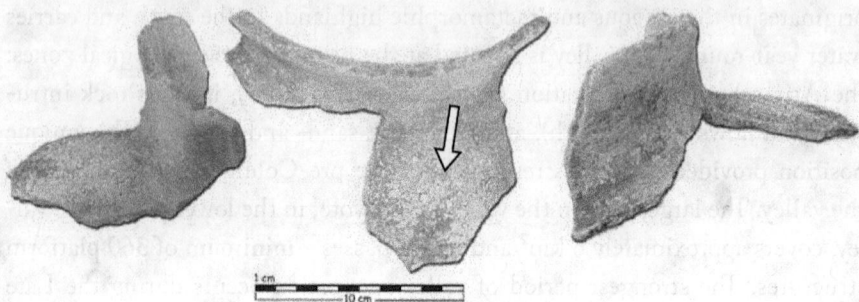

Figure 8.2. Example of a ceramic potstand with an arrow indicating the clay 'globules' on the exterior surface (Photograph by Dr. David Small 2003).

STAGES AND PURPOSE OF PETROGRAPHIC ANALYSIS

The following analysis addresses the question of pottery manufacture at Rancho del Rio during the late facet of the Late Classic Period (for complete analysis results and interpretations, see Peuramaki-Brown 2004). Petrographic analysis was chosen above other analytical techniques due to the large number of inclusions found in ceramics from the site. The analysis is composed of three stages:

Stage 1 consisted of the preliminary identification and description of the various petrofabrics observed from twenty ceramic sherd samples. These consisted of five jar rim sherds from each of the four most abundant macrovisual paste groups found at Rancho del Rio (Cacaulapa, San Joaquin, Pueblo Nuevo, and Pitones) and their relationship to the established macrovisual type-variety-mode system employed in the Valley of Cacaulapa. This will provide a pedestal for the further study of ceramic manufacture at the site. This stage comprises Arnold's (1991) previously mentioned third class of data.

Stage 2 consisted of the petrographic analysis of clay 'globules' on potstands from Rancho del Rio. Thin sections were made of five identified potstand sherds with globules representing two macrovisually different types of residues in an attempt to match this manufacturing waste to the identified petrofabrics. This accounts for Arnold's (1991) first and second classes of data.

Stage 3 consisted of the identification of the environment and/or source from which the clay and possible tempers used in pottery manufacture at Rancho del Rio were obtained. Three clay sources were tested through briquette manufacture and firing, along with the addition of crushed schist from courtyard excavations to a fourth briquette. This, along with the final product, satisfies Arnold's (1991) third class of data.

RESULTS AND DISCUSSION OF PETROGRAPHIC ANALYSIS

Petrofabrics. From the four type-variety paste groups represented in the Rancho del Rio ceramic sample, five petrofabric groups were identified: Volcanic Ash 1, Volcanic Ash 2, Volcanic Ash 3, Muscovite 1, and Muscovite 2 (Table 8.1; Table 8.2; Figure 8.3). The clay bodies appear very similar in aplastic content, including volcanic ash and many fine particles of muscovite and polycrystalline quartz, and are likely derived from similar environments. The clay bodies are secondary and likely of metamorphic and igneous origin, indicated by metamorphic and igneous rock fragments within the clay body (natural inclusions), volcanic ash, and polycrystalline quartz (MacKenzie and Adams 1994:48,153–155; MacKenzie and Guilford 1980:71). This would seem typical of the Chamelecón River based on its origins.

Although very similar in aplastic content, roughly representing a continuum, differences in ratios of aplastics, grain size, as well as shape, provide rationale for division of the petrographic groups. All contain a high percentage of volcanic ash, though only Volcanic Ash 1 appears to have ash that may have been added as a temper. The 'crisp' edges of the ash within the clay body, unlike the 'blended' ash borders seen in Volcanic Ash 2 and 3 and Muscovite 1 and 2, together with the great abundance of ash, lends credence to this premise (for similar observations, see Jones 1991:172). Volcanic ash is a desirable inclusion due to its low level of thermal expansion and irregular particle shapes allowing for stronger bonds with clay (Arnold 1991:23–24). Overall, Volcanic Ash 1 is extremely homogenous when compared with the other petrofabrics represented in the sample. The relatively fine grain size of all inclusions and the abundance

Table 8.1. Descriptions of volcanic ash petrofabric aplastics.

Petrofabric	Aplastics	Percentage	Shape	Sorting	Grain size
VOLCANIC ASH 1	volcanic ash	39	angular	well	fine to medium sand
	plagioclase	1	subrounded to subangular	poorly	very fine to medium sand
	gypsum	less than 1	subangular to angular	moderately	very fine to medium sand
	schist	less than 1	subrounded to subangular	poorly	very fine to coarse sand
	polycrystalline quartz	5	subangular to angular	poorly	very fine to coarse sand
	opaques	less than 1	rounded	well	fine to medium sand
	basalt	less than 1	subangular	moderately	medium to coarse sand
	chert	less than 1	subangular	moderately	medium to coarse sand
	muscovite	5	subangular	poorly	silt to medium sand
	grog	0			
	chlorite	0			
	pseudobone	1	angular	well	medium to coarse sand
	granite/gneiss	less than 1	subangular to angular	well	medium to coarse
VOLCANIC ASH 2	volcanic ash	32	angular	moderately	fine to coarse sand
	plagioclase	3	subangular	poor	very fine to coarse sand
	gypsum	1	subangular to angular	moderately	very fine to medium sand
	schist	3	subangular	poor	very fine to very coarse sand
	polycrystalline quartz	10	subangular to angular	poor	very fine to medium sand
	opaques	5	rounded	moderately	very fine to medium sand

MEAGHAN M. PEURAMAKI-BROWN

Table 8.1. (cont'd)

PETROFABRIC	APLASTICS	PERCENTAGE	SHAPE	SORTING	GRAIN SIZE
	basalt	less than 1	subangular	well	medium to very coarse sand
	chert	less than 1	subrounded to subangular	well	medium to coarse sand
	muscovite	5	subangular	moderately-well	medium sand
	grog	1	angular	well	medium to coarse sand
	chlorite	0			
	pseudobone	3	angular	well	coarse sand
	granite/gneiss	less than 1	subangular to angular	well	medium to coarse
VOLCANIC ASH 3	volcanic ash	32	angular	moderately	fine to medium sand
	plagioclase	3	subangular	moderately	very fine to fine sand
	gypsum	1	subangular to angular	moderately	very fine to fine sand
	schist	3	subangular	poor	very fine to coarse sand
	polycrystalline quartz	8	subangular to angular	poor	very fine to fine sand
	opaques	2	rounded	moderately	very fine to medium sand
	basalt	less than 1	subangular	well	medium to very coarse sand
	chert	3	subrounded to subangular	well	medium to coarse sand
	muscovite	3	subangular	well	fine sand
	grog	less than 1	angular	well	medium sand
	chlorite	none			
	pseudobone	3	angular	well	medium to coarse sand
	granite/gneiss	less than 1	subangular to angular	well	medium to coarse

Table 8.2. Descriptions of muscovite petrofabrics aplastics.

PETROFABRIC	APLASTICS	PERCENTAGE	SHAPE	SORTING	SIZE
MUSCOVITE 1	volcanic ash	25	angular	poorly	fine to very coarse sand
	plagioclase	1	angular	poorly	fine to coarse sand
	gypsum	less than 1	subangular to angular	moderately	fine to coarse sand
	schist	15	subrounded to angular	poorly	medium to very coarse sand
	polycrystalline quartz	15	subangular to angular	poorly	very fine to coarse sand
	opaques	7	rounded to subangular	moderately	very fine to medium sand
	basalt	less than 1	subrounded	well	coarse to very coarse sand
	chert	1	subrounded	poorly	fine to coarse sand
	muscovite	15	subangular to angular	moderately	fine to medium sand
	grog	2	subangular to angular	moderately	fine sand to grit
	chlorite	less than 1	angular	very well	coarse sand
	pseudobone	5	angular	well	coarse sand
	granite/gneiss	less than 1	subangular to angular	well	medium to coarse
MUSCOVITE 2	volcanic ash	15	angular	moderately	very fine to medium sand
	plagioclase	2	angular	poor	fine to coarse sand
	gypsum	1	subangular to angular	moderately	fine to coarse sand
	schist	10	subrounded to angular	poor	fine to coarse sand
	polycrystalline quartz	10	subangular to angular	poor	very fine to coarse sand
	opaques	7	subrounded	moderately	very fine to medium sand

MEAGHAN M. PEURAMAKI-BROWN

Table 8.2. (cont'd)

PETROFABRIC	APLASTICS	PERCENTAGE	SHAPE	SORTING	SIZE
	basalt	less than 1	subrounded	well	coarse
	chert	1	subrounded	well	coarse to very coarse sand
	muscovite	10	subangular to angular	moderately	fine sand
	grog	less than 1	angular	moderately	medium sand
	chlorite	less than 1	angular	very well	fine to medium sand
	pseudobone	5	angular	well	coarse sand
	granite/gneiss	less than 1	subangular to angular	well	medium to coarse

of volcanic ash suggest that this paste was carefully prepared, possibly by sieving the clay prior to manufacture and/or addition of ash temper.

Volcanic Ash 2 and 3 are similar to Volcanic Ash 1 in their high content of volcanic ash and their relatively porous body; however, the ash in these petrofabrics is more similar to that of Muscovite 1 and 2. The borders of the ash are 'blended', making it appear that the ash is a natural part of the clay. They also possess a slightly higher percentage of inclusions (other than ash) when compared with Volcanic Ash 1, though less than the Muscovite petrofabrics. They are slightly coarser than Volcanic Ash 1 and the lighter tan colour of Volcanic Ash 2 as compared with Volcanic Ash 1 and 3 may be due to its higher content of muscovite and polycrystalline quartz. When fired, higher silica contents produce a cream to light brown colour (Fuente 2004:6).

While the most abundant inclusion in Muscovite 1 and 2 is volcanic ash, they differ significantly from their Volcanic Ash counterparts in their very high content of muscovite mica, polycrystalline quartz, and micaceous schist. The presence, although small, of chlorite (likely part of the schist) also distinguishes these petrofabrics from the three Volcanic Ash groups. The abundance of these three inclusions, as well as their more angular and coarse nature when compared with the previous three petrofabrics, suggest their possible addition as

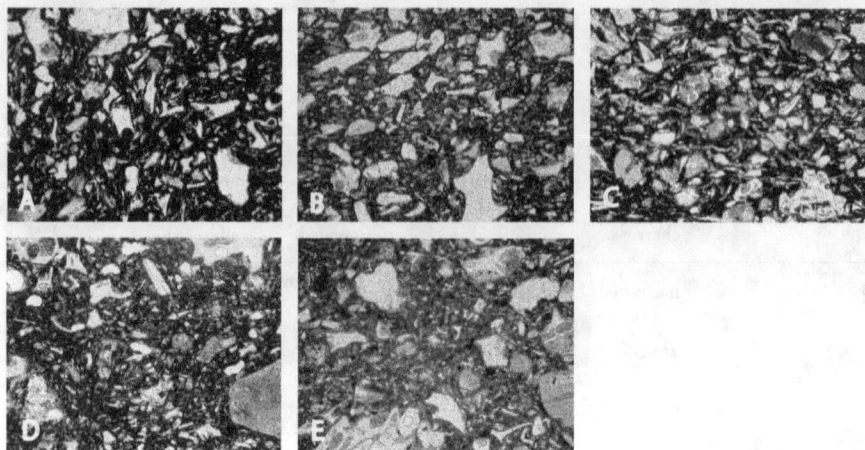

Figure 8.3. Five identified petrofabrics, photographed in plane-polarized light at 10x magnification; (A) Volcanic Ash 1, (B) Volcanic Ash 2, (C) Volcanic Ash 3, (D) Muscovite 1, (E) Muscovite 2 (Photographed by Meaghan Peuramaki-Brown 2004).

temper (Rye 1981:37). During excavations of the courtyard, lumps of easily flaked, low-grade metamorphic, micaceous schist were recovered in association with other ceramic debris. Schist is not seen in the architecture of the Valle de Cacaulapa, nor have known source outcrops been identified to date. The nearby valley of Naco does have schist sources, and pre-Columbian inhabitants there used varieties of the stone in the construction of their structures. As will be explained below, experimentation with the schist found at the site produced results similar to those observed in the Muscovite petrofabrics. The possibility of trade in schist between the two valleys is a subject that could be investigated in the future. Finally, the differences in ratios of muscovite, polycrystalline quartz, and micaceous schist between Muscovite 1 and Muscovite 2 may account for the colour differentiation between the two petrofabrics, as it does between Volcanic Ash 2 and Volcanic Ash 3.

Potstands. When the potstand thin sections were examined (Figure 8.4), the material found coating Potstands 1, 2, and 3 did not resemble any of the petrofabrics represented in the Rancho del Rio ceramic thin sections. It is possible that this 'silt-like' material was the result of past flooding in the courtyard, resulting from a rise in water levels in the nearby Chamelecón River. The high quantity of calcite in the silt could be related to the calcite observed in the clay sources analyzed from the valley. Potstands 4 and 5 are much more 'typical' of the appearance of potstands with globules observed at other sites in the valley. The matching of the globules with two of the petrofabrics (Volcanic Ash 2 and 3, respectively) represented in the Rancho del Rio ceramic material suggest that manufacture was indeed occurring at the site; however, it is important to remember that these are only preliminary studies and other potstands similar to these should be analyzed before any firm conclusions are drawn.

Clay sources. Although none of the clay sources analyzed were an exact match to the ceramic petrofabrics, some similarities were observed. Muscovite, polycrystalline quartz, micaceous schist, plagioclase feldspar, basalt, and gypsum are all rocks and minerals found in both the Rancho del Rio petrofabrics and the three clay sources. The lack of ash within the sources, except for a small amount in Source B, could be due to the temporal distribution of volcanic ash deposits. The high content of calcite, possibly due to shell within the river sediments, may also be a temporal characteristic.

Overall, the particular minerals and rocks found within the clay sources (metamorphic and igneous/volcanic), as well as their angularity, suggest a possible match in environmental sourcing. However, there can be no definite conclusion drawn as analyses of more source and sherd samples are required. Based on ethnographic studies of distances between clay sources and vessel manufacture locations (D. E. Arnold 1971, 1985), it is reasonable to still assume clays were collected near the site.

When some of the easily-flaked muscovite schist (a low-grade metamorphic) that was recovered from courtyard excavations was crushed and added to a test briquette with Clay Source C, some interesting observations were made. The overall percentage of muscovite (common in schistose rock [Adams et al. 1984:14]), polycrystalline quartz, and micaceous schist increased. Also present after the addition of the temper was chlorite, which is found primarily within the identified schist fragments.

Numerous observations imply the addition of this material as temper by Late Classic potters. First, the presence of this rock associated with pottery sherds, possible ceramic manufacturing tools, and manufacture residue within the late facet of the Late Classic courtyard suggest associate use patterns. The absence of known outcropping in the valley and the lack of use of this type of rock in Late Classic valley architecture suggests an anomalous use pattern for

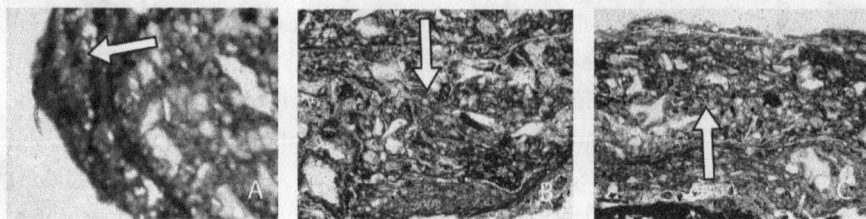

Figure 8.4. Thin sections of potstands with arrows indicating 'globule' layers on exteriors, photographed in plane-polarized light at 10x magnification; (A) example of Potstands 1 to 3, (B) Potstand 4, and (C) Potstand 5 (Photographed by Meaghan Peuramaki-Brown 2004).

such stone sources. Finally, the increased presence of muscovite, polycrystalline quartz, micaceous (muscovite) schist, and chlorite within two of the petrofabrics from the Rancho del Rio sample and the angular nature of these inclusions suggest addition of schist temper.

Why schist was added, given that it has no known advantage in pottery manufacture, is uncertain. However, the additional 'sparkle' that the muscovite in the schist provides may have been a desired characteristic, exemplified by other high micaceous content paste groups from the valley such as Joya (Pat Urban and Edward Schortman, personal communication 2004).

Finally, the addition of the schist to Clay Source C also created a postfiring colour change not observed in the briquette made only of Clay Source C. The addition of the schist caused a colour change from a yellow to a light brown, similar to that observed in Muscovite 1, Muscovite 2, and Volcanic Ash 2, all of which have more schist, muscovite, and polycrystalline quartz than the other petrofabrics.

CONCLUDING REMARKS

Research at the site of Rancho del Rio in the Valle de Cacaulapa, Northwest Honduras has the potential to uncover critical information concerning the *chaîne opératoire* of ceramic manufacture in this corner of Mesoamerica. Preliminary analysis of the 'final product' of manufacture is the most logical starting point and the results encourage future investigation into ceramic manufacture and production at the site of Rancho del Rio.

Further questions resulting from the present analysis may address issues such as inter-valley trade of raw materials (i.e., schist) used in pottery manufacture and degree of production as represented by the relationship between vessel form and petrofabric, along with the standardization of tool and potstand forms. The petrographic comparison of the Rancho del Rio fabrics and clay sources with those of other sites within the valley and beyond would also shed light on regional ceramic manufacture practices. The results would greatly contribute to our understanding of inter- and intra-valley relationships regarding ceramic manufacture and production in this region, and possibly within Mesoamerica in general.

Acknowledgments: I would like to thank the Institute of Archaeology, University College London, and particularly Dr. Bill Sillar and Dr. Elizabeth Graham, for allowing me the opportunity (and encouraging me) to conduct my dissertation research in Honduras. Sincere gratitude to the Instituto Hondureño de Antropología e Historia for granting permission for the export of my samples. Thanks are due to: Dr. David Small and Dr. Aaron Shugar (Lehigh University) for inviting me to join the Rancho del Rio project for the 2004 field season. Thanks to Lehigh University for funding my travel expenses, room and board, and laboratory costs. A very special thank you to Dr. Edward Schortman and Dr. Patricia Urban (Kenyon College) for guiding me in my research and teaching me the 'ins and outs' of ceramic identification in the Cacaulapa Valley. Also thanks to Rob Ixer and Simon Groom for their schooling in the elementaries of petrography. Thanks to the University College London and the Institute of Archaeology for honouring me with two scholarships towards my year of study in London.

References Cited

Arnold, Dean E.

1971   Ethnomineralogy of Ticul, Yucatan potters. *American Antiquity* 36:20–40.

1985   *Ceramic Theory and Cultural Process.* Cambridge University Press, Cambridge.

Arnold, Philip J.

1991   *Domestic Ceramic Production and Spatial Organization: A Mexican Case Study in Ethnoarchaeology.* Cambridge University Press, Cambridge.

Barclay, Katherine

   2001   *Scientific Analysis of Archaeological Ceramics: A Handbook of Resources*. Oxbow Books, Oxford.

Bishop, Ronald L., Robert L. Rands, and George R. Holley

   1982   Ceramic Compositional Analysis in Archaeological Perspective. In *Advances in Archaeological Method and Theory*, vol. 5, edited by M.B. Schiffer, pp. 275–330. Academic Press, New York.

Cresswell, R.

   1976   Avant-propos. *Techniques et culture* 1:5–6.

Fuente, Guillermo A. de la

   2004   Technological Characterization of Inka and Pre-Inka Pottery: A Ceramic Petrology Approach. *The Old Potter's Almanack* 12(1), May:1–14.

Gribble, Colin D., and Allan J. Hall

   1992   *Optical Mineralogy: Principles and Practice*. UCL Press, London.

Jones, Lea D.

   1991   Tempering Trends in Lowland Mayan Pottery. In *Recent Developments in Ceramic Petrology*, British Museum Occasional Paper No. 81, edited by A. Middleton and I. Freestone, pp. 165–182. British Museum Research Laboratory, London.

Lemonnier, Pierre

   1992   *Elements for an Anthropology of Technology*. Anthropological Papers, Museum of Anthropology, University of Michigan, No. 88, Ann Arbor, Michigan.

MacKenzie, W.S., and A.E. Adams

   1994   *A Colour Atlas of Rocks and Minerals in Thin Section*. Manson Publishing, London.

MacKenzie, W.S., and C. Guilford

   1980   *Atlas of Rock-Forming Minerals in Thin Section*. Longman Group Limited, Essex, UK.

Peuramaki-Brown, Meaghan

   2004   The *Chaîne Opératoire* of Ceramic Manufacture and Production: Preliminary Analysis through Ceramic Petrography at Rancho del Rio, Valle de Cacaulapa, Santa Barbara District, Honduras. M.A. dissertation, University College London, Institute of Archaeology, London.

Rice, Prudence M.

1987   *Pottery Analysis: A Sourcebook*. University of Chicago Press, Chicago.

1996   Recent Ceramic Analysis: 2. Composition, Production, and Theory. *Journal of Archaeological Research* 4:165–202.

Rye, Owen S.

1981   *Pottery Technology: Principles and Reconstruction*. Manuals on Archaeology 4. Taraxacum, Washington.

Shepard, Anna O.

1965   *Ceramics for the Archaeologist*, 5th ed. Publication 609, Carnegie Institution of Washington, Washington, D.C.

Small, David, and Meaghan Peuramaki-Brown

2004   Excavaciones Arqueológicas en Rancho del Rio, Santa Barbara. Paper presented at the VIII Seminario de Antropologia Hondurena, Tegucigalpa, Honduras.

Small, David, and Aaron Shugar

2004   National Science Foundation Grant Proposal: Rancho del Rio 2004. Electronic document, http://www.lehigh.edu/~inarch/, accessed May 15, 2004.

Stockett, Miranda

2005   Approaching Social Practice through Access Analysis at Las Canoas, Honduras. *Latin American Antiquity* 16(4):385–407.

Tite, M. S.

1999   Pottery Production, Distribution, and Consumption – The Contribution of the Physical Sciences. *Journal of Archaeological Method and Theory* 6(3):181–233.

Varela, Sandra L. Lopez, Patricia A. McAnany, and Kimberly A. Berry

2001   Ceramic Technology at Late Classic K'axob, Belize. *Journal of Field Archaeology* 28:177–191.

Vince, Alan

2003   Ceramic Petrology – An Introduction. Electronic document, http://www.postex.demon.co.uk/petrology.htm, accessed May 15, 2004.

Wardle, Peter

1992   *Earlier Prehistoric Pottery Production and Ceramic Petrology in Britain*. BAR British International Series 225, Oxford.

9

ARCHAEOMETRIC AND NON-ARCHAEOMETRIC TECHNIQUES AND THEIR RELEVANCE TO UNDERSTANDING HUMAN BEHAVIOUR

Leslie G. Cecil

Abstract. A review of current research concerning pottery analysis done by an-thropologically oriented archaeologists elucidates the almost exclusive reliance on archaeometric techniques (e.g., INAA and ICPS) for attempting to understand human behaviour. Because of the notoriety and value of archaeometric techniques for archaeological research, we are often drawn away from the more basic, non-technical kinds of analyses (colour and form measurements and petrography), thus missing opportunities to more fully understand the cultures we study. There-fore, by conjoining archaeometric and non-archaeometric techniques of analyses, archaeologists can better interpret the complexity of past human events that may not have been apparent using only archaeometry. I demonstrate the value of this type of research by presenting a case study of the Petén Postclassic Maya pottery manufacturing traditions (clay and pigment sources and decorative programs) and changing trade patterns before and during the socio-politically complex milieu of Spanish contact.

INTRODUCTION

The analysis of a collection of pottery can be accomplished by a myriad of techniques that include, but are not limited to, classification (devised and folk), colour and form measurements, re-firing experiments, strength and hardness measurements, thin-section (petrographic), X-ray diffraction (XRD), scanning electron microscopy (SEM), energy dispersive spectroscopy (EDS), X-ray fluorescence (XRF), neutron activation analysis (INAA or NAA), and inductively coupled plasma spectroscopy (ICPS or some variation thereof). Each technique has its strengths and weakness and is appropriate for addressing different research questions.

Analyzing pottery through a visual examination (e.g., decorative styles, estimations of firing temperatures and slip and paste colour measurements) provides qualitative information about technology (Orton et al. 1993; Rice 1987b). By beginning an analysis with these "low-tech" methods, the archaeologist gathers objective qualitative data to evaluate technological characteristics as well as the operational choices that may be embedded in pottery production. Alone, these data may not contribute "earth-shattering" results, but when conjoined with archaeometric techniques, the archaeologist has a much more powerful dataset from which to draw conclusions about behavioural choices as well as how an ancient culture may have seen its past, present, and future.

To more fully understand human behaviours and choices during pottery manufacture, it is almost impossible not to include mineralogical and/or chemical methods of analysis. While many current projects, but by no means all, employ INAA and ICPS as the archaeometric standard for obtaining the chemical composition of pottery, petrographic thin-section analysis was the norm. Many petrographic analyses, in both past and current research, can distinguish between source materials, and the researchers are then able to determine trade patterns, reciprocity patterns, and "mother cultures" (Flannery et al. 2005). Petrography also allows for the study of pottery manufacturing processes such as slipping, painting, and forming methods (e.g., Dickinson et al. 2001; Middleton et al. 1985).

By the 1980s, INAA became the standard for quantifying trace and rare earth elements in ceramic pastes. Because of its high precision and sensitivity and ability to discriminate pottery groups and clay sources, many archaeologists turned to this technique to answer questions previously addressed by petro-

LESLIE G. CECIL

graphic analysis (e.g., Adan-Bayewitz and Weider 1992; Blomster et al. 2005). As a result, INAA became the technique of choice. Some archaeologists would, and still do, submit samples to see what the chemistry "says" and then they formulate research questions to fit their data. Additionally, many projects that involve INAA do not use other techniques of analysis to provide additional, equally valuable data to their research projects. More recently, ICPS has been added to the list of successful techniques for determining the chemical composition of ceramic pastes and slips (e.g., Neff 2003; Speakman 2005).

Because many researchers use solely archaeometric techniques for the analysis of their data set, antagonism has developed among archaeologists (e.g., Blomster et al. 2005; Flannery et al. 2005). While this trend is unfortunate and does not necessarily advance the field, using as many techniques as possible to gather data at all levels – stylistic, mineralogical, and chemical – provides a middle ground as well as providing data that may be able to more completely address questions of how and why people manufactured material culture in the manner that they did. Ultimately, it allows archaeologists to answer emic behaviour based on the etic phenomenon of the material record (e.g., Cecil 2001; Lechtman 1977; Lemonnier 1992).

The case study that follows is an attempt to demonstrate that neither non-archaeometric nor archaeometric analyses alone would be able to answer how Petén Postclassic potters defined themselves through their material culture. I conjoin classification, hardness, colour, and form measurements with mineralogical and chemical analyses to define the technological styles of the two main warring Petén Postclassic socio-political groups at the time of the Spanish conquest.

CASE STUDY

The Postclassic (AD 900–1525) and Contact (AD 1525–1697) periods in central Petén are characterized by numerous socio-political groups migrating to and from northern Yucatán to the central Petén region (Figure 9.1) and co-existing in a relatively isolated area (Bullard 1970; Cecil 2001, 2004; Chase 1983; Jones 1989, 1998; Jones et al. 1981; Rice et al. 1996; P. M. Rice 1987a). While the Itzá, Kowoj, Mopan, and Kejach may have co-existed, they were not peaceful (Jones 1998). Instead, the socio-political groups fought wars with each

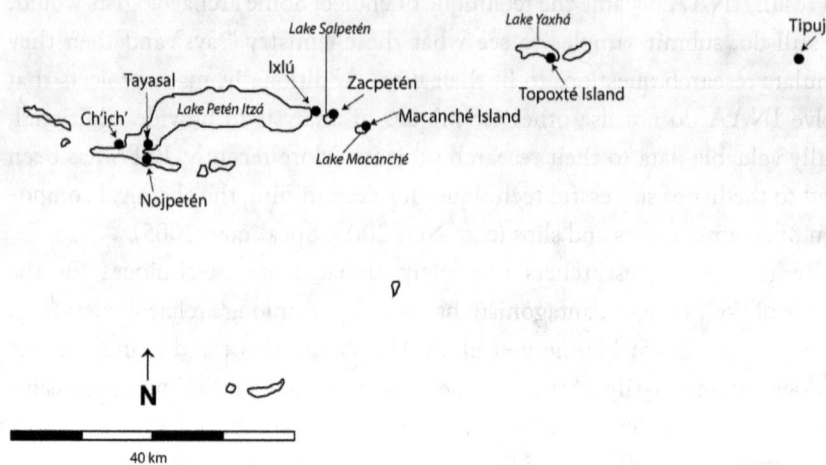

Figure 9.1. Postclassic Archaeological Sites in the Central Petén Lakes Region.

other and gained and lost territory and political dominance. As a result, social and political boundaries may have been created to enhance and enforce social differences.

Although a number of socio-political groups may have lived in the central Petén lakes region, the Itzá and Kowoj were best documented by the Spanish. The Itzá dominated territory west and south of Lake Petén Itzá. They claimed ancestry from the archaeological site of Chich'en Itzá in northern Yucatán and are said to have migrated from there to the Petén lakes region before the Spanish conquest (Jones 1998:22). The head of the ruling Kan Ek' lineage of the Petén Itzá also stated that his family still lived there (Jones 1998:11). In Petén, the Itzá made their capital at Nojpeten (modern-day Flores Island) and may have controlled the archaeological sites of Ch'ich,' Tayasal, Ixlú, Macanché Island, Yalain, and Tipuj. Their absolute control of Ixlú, Yalain, and Tipuj is questionable as these sites may have changed hands when borders were contested and redrawn (Cecil and Neff 2006; Jones 1998:6, 11). Architecture and burial/cache patterns at sites in the Itzá territory are similar to architecture and burial patterns found at Chich'en Itzá (Duncan 2005; Proskouriakoff 1962; Rice 1986; Rice et al. 1996).

The Kowoj occupied the northern and eastern part of Lake Petén Itzá and Lake Salpetén. They claimed to have migrated from Mayapán around AD 1530 as a result of Spanish contact and political turmoil (Jones 1998:27–28). However, the earliest migration may have been at approximately AD 1200 given that Kowoj architecture with that date exists at Topoxté Island (Hermes and Noriega 1997). The Kowoj may have controlled the sites of Zacpetén, Topoxté Island, and possibly Ixlú and Tipuj. Petén Kowoj architecture and burial/cache patterns are similar to those found at Mayapán (Duncan 2005; Proskouriakoff 1962; Pugh 2001).

In order to identify pottery manufacturing patterns of the Kowoj, and to some extent the Itzá, I conducted non-archaeometric and archaeometric analyses of the three Petén Postclassic slipped wares: Clemencia Cream Paste, Vitzil Orange-Red, and Snail Inclusion Paste (Cecil 2001, 2004; Cecil and Neff 2006). The resulting data from each technique provided results that by themselves did not produce much information about behavioural choices during the manufacturing process, but by conjoining the non-archaeometric and archaeometric data I was able to conclude something more meaningful about socio-political identities and pottery manufacture during the Postclassic period.

METHODS OF ANALYSIS

The first level of analysis, non-archaeometric, consisted of a typological examination (type variety system) of all Postclassic sherds excavated from the archaeological sites of Ch'ich,' Ixlú, Zacpetén, and Tipuj (Smith et al. 1960). The data gathered by the type variety system include observations about ceramic pastes, degree of dark coring, core colour, hardness, and firing temperatures, slips (colour, hardness, and firing temperatures), forms and form measurements, and regional and inter-regional distribution. Through the examination of pottery at this preliminary level of analysis, I was able to note the variation in the painted and incised decorations, the presence and absence of decorative motifs, the number of form categories and the range of sizes, and the firing and slip technologies in the Petén lakes region during the Postclassic period (Cecil 2001). While the differences were not numerous, variations in pastes, slips, and decorations of the different types and varieties suggested that while the Petén Postclassic potters may have not perfected their manufacturing process, their decorative program was well established.

Since these conclusions did not fully answer the research questions asked, I incorporated archaeometric techniques. Based on the preliminary technological style groups developed from the non-archaeometric analyses, I selected a sample of sherds for further petrographic thin-section analysis to better identify slip characteristics and non-plastic inclusions, minerals, and rock fragments in the clay paste (Cecil 2001). In addition to identifying the presence of various minerals, I also recorded the abundance, association, granulometry, and shape of the minerals and other inclusions in the clay paste (Cecil 2001; Childs 1989; Middleton et al. 1985; Orton et al. 1993).

As a result of the petrographic analysis, I identified multiple compositional groups within each ceramic ware (Cecil 2001:422–424). Clemencia Cream Paste wares form three mineralogical groups: clay pastes that lack mineral inclusions and have an abundance of pores (volcanic ash); clay pastes with biotite; and clay pastes with biotite, chert, chalcedony, and quartz. Vitzil Orange-Red ware sherds form two basic groups: those with an abundance of pores (volcanic ash); and pastes with minerals. The second group may be divided further to those with an abundance of quartz and those with an abundance of calcite; however, the division was not made because of the small number of sherds with quartz inclusions. Finally, Snail Inclusion Paste ware sherds also formed two basic groups: pastes with biotite, chert, and chalcedony; and those lacking biotite, chert, and chalcedony.

While the petrographic analysis provided information concerning manufacturing details (clay recipes), I added acid-digestion inductively coupled plasma spectroscopy (ICP-ES) to analyze the sherd pastes (Burton and Simon 1996) and laser-ablation inductively coupled plasma spectroscopy (LA-ICP-MS) to analyze the exterior slips and red and black pigments used for decoration (Neff 2003). These differences indicated subtle variations in the manufacturing processes that may designate different technological styles, socio-political identities, resource restrictions due to territorial boundaries, and Postclassic trade.

When the chemical compositions of the ceramic pastes were analyzed using multivariate analyses (principle component analysis and cluster analysis), seven groups occurred (Cecil 2001). For the most part, the division of the seven groups cannot be confirmed with Mahalanobis distance statistics, but the differences appear to be emically significant. The seven chemical compositional groups conform to Petén Postclassic ware categories: Groups 1, 6, and 7 are the Clemencia Cream Paste ware samples; Groups 2 and 3 represent the Vitzil Orange-Red ware sherds; and Groups 4 and 5 consist of the Snail Inclusion Paste ware samples.

While the paste chemical composition data do not add an entirely new set of characteristics to the previously established groups based on the other techniques discussed above, the chemical composition analysis of the exterior slips and red and black pigments used for decoration do (Cecil and Neff 2006). Postclassic Maya potters used different exterior red slips for different vessel forms (jars and bowls versus tripod plates) in the Vitzil Orange-Red and Clemencia Cream Paste wares. Perhaps this difference has to do with vessel function. Additionally, they used different exterior red slips for decorated and undecorated, but slipped vessels.

Red and black paint pigments are also chemically distinct from those used for exterior slips (Cecil and Neff 2006). Not only were the exterior slip pigments different than those used for decoration, but the red pigments used to decorate in red-and-black decorative programs were also chemically distinct from those used to decorate only in red. Additionally, red decoration on the higher quality Clemencia Cream Paste ware pottery also has a different chemical composition than that on lower quality pottery. Maya Postclassic potters also used different black pigments depending on the motif used (hooks and reptiles versus mats, circles, and birds) and if the black pigment was part of a red-and-black decorative program.

PUTTING IT ALL TOGETHER

When data from the non-archaeometric and archaeometric analyses were combined, seven interesting technological and stylistic combinations occur that reflect operational sequence choices and may reflect different social/ethnic identities (Cecil 2001). While the technological style groupings were not dependent on the acid-digestion ICP-ES analysis, the technological style group numbering follows the numbering for the sherd paste chemical composition groups (Groups 1–7). Table 9.1 illustrates the combination of technological and stylistic characteristics of the seven distinct groups.

Table 9.1. Technological Style Groups and Their Associated Non-Archaeometric and Archaeometric Characteristics.

	GROUP						
	1	2	3	4	5	6	7
CERAMIC WARE							
Clemencia Cream Paste	X					X	X
Vitzil Orange-Red		X	X				
Snail Inclusion Paste				X	X		
DECORATION							
Slipping Only	X	X			X	X	X
Black Paint		X	X	X			X
Red Paint				X		X	
Red and Black Paint			X	X			
Incising			X	X			
PETROGRAPHY							
Volcanic Ash	X	X					
Biotite			X	X		X	X
Chert			X	X			X
Chalcedony			X	X			X
Quartz	X		X	X	X		X
ARCHAEOLOGICAL SITE							
Ch'ich'		X	X	X	X		
Ixlú	X	X	X	X	X	X	
Zacpetén		X	X	X	X	X	X
Tipuj	X		X	X	X		X
ETHNICITY							
Kowoj	X			X		X	X
Itzá		X	X	X	X		

When the technological style groups are examined together with ethnohistorical, architectural, burial, and decoration colour and motif data from archaeological sites in Petén and compared to descriptive data from northern Yucatán, I can suggest which socio-political group may have produced each technological style. This is because technological styles result from choices made by Postclassic Petén Maya potters within a social structure that embodies their identity. As such, the patterns of manufacture are not merely "'added on' in order to signal group identity" but are choices made by the potter "by which a sense of group identity is formed and transformed as being coeval with and identical to the process by which a sense of technique is formed and transformed" (Dietler and Herbich 1998:247). A sense of group identity may have been important in Postclassic Petén because of the unstable conditions brought on by wars, changing social boundaries, and changing positions of dominance. As such, Maya potters, as well as other members of Maya society, may have continually constructed and reconstructed their identity by creating and recreating their social structures through daily activities such as pottery manufacture (Giddens 1984:17).

The "hallmark" signature of Kowoj pottery is red-on-paste decoration that first appears on Clemencia Cream Paste ware pottery with the florescence of Chompoxté Red-on-paste pottery (Figure 9.2). Clemencia Cream Paste ware pottery is thought to have been produced at and traded from the Kowoj site of Topoxté Island from the Early to early Late Postclassic periods (ca. AD 900–1450) and is traded to sites in the eastern portion of the Petén lakes region and Tipuj. Interestingly, the majority of Clemencia Cream Paste ware pottery at Tipuj is of inferior quality, whereas the majority of this pottery at Zacpetén is of a higher quality. This may suggest closer ties between the inhabitants at Topoxté Island and Zacpetén than those between Topoxté Island and Tipuj. I believe that this pottery and the civic-ceremonial architecture that resembles that of Mayapán represent Kowoj social identity and Kowoj occupation at Topoxté, Zacpetén, and Tipuj. This pottery does not appear at archaeological sites in the western portion of the Petén lakes region, suggesting that socio-political boundaries had been established to separate the Itzá and Kowoj.

The Kowoj traditions/customs began at Topoxté Island continued at Zacpetén (when Topoxté was abandoned) throughout the Postclassic period. At Zacpetén, the Kowoj recreated red-on-paste decoration on local clays with gray pastes (Snail Inclusion Paste ware) to reinforce their social/ethnic identity. In addition to red-on-paste decoration, red-and-black decoration also indicates Kowoj social identity. These same traits are seen at Mayapán in their buff-coloured pottery (Smith 1971).

On the other hand, Itzá socio-political identity may be represented by Vitzil Orange-Red and Snail Inclusion Paste wares with the presence of black painted reptilian (*kan*) and hook motifs that may reflect the ruling Kan Ek' lineage of the Petén Itzá. More research needs to be conducted at Itzá archaeological sites before this category can be expanded.

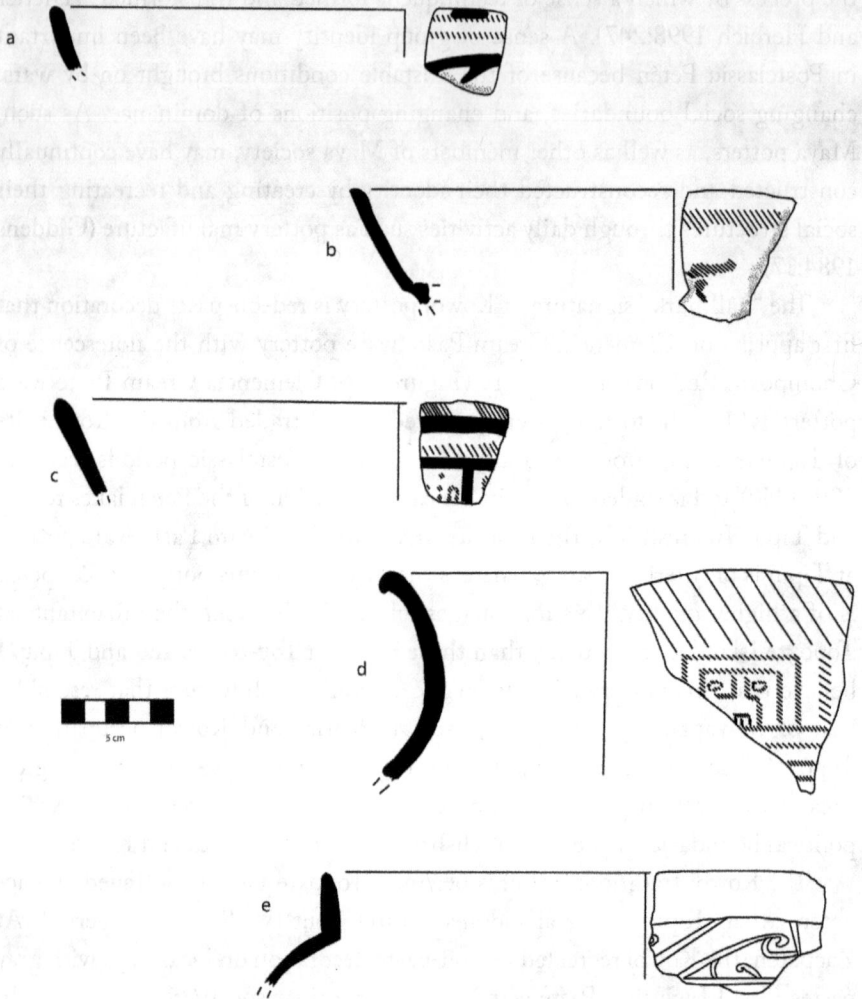

Figure 9.2. Kowoj Pottery: a): Pastel Polychrome from Tipuj; b) Chompoxté Red-on-paste: Akalché Variety from Tipuj; c) Sacá Polychrome from Zacpetén; d) Chompoxté Red-on-paste:Alkaché Variety from Zacpetén; e) Picú Incised: Picú Variety (*ilhuitl* glyph) from Tipuj.

In sum, my comparison of pottery technological style data with multiple lines of evidence from the archaeological sites of Ch'ich,' Ixlú, Zacpetén, and Topoxté Island in Petén and Tipuj in Belize suggest that Petén Postclassic potters produced and reproduced pottery technological styles as part of the social identities. In addition to defining technological styles and determining their socio-political affiliation, this study demonstrates that the analysis of technological style and the interpretations concerning the complex socio-political milieu could not have been made without the contribution of both non-archaeometric and archaeometric analyses. While non-archaeometric techniques are not *en vogue*, they are the base from which sampling occurs for the archaeometric techniques and do contribute to an archaeologist's understanding of ancient potters' actions and their socio-political milieu and should not be dismissed as useless and time-consuming.

Acknowledgments: The author would like to that the University of Calgary's Chacmool Conference for the invitation to present an abbreviated version of the above paper. This research was supported by funding by the National Science Foundation grants BCS-0228187 and SBR-9816325 (Dissertation Improvement Grant), Proyecto Maya Colonial of Southern Illinois University Carbondale, and Sigma Xi Grants-in-Aid of Research. All errors and omissions are those of the author.

References Cited

Adan-Bayewitz, David, and Moshe Weider

    1992   Ceramics from Roman Galilee: A Comparison of Several Techniques for Fabric Characterization. *Journal of Field Archaeology* 19:189–205.

Blomster, Jeffrey P., Hector Neff, and Michael D. Glascock

    2005   Olmec Pottery Production and Export in Ancient Mexico Determined through Elemental Analysis. *Science* 307:1068–1072.

Bullard, William R.

    1970   Topoxté: A Postclassic Maya Site in Petén, Guatemala. In *Monographs and Papers in Maya Archaeology*, edited by William R. Bullard, pp. 245–308. Papers of the Peabody Museum of Archaeology and Ethnology, No. 61. Harvard University, Cambridge.

Burton, James H., and Arleyn W. Simon

1996   A Pot is Not a Rock: A Reply to Neff, Glascock, Bishop, and Blackman. *American Antiquity* 61:405–413.

Cecil, Leslie G.

2001   The Technological Styles of Late Postclassic Slipped Pottery Groups in the Petén Lakes Region, El Petén, Guatemala. PhD dissertation, Department of Anthropology, Southern Illinois University Carbondale, Carbondale.

2004   Inductively Coupled Plasma Emission Spectroscopy and Postclassic Petén Slipped Pottery: An Examination of Pottery Wares, Social Identity and Trade. *Archaeometry* 46:385–404.

Cecil, Leslie G., and Hector Neff

2006   Postclassic Maya Slips and Paints and Their Relationship to Socio-Political Groups in El Petén, Guatemala. *Journal of Archaeological Sciences* 33:1482–1491.

Chase, Arlen F.

1983   A Contextual Consideration of the Tayasal-Paxcamán Zone, El Petén, Guatemala. PhD dissertation, Department of Anthropology, University of Pennsylvania, Philadelphia.

Childs, S.T.

1989   Petrographic Analysis of Archaeological Ceramics. *Material Research Science* 25:24–29.

Dickinson, William R., Brian M. Butler, Darlene R. Moore, and Marilyn Swift

2001   Geologic Source and Geographic Distribution of Sand Tempers in Prehistoric Potsherds from the Mariana Islands. *Geoarchaeology* 16:827–854.

Dietler, Michael, and Ingrid Herbich

1998   Habitus, Techniques, Style: An Integrated Approach to the Social Understanding of Material Culture and Boundaries. In *The Archaeology of Social Boundaries*, edited by Miriam T. Stark, pp. 232–263. Smithsonian Institution Press, Washington, D.C.

Duncan, William N.

2005   Understanding Ritual Violence in the Archaeological Record. In *Interacting with the Dead: Perspectives on Mortuary Archaeology for the New Millennium*, edited by Gordon F.M. Rakita, Jane E. Bukstra, Lane A. Beck, and Sloan R. Williams, pp. 207–222. University of Florida Press, Gainesville.

Flannery, Kent V., Andrew K. Balkansky, Gary M. Fienman, David C. Grove, Joyce
Marcus, Elsa M. Redmond, Robert G. Reynolds, Robert J. Sharer, Charles S.
Spencer, and Jason Yaeger

2005   Implications of New Petrographic Analysis for the Olmec "Mother Culture"
Model. *Proceedings of the National Academy of Science* 102:11219–11223.

Giddens, Anthony

1984   *The Constitution of Society: Outline of the Theory of Structuration.* University of
California Press, Berkeley.

Hermes, Bernard, and Raúl Noriega

1997   El período Postclásico en el area de la Laguna Yaxhá: Una vision desde Topoxté.
In *XI Simposio de Investigaciones Arqueologicas en Guatemala*, edited by Juan
Pedro LaPorte and Hector L. Escobedo, pp. 755–778. Ministerio de Cultura de
Desportes, Instituto de Antropología e Historia, Asociacion Tikal, Guatemala.

Jones, Grant D.

1989   *Maya Resistance to Spanish Rule: Time and History on a Colonial Frontier.* University of New Mexico Press, Albuquerque.

1998   *The Conquest of the Last Maya Kingdom.* Stanford University Press, Stanford.

Jones, Grant D., Don S. Rice, and Prudence M. Rice

1981   The Location of Tayasal: A Reconsideration in Light of Petén Maya Ethnohis-
tory and Archaeology. *American Antiquity* 46:530–547.

Lechtman, Heather

1977   Style in Technology – Some Early Thoughts. In *Material Culture: Styles, Organization, and Dynamics of Technology*, edited by Heather Lechtman and Robert S.
Merrill, pp. 3–20. West Publishing Company, St. Paul.

Lemonnier, Pierre

1992   *Elements for an Anthropology of Technology.* Anthropological Papers No. 88,
Museum of Anthropology, University of Michigan, Ann Arbor.

Middleton, A.P., Ian C. Freestone, and Morven N. Lesse

1985   Textural Analysis of Ceramic Thin Sections: Evaluations of Grain Sampling
Procedures. *Archaeometry* 27(1):64–74.

Neff, Hector

2003   Analysis of Mesoamerican Plumbate Pottery Surfaces by Laser Ablation-
Inductively Coupled Plasma-Mass Spectrometry (LA-ICP-MS). *Journal of
Archaeological Science* 30:21–35.

Orton, Clive, Paul Tyers, and A. G. Vince

1993   *Pottery in Archaeology.* Cambridge University Press, Cambridge

Proskouriakoff, Tatiana

1962   Civic and Religious Structures of Mayapán. In *Mayapán, Yucartán, Mexico*, edited by HED Pollock, Ralph L. Roys, Tatiana Proskouriakoff, and A. Ledyard Smith, pp. 87–164. Carnegie Institution of Washington, Washington, D.C.

Pugh, Timothy W.

2001   Architecture, Ritual, and Social Identity at Late Postclassic Zacpetén, Petén, Guatemala: Identification of the Kowoj. PhD dissertation, Southern Illinois University Carbondale. University Microfilms, Ann Arbor, Michigan.

Rice, Don S.

1986   The Petén Postclassic: A Settlement Perspective. In *Late Lowland Maya Civilization: Classic to Postclassic*, edited by Jeremy A. Sabloff and E.W. Andrews V, pp. 301–344. University of New Mexico Press, Albuquerque.

Rice, Don S., Prudence M. Rice, Romulo Sánchez-Polo, and Grant D. Jones

1996   *Proyecto Maya-Colonial: Geografía Política de Siglo XVII en el Centro del Petén, Guatemala*, Informe Preliminary al Instituto de Anthropología e Historia de Guatemala Sobre Investigaciones del Campo en los Años 1994 y 1995.

Rice, Prudence M.

1987a   *Macanché Island, El Petén, Guatemala*. University of Florida Press, Gainesville.

1987b   *Pottery Analysis: A Sourcebook*. University of Chicago, Chicago.

Smith, Robert E.

1971   *The Pottery of Mayapán, Including Studies of Ceramic Material from Uxmal, Kabah, and Chichen Itza*. Papers of the Peabody Museum of Archaeology and Ethnology, vol. 66. Harvard University, Cambridge.

Smith, Robert E., Gordon R. Willey, and James C. Gifford

1960   The Type-Variety Concept as a Basis for the Analysis of Maya Pottery. *American Antiquity* 25:330–340.

Speakman, Robert J.

2005   Chemical Characterization of Mesa Verde and Mancos Black-on-White Pottery Pigments by LA-ICP-MS. In *Laser Ablation ICP-MS in Archaeological Research*, edited by Robert J. Speakman and Hector Neff, pp. 167–186. University of New Mexico Press, Albuquerque.

10

STABLE ISOTOPE ANALYSIS OF MARINE SHELL TO DETERMINE GEOGRAPHIC PROVENIENCE: IMPLICATIONS FOR PREHISTORIC TRADE ROUTE RESEARCH

Tobin C. Bottman

Abstract. For more than 10,000 years, North American coastal peoples traded with groups from the interior. Archaeological excavations provide a material record of these interactions, generally in the form of marine shell objects found at inland sites and obsidian toolstone at coastal sites. Numerous trade route proposals have been formulated for the procurement and movement of these goods. While geochemical analysis has been used for decades to source obsidian artefacts, the same has not been possible for shell artefacts. With such a large distribution along the coast and no reliable sourcing techniques, locating the geographic origin of spire-lopped *Olivella biplicata* beads has been problematic. Past research has proven oxygen and carbon isotope analysis to be successfully utilized in estimating the seasonality of marine shell collection and recreating palaeo-environments. Since oxygen and carbon isotope levels in shell are related to the water parameters from which the shells originate, analysis of these isotopes can also be used to determine the relative geographic provenience of specific shells. Isotopic analyses of 23 *O. biplicata* beads collected from five Northern Great Basin archaeological sites predominantly suggest Southern California as a primary shell collection source. Utilizing this process, current and future models of prehistoric trade and interaction can be refined.

INTRODUCTION

For thousands of years, the peoples of the Pacific Coast and the Great Basin exchanged technology, art, and goods. Archaeological excavations from within this vast geographic region have provided material record of this cultural interaction, generally in the form of marine shell objects found at inland sites and obsidian tools excavated in coastal sites. For years, obsidian trace element analysis has been used to source the obsidian to specific flows, each of which have their own unique chemical signature. Unfortunately, this has not been the case for marine shell artefacts found inland. Many of the molluscan species used in the manufacture of shell tools and ornaments, particularly *Olivella biplicata* shells, naturally occur along large sections of the Pacific coast, from present-day Alaska to Mexico. With such a large distribution along the coast and no reliable sourcing techniques, geographic positioning for the origin of shell artefacts has remained problematic.

Over the last twenty years, Bennyhoff and Hughes (1987) and Galm (1994), among others, have studied prehistoric artefact exchange patterns between the coast and the interior. This research has most often been accomplished by analyzing artefact typologies and comparing them to patterns discerned in adjacent areas. Unfortunately, given the wide geographic range of *O. biplicata*, coupled with the long temporal span of the spire lopped bead variety, typological dating and sourcing has been impossible.

Oxygen and carbon isotopic analysis has been used for many years to estimate seasonality of marine shells found in archaeological contexts (see Kennett and Voorhies 1996; Shackleton and Renfrew 1970). Levels of these elements are related to the water conditions in which the shell formed. As such, these isotopic parameters may also be used to determine the relative geographic origin of specific shells as there is little overlap in oxygen and carbon isotope values between different coastal areas. Consequently, by comparing oxygen and carbon isotope levels in archaeological specimens recovered from provenience-

TOBIN C. BOTTMAN

controlled contexts to natural specimens collected along the Pacific Coast, it may be possible to discern changing patterns of shell ornament acquisition through space and time. Applying a similar method, Shackleton and Renfrew (1970) successfully sourced *Spondylus* artefacts to reconstruct Neolithic trade routes in Europe.

Shell sourcing research conducted by Eerkens et al. (2005) has focused primarily on *Olivella biplicata* beads from Late Holocene deposits in California. This research includes the construction of a modern *O. biplicata* shell oxygen and carbon isotope profile for the Oregon and California coastlines to aid in determinations of geographic provenience. This baseline data permits the comparison of *O. biplicata* beads from other time periods and cultural areas. As the bulk of the *O. biplicata* beads excavated in Oregon date to the Middle Holocene (7,600 to 3,000 cal. BP), my research was focused on beads from this period that were recovered from archaeological sites located just a few kilometres from one another in the lowlands of the Fort Rock Basin, in the Northern Great Basin of Oregon, and housed in collections at the University of Oregon Museum of Natural and Cultural History. Hypotheses concerning the prehistoric trade routes that conveyed shell beads hundreds of kilometres inland have generally been limited by a lack of scientific evidence. Stable isotope analysis of shell beads proves to be a reliable way to test these hypotheses by providing an additional tool to decipher prehistoric exchange patterns and routes of acquisition from the Pacific Coast to the interior for any type of shell artefact.

BACKGROUND

Cultural Setting

Located in the northwestern corner of the Great Basin, the Fort Rock Basin has long supported various groups of people. In fact, archaeological evidence suggests over 13,000 years of human occupation in and around the basin (Bedwell 1973; Wingard 2001). Formed of upthrust volcanic tuff and worn by waves from Palaeo Fort Rock Lake (Freidel 1994:32), Fort Rock is the focal point of the area. The Fort Rock Basin is divided by two low ridges into three, discrete, sub-basins (Freidel 1994:22) (Figure 10.1). The northernmost sub-basin is the

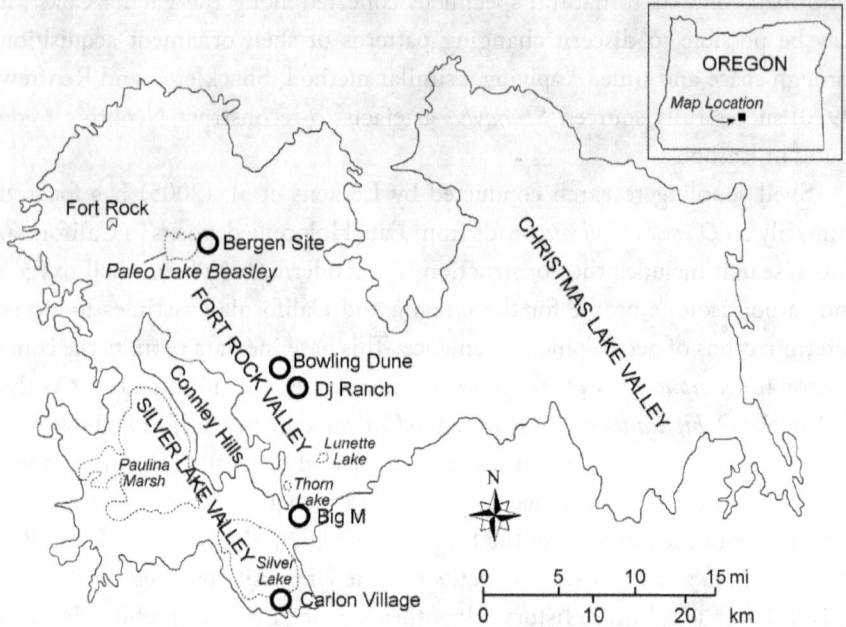

Figure 10.1. Map of the Fort Rock Basin located in the Northern Great Basin of Oregon showing archaeological sites and associated geographic features.

Fort Rock Valley, with Christmas Valley to the east and Silver Lake Valley to the south. Fort Rock and Silver Lake valleys are connected by a series of channels that once filled a chain of freshwater lakes and marshes during periods of increased precipitation (Jenkins 1994a:601; Jenkins et al. 2004b). For unlike the arid desert conditions present today, moist climatic conditions common to the Middle Holocene supported this channel system (Jenkins et al. 2004b). The archaeological sites included in this study are located along this system of channels. The Bergen, Big M, Bowling Dune, Carlon Village, and DJ Ranch sites are all lowland sites and all located within a few kilometres of the others (see Figure 10.1).

Archaeological evidence suggests varying occupational patterns throughout the last 13,000 years, often hinging on ecological and demographic fluctuations (Jenkins et al. 2004a). There is very little evidence to suggest long-term habitation during the Early Holocene as most sites appear to have been stops on the seasonal rounds of small populations of people (Jenkins et al. 2004a). However, evidence from the latter portion of the Middle Holocene (6,000 to 3,000 cal. BP) lowland basin lakeshore sites illustrates more comprehensive settlement patterns (Jenkins et al. 2004a). It was at this time that substantial houses, large storage pits, and imported items such as beads appear in the archaeological record (see Helzer 2004; Jenkins 1994b, 2000, 2004; Jenkins et al. 2004c; Largaespada 2001; Moessner 2004). At around 3,000 cal. BP, evidence of these comprehensive occupations is no longer visible, coinciding initially with an intense regional drought (Wigand 1987). This drought likely affected food resources and initiated a seasonal movement of peoples to exploit root crops (Jenkins et al. 2004b).

Although many archaeologists consider shell beads to be identifiers of wealth, social status, and group affiliation, their actual value and utility during prehistory is unknown. King has argued that beads are representative of a currency that can be saved as a form of excess energy and as such had an innate value to many populations (1974:80). The fact that shell beads, originating from sources on the Pacific Coast, are excavated from archaeological deposits located hundreds of kilometres inland attests to this. During ethnographic times, beads were traded widely between distinct regions of North America. This was also the case during the Middle and Late Holocene as beads manufactured out of exotic materials are present in the archaeological record (Jenkins and Wimmers 1994). The presence of shell beads at archaeological sites indicate the existence of sophisticated trade alliances and levels of social complexity that few other artefacts provide. This has prompted the construction of numerous trade route proposals and hypotheses based at least in part on shell beads (Bennyhoff and Hughes 1987; Erickson 1990; Galm 1994; Hughes and Bennyhoff 1986; Jenkins and Erlandson 1997; Raab and Howard 2000) (Figure 10.2).

Bennyhoff and Hughes (1987) identified four California trade centres active by the Late Holocene. They proposed that trade centres were located in northern, central, and southern California, as well as the Gulf of California (Bennyhoff and Hughes 1987:154–155) with the western sector of the Great Basin serving as the primary shell redistribution centre by about 8,000 BP. They proposed that these four exchange networks had little if any impact on the Northern Great Basin during the Middle Holocene; however, it must be noted that, at the time Bennyhoff and Hughes (1987) was published, they considered the Northern Great Basin in Oregon to be a peripheral area as only three sites

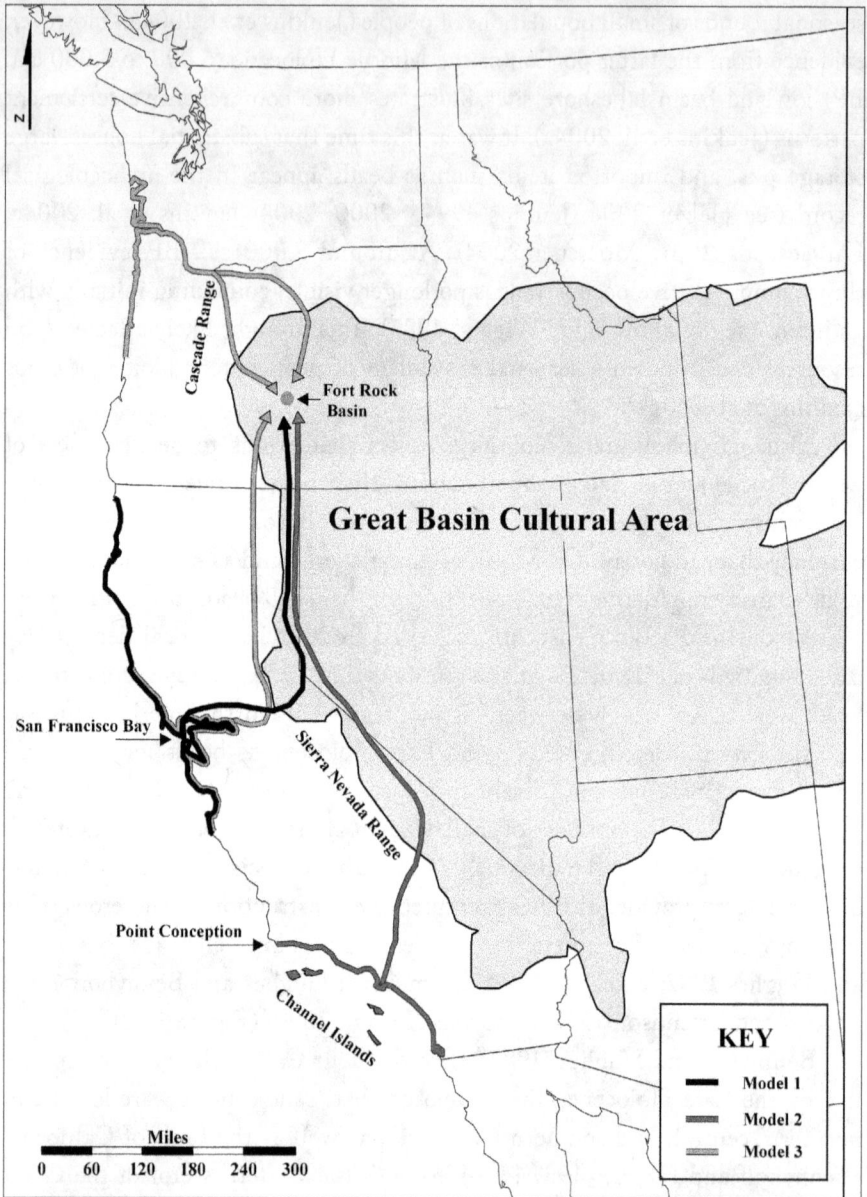

Figure 10.2. Map of western North America showing the physiographic Great Basin, hypothesized shell collection centers and trade routes.

TOBIN C. BOTTMAN

yielding eight shell beads were known to exist (1987:156). The northern California network provides the shallowest time depth, with the exception of some beads recovered from the Snake River region in Idaho (Bennyhoff and Hughes 1987:154). The southern California exchange network was deemed to be most important to groups living in the southwestern areas of the Great Basin like Death and Owens valleys (Bennyhoff and Hughes 1987:155). Bennyhoff and Hughes concluded that the Gulf of California exchange network was of the least significance to Great Basin peoples (1987:155).

By the beginning of the Late Holocene, Bennyhoff and Hughes posited that the Central California exchange network was dominant (between 4,000 and 2,200 BP) and that the *O. biplicata* A1 and B2 bead types were originating there, with a few large specimens likely collected from northern Californian waters (1987:160). They also proposed that beads from this early Middle Archaic Period were likely traded along the same trans-Sierran trail network as obsidian (Hughes and Bennyhoff 1986:255). However, in the Fort Rock Basin, *Olivella* beads have been most commonly encountered in Early and Middle Holocene deposits (Largaespada 2001). Bennyhoff and Hughes speculated that beads recovered from Early Holocene deposits (excavated in the Lower Snake River region) were derived from the Oregon or Washington coast (1987:154).

Hughes and Bennyhoff (1986:246) have also suggested a non-California-based network centred on the Columbia River Plateau area. This exchange route consisted of shell goods collected along northern California, Oregon, and southern Washington coasts coming inland along the Columbia River and distributed along the Deschutes and Umpqua rivers down into the Northern Great Basin (Hughes and Bennyhoff 1986:Figure 1). They proposed that spire lopped *O. biplicata* beads in the Northern Great Basin likely originated in northern California (Hughes and Bennyhoff 1986:247).

Raab and Howard (2000) have proposed a "Uto-Aztecan Interaction Sphere" involving Southern Channel Island populations from the Santa Barbara Channel in direct contact with groups in the Western Great Basin during the Middle Holocene. This hypothesis is based specifically on the recovery of *Olivella* Grooved Rectangle (OGR) (Type N, Bennyhoff and Hughes 1987) beads from sites in the Northern Great Basin (Jenkins and Erlandson 1997) and the Southern Channel Islands (Vellanoweth 1995). They have hypothesized that related Takic-speaking peoples from the Southern Channel Islands were in contact with other Uto-Aztecan language family speakers throughout the

Northern Great Basin (Raab and Howard 2000:595). They believe this Uto-Aztecan language family route followed the western Numic frontier in eastern California south of the Sierra Nevada's and continuing up into Oregon (Raab and Howard 2000:595). Jenkins et al. (2004c) hypothesized that the most direct route into the Great Basin, along the eastern Sierra Nevada – Cascade Front, would have likely been utilized. This route, leading through the Owens Valley, into the Carson sink, and north to the Fort Rock Basin, would have been quite hospitable for travel during the moist climatic conditions common during the Middle Holocene in the Northern Great Basin (Jenkins et al. 2004c:264).

Rather than a strict focus on the Great Basin, Galm (1994) and Erickson (1990) have focused their efforts in discerning trade patterns within the greater Columbia Plateau region. However, these trade postulations either directly or indirectly include involvement of Great Basin populations. Central to their models is the concept of multiple trade routes. Galm (1994) has proposed "The Dalles – Deschutes" trade network extending across the Southern Columbia Plateau to the north of the Fort Rock Basin during the Middle Holocene. While citing no direct evidence for trade into the Fort Rock area, Galm has also proposed a Great Basin exchange network for the movement of beads and obsidian into the Columbia Plateau region (1994:297) as well as the coastal trade network travelling inland along the Columbia River (1994:298). Erickson (1990:131) has proposed a similar trade model for the Middle Holocene, one that is dependant upon trade material source. He posited that the most direct route into the Plateau area would be from Oregon or Washington coast sources, travelling along the Columbia River Gorge, while acknowledging that finds in the Northern Great Basin would indicate a trans-Sierran movement (*sensu* Bennyhoff and Hughes 1987) from the central California coast towards the interior. Like Galm, he questions the feasibility of assuming a single point of origin for shell bead trade for both the Great Basin and Southern Plateau (Erickson 1990:131).

Contemporary Trade Models

The above hypotheses can be summarized by the formation of three primary shell acquisition models (see Figure 10.2). The specific parameters of these three models can then be tested by oxygen and carbon stable isotope analysis in order to determine the movements of shell ornaments and their possible trade routes into and through the Northern Great Basin.

Model #1 – By the end of the Middle Holocene, a Central California exchange network, centred around San Francisco Bay, was dominant (between 2000 and 200 B.C.) and that the *O. biplicata* A1 and B2 bead types were originating there, with a few large specimens originating from northern Californian waters (Bennyhoff and Hughes 1987:160). These beads were then traded through a Western Great Basin exchange hub (Hughes and Bennyhoff 1986:255).

Model #2 – A "Uto-Aztecan Interaction Sphere" involving Southern Channel Island peoples were in direct contact with groups in the Western Great Basin during the Middle Holocene (Raab and Howard 2000). These beads would then follow a route into the Great Basin along the eastern Sierra Nevada–Cascade front. Previous research has indicated that temporally and geographically sensitive *Olivella* Grooved Rectangle beads were manufactured in the Southern Channel Islands and followed a similar route of dispersal (Jenkins and Erlandson 1997; Raab and Howard 2000; Vellanoweth 1995; Vellanoweth et al. 1996).

Model #3 – This model relies upon the utilization of multiple trade routes involving coastal as well as Great Basin routes. "The Dalles – Deschutes" (Galm 1994:298) trade network, featuring goods travelling inland along the Columbia River and extending across into the Southern Columbia Plateau during the Middle Holocene, as well as a Great Basin exchange network for the movement of beads and obsidian into the Columbia Plateau region (Galm 1994:297; Hughes and Bennyhoff 1986), has been proposed. A trans-Sierran trade route from the central Californian coast may have supplied this Great Basin network (Erickson 1990:131).

These models of Great Basin bead trade patterns have depended on assumptions concerning the provenience of the raw materials acquired. This is particularly problematic for spire lopped *O. biplicata* beads due to their exceptionally wide geographic and temporal distributions. The ability to source the shell beads to general geographic sources will have dramatic consequences for these and future trade route proposals.

METHODS

Bead Data

Olivella biplicata beads are manufactured from the shell of a small (8 to 38 mm) gastropod living in the Pacific Ocean. They have a wide geographic distribution and can be found in marine waters stretching from Baja, Mexico, to Sitka Alaska (Sept 2001:77). *O. biplicata* occupy sandy strata from low tide level to depths of 46 metres (Sept 2001:77) often in groups of hundreds or thousands of individuals. Shell coloration varies, but purple- and cream-coloured bodies are common and often feature orange, purple, or blue striping. Archaeological specimens are generally cream- to white-coloured.

O. *biplicata* beads were manufactured in many different styles. Bennyhoff and Hughes identified seventeen different classes of beads manufactured from Olivella shells, notated A through Q (1987:85). Bead classes are delineated by the construction methods and shell parts utilized and include spire altered, wall, shelf, callus, and columella type beads (see Bennyhoff and Hughes 1987:89, Figure 10.1). These bead types were manufactured at different times by different populations throughout the Holocene.

The majority of the twenty-three *O. biplicata* beads analyzed are all classified per the Bennyhoff and Hughes (1987) typology as being of the Class A variety (Table 10.1). Class A denotes a nearly complete *Olivella* shell with only the spire removed either by grinding, breaking, or natural water-wear (Bennyhoff and Hughes 1987:116). Further subdivision of Class A beads into types *a* (small), *b* (medium) and *c* (large) is based on size using maximum diameter as a measure (Bennyhoff and Hughes 1987:117). While type A beads were manufactured using six different species of *Olivella*, only beads manufactured from *O. biplicata* were used for this study.

BEAD NO.	SITE	TYPE	DATE (CAL. BP 2 SIGMA)	SOURCE	NO. SAMPLES TAKEN	SAMPLE SPACING (MM)	18 O RANGE	18 O AVERAGE	13 C RANGE	13 C AVERAGE	INFERRED SOURCE
1	Carlon Village	A2a	1,650	Wingard 2001	3	2	[-0.650,-0.740]	-0.707	[0.728,0.635]	0.669	So. CA
2	Carlon Village	A1a	600	Wingard 2001	3	2	[0.598,0.187]	0.478	[1.760,1.284]	1.547	So. CA
3	Carlon Village	A1a	600	Wingard 2001	3	2	[0.948,0.708]	0.789	[1.978,1.274]	1.518	So. CA
4	Bergen	A1b	4,420	Helzer 2001	3	3	[0.170,-0.082]	0.789	[1.780,0.582]	1.240	So. CA
5	Bergen	A2	6,110	Largaespada 2001	3	3	[-0.268,-0.683]	-0.118	[1.835,0.952]	1.361	So. CA
6	Bergen	A1a	5,320	Largaespada 2001	3	2	[0.265,-0.269]	-0.012	[1.128,-0.187]	0.470	So. CA
7	Bergen	A1a	5,450	Largaespada 2001	3	2	[1.936,1.591]	1.808	[2.131,1.819]	1.930	No. CA
8	Bergen	A2a	3,820	Largaespada 2001	3	2	[1.418,1.295]	1.239	[0.166,0.146]	1.372	So. CA/No. CA
9	Bergen	A1b	5,740	Largaespada 2001	3	2	[1.664,1.347]	-0.130	[0.149,0.102]	1.538	So. CA
10	Bergen	A2a	3,820	Largaespada 2001	3	2	[1.053,0.449]	0.801	[1.648,1.535]	1.575	So. CA/No. CA
11	Bergen	A1a	5,930	Helzer 2001	3	2	[1.711,1.282]	1.565	[1.978,1.827]	1.879	So. CA/No. CA
12	Big M	A1a	5,525	Jenkins 1994b	3	2	[0.074,-0.274]	-0.136	[0.831,0.651]	0.769	So. CA
13	Big M	A1c	5,610	Jenkins 1994b	2	3	[1.133,0.755]	0.944	[1.924,1.621]	1.773	So. CA/No. CA
14	Big M	A1a	5,610	Jenkins 1994b	2	2	[0.777,0.752]	0.765	[2.209,1.537]	1.873	So. CA
15	Big M	A1b	5,525	Jenkins 1994b	3	2	[-0.132,-0.826]	-0.482	[1.843,1.631]	1.710	So. CA
16	Big M	A1a	5,610	Jenkins 1994b	3	2	[0.404,-0.053]	0.182	[1.819,0.827]	1.213	So. CA
17	Big M	A1b	5,525	Jenkins 1994b	3	2	[-0.123,-0.325]	-0.224	[1.192,0.711]	1.007	So. CA
18	Big M	A2a	5,650	Jenkins 1994b	3	2	[0.654,0.421]	0.567	[1.904,1.677]	1.756	So. CA
19	Big M	A2	5,650	Jenkins 1994b	3	2	[1.117,-0.410]	0.351	[2.068,1.851]	1.989	Not Olivella
20	Big M	NA	5,640	Jenkins 1994b	3	3	[0.860,-0.250]	0.467	[1.097,0.848]	0.988	So. CA
21	Bowling Dune	B3	2,980	Jenkins 2004	3	2	[1.278,0.792]	0.963	[2.286,1.961]	2.089	So. CA
22	Bowling Dune	A1a	5,310	Jenkins 2004	3	2	[1.300,0.681]	0.896	[1.766,1.683]	1.733	So. CA/No. CA
23	DJ Ranch	B3	~3,700	Moessner 2004	3	2	[0.924,0.258]	0.520	[2.071,1.640]	1.838	So. CA
24	DJ Ranch	A1a	~3,700	Moessner 2004	3	2	[1.529,1.210]	1.387	[1.837,1.559]	1.722	So. CA

STABLE ISOTOPE ANALYSIS

Previous studies have shown that oxygen and carbon isotopic analysis of marine shell is an effective method for reconstructing sea-surface temperature (Epstein et al. 1953), changes in salinity (Kennett and Voorhies 1995), seasonality studies (Killingley 1981; Shackleton 1973; Kennett and Voorhies 1996), and fluctuations in upwelling (Glassow et al. 1994; Killingley 1979). The ratio of ^{16}O and ^{18}O in shell carbonate (aragonite and/or calcite) depends on the temperature and salinity of the seawater in which the shell formed (Urey 1947). The salinity and temperature gradients of the ocean vary depending on both geographic positioning and seasonal fluctuations. These ambient ocean conditions are 'recorded' in the chemical signature of mollusc shells. Unique regional patterns can be discerned by taking multiple incremental samples of the shell carbonate across growth lines, thus mitigating seasonal fluctuations.

Shell ^{18}O levels are primarily affected by temperature and salinity and these gradients are quite distinct along the Pacific Coast. While there is some seasonal sea surface temperature (SST) overlap, overall coastal temperature signatures are distinct over larger geographic areas. Summer ocean temperatures in the waters of the Santa Barbara area peak between 16° and 20° Celsius, between 12° and 14° Celsius in Monterey Bay and between 9° and 12° Celsius around southern Oregon (Eerkens et al. 2005). Given the scarcity of freshwater outlets into the Pacific, fluctuations in salinity are slight in southern Californian waters; however, north of Point Conception, slightly lower salinities occur in the winter months due to increased freshwater input from streams and rivers (Eerkens et al. 2005). Seasonal upwelling events, initiated by dissolved inorganic carbon, have been found to affect shell ^{13}C (Shackleton and Renfrew 1970). These upwelling events are common in parts of the California coast and generally occur between the months of April and July (Eerkens et al. 2005). More negative oxygen isotope values indicate warmer ocean temperatures; more positive values signify cooler temperatures. More negative carbon isotope values indicate more extensive upwelling events; more positive values suggest less intense upwelling.

Eerkens et al. (2005) have analyzed numerous modern *O. biplicata* shells collected from southern Oregon, northern California, and the Santa Barbara Channel. Three distinct isotopic signatures have been identified: a northern California/southern Oregon signature, a Santa Rosa/Santa Barbara Mainland signature, and a Santa Cruz Island signature. While there is some overlap of isotopic values, Eerkens et al. (2005) have demonstrated that the [18]O present in *Olivella biplicata* shells are affected by the interplay of sea temperature and salinity, and ^{13}C levels by upwelling events and that these water parameter levels have little overlap along the California and Oregon coasts. By extracting multiple samples per shell, seasonal SST overlap can be accounted for and oxygen and carbon isotopes can be geographically sensitive (Eerkens et al. 2005). While the overall resolution and accuracy of geographic provenience determinations via oxygen and carbon isotopic data is still being investigated, isotopic values from north and south of Point Conception are readily discernable and *O. biplicata* shells can be reliably sourced to at least that level of resolution (Eerkens et al. 2005:4).

Despite the relatively stable nature of marine parameters since the beginning of the Middle Holocene, research by Kennett and Kennett (2000) has shown that there have been millennial scale SST oscillations during this time. There have been warm and cool water temperature intervals throughout the Holocene and these periods may have had an effect on oxygen isotopic levels present in prehistoric shells and beads. The coldest SSTs occurred between 1500 and 500 BP and the warmest between 5,900 and 3,800 BP (Kennett 2005:67). The resolution of the SST records is more refined than that of radiocarbon dates, but impacts to shell isotope values from these SST fluctuations can be approximated.

For the present study, three samples were taken per bead at 2–3 millimetre increments, depending on overall shell size. Extracting three samples across growth lines mitigates the effects of natural seasonal fluctuations in isotopic values. Into the Early Holocene, large fluctuations in isotopic values had occurred due to post-glacial sea-level rise. Global sea levels rose from approximately −60 metres 12,000 years ago to near present levels by about 6,000 years ago (Stott et al. 2004). To avoid problems related to changing ocean chemistry through time, only Middle and Late Holocene aged beads (less than 7,600 cal. BP) recovered from carefully excavated, undisturbed, and dated contexts were utilized in the present research.

The shell beads were prepared for sampling by a thorough cleansing process. They were rinsed with deionized water to remove loose surface dirt and debris, dried in an oven, and the process repeated until all visible organic material was removed. The shells were then etched with a solution of 5 per cent hydrochloric acid to remove any diagenetically altered carbonate and then rinsed again and dried. Samples were extracted with a dental drill equipped with 1/32-inch bits. Each sample was screened for impurities under a microscope before being transferred to a glass vial. Samples were then sent to stable isotope laboratories located at the College of Oceanic and Atmospheric Science at Oregon State University and the Marine Science Institute at the University of California, Santa Barbara. Both laboratories utilize a Finnegan-MAT 252 mass spectrometer with a kiel carbonate inlet system ensuring comparable results.

RESULTS

The oxygen and carbon isotopic data from the twenty-three *Olivella biplicata* beads were compared to the *O. biplicata* baseline shell data published by Eerkens et al. (2005) (Figure 10.3). The initial results indicated strong evidence for southern California as the primary *O. biplicata* shell collection centre for the beads analyzed from the five Northern Great Basin sites. Thus, SST records from the Santa Barbara Channel were utilized to correct the oxygen (^{18}O) isotopic results. Some isotopic values suggest shell collection from waters warmer than those present in the Northern Channel Islands, but data for the Southern Channel Islands and points south were unavailable at the time of writing. The results are organized into arbitrary time periods only in an attempt for simplicity and clarity and are not indicative of any established periods.

Isotopic results from the three beads dating to the Late Holocene (Figure 10.4) are consistent with values garnered from southern California. Bead number 1, excavated from the Carlon Village site and dating to approximately 1650 cal. BP, appears to have been gathered from waters south of the Northern Santa Barbara Channel. This time period featured normal SST levels and isotopic skew is unlikely. Bead numbers 2 and 3 are also from the Carlon Village site but date to approximately 600 cal. BP. These two beads likely originated from the same occupational period and their isotopic values accordingly cluster rather tightly together. This time period exhibited colder than present SST levels, which may have skewed the oxygen isotopic values up to three parts per mil more than the oxygen isotopic results indicate. This would indicate isotopic values completely in the range common to Santa Barbara and the Northern Channel Islands.

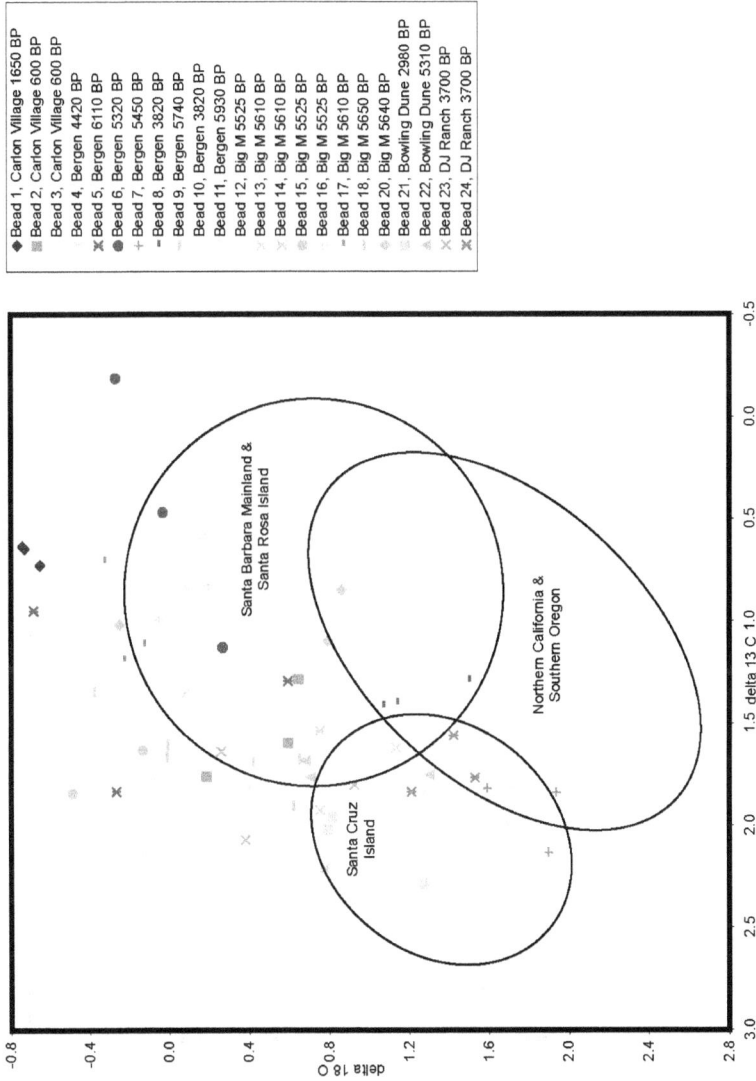

Figure 10.3. Oxygen and carbon isotope values from all twenty-three beads analyzed compared to Eerkens et al. (2005) modern *O. biplicata* data set.

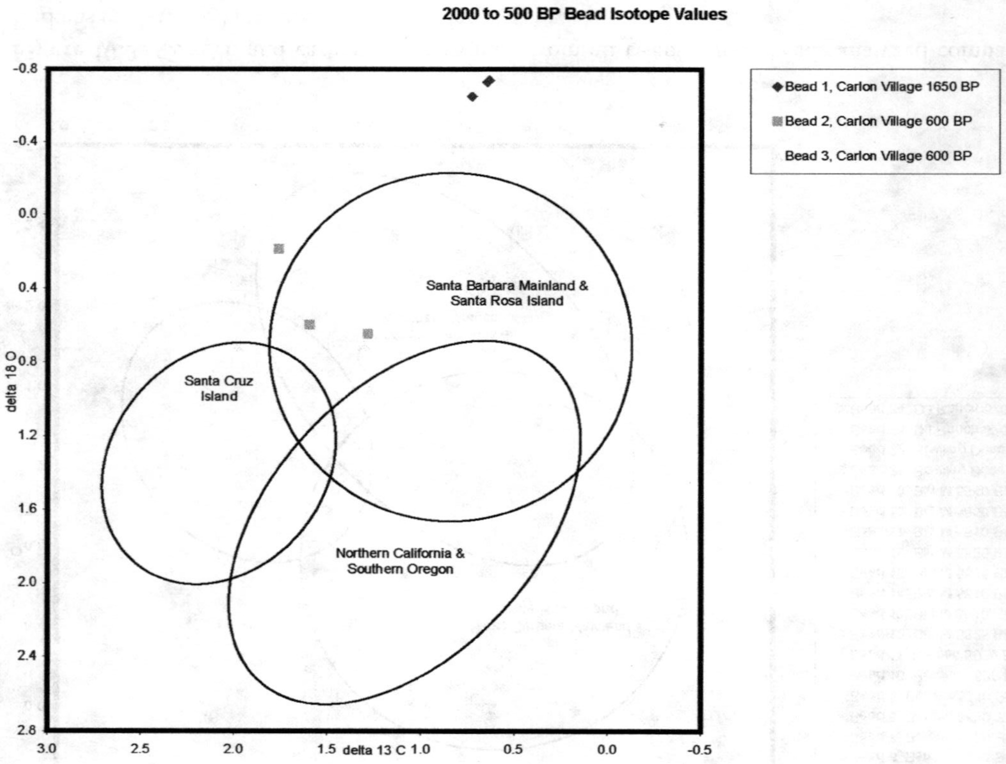

Figure 10.4. 2000 to 500 BP Bead Isotope Values.

TOBIN C. BOTTMAN

Beads recovered from 4,000- to 3,000-year-old deposits (Figure 10.5) generally displayed greater 13 C values than the beads from the Late Holocene. Bead numbers 8 and 10 were recovered from the Bergen Site and date to approximately 3,820 cal. BP. SST levels at this time were in a transitional phase, but an ^{18}O shift of more than one or two mil in either direction is unlikely. This places bead numbers 8 and 10 in the isotopic range of both the Santa Barbara Channel area, as well as the warmest limits of the northern California levels. Bead number 21 (2,980 cal. BP), from the Bowling Dune site, appears to originate from southern California waters. There were slightly cooler SST's during this time, but the impacts to the oxygen isotopic signature are slight and only more fully support the Santa Barbara Channel as the likely shell source. Beads numbers 23 and 24, from DJ Ranch, date to 3,700 cal. BP. This coincides with cooler than normal sea surface temperatures and suggests that oxygen isotope values may be skewed up to one to two mil 'cooler' than they appear. This would more strongly suggest a shell source in southern California such as the Santa Barbara Channel.

The isotopic results from the bead dating to between 5,000 and 4,000 BP (Figure 10.6) are strongly suggestive of a point of origin in southern California. This period coincides with a shift to warmer SST levels, influencing ^{18}O values no more than approximately two per mil more positive. This would suggest that bead number 4 from the Bergen site (4,420 cal. BP) originated from an area south of Point Conception. Little to no overlap into northern California and southern Oregon isotopic values is expected, even in the event of a two-per-mil oxygen isotope value SST shift.

The isotopic values of beads dating between 6,500 and 5,000 BP (Figure 10.7) indicate a wider range than any other period. This period of time represents periods of both warmer and cooler overall SST levels. Beads 6, 7, and 9 from Bergen, 12, 13, 14, 15, 16, 17, 18, and 20 from Big M, as well as bead number 22 from Bowling Dune, date to the period of warmer overall SST levels. Of these, the isotopic results of beads 6, 9, 12, 14, 15, 16, 17, 18, and 20 are strongly suggestive of a source in southern California, likely the Santa Barbara Channel itself. However, the isotopic values for beads 13 and 22 overlap slightly with values associated with more northerly areas, suggesting a central or northern California source. The isotopic values for bead number 7 are quite indicative of those associated with northern California and southern Oregon. While SST levels were only marginally lower at this time (on the order of 0.5 to 1 per mil

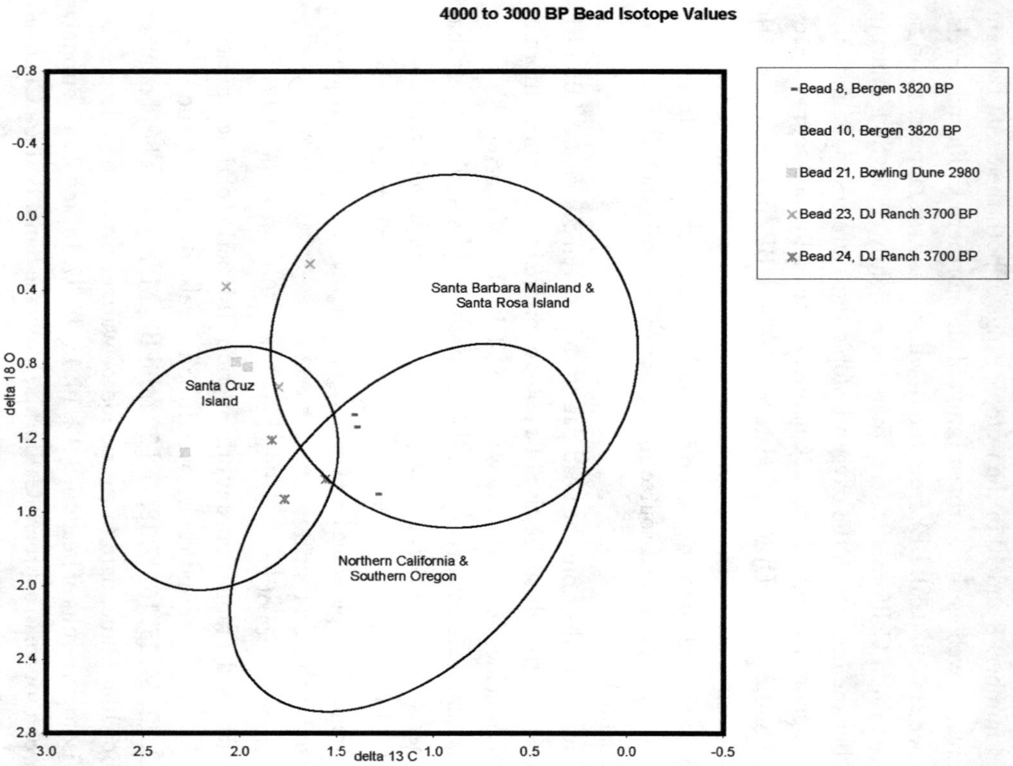

Figure 10.5. 4000 to 3000 BP Bead Isotope Values.

TOBIN C. BOTTMAN

5000 - 4000 BP Bead Isotope Values

Bead 4, Bergen 4420 BP

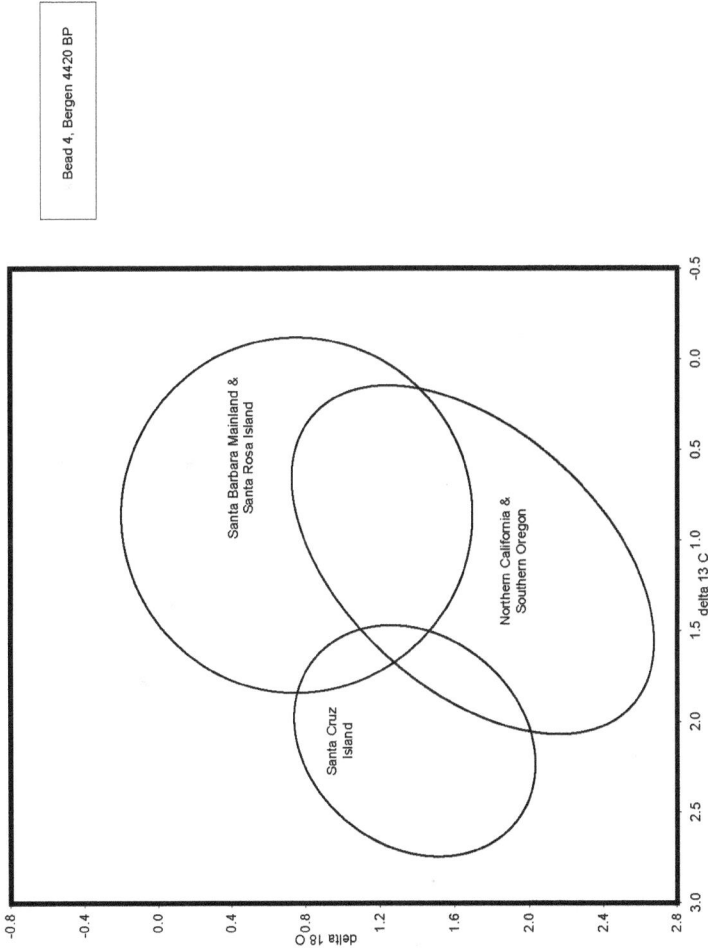

Figure 10.6. 5000 to 4000 BP Bead Isotope Values.

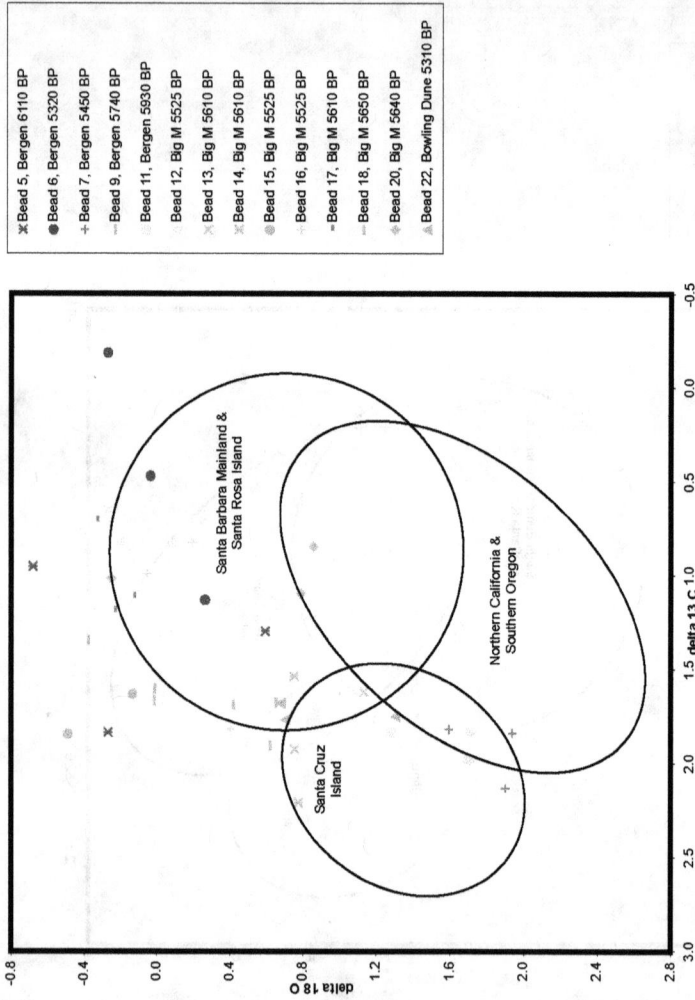

6500 - 5000 BP Bead Isotope Values

Legend:
- ✷ Bead 5, Bergen 6110 BP
- ● Bead 6, Bergen 5320 BP
- + Bead 7, Bergen 5450 BP
- — Bead 9, Bergen 5740 BP
- Bead 11, Bergen 5930 BP
- Bead 12, Big M 5525 BP
- ✕ Bead 13, Big M 5610 BP
- ✷ Bead 14, Big M 5610 BP
- ⊛ Bead 15, Big M 5525 BP
- + Bead 16, Big M 5525 BP
- — Bead 17, Big M 5610 BP
- Bead 18, Big M 5650 BP
- ◆ Bead 20, Big M 5640 BP
- ▲ Bead 22, Bowling Dune 5310 BP

Santa Barbara Mainland & Santa Rosa Island

Northern California & Southern Oregon

Santa Cruz Island

delta 13 C

delta 18 O

Figure 10.7. 6500 to 5000 BP Bead Isotope Values.

TOBIN C. BOTTMAN

greater [18]O value), a shell source north of Point Conception is still supported. Beads 5 and 11 from the Bergen site (6,110 and 5,930 cal. BP, respectively) date from the latter part of this period, a time of cooler SST levels. Both beads likely originated in southern California waters, though the isotopic values of bead 11 does overlap slightly into values associated with more northerly waters.

DISCUSSION

Oxygen and carbon isotopic values from the twenty-three analyzed beads strongly indicate a southern California point of origin; many suggest procurement from the Santa Barbara Channel region specifically. The above results have interesting consequences for the existing trade route models discussed earlier.

Models 1 and 3 feature trade networks centred north of Point Conception. While the isotopic data suggests that up to six beads (numbers 7, 8, 10, 11, 13, and 22) may have originated from more northerly waters, the current isotopic data strongly suggests a southern California point of origin. Bennyhoff and Hughes (1987) proposed a southern California exchange network, though it was thought to be most important only for areas in the southwestern sector of the Great Basin like Death Valley during the Late Holocene.

The southern California-based trade network of Model 2 is very well supported by the isotopic evidence obtained in the current research. This conclusion is also supported by the available evidence concerning the collection and dispersal of OGR beads (Jenkins and Erlandson 1997; Raab and Howard 2000; Vellanoweth 1995; Vellanoweth et al. 1996). While isotopic data for Southern Channel Islands *O. biplicata* are not currently available, a shell source zone located south of Point Conception, in the vicinity of the Northern and Southern Channel Islands, is very likely. North of Point Conception, marine isotopic values have been found to be distinct enough from the Santa Barbara Channel to strongly suggest such a conclusion.

However, this shell sourcing technique is not free of complications and shortcomings. Overlapping modern shell isotopic values, sea water parameter changes through time, radiocarbon dating accuracy, a geographically limited modern shell data set, and a small archaeological bead sample size are some of the primary problems surrounding the process. Future research must address these and other issues. These issues can be resolved in part by refining and expanding the modern *O. biplicata* data set, compiling comprehensive SST records for other coastal areas and sampling additional *O. biplicata* beads from more locales within the Great Basin.

CONCLUSION

The results of this research corroborate with previous research (i.e., Eerkens et al. 2005; Shackleton and Renfrew 1970) proving that shell sourcing via oxygen and carbon isotope analysis is a viable technique. The current isotopic data confirm that at least seventeen, but likely twenty-two, of the twenty-three *O. biplicata* beads analyzed from sites in the Fort Rock area of the Northern Great Basin of Oregon were of southern California origin. This research supports a shell trade network likely located in the vicinity of the Santa Barbara Channel area of southern California. This method of shell isotopic sourcing has proven to be an additional tool in the decipherment of the procurement and movement of prehistoric trade goods.

Acknowledgments: Many people enabled this project to succeed. In particular, I would like to thank Dr. Douglas Kennett, Dr. Jelmer Eerkens, and Dr. Dennis Jenkins for their help, guidance, and support throughout the entire process. I would also like to thank the staff members of the stable isotope laboratories at Oregon State University and University of California, Berkeley. Shell analysis was made possible due to the generosity of the Edna English Fund from the University of Oregon. The University of Oregon Department of Anthropology and Museum of Natural and Cultural History provided the travel and lodging funds for the Chacmool conference.

REFERENCES CITED

Bedwell, Stephen F.

1973   *Fort Rock Basin: Prehistory and Environment*. University of Oregon Books, Eugene.

Bennyhoff, James A., and Richard E. Hughes

1987   *Shell Bead and Ornament Exchange Networks between California and the Western Great Basin*. Anthropological Papers, vol. 64, pt. 2. American Museum of Natural History, New York.

Eerkens, Jelmer W., Gregory S. Herbert, Jeffrey S. Rosenthal, and Howard J. Spero

2005   Provenance Analysis of *Olivella biplicata* Shell Beads from the California and Oregon Coast by Stable Isotope Fingerprinting. *Journal of Archaeological Science* 32(10):1501–1514.

Epstein, Samuel, Ralph Buchsbaum, Heinz A. Lowenstam, and Harold C. Urey

1953   Revised Carbonate-Water Isotopic Temperature Scale. *Bulletin of the Geologic Society of America*. 64:1315–1326.

Erickson, Kevin

1990   Marine Shell Utilization in the Plateau Culture Area. *Northwest Anthropological Research Notes* 24(1):91–144.

Freidel, Dorothy E.

1994   Paleolake Shorelines and Lake Level Chronology of the Fort Rock Basin, Oregon. In *Archaeological Researches in the Northern Great Basin: Fort Rock Archaeology since Cressman*, edited by C. Melvin Aikens and Dennis L. Jenkins, pp. 21–40. University of Oregon Anthropological Papers 50. Eugene.

Galm, Jerry R.

1994   Prehistoric Trade and Exchange in the Interior Plateau of Northwestern North America. In *Prehistoric Exchange Systems in North America*, edited by Timothy G. Baugh and Jonathon E. Ericson, 275–305. Plenum Press, New York.

Glassow, Michael A., Douglas J. Kennett, James P. Kennett, and Larry R. Wilcoxon

1994   Confirmation of Middle Holocene Ocean Cooling Inferred from Stable Isotopic Analysis of Prehistoric Shells from Santa Cruz Island, California. In *The Fourth California Islands Symposium: Update of the Status of Resources*, edited by W.L. Halvorson and G.J. Maender, pp. 223–232. Santa Barbara Museum of Natural History, Santa Barbara.

Helzer, Margaret M.

2004   Archaeological Investigations at the Bergen Site: Middle Holocene Lakeside Occupations Near Fort Rock, Oregon. In *Early and Middle Holocene Archaeology of the Northern Great Basin*, edited by Dennis L. Jenkins, Thomas J. Connolly, and C. Melvin Aikens, pp. 77–94. University of Oregon Anthropological Papers 62, Eugene.

Hughes, Richard E., and James A. Bennyhoff

1986   Early Trade. In *Great Basin*, edited by Warren L. D'Azevedo, pp. 238–255, Handbook of North American Indians, Vol. 11, William C. Sturtevant, general editor. Smithsonian Institution, Washington, D.C.

Jenkins, Dennis L.

1994a   Settlement-Subsistence Patterns in the Fort Rock Basin: A Cultural-Ecological Perspective on Human Responses to Fluctuating Wetlands Resources of the Last 5000 Years. In *Archaeological Researches in the Northern Great Basin: Fort Rock Archaeology Since Cressman*, edited by C. Melvin Aikens and Dennis L. Jenkins, pp. 599–628. University of Oregon Anthropological Papers 50, Eugene.

1994b   Archaeological Investigations at Three Wetlands Sites in the Silver Lake Area of the Fort Rock Basin. In *Archaeological Researches in the Northern Great Basin: Fort Rock Archaeology Since Cressman*, edited by C. Melvin Aikens and Dennis L. Jenkins, pp. 213–258. University of Oregon Anthropological Papers 50, Eugene.

2000   Early to Middle Holocene Cultural Transitions in the Northern Great Basin of Oregon: The View from Fort Rock. In *Archaeological Passages: A Volume in Honor of Claude Nelson Warren*, edited by Joan S. Schneider, Robert M. Yohe II, and Jill Gardner, pp. 69–109. Publications in Archaeology, vol. 1. Western Center for Archaeology and Paleontology, Hemet, California.

2004   The Grasshopper and the Ant: Middle Holocene Occupations and Storage Behavior at the Bowling Dune Site in the Fort Rock Basin, Oregon. In *Early and Middle Holocene Archaeology of the Northern Great Basin*, edited by Dennis L. Jenkins, Thomas J. Connolly, and C. Melvin Aikens, pp. 123–156. University of Oregon Anthropological Papers 62, Eugene.

Jenkins, Dennis L., and Jon M. Erlandson

1997   Olivella Grooved Rectangle Beads from a Middle Holocene Site in the Fort Rock Valley, Northern Great Basin. *Journal of California and Great Basin Anthropology* 19(2):296–302.

Jenkins, Dennis L., and Nina Wimmers

1994   Beads as Indicators of Cultural and Chronological Change in the Fort Rock Basin. In *Archaeological Researches in the Northern Great Basin: Fort Rock Archaeology Since Cressman*, edited by C. Melvin Aikens and Dennis L. Jenkins, pp. 107–123. University of Oregon Anthropological Papers 50, Eugene.

Jenkins, Dennis L., Thomas J. Connolly, and C. Melvin Aikens

2004a Early and Middle Holocene Archaeology in the Northern Great Basin: Dynamic Natural and Cultural Ecologies. In *Early and Middle Holocene Archaeology of the Northern Great Basin*, edited by Dennis L. Jenkins, Thomas J. Connolly, and C. Melvin Aikens, pp. 1–20. University of Oregon Anthropological Papers 62, Eugene.

Jenkins, Dennis L., Michael S. Droz, and Thomas J. Connolly

2004b Geoarchaeology of Wetland Settings in the Fort Rock Basin, South-Central Oregon. In *Early and Middle Holocene Archaeology of the Northern Great Basin*, edited by Dennis L. Jenkins, Thomas J. Connolly, and C. Melvin Aikens, pp. 31–52. University of Oregon Anthropological Papers 62, Eugene.

Jenkins, Dennis L., Leah L. Largaespada, Tony D. Largaespada, and Mercy A. McDonald

2004c Early and Middle Holocene Ornament Exchange Systems in the Fort Rock Basin of Oregon. In *Early and Middle Holocene Archaeology of the Northern Great Basin*, edited by Dennis L. Jenkins, Thomas J. Connolly, and C. Melvin Aikens, pp, 251–270. University of Oregon Anthropological Papers 62, Eugene,

Kennett, Douglas J.

2005 *The Island Chumash: Behavioral Ecology of a Maritime Society*. University of California Press, Berkeley.

Kennett, Douglas J., and James P. Kennett

2000 Competitive and Cooperative Responses to Climatic Instability in Southern California. *American Antiquity* 65(2):379–395.

Kennett, Douglas J., and Barbara Voorhies

1995 Middle Holocene Periodicities in Rainfall Inferred from Oxygen and Carbon Isotopic Fluctuations in Prehistoric Tropical Estuarine Mollusc Shells. *Archaeometry* 37(1):157–170.

1996 Oxygen Isotopic Analysis of Archaeological Shells to Detect Seasonal Use of Wetlands on the Southern Pacific Coast of Mexico. *Journal of Archaeological Science* 23:689–704.

Killingley, John S.

1979 Stable Isotopes in a Mollusk Shell: Detection of Upwelling Events. *Science* 205:186–188.

1981 Seasonality of Mollusk Collecting Determined from ^{18}O Profiles of Midden Shells. *American Antiquity* 48:152–158.

King, Chester D.

1974 The Explanation of Differences and Similarities among Beads Used in Prehistoric and Early Historic California. In *Antap: California Indian Political and*

Economic Organization, edited by L.J. Bean and T.F. King, pp. 75–92. Anthropological Papers 2, Ballena Press, Ramona.

Largaespada, Leah L.

2001   From Sand and Sea: Marine Shell Artifacts from Archaeological Sites in the Fort Rock Basin, Northern Great Basin. Master's paper, Department of Anthropology, University of Oregon, Eugene.

Moessner, Jean

2004   DJ Ranch: A Mid- to Late Holocene Occupation Site in the Fort Rock Valley, South Central Oregon. In *Early and Middle Holocene Archaeology of the Northern Great Basin*, edited by Dennis L. Jenkins, Thomas J. Connolly, and C. Melvin Aikens. pp. 95–122. University of Oregon Anthropological Papers 62, Eugene.

Raab, L. Mark, and William J. Howard

2000   Modeling Cultural Connections between the Southern Channel Islands and the Western United States: The Middle Holocene Distribution of Olivella Grooved Rectangle Beads. *Proceedings of the Fifth California Channel Islands Symposium*, edited by D. Brown, K. Mitchell, and H. Chaney, pp. 590–597. Santa Barbara Museum of Natural History, California.

Sept, J. Duane

2001   *The Beachcombers Guide to Seashore Life in the Pacific Northwest*. Harbour Publishing, Madeira Park, British Columbia.

Shackleton, Nicholas J.

1973   Oxygen Isotope Analysis as a Means of Determining Season of Occupation of Prehistoric Midden Sites. *Archaeometry* 15:133–141.

Shackleton, Nicholas J., and Colin Renfrew

1970   Neolithic Trade Routes Realigned by Oxygen Isotope Analyses. *Nature* 228:1062–1065.

Stott, Lowell, Kevin Cannariato, Robert Thunell, Gerald H. Haug, Athanasios Koutavas, and Steve Lund

2004   Decline of Surface Temperature and Salinity in the Western Tropical Pacific Ocean in the Holocene Epoch. *Nature* 431:56–59.

Urey, Harold C.

1947   The Thermodynamic Properties of Isotopic Substances. *Journal of the Chemical Society*, pp. 562–581.

Vellanoweth, Rene L.

1995   New Evidence from San Nicolas Island on the Distribution of Olivella Grooved Rectangle Beads. *Pacific Coast Archaeological Society Quarterly* 31:13–22.

TOBIN C. BOTTMAN

Vellanoweth, Rene L., L. Mark Raab, Jon M. Erlandson, and Dennis L. Jenkins

1996   Olivella Grooved Rectangle Beads in Southern California and the Great Basin. Paper presented at the Twenty Fifth Biannual Great Basin Anthropological Conference, Kings Beach, California.

Wigand, Peter E.

1987   Diamond Pond, Harney County, Oregon: Vegetation History and Water Table in the Eastern Oregon Desert. *Great Basin Naturalist* 47:427–458.

Wingard, George F.

2001   *Carlon Village: Land, Water, Subsistence and Sedentism in the Northern Great Basin.* University of Oregon Anthropological Papers 57. Eugene.

Molecular Analysis of Ancient Cervid Remains from Two Archaeological Sites: Banff National Park and Rocky Mountain House National Historic Site, Alberta

Maria Victoria Monsalve, Dongya Y. Yang, and E. Gwyn Langemann

Abstract. Identification of cervid remains from archaeological sites can be challenging due to the lack of morphological criteria needed to determine the species and subspecies level. Such difficulty of identification significantly limits our ability to study the distribution of cervid species in the past, prior to the extensive alteration of their ecosystems and distributions in historic times. We used ancient DNA techniques in an attempt to obtain more accurate species identification from archaeological cervid bone samples. Four bone samples were recovered from a precontact kill site (EhPv-126) near Banff town site, Banff National Park, and one from Rocky Mountain House National Historic Site (FcPr-4). The bone samples from Banff were in a component radiocarbon dated to 720 ± 40 BP; the sample from Rocky Mountain House came from a feature that was in use between AD 1799 and 1821. DNA was successfully extracted from the remains; the analysis of the mtDNA control region indicates that four of the samples belong to elk (Cervus elaphus) and one to moose (Alces alces). Four samples match the mtDNA control region sequence found in the Genbank data, pointing to the likelihood of Cervus elaphus nelsoni (elk). Although longer mtDNA might be needed to confirm the subspecies status of Cervus elaphus nelsoni and more bone samples are needed to examine the existence of other subspecies in the region, our results have clearly illustrated the potential to use molecular analysis to distinguish species in archaeological faunal assemblages where morphological identification is difficult. Elk and moose are seldom identified in precontact archaeological material from the Canadian Rocky Mountains. More accurate species identification will help conservation biologists to make more informed decisions about managing modern ungulate populations for ecological integrity.

INTRODUCTION

Banff National Park of Canada is actively developing an integrated set of measures to restore bison to the ecosystem, to manage the concentrated occurrence of elk at the Banff town-site, to re-establish wildlife corridors connecting predators and prey, and to reintroduce fire to the landscape (Parks Canada 1997, 2004; White 2001). Zooarchaeological evidence can help in this process by supplying evidence for the former temporal and spatial range of various ungulate species (Kay et al. 1999; Langemann 2004; Lyman 2004; Shapiro et al. 2004; White et al. 2001).

It is clear that accurate species and subspecies identification of archaeological remains would be very useful for conservation biologists to make more informed decisions about which species, subspecies, and populations should be reintroduced for managing modern ungulate populations for ecological integrity.

Visual inspection cannot always identify the fragmented and poorly preserved bones that are usually found in mountain archaeological sites. Commonly, the small portion of an assemblage that is identifiable has only been identified to the level of "large ungulate" or "small cervid." Therefore the relative abundance of species over time or space is difficult to assess.

Elk were nearly extirpated in Banff and southern Alberta by the late 1800s, due to hunting pressure and habitat change. Modern elk populations are the result of restocking from populations in Manitoba and Yellowstone National

Park in Wyoming, as well as elk returning from British Columbia (Holroyd and Van Tighem 1983). Species and subspecies identification of archaeological elk remains will provide direct evidence and specific information about the presence of such species in the region.

Using molecular analysis as a tool in the field of zooarchaeology, accurate identification of ancient biological remains has become possible (Bar-Gal et al. 2002; Barnes et al. 2000; Loreille et al. 1997). In this paper, we present the analysis of mtDNA from five zooarchaeological cervid bone fragments and address the question of which species are actually present in the otherwise unidentifiable archaeological bone assemblages.

Materials and Methods

In 1998 and 1999, archaeologists from Parks Canada recovered the remains of a late precontact period elk kill at a site beside the Golf Loop road, near Banff town-site in Banff National Park, Alberta, Canada (Site EhPv-126, or 1210R in the Parks Canada system) (see Figure 11.1). At least five elk ranging in age between two and eight years had been intensively butchered. A calibrated and corrected radiocarbon date of 720 BP ± 40 (BGS 2147) was obtained from an elk radius shaft bone. The bone layer is a tight component within the site, sealed above and below by sterile layers, and the bones of the different individuals are all mixed together in the archaeological floor. The bones from EhPv-126 were in an excellent state of preservation, but because they were intensively butchered, in most cases they could only be visually identified as large ungulate, probably cervid.

Historic site 16R (FcPr-4) is one of several fur trading posts that are part of Rocky Mountain House National Historic Site of Canada, located in the foothills of west central Alberta (see Figure 11.1). The elk bone in question came from a cellar feature, which is interpreted as a trading room and hall building within the fort. This structure overlaps earlier pit features and so probably dates from the later period of the fort occupation (Steer and Rogers 1978). The bones were in an excellent state of preservation (see Figure 11.2).

For this study, four large cervid bone samples were chosen from the precontact kill site 1210R. A distal humerus that was clearly elk was chosen from the Rocky Mountain House site. Table 11.1 presents a summary of the samples.

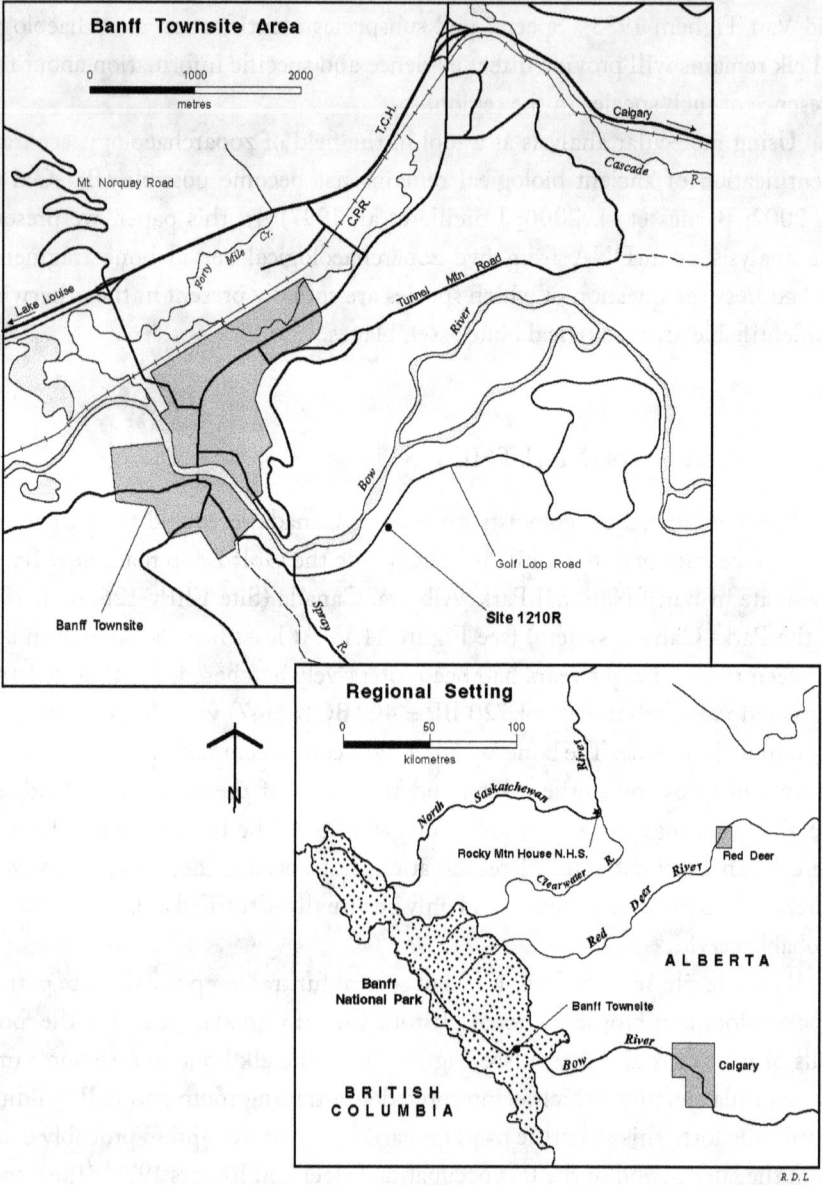

Figure 11.1. Locations of Site 1210R and Rocky Mountain House National Historic Site.

Maria Victoria Monsalve,
Dongya Y. Yang, and E. Gwyn Langemann

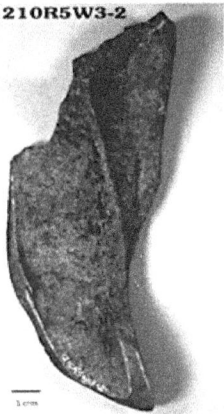

Figure 11.2. Elk and moose bones from Site 1210R. 1210R5W3-2: tibia shaft, elk; 1210R5Z3-12: metacarpal shaft, elk; 1210R5Z3-50: metacarpal shaft, moose; 1210R6J4: tibia shaft, elk.

Table 11.1. Cervid bone samples and their DNA ID.

LAB#	SAMPLE#	SITE	BONE	DNA ID	PERIOD
EK-1	1210R5W3-2	Banff	tibia shaft	elk	720 ± 40 BP
EK-2	1210R5Z3-12	Banff	metacarpal shaft	elk	720 ± 40 BP
EK-3	1210R5Z3-50	Banff	metacarpal shaft	moose	720 ± 40 BP
EK-4	1210R6J4	Banff	tibia shaft	elk	720 ± 40 BP
EK-5	16R8B4-21	Rocky Mountain House	distal humerus	elk	AD 799 to 1821

A cryogenic grinding method, described previously (Sweet and Hildebrand 1998), was used to pulverize the ancient bones. Each bone sample was cleaned and pulverized separately. Small sections of bone were removed from each of the samples, totalling approximately 4 to 8 grams.

Extraction of ancient DNA and PCR Amplification at the University of British Columbia (UBC) was carried out in a laminar flow according to the methodology used (Yang et al. 1998). Double strands of the mtDNA control region from the samples were amplified using two sets of primers (CST15-CST467 and MST29-MST24). PCR was run for 40 cycles.

Ancient DNA extraction and PCR Amplification at Simon Fraser University (SFU) was conducted in a dedicated DNA laboratory built specifically for the ancient DNA analysis. A modified silica-spin column method (Yang et al. 1998) was employed for extracting DNA. PCR amplification was done using primers F136 and R316 in addition to the two sets of primers used at UBC. PCR was run for 50 cycles (see Figure 11.3). PCR products were purified and were subjected to direct sequencing. (Primer sequences are available upon request.)

Sequences obtained on the amplification of three different fragment sizes of the mtDNA were aligned using the program ClustalW and search for identification of species and subspecies were made using the BLAST program (see Figure 11.4).

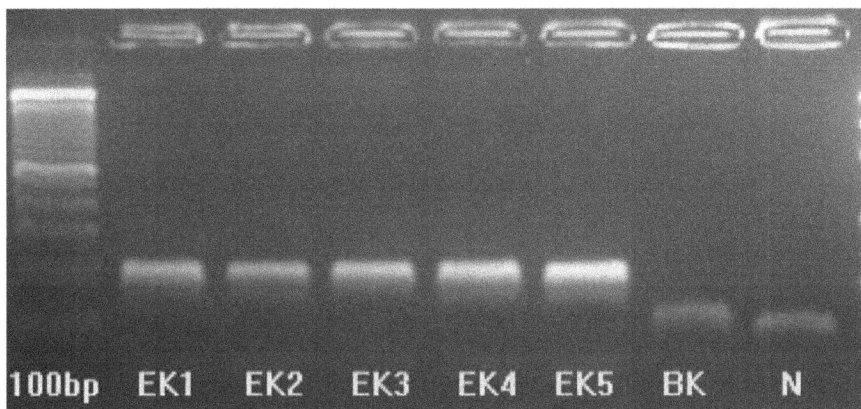

Figure 11.3. Image of SYBR-Green stained 2% agarose gel of PCR products amplified from primers F136/R316 at SFU. EK1, EK2, EK3, EK4 and EK5 are DNA samples (Table 11.1), BK is blank extract, N is PCR negative control, and 100bp is 100bp ladder from Invitrogen. Note: faint bands in BK and N are primer dimmers.

RESULTS

Samples of DNA extracted from ancient bones were analyzed separately at UBC and SFU for this study. Sequences matched were searched in the Genbank data using the BLAST program (NCIB). The DNA extracted at UBC provided a 111 bp fragment of the control region of the mtDNA in five bones by PCR amplification using the primers MST29 and MST84. The amplification of these DNA samples was also successful at SFU and sequencing of PCR products indicated that all the samples belonged to the Cervidae family.

Using primers CST15 and CST 467, PCR amplified products of 266 bp were obtained at UBC in all the samples. Only EK-3 and EK-5 gave readable sequences. Re-extraction of DNA of all five samples was carried out at SFU. Control mtDNA sequences were obtained in the other three cervid samples. Although the BLAST search revealed general match to those of elk, the poor quality of the sequences prevents a reliable base-to-base comparison with the elk DNA sequences used as references in GenBank.

Using primers F136 and R319, PCR amplified products of 181 bp were obtained at SFU from supernatant DNA extractions performed at UBC.

```
Elk¹   TGTACTTCTCATTATTTAAAGTACATAGTACATAATGTTGTTCATCGTACATAGCGCATT  60
EK-1   ............................................................  60
EK-2   ............................................................  60
EK-4   ............................................................  60
EK-5   .......T...C...C..........................................TA....  60

Elk    AAGTCAAATCAGTCCTTGTCAACATGCGTATCCCGTCCCCTAGATCACGAGCTTAATTAC  120
EK-1   ............................................................  120
EK-2   ............................................................  120
EK-4   ............................................................  120
EK-5   ............................................................  120

Elk    CATGCCGCGTGAAACCAGCAACCCG  145
EK-1   .........................  145
EK-2   .........................  145
EK-4   .........................  145
EK-5   .........................  145


Moose² CAAGTACATGACATTATTAATAGTACATAGTACATATTATTATTGATCGTACATAGCACA  60
EK-3   ...................................................G.....  60

Moose  TTATGTCAAATCCATTCTTGTCAACATGCGTATCCCGTCCATTAGATCACGAGCTTAATT  120
EK-3   ...............CA...........................................  120

Moose  ACCATGCCGCGTGAAACCAACAACCCG  145
EK-3   ..................G.......  145
```

Figure 11.4. Comparison of the ancient mtDNA sequences (amplified from primers F136/R316) with the reference sequences from GenBank (1 *Cervus elaphus nelsoni*, accession no. AF16964 and 2 *Alces alces*, accession no. AF412267).

Comparisons of the fragment sequences of the samples studied and sequences obtained in elk and moose (Polziehn and Strobeck 1998) indicated the following: 1) EK-1, EK-2, EK-4 share identical mtDNA sequences and the same DNA sequence as AF16964; 2) EK-5 shares the same mtDNA sequence as *C. e nelsoni* (AF16964) with the exception of a transition (C→T) at positions 8 and 55, a transition (T→C) at positions 12 and 16, and a transition (G→A) at position 56; 3) EK-3 shares the same mtDNA sequences as *Alces alces* (Yakutia AF412267, North American AF412240 and AF412244 samples) with the exception of a transition (A→G) at positions 55 and 140, a transition (T→C) at position 76, and a transversion (C→A) at position 77 (see Figure 11.4).

MARIA VICTORIA MONSALVE,
DONGYA Y. YANG, AND E. GWYN LANGEMANN

DISCUSSION

It is well known that ancient DNA research presents extreme difficulties because of the small amount of DNA that survives and the risks of contamination. This study followed the necessary steps described by Cooper and Poinar (2000) to avoid problems that are inherent in working with ancient DNA as follows: 1) dedicated areas for working with ancient DNA were independent of areas used for PCR amplification; 2) duplicate extractions with controls were carried out to detect contamination; 3) positive controls were avoided; 4) results were reproduced from the same and different DNA extracts from each specimen; 5) different primers were used to increase the chance of detecting contamination by PCR products; 6) independent laboratories extracted samples of the specimens.

Analysis of mtDNA in archaeological bones has been applied to a variety of faunal species (Barnes et al. 2000; Loreille et al. 1997; Yang et al. 2004). Our study also demonstrates that the techniques used for working with ancient DNA might help to identify faunal remains to the level of sub-species in bone samples in which morphology has been ambiguous. Assignment of the elk sample as *C. e. nelsoni* (Rocky Mountain elk) might need confirmation by amplifying a longer DNA sequence, and DNA sequences from more samples, since 181 bp might be limited in securing such determination of subspecies. Nevertheless, this identification is consistent with the current distribution of Rocky Mountain elk (Hebblewhite et al. 2002; Polziehn et al.1998; Polziehn and Strobeck 2002).

The use of DNA to identify excavated cervid remains in the Canadian Rockies is a valuable tool to make inferences about ecosystems in pre-Columbian times. It may support or refute hypotheses respecting occupancy by specific species in this region. Elk is rarely reported, but clearly, as the archaeological data show, elk was present 740 years ago in the Bow River valley. The identification of an ancient bone belonging to an *Alces alces* (moose) suggests the existence of a species seldom reported in pre-Columbian times. Moose and elk are both commonly identified in the historic archaeological assemblages at Rocky Mountain House (Nicol 1978, 1979). We determined that some of the ungulate long bones are in fact moose and not elk. This was a significant result. An elk site is rare enough, but it is extremely uncommon to find butchered moose bones in a pre-contact site in the Rocky Mountains. The study presented here is the first describing a pre-contact archaeological site in Banff that includes firmly identified butchered moose bones.

Recent studies have established the habits and ecology of elk in the eastern Rocky Mountains and the foothills east of Banff and Jasper National Parks, extending east nearly to Rocky Mountain House (Central East Slopes Elk Study 2004; Hebblewhite 2002; Hebblewhite et al. 2002, 2005; Morgantini 1988). In the Bow River valley near Banff town-site and site 1210R, elk have recently become highly concentrated, where they are protected from predators. Recent changes in elk management through aversive conditioning and fencing, and predator restoration, have reduced the concentrations of elk in this part of the valley and moved them out more widely (Hebblewhite et al. 2002; Parks Canada 2004). Clearly, as the archaeological data show, elk were present in some numbers 740 years ago at this same location in the Bow River valley.

The total number of fragments identifiable at least to element (NISP) in site EhPv-126 is 256, out of a total of 2,171. Because nearly all of the visually iden-tifiable fragments were elk for a minimum number of individuals of five (based on the number of tooth rows), and only one fragment was moose (an incisive), the assumption could have been made in a standard visual analysis that the unidentifiable fragments are predominately elk as well, in a comparable ratio. However, one out of four samples in this study were identified by their DNA as moose, which gives a much larger relative proportion of moose to elk within the zooarchaeological assemblage than the visual identification. It will be neces-sary to re-examine the faunal assemblage, with a more careful comparison of the available moose and elk material. DNA allowed us to accurately identify which species were present in Banff National Park and Rocky Mountain House National Historic sites.

In Banff, the reason that elk and moose have seldom been identified in sites may well be due to the poor preservation and extremely fragmented nature of bone, so that diagnostic anatomical features are not present on the small bits of bone; it may be due to the inexperience of analysts; or it may reflect a real short-age of elk and moose. These reasons all need to be more carefully considered. Some reviews of the zooarchaeological literature have used the absence of elk to argue that elk were not in fact ever present in any numbers (Kay et al. 1999). However, in EhPv-126 there is in fact a site where elk are by far the most abundantly represented species.

The historic fur trade sites are a different situation. Bone is often well-preserved here because it is more recent and often deliberately buried in cellars or pits for hygiene. The species in these sites reflect animals hunted for food by inhabitants of the fort, as well as animals trapped for their furs. There is often a tighter time control, given the datable features at a historic site. At a site such as Rocky Mountain House, where there is a series of forts built over the years, comparison of the fauna may reflect the changes in abundance of local species over time.

Studies of DNA in conjunction with archaeozoological data allow more precise identification of species and subspecies than was previously possible. Thus EK-5, identified as belonging to *C. e nelsoni* has a different haplotype than EK-1, EK-2, and EK-4. Interestingly, the EK-5 sample dated in the early 1800s was found in the Rocky Mountain House historic fur trade site located 140 km from EhPv-126. There are different rationales for this. Geographic isolation may account for different haplotypes in each of the two sites, or different elk haplotype frequencies may have predominated in pre-Columbian and post-Columbian periods.

DNA analysis of archaeological samples has been proven to be useful in determining how closely related various individuals were, at different places and times (Shapiro et al. 2004). It could also allow us to consider if elk populations before the local extirpation moved as widely and rapidly as some individuals do today in regions of the Rocky Mountains (Central East Slopes Elk Study 2004; Hebblewhite et al. 2002). Unfortunately, it is not common to find elk bones in a good excavated pre-contact archaeological context in the central Rocky Mountains, and our present sample is a small one.

It is quite possible that at the time site EhPv-126 was occupied, 740 years ago, moose were more abundant in the Bow River valley than now. Human-ignited fires were then more frequent (White 2001), renewing the early succession vegetation that moose prefer (Hurd 1999). It would be useful to attempt further molecular analysis of the bone fragments in order to see if more moose are present in the archaeological assemblage.

Acknowledgments: We are grateful to UBC Bureau for Forensic Dentistry for some sample preparation; to Karl Hillis, Camilla Speller and Kathy Watt of D. Y. Yang's Ancient DNA Laboratory at SFU for pre-PCR and post-PCR technical assistance; and to Lisa Schattman at UBC for editing work. This research was in part supported by grants to D. Y. Yang from the Social Science and Humanities Research Council of Canada. Rick Lalonde drafted the location figure.

REFERENCES CITED

Bar-Gal, G. Kahila, H. Khalaily, O. Mader, P. Ducos, and L. Kolska Horwitz

2002 Ancient DNA Evidence for the Transition from Wild to Domestic Status in Neolithic Goats: A Case Study from the Site of Abu Gosh, Israel. *Ancient Biomolecules* 4:9–17.

Barnes, Ian, J. Peter W. Young, and Keith M. Dobney

2000 DNA-Based Identification of Goose Species from Two Archaeological Sites in Lincolnshire. *Journal of Archaeological Science* 27:91–100.

Central East Slopes Elk Study

2004 Project Overview. Electronic document, http://ursus.biology.ualberta.ca/elk/overview.htm, accessed January 22, 2007.

Cooper, Alan, and Hendrik N. Poinar

2000 Ancient DNA: Do it right or not at all. *Science* 289:1139–1140.

Hebblewhite, Mark

2002 No Park, or Elk, is an Island. Electronic document, http://ursus.biology.ualberta.ca/yhtelkwolfproject/Reports.htm, accessed January 22, 2007.

Hebblewhite, Mark, Daniel H. Pletscher, and Paul C. Paquet

2002 Elk Population Dynamics in Areas with and without Predation by Recolonizing Wolves in Banff National Park, Alberta. *Canadian Journal of Zoology* 80:789–799.

Hebblewhite, Mark, Clifford A. White, Clifford G. Nietvelt, John A. McKenzie, Thomas E. Hurd, John M. Fryxell, Suzanne E. Bayley, and Paul C. Paquet

2005 Human Activity Mediates a Trophic Cascade Caused by Wolves. *Ecology* 86:2135–2144.

Holroyd, Geoffrey L., and K. J. Van Tighem

1983 *The Wildlife Inventory.* Ecological (Biophysical) Land Classification of Banff and Jasper National Parks, vol. III, edited by W. D. Holland and G. M. Coen. Canadian Wildlife Service, Edmonton, Alberta.

Hurd, Thomas E.

1999   Factors Limiting Moose Numbers and Their Interactions with Elk and Wolves in the Central Rocky Mountains, Canada. Master's thesis, Department of Forest Sciences, University of British Columbia, Vancouver.

Kay, Charles E., Clifford A. White, Ian R. Pengelly, and Brian Patton

1999   Assessment of Long-Term Ecosystem States and Processes In Banff National Park and the Central Canadian Rockies. Occasional Paper No. 9. Parks Canada, National Parks, Ottawa.

Langemann, E. Gwyn

2004   Zooarchaeological Research in Support of a Reintroduction of Bison to Banff National Park, Canada. In *The Future from the Past: Archaeozoology in Wildlife Conservation and Heritage Management*, edited by Roel C.G.M. Lauwerier and Ina Plug, pp. 79–89. Proceedings of the 9th International Council of Archaeozoology Conference, Durham 2002, Umberto Albarella, Keith Dobney, and Peter Rowley-Conway, series editors. Oxbow Books, Oxford.

Loreille, Odile, Jean-Denis Vigne, Chris Hardy, Cecille Callou, Françoise Treinen-Claustre, Nicole Denebouy, and Monique Monnerot

1997   First Distinction of Sheep and Goat Archaeological Bones by the Means of their Fossil mtDNA. *Journal of Archaeological Science* 24:33–37.

Lyman, R. Lee

2004   Aboriginal Overkill in the Intermountain West of North America: Zooarchaeological Tests and Implications. *Human Nature* 15(2):169–208.

Morgantini, Luigi

1988   Behavioral Adaptive Strategies of Wapiti (*Cervus elaphus*) in the Canadian Rocky Mountains. PhD dissertation, Department of Animal Science, University of Alberta, Edmonton, Alberta.

Nicol, Heather

1978   Analysis of Faunal Remains from Site 16R, Rocky Mountain House. In *Archaeological Investigations at an Early Nineteenth Century Fur Trading Fort, Rocky Mountain House National Historic Park, 1975–1977*, edited by Donald N. Steer and Harvey J. Rogers, pp. 429–474. Microfiche Report Series No. 35. Parks Canada, Ottawa.

1979   Analysis of Faunal Remains from Site 15R, Rocky Mountain House. In *Archaeological Investigations at the Hudson's Bay Company Rocky Mountain House, 1835–61*, edited by Donald N. Steer, Harvey J. Rogers, and Gregory J. Lutick, vol. 1, pp. 221–249. Manuscript Report Number 445, Environment Canada, Parks, Ottawa.

Parks Canada

1997 Banff National Park Management Plan. Electronic document, http://www.
pc.gc.ca/pn-np/ab/banff/docs/plan1/plan1a_e.asp, accessed February 20, 2007.

2004 Elk Management in Banff National Park. Electronic document, http://www.
pc.gc.ca/pn-np/ab/banff/plan/plan23a_E.asp, accessed January 22, 2007.

Polziehn, Renee O., and Curtis Strobeck

1998 Phylogeny of Wapiti, Red Deer, Sika Deer, and Other North American Cervids
as Determined from Mitochondrial DNA. *Molecular Phylogenetics and Evolution*
10(2):249–258.

2002 A Phylogenetic Comparison of Red Deer and Wapiti Using Mitochondrial
DNA. *Molecular Phylogenetics and Evolution* 22(3):342–356.

Polziehn, Renee O., Josef Hamr, Frank F. Mallory, and Curtis Strobeck

1998 Phylogenetic Status of North American Wapiti (*Cervus elaphus*) Subspecies.
Canadian Journal of Zoology 76:998–1010.

Shapiro, Beth, Alexei J. Drummond, Andrew Rambaut, Michael C. Wilson, Paul E.
Matheus, Andrei V. Sher, Oliver G. Pybus, M. Thomas P. Gilbert, Ian Barnes,
Jonas Binladen, Eske Willerslev, Anders J. Hansen, Gennady F. Baryshnikov,
James A. Burns, Sergei Davydov, Jonathan C. Driver, Duane G. Froese, C.
Richard Harington, Grant Keddie, Pavel Kosintsev, Michael L. Kunz, Larry
D. Martin, Robert O. Stephenson, John Storer, Richard Tedford, Sergei Zimov,
and Alan Cooper

2004 Rise and Fall of the Beringian Steppe Bison. *Science* 306:1561–1565.

Steer, Donald N., and Harvey J. Rogers

1978 *Archaeological Investigations at an Early Nineteenth Century Fur Trading Fort,
Rocky Mountain House National Historic Park, 1975–1977.* Microfiche Report
Series No. 35. Parks Canada, Ottawa.

Sweet, David, and Dean Hildebrand

1998 Recovery of DNA from Human Teeth by Cryogenic Grinding. *Journal of Forensic Sciences* 43:1199–1202.

White, Clifford A.

2001 Aspen, Elk and Fire in the Canadian Rocky Mountains. PhD dissertation,
Department of Forest Sciences, University of British Columbia, Vancouver.

White, Clifford A., E. Gwyn Langemann, C. Cormack Gates, Charles E. Kay, Todd
Shury, and Thomas E. Hurd

2001 Plains bison restoration in the Canadian Rocky Mountains? Ecological and
management considerations. In *Crossing Boundaries in Park Management: Proceedings of the 11th Conference on Research and Resource Management in Parks and
on Public Lands*, edited by David Harmon, pp. 152–160. George Wright Society,

Hancock, MI. Electronic document, http://www.georgewright.org/25white.pdf, accessed January 22, 2007.

Yang, Dongya Y., Barry Eng, John S. Waye, J. Christopher Dudar, and Shelley R. Saunders

1998   Technical Note: Improved DNA Extraction from Ancient Bones Using Silica-Based Spin Columns. *American Journal of Physical Anthropology* 105:539–543.

Yang, Dongya Y., Aubrey Cannon, and Shelley R. Saunders

2004   DNA Species Identification of Archaeological Salmon Bone from the Pacific Northwest Coast of North America. *Journal of Archaeological Science* 31:619–631.

12

Tools for Interpreting Past Plant Use by Subarctic and Northern Northwest Coast Peoples

Leslie Main Johnson

Abstract. Although subarctic Athapaskan and northern Northwest Coast cultures are known more for their fisheries and hunting than plant use, plants formed a significant component of the resource base. I describe types of plant uses and species used for food and technology and review the kinds of evidence that might be encountered that would provide evidence of past plant use. Evidence on the land comprises culturally modified trees [CMT's] and remains of *in situ* structures. CMT's can provide evidence of bark stripping, plank removal, and old tree cutting and can reveal both spatial and chronological patterns of use. Bark may be stripped for technological uses [mats, basketry, cordage, roofing], for food [edible hemlock or pine cambium], or for medicinal uses [pine, spruce, and true fir barks and pitches]. Other evidence of past plant use on the land includes remains of dwellings, berry-drying racks, fish traps, caribou fences, deadfall traps, and the like. Anomalies in distributions of culturally significant plants such as Pacific crabapple may also indicate past management and/or cultivation. Archaeobotanical methods, including recovery of remains from conventional archaeological sites, and the spectacular finds of organic remains melting out of ice fields and glaciers, have also yielded insights into past plant uses, both corroborating ethnographic uses and revealing previously unknown uses.

INTRODUCTION

Plant use by subarctic Athapaskan and northern Northwest peoples must be considered as an integral aspect of their cultures and in ecological context, incorporated in the seasonal round and all kinds of cultural activities. Although subarctic Athapaskan and northern Northwest Coast cultures are known more for their fisheries and hunting than plant use, plants formed a significant component of the resource base. In this largely forested and cool temperate to subarctic region, trees and woody shrubs were vital for construction materials, implements and containers, fuel, food resources and medicines. Various kinds of berries, especially species of the Ericaceae, were the most important plant foods; these were supplemented by spring greens and a few root foods in season. Bryophytes and lichens also contributed materials for technology and healing. In this paper I focus on the kinds of evidence that can indicate past plant uses by Subarctic Dene and northern Northwest Coast peoples. I have organized this paper by categories of evidence, moving across use classes and cultures throughout the discussion.

EVIDENCE OF PAST PLANT USES

Chief classes of evidence of past plant use for northern Northwest Coast and subarctic Athapaskan peoples include: evidence on the land (culturally modified trees and remains of *in situ* structures), evidence from archaeological contexts (remains from wet sites and archaeobotanical evidence), and other evidence from ice fields and glaciers.

CULTURALLY MODIFIED TREES

Culturally Modified Trees (or CMTs) preserve records of bark use for various purposes, wood use, and 'miscellaneous use' where the CMT itself is the "use," as in dendroglyphs used as boundary markers and message boards (Figure 12.1d) (cf. Blackstock 1996). CMTs record types of use only within the period that living or recently dead trees remain on the landscape, and they are subject to destruction by forest clearance and other development, having been only recently accorded a degree of protection. Nonetheless, they can document presence and resource use of local aboriginal populations in their traditional homelands (Muir and Moon 2000).

Bark and wood use in technology. Western red cedar is utilized wherever it occurs for bark and for wood. Two main types of cedar CMTs in northwestern British Columbia are those scarred by removal of cedar planks (Figure 12.1a), and those scarred by removal of whole bark or inner bark (Figure 12.1b,c). Cedar planks, highly valued for construction, could be removed from living trees with a combination of adzes, stone mauls, and wedges. Such trees are predominantly found on the coast where very large and long-lived cedar trees were suitable for this activity and may still be present to preserve a record. Cedar bark on the northwest coast served many uses (Gottesfeld 1992; Stewart 1984; Turner 1998, 2004). Whole bark could be used for a relatively durable roofing and served as waterproof covering (Johnson 1997). Cedar inner bark had innumerable uses for clothing, basketry, mat making, and lashing (LaForet 1984; Stewart 1984). When bark is removed from a cedar tree, the wood dies in the area that is uncovered, allowing the use of dendrochronology to age the regrowth lobe (Mobley and Eldridge 1992).

Spatial and temporal information about bark use may be recoverable by considering the context of bark use and employing survey techniques coupled with dendrochronology and measurement of scars. Studies of this sort have been carried out on Meares Island and other locations in Coastal British Columbia (Arcas Associates 1984) and in Northern Sweden, where spatial and temporal patterning of Saami use of edible inner bark of Scots Pine around Lake Sädvajaure was studied (Niklasson et al. 1994).

In the North, including the Mackenzie Delta region (Andre and Fehr 2001) and the Yakutat Bay area in Alaska (De Laguna 1972), spruce bark was used to make smoke houses and shelters. Use of spruce bark for canoes is also documented ethnographically for Athapaskans of the B.C. Interior (Gottesfeld 1994) and for Dogrib, Mountain, and Slavey peoples of the subarctic Mackenzie (Industry Canada n.d.). As trees are relatively small, harvest of spruce bark for these purposes typically involved girdling (and thus killing) the tree. Girdled trees also provided firewood, as girdled trees dry where they stand and can be cut down for fuel when needed.

Except in the Coastal Zone, birch bark is the most important bark for technological use in the region. Birch bark is used from central British Columbia

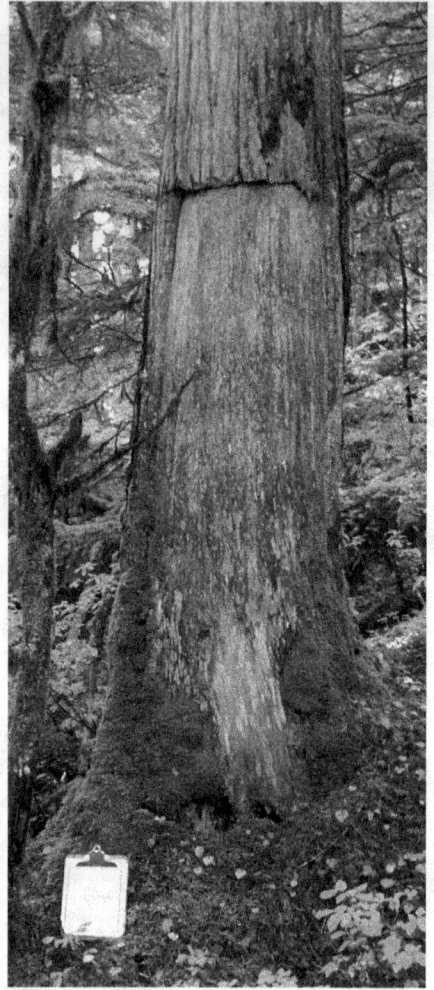

a

b

Figure 12.1. Types of culturally modified trees. a. large standing red cedar plank tree near Weewanee Hotsprings, Douglas Channel, B.C. (Haisla). Photographed August 1997. b. rectangular red cedar bark stripping scar, coastal forest, (Haisla) Douglas Channel, B.C. Photographed August 1997. c. triangular bark stripping scar on red cedar, (Gitksan) near Hazelton B.C. Photographed 1987. d. dendroglyph on western hemlock tree, Upper Skeena River. Photographed 1995 by Darlene Vegh.

c

d

into the southern Yukon and down the Mackenzie drainage to the Delta. It is also widely used in mainland Alaska (Kari 1987). Birch bark can be used for containers, wrapping food, in pit cooking, and for canoes (Andrews and Zoe 1998). Its burning properties also make it a valued fire starter, and Gitksan used it for torches ("Git an Maaxs," a village name, means people of the birch bark torches and alludes to an oral history that involves fishing by torchlight).

Unlike harvest of other types of barks, birch bark collection does not normally allow aging by dendrochronological techniques. However, the birch tree continues to increase in girth, and the exposed inner bark undergoes a series of changes in appearance, allowing a rough estimation of the time of bark collection (Figure 12.2). A freshly peeled tree will have fresh, uncheckered orange inner bark exposed. After some time, the exposed inner bark darkens to nearly black and exhibits a fine, checkered texture caused by growth in girth of the tree. After decades, this dark inner bark fades to a chalky grey colour, and the "checkers" grow large and irregular. The marking on the bark can remain even after the tree has died and only a cylinder of bark remains around the now rotten trunk wood. This would indicate very old birch collection (perhaps >100 years on the Skeena River).

Evidence of medicinal bark use. More rarely, one may encounter evidence of bark stripping for medicinal purposes. Here ethnographic data are important in deducing the use. Balsam or subalpine fir bark (*Abies lasiocarpa*) has no technological uses but is widely collected for medicine. Spruce bark can also be stripped for medicinal preparations; I have observed both Wet'suwet'en and Slavey (at Great Bear Lake) stripping bark from a young spruce (or "green tree") for medicine. This procedure involves young trees, which are not usually girdled standing, though they may be cut down and stripped.

Bark collection for food. The edible inner bark or "cambium" of lodgepole pine has been a frequently collected seasonal food and a welcome source of sugars in the spring season. Cambium collection has a very short season, less than three weeks at any given site, during which the digestibility of the newly formed cambium and inner bark is high, sugar content is high, and resin content very low (Gottesfeld 1995; Johnson 1997). Trees scarred by pine cambium collection show cut marks at the top of the rectangular or elongated scar at a height convenient to the harvester and may show branch stubs removed by axe. Dendrochronology of the regrowth lobe can date the harvest year (Niklasson et al. 1994; cf. Swetnam 1984). Specific bone, antler, or wooden tools for collect-

a

b

c

Figure 12.2. Relative ages of birch bark collection scars. a. stage 1 fresh birch bark collection scar, less than five years old Kispiox Valley, B.C. Photographed 1988. b. stage 2 scar, dark with fine checkers perhaps 20–40 years old Skeena Valley B.C. c. stage 3 scar, grey with large irregular checkers, estimated at 60–80+ years old Skeena Valley B.C. Photographed 1989.

ing edible inner bark resources had distinctive shapes depending on the species harvested. As the edible tissue sticks to the wood rather than bark in the case of lodgepole pine, the tools may exhibit a concave curvature to match the shape of the trunk (Morice 1892–93:Figures 64 and 65) while harvest of hemlock inner bark requires a convex tool as it adheres to the removed bark strips (Johnson 1997:Figure 4–3).

On the northwest coast and extending up the Skeena River, western hemlock provided an important seasonal food resource, collected in large quantities in season, processed by pounding and pit cooking before drying into molded cakes, which could be stored indefinitely, and which were an important trade item (Boas 1916; Gottesfeld 1992; People of Ksan 1980). Mature trees might be girdled, or more recently, felled and stripped to maximize the amount of edible bark *xsu'uu*. The Tsimshian had a special tool for gauging the thickness of hemlock cambium to ensure that an adequate thickness of harvestable inner bark was present to warrant harvesting (sketch by George MacDonald figured in Eldridge 1982). Evidence at a hemlock processing camp could include remains of wooden mortars to pound the cambium, cooking pits, or drying racks or molds for cambium cakes. Other species harvested for cambium, such as aspen and black cottonwood, appear to leave infrequent evidence of past use.

EVIDENCE ON THE LAND

In the subarctic, remains of former camps, frames for working hides, sweathouse pits, or ancient wooden fish traps can be encountered on the land. As wood rots slowly in the cold and relatively dry climate, old wooden items can be found *in situ* on the surface, including the remains of brush houses (Hare and Greer 1994); such shelters were made by Tutchone, Tahltan (Emmons 1911), and Wet'suwet'en (Morice 1892–93; Gottesfeld 1994). Remains of a variety of deadfall traps and cut stumps of varying ages may also be encountered (Emmons 1911; Morice 1892–93). In Gitksan and Wet'suwet'en territory, harvest of black huckleberry was an integral part of the season round, and berry camps were established on the land near or within named, owned, and managed berry patches (Johnson 1997; Trusler and Johnson 2008). Berry camps may be recognized, even where vegetation succession has occurred, by remains of implements used in berry processing such as berry drying racks or large bentwood boxes at the site (Trusler 2002; Trusler and Johnson 2008).

Anomalies in plant distribution. Certain plants have unusual ranges that appear to be correlated with anthropogenic environments or travel corridors. Rice root lily [*Fritillaria camschatcensis*] is common on the coast, and its bulbs are a widely used carbohydrate source (Kuhnlein and Turner 1991). Along the Skeena River corridor, the lily is found far upriver, especially in areas burned for garden sites and in the fields surrounding village sites (Johnson 1999). Pacific crabapple (*Malus fuscus*) shows a similar anomalous distribution. It is frequent near habitation sites and camps along the coast. Ken Downs has located stands that appear to be orchards in Kalum Canyon, an ancient Tsimshian habitation site about 90 kilometres from the coast which was abandoned about a hundred years ago (Downs 2006). McDonald (2005) has documented Tsimshian accounts of transplanting crabapple and hazelnut, and tending riceroot lily from Kitsumkalum elders. Crabapple is also sporadically present farther up the Skeena River along major indigenous travel corridors in certain sites in the Kispiox Valley and along the Telegraph Trail to Kuldo (Galdo'o) on the upper Skeena, where a traditional place name, *Milkst* 'crabapple,' records its presence (Jeff Harris Sr., personal communication 1987; Ralph Michell, personal communication 2005).

EVIDENCE FROM ARCHAEOLOGICAL CONTEXTS

Evidence from wet sites. Remarkable insights into ancient plant use have come from a handful of sites with waterlogged soils, which can preserve plant remains for long periods of time. Croes (2001), MacDonald and Cybulski (2001), and Fladmark (1986) give good reviews of wet sites and recovered plant artefacts on the North Coast. These sites demonstrate lengthy cultural continuity in the region (±6,000 years), as well as ancient cultural diversity, and suggest that extrapolation from ethnographic data is likely to be useful.

Potential of analysis of microfossils and macrofossils. Another strand of evidence of plant use from sites is archaeobotanical analysis. Lepofsky et al. (2001) lament the paucity of palaeoethnobotanical studies in northwestern North America and call attention to the potential range of information such studies can provide. They describe and analyze an archaeobotanical assemblage of human-transported plant remains in a rock shelter shell-midden deposit on a small island west of Prince of Wales Island, in an area settled historically by Tlingit and then Haida. Archaeobotanical evidence suggests that the shelter was occupied during the spring and summer months. Among the surprises that this investigation revealed was the use of *Armeria maritima*, an edible plant not reported to be used locally in the ethnographic literature, and the use of Douglas fir wood for fuel, apparently recovered from driftwood transported north from its natural limit at latitude 53°. A problem noted by Lepofsky et al. (2001) is the paucity of reference materials of tissues such as roots for comparison of archaeobotanical SEMs.

McAndrews and Fecteau (1989) studied a dry non-coastal site in the Skeena River drainage in conjunction with the excavation of the historic Kitwanga Fort, well recorded in local Gitksan oral histories. They report a number of taxa present in screened soil samples from house interiors and hearths and within the palisade, including charred and uncharred seeds of a variety of berries and fruits known to have been used by the Gitksan. Other seeds present represent herbaceous weedy taxa, windblown tree seeds, and a few dogwood seeds (*Cornus* sp.). If the dogwood seeds represent bunchberry *Cornus canadensis*, this would be another edible berry species reported ethnographically (Johnson 1997; People of Ksan 1980). Pollen analysis indicates a vegetative environment largely similar to the present area. Some of the reported spore types may be from economic plants; *Dryopteris*-type fern spores were present, which could possibly indicate use of the carbohydrate-rich rhizomes as food (cf. Turner et al. 1992), while sphagnum spores might represent moss used for diapering babies and for menstrual needs (Johnson-Gottesfeld and Vitt 1996) as it is unlikely to have been part of the local site vegetation.

Zutter's (2000) work on a house site in Labrador in the eastern Canadian subarctic also suggests the potential of archaeobotany to add detail to the archaeological record of plant uses; evidence of spruce bough flooring was particularly interesting and consistent with ethnographic data. In a more southerly study, Lepofsky et al. (1996) also found remains of conifer bough floor covering in a pit house in Keatly Creek, B.C. These studies support the potential of palaeoethnobotanical analysis to augment the information collected through other forms of archaeological analysis.

EVIDENCE FROM ICE FIELDS AND GLACIERS

The remarkable artefacts being recovered from melting ice fields and glaciers in the mountainous region of the southwestern Yukon and adjacent British Columbia give an unexpected window on activities of people in that region dating back to around 8,000 BP in some sites (Hare et al. 2004). Perishable materials of both plant and animal origin are melting out of retreating icefields, which have been present for more than 4,000 years (Kuzyk et al. 1998; Hare et al. 2004; Farnell et al. 2004). The oldest artefact yet recovered, a dart shaft, dates to 8,360 BP (Hare et al. 2004). This ecological zone was extensively used for hunting caribou (as it still is to the east near the NWT border, and to the north along the Dempster corridor in the northern Yukon). Materials recovered from ice fields include a variety of wooden artefacts, such as dart shafts and arrow shafts, and allow the shift in technology from atlatl to bow and arrow in the area to be dated (Hare et al. 2004). Though the types of plant remains thus far recovered are relatively few, the direct evidence of the form and nature of wooden dart and arrow shafts, including the lashing and fletching, extends back thousands of years and helps to refine interpretations of the purposes of various points. The species of woods used are not reported in the articles I have reviewed but should be determinable in such well-preserved material. The spectacular find of Kwaday Dän Ts'ìnchí, 'Long Ago Person Found,' the young man who died in a glacier crevasse about AD 1450, allows yet further insight into use of plants and animals (Dickson et al. 2004; Mudie et al. 2005). The man wore a coastal-style spruce root hat, consistent with what one might have expected of a traveller coming from the rainy coast, though his fur robe was of interior Athapaskan style, attesting to trade and probably kin relations across the mountains (cf. Cruikshank 2005). The surprise, however, was the large amount of *Salicornia* pollen in his intestinal tract, suggesting a meal of glasswort or samphire picked on the coast (Mudie et al. 2005), a finding not predicted by extrapolation backward from ethnographic records of plant use in the region. As glaciers and ice fields continue to melt in the region, further spectacular finds are likely which will yield a great amount of information if they can be recovered and studied before they begin to deteriorate.

PUTTING THE EVIDENCE TOGETHER

Interpreting evidence of past plant use requires bringing together a number of threads of evidence. The evidence from contemporary ethnobotany and ethnographic and ethnohistoric evidence provides a rich lens of interpretation of evidence on the land, from sites and from palaeoenvironmental data, but must be used with a degree of circumspection, as the unexpected findings from Kwaday Dän Ts'ìnchí and other archaeobotanical contexts remind us. In this paper I have reviewed a number of kinds of evidence of past plant use, concentrating on evidence on the land, which records evidence of the recent past but which also gives a sense of the spatial and sometimes seasonal patterning of use, and on the relatively rare plant remains from archaeological contexts. Wet sites have offered remarkable insights into past plant use, especially for technology, and have allowed interpretations both of contemporaneous cultural diversity and of noteworthy cultural continuity, belying the evidence of discontinuity or change from the lithic evidence. Archaeobotany also offers significant possibilities in northwest coast and subarctic and arctic sites, as Zutter (2000) has demonstrated from Labrador and Lepofsky et al. (2001) demonstrated from the Prince of Wales Island in southeast Alaska, both confirming what one would expect to find (e.g., spruce boughs covering living floors) and surprising us with unexpected evidence such as the previously unreported use of *Armeria maritima*.

Extending evidence of past plant use by looking for distinctive residue signatures, perhaps on suspected cooking or sweatlodge rocks, for example, remains to be attempted. The last, and rather spectacular archaeological strand of evidence for past plant use comprises the remarkable preserved organics from the Yukon ice patches, and the rarer remains from glaciers, which allow recovery of datable wooden and other plant-related artefacts from alpine hunting areas and from trans-mountain travel corridors. The artefacts recovered with Kwaday Dän Ts'ìnchí (his spruce root hat) and the analysis of his gut contents provided remarkable evidence of plant use and both continuity with and distinction from recorded ethnographic and ethnohistoric evidence.

Acknowledgments: I would like to thank the Social Science and Humanities Research Council, the Canadian Circumpolar Institute, the Gwich'in Renewable Resource Board, and the Athabasca Research Fund for research support; my local teachers and elders; my local collaborators; my patient colleagues; and Ken Downs, and Darlene Vegh for use of photographs, and Lisa Mutch for review of a draft of this manuscript. Space limitations make it impossible to acknowledge all of my teachers, elders, and local collaborators by name here, but I would have nothing to report without their teachings and assistance.

REFERENCES CITED

Andre, Alestine, and Alan Fehr
   2001   *Gwich'in Ethnobotany, Plants Used by the Gwich'in for Food, Medicine, Shelter and Tools.* Gwich'in Social and Cultural Institute and Aurora Research Institute, Inuvik.

Andrews, Tom, and John B. Zoe
   1998   The Dogrib Birchbark Canoe Project. *Arctic* 51(1):75–81.

Arcas Associates Heritage Resource Consultants
   1984   *Meares Island Aboriginal Tree Utilization Study.* Consulting report prepared for MacMillan Bloedel Limited, Nanaimo, B.C., by Arcas Associates Heritage Resource Consultants. On file, Resource Information Centre, Heritage Conservation Branch, Parliament Buildings, Victoria B.C.

Blackstock, Michael D.
   1996   *Gyetim Gan: Faces in the Forest.* Master's thesis, University of Northern British Columbia, Prince George, B.C.

Boas, Franz
   1916   *Tsimshian Mythology.* In 31st Report of the American Bureau of Ethnology 1909–10. Government Printing Office, Washington.

Croes, Dale R.
   2001   North Coast Prehistory – Reflections from Northwest Coast Wet Site Research. In *Perspectives on Northern Northwest Coast Prehistory*, Mercury Series Paper 160, edited by Jereome S. Cybulski, pp. 145–171. Canadian Museum of Civilization, Archaeological Survey of Canada, Hull.

Cruikshank, Julie
   2005   *Do Glaciers Listen? Local Knowledge, Colonial Encounters and Social Imagination.* UBC Press, Vancouver.

de Laguna, Frederika
   1972   *Under Mount St. Elias: The History and Culture of the Yakutat Tlingit.* (Three parts) Smithsonian Contributions to Anthropology, vol. 7. Smithsonian Institution Press, Washington.

Dickson, James H., Michael P. Richards, Richard J. Hebda, Petra J. Mudie, Owen Beattie, Susan Ramsay, Nancy J. Turner, Bruce J. Leighton, John M. Webster, Niki R. Hobischak, Gail S. Anderson, Peter M. Troffe, and Rebecca J. Wigan
    2004   Kwäday Dän Ts'ìnchí, the First Ancient Body of a Man from a North American Glacier: Reconstructing His Last Days by Intestinal and Biomolecular Analyses. *The Holocene* 14(4):481–486.

Downs, Ken
    2006   Tsimshian: A Prehistoric Cultural Landscape: Deconstructing the "Pristine Myth" in Northwestern British Columbia. Master of Arts Integrated Studies Final Project, Athabasca University, Athabasca, Alberta.

Eldridge, Anne
    1982   Cambium Resources of the Pacific Northwest: An Ethnographic and Archaeological Study. Unpublished report, Department of Archaeology, Simon Fraser University, Burnaby, B.C.

Emmons, G.T.
    1911   *The Talhtan Indians.* University of Pennsylvania, The Museum Anthropological Publications, vol. IV, no. 1. The University Museum, Philadelphia.

Farnell, Richard, P. Gregory Hare, Erik Blake, Vandy Bowyer, Charles Schweger, Sheila Greer, and Ruth Gotthardt
    2004   Multidisciplinary Investigations of Alpine Ice Patches in Southwest Yukon, Canada: Paleoenvironmental and Paleobiological Investigations. *Arctic* 57(3):247–259.

Fladmark, Knut R.
    1986   *British Columbia Prehistory.* National Museum of Man, National Museums of Canada, Ottawa.

Gottesfeld, Leslie M. Johnson
    1992   The Importance of Bark Products in the Aboriginal Economies of Northwestern British Columbia. *Economic Botany* 46(2):148–157.

    1994   Wet'suwet'en Ethnobotany: Traditional Plant Uses. *Journal of Ethnobiology* 14(2):185–210.

    1995   The Role of Plant Foods in Traditional Wet'suwet'en Nutrition. *Ecology of Food and Nutrition* 34:149–169.

Hare, Greg, and Sheila Greer
    1994   *Désdélé Méné, The Archaeology of Annie Lake.* Carcross/Tagish First Nation.

Hare, P. Gregory, Sheila Greer, Ruth Gotthardt, Richard Farnell, Vandy Bowyer, Charles Schweger, and Diane Strand
    2004   Ethnographic and Archaeological Investigations of Alpine Ice Patches in Southwest Yukon, Canada. *Arctic* 57(3):260–272.

Industry Canada, Schoolnet Digital Collections
  n.d.   Canoe. Electronic document, http://collections.ic.gc.ca/canoe/Vtour/canoe.htm,
         accessed 2/2/06.

Johnson, Leslie Main
  1997   Health, Wholeness, and the Land: Gitksan Traditional Plant Use and Healing.
         PhD dissertation, University of Alberta, Edmonton.

  1999   Aboriginal Burning for Vegetation Management in Northwest British Colum-
         bia. in *Indians, Fire and the Land in the Pacific Northwest*, edited by Robert Boyd,
         238–254. Oregon State University Press, Corvallis.

Johnson-Gottesfeld, Leslie M. Johnson, and Dale H. Vitt
  1996   *Sphagnum*: Its Identification for Diapers by Indigenous North Americans. *Evan-
         sia* 13(3):103–108.

Kari, Priscilla Russell
  1987   *Tanaina Plantlore, Dena'in ket'una*, 2nd ed. National Park Service, Alaska
         Region.

Kuhnlein, Harriet, and Nancy J. Turner
  1991   *Traditional Plant Foods of Canadian Indigenous Peoples, Nutrition, Botany and Use.*
         Food and Nutrition in History and Anthropology, vol. 8. Gordon and Breach,
         Philadelphia.

Kuzyk, Gerald W., Donald E. Russell, Richard S. Farnell, Ruth M. Gotthardt , P. Gregory
  Hare, and Erik Blake
  1998   In Pursuit of Prehistoric Caribou on Thandlät, Southern Yukon. *Arctic*
         52(2):214–219.

LaForet, A.
  1984   Tsimshian Basketry. In *The Tsimshian, Images of the Past: Views for the Present*,
         edited by M. Seguin, pp. 215–280. University of British Columbia Press, Van-
         couver.

Lepofsky, Dana, Karla Kusmer, Brian Hayden, and Kenneth B. Lertzman
  1996   Reconstructing Prehistoric Socioeconomies from Paleoethnobotanical and Zoo-
         archaeological Data: An Example from the British Columbia Plateau. *Journal of
         Ethnobiology* 16(1):31–62.

Lepofsky, Dana, Madonna L. Moss, and Natasha Lyons
  2001   The Unrealized Potential of Paleoethnobotany in the Archaeology of North-
         western North America: Perspectives from Cape Addington, Alaska. *Arctic
         Anthropology* 38 (1):48–59.

MacDonald, George F., and Jerome S. Cybulski
  2001   Introduction: The Prince Rupert Harbour Project. In *Perspectives on Northern
         Northwest Coast Prehistory*, edited by Jereome S. Cybulski, Mercury Series Paper
         160, pp. 1–23. Canadian Museum of Civilization, Archaeological Survey of
         Canada, Hull.

McAndrews, J.H., and R.D. Fecteau
1989   Appendix IV. Archaeobotany of the Kitwanga Fort Project, Skeena River,
        British Columbia. In *Kitwanga Fort Report*, edited by George MacDonald,
        Mercury Series Directorate Paper No. 4., pp. A-29–A40. Canadian Museum of
        Civilization, Hull.

McDonald, Jim
2005   Cultivating in the Northwest, Early Accounts of Tsimshian Horticulture. In
        *Keeping It Living, Traditions of Plant Use and Cultivation on the Northwest Coast
        of North America*, edited by Douglas Deur and Nancy J. Turner, pp. 240–271.
        University of Washington Press, Seattle, and UBC Press, Vancouver.

Mobley, Charles M., and Morely Eldridge
1992   Culturally Modified Trees in the Pacific Northwest. *Arctic Anthropology*
        20(1):91–110.

Morice, A.G.
1892–93 Notes Archaeological, Industrial and Sociological on the Western Dénés with
        an Ethnographic Sketch of the Same. *Transactions of the Canadian Institute*, vol.
        IV, pp. 5–221.

Mudie, Petra J., Sheila Greer, Judith Brakel, James H. Dickson, Clara Schinkel, Ruth
        Peterson-Welsh, Margaret Stevens, Nancy J. Turner, Mary Shadow, and Rosalie
        Washington
2005   Forensic Palynology and Ethnobotany of *Salicornia* Species (Chenopodiaceae) in
        Northwest Canada and Alaska. *Canadian Journal of Botany* 83:111–123.

Muir, Robert J., and Heather Moon
2000   *Sampling Culturally Modified Tree Sites, Final Report*. Prepared for British
        Columbia Ministry of Forests, Aboriginal Affairs. Electronic document, http://
        srmwww.gov.bc.ca/arch/research/Sampling_CMTs.pdf, accessed 2/13/06.

Niklasson, Mats, Olle Zackrisson, and Lars Östlund
1994   A Dendroecological Reconstruction of Use by Saami of Scots Pine (*Pinus sylves-
        tris* L.) Inner Bark over the Last 350 Years at Sädvajaure, N. Sweden. *Vegetation
        History and Archaeobotany* 3:183–190.

People of Ksan
1980   *Gathering What the Great Nature Provided*. Douglas & McIntyre, Vancouver.

Stewart, Hilary
1984   *Cedar*. Douglas & McIntyre, Vancouver.

Swetnam, Thomas W.
1984   Peeled Ponderosa Pine Trees: A Record of Inner Bark Utilization by Native
        Americans. *Journal of Ethnobiology* 4(2):177–190.

Trusler, Scott
2002   Footsteps amongst the Berries: The Ecology and Fire History of Traditional
        Gitxsan and Wet'suwet'en Huckleberry Sites. MSc. thesis, Environmental Stud-
        ies, University of Northern British Columbia, Prince George, B.C.

Trusler, Scott, and Leslie M. Johnson
  2008 "Berry Patch" as a Kind of Place – The Ethnoecology of Black Huckleberry in Northwestern Canada. (In press, *Human Ecology* 36).

Turner, Nancy J.
  1998 *Plant Technology of First Peoples in British Columbia.* Vancouver: UBC Press.

  2004 *Plants of Haida Gwaii.* Sono Nis Press, Winlaw.

Turner, Nancy J., Leslie M. Johnson Gottesfeld, Harriet V. Kuhnlein, and Adolf Ceska
  1992 Edible Wood Fern Rootstocks of Western North America: Solving an Ethnobotanical Puzzle. *Journal of Ethnobiology* 12(1):1–34.

Zutter, Cynthia
  2000 Archaeobotanical Investigations of the Uivak Archaeological Site, Labrador, Canada. Manuscript in possession of author.

13

VARIABLE WETLAND USE AT THE MONO LAKE BASIN, EASTERN CALIFORNIA: PERSPECTIVES FROM A NON-SITE APPROACH

Ryan T. Brady

Abstract. Site-based scales of analysis are often the dominant units of archaeological inquiry. Difficulty arises when a small number of sites are used to interpret mobile hunter-gatherer land use across a region. More ephemeral patterns of tool use and discard represented across the landscape may be overlooked. A non-site-based approach to regional surface survey, emphasizing the character of artefact distributions, can provide a dynamic perspective to the study of prehistoric settlement and subsistence. Mono Lake, located at the western extent of the North American Great Basin, is an area with variable wetland resource patches that were differentially targeted by hunter-gatherers throughout the Holocene. Prehistoric land use is understood through environmentally stratified surface survey, in addition to accounting for past lake elevation fluctuation on wetland productivity. An artefact-focused approach to archaeological analysis demonstrates that Mono Lake's wetlands were not targeted for the same reasons throughout prehistory, nor were all wetlands used in the same manner.

INTRODUCTION

The environment is often viewed as an important factor affecting settlement and mobility patterns of hunter-gatherers in the North American Great Basin. Located between the Sierra Nevada mountains to the west and the Rocky Mountains in the east, the Great Basin is predominated by sagebrush scrub habitat, interspersed with more than thirty-three mountain ranges, and scattered internally draining rivers, lakes, and marshes (Grayson 1993:11–23). As an arid region, the presence of water is often seen as an important factor affecting human settlement and may also be viewed as a proxy for general environmental productivity.

Earlier archaeological research focusing on the central-western Great Basin had put forth two opposing models of settlement organization relative to wetland habitats. These have come to be known as the "limnosedentary" and "limnomobile" hypotheses (e.g., Thomas 1985:19–20). The first proposes that wetlands were such productive habitats relative to the surrounding environment that hunter-gatherers would map onto these resources for periods of time, potentially throughout the year. Alternatively, the limnomobile hypothesis argues that Great Basin wetlands were not productive enough to support sedentary populations. In the face of archaeological variability, these views have proven overly simplistic (Bettinger 1993:45; Madsen 2002). Further research argues that one must also consider factors relating to gendered work differentiation and central place foraging (Zeanah 1996) in addition to population mobility and the viability of other foraging options when considering the importance of a given habitat for hunter-gatherer groups (Kelly 2001). As such, the factors affecting Great Basin wetland use still have much to be learned. The present research investigates how variable wetland habitats were used within a single region.

RESEARCH CONTEXT

The Mono Lake basin, located east of the Sierra Nevada mountains, at the western extent of the North American Great Basin is a unique setting to test propositions about the aboriginal importance of wetlands (Figure 13.1). The basin itself is large, covering more than 650 km² (Stine 1987:14). Peaks in the west exceed 3,900 m asl, yet are considerably lower around the other basin margins. In the central-western portion of the basin is Mono Lake, a large, hypersaline lake that is inhospitable for fish. Instead, aquatic resources are restricted to brine shrimp, and pupae of the brine fly that develop in the lake's waters (National Academy of Sciences [NAS] 1987:13–14). Lake elevation is presently 1,945 m asl, although it undergoes natural fluctuations due to changes in the rate of evaporation and water inflow. In the past 3,500 years, lake elevation has ranged between 1,940 m and 1,981 m asl (Stine 1990). This range frames much of the time period in question.

Ethnographically, the Mono Basin was inhabited by the *Kutzadika'a* Paiute. The *Kutzadika'a* appear to have practised a fission-fusion settlement pattern typical of many Great Basin groups. Although generally residing in the Basin year-round, individuals and families were known to come and go as they pleased depending on seasonal resource availability or other social obligations (Davis 1965:15–16). The ethnographically described annual subsistence round depicts Mono Lake basin's inhabitants making seasonal use of the wetlands where in the spring and early summer they would move down to the wet meadows and marshes on the western portion of the lake to gather roots, greens, and seeds (Davis 1965:29–36). Populations would disperse in the summer, and autumn was often spent collecting pine nuts in the mountains fringing the basin. The *Kutzadika'a* generally lived off stored resources throughout the winter (Davis 1964, 1965).

Physical geography affects the resource structure of the Mono Basin. Most water entering the Basin does so in the form of snowmelt flowing to the western shore of Mono Lake through five main riparian corridors. Due to the rainshadow effect of storms passing over the Sierra Nevada, precipitation falling in the eastern Basin is meagre at 14 cm, compared to 38.5 cm in the west (Stine 1987:16). Other sources of freshwater entering the lake are through slope runoff and artesian and groundwater springs. Type of water inflow, in addition to slope and sediment leaching create variable wetland habitats that fringe the lake (Jones & Stokes Associates 1993; NAS 1987; Stine 1993). Based on these characteristics as well as vegetation distributions, wetlands have been grouped into three different types: freshwater, brackish, and saline.

Of these habitats, freshwater wetlands in the west contain a greater diversity and density of plant and animal resources for people to exploit (Constantine 1993; NAS 1987:Figure 5.5). Vegetation in the eastern saline habitats

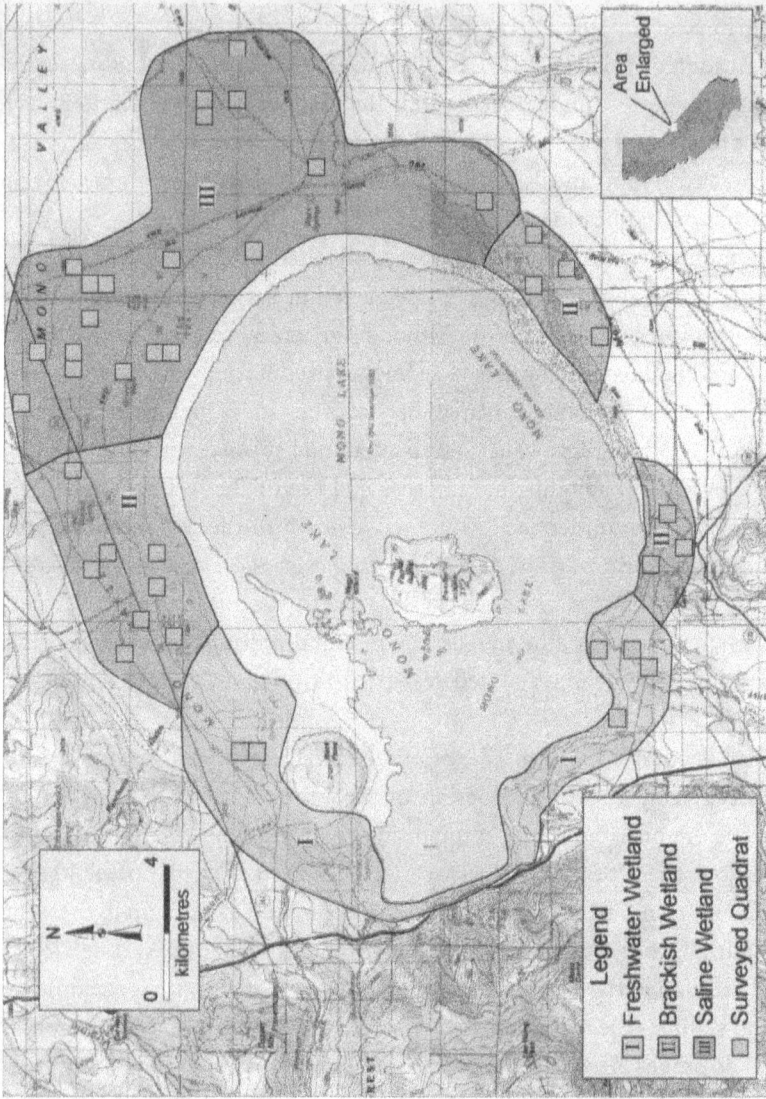

Figure 13.1. Map of the Mono Lake basin with wetland habitats and surveyed quads.

RYAN T. BRADY

is more sparse, comprised mainly of salt-tolerant plants such as greasewood and saltgrass. They attract fewer animals and are viewed as low ranked relative to the other wetland types. Brackish wetlands, on the northern and southern shores, fall somewhere between these two, containing a mixture of environmental characteristics that may fluctuate more readily than freshwater or saline wetlands.

Foraging theory predicts that hunter-gatherers will exploit resources that provide the highest caloric return for the effort invested in procurement and processing (Kelly 1995:83). As highly ranked foods become depleted, people will either travel to other areas where those resources can be obtained or include lower ranked resources in the diet that provide fewer calories for the effort invested. Importance of a given resource may be related not only to intrinsic properties of energetic returns but also to ease of capture, size, and density of a given resource patch, among other factors (Bettinger 1991:84). Generally, large game such as mule deer or bighorn sheep are viewed as high ranked, while plant resources like rice and salt grass are lower ranked.

Predominant questions driving the present research are: how did hunter-gatherers in the Mono Basin use the varied wetland habitats? Were some wetland types ignored while others were more intensively used? How were the wetlands exploited, through residential "mapping on," logistical mobility, or from within a daily foraging radius of the residential base? These questions are used to understand how different Great Basin wetlands provided for hunter-gatherer populations over a long or short-term basis.

Initial predictions were that freshwater wetlands would exhibit the greatest diversity of artefacts and represent the most intensive use through time due to increased environmental productivity. Likewise, the decreased productivity and diversity of saline habitats may result in them being used predominantly in more recent times for short periods, when regional populations are believed to have had a more expanded diet breadth (Bettinger 1999:41; Carpenter 2001:12–13).

Methods

To investigate differential use of the wetlands, it was necessary to sample multiple areas and pertinent elevation zones around the Basin. To achieve this goal, a non-site approach to surface survey was undertaken to collect data from the different wetland habitats.

Proponents of what is often termed non-site (Dunnell 1992; Thomas 1975), off-site (Foley 1981), or distributional archaeology (Ebert 1992) argue that the sites are often the result of a palimpsest of archaeological accumulations, resulting from multiple, often unrelated activities. They contend that site-based records are too mixed to be able to interpret on their own. Rather, surface artefact distributions across large landscapes should be studied to identify patterns of tool use and discard at multiple scales and across regions. The present study focuses on the distribution of artefacts across the landscape without biasing the data set toward large artefact accumulations at the expense of overlooking smaller ones.

Forty 500 m x 500 m survey units were selected from a stratified sample of 461 that covered the extent of the delineated wetland habitats from the current lake elevation up to 2,025 m asl (Figure 13.1). This sample covers the extent of lake fluctuations over the past 3,500 years and also provides a 30 m elevation buffer zone to include potential activity areas related to the lake's high stand. These lands were also likely exposed in earlier times. Survey transects were spaced 25 m apart with each surveyor plotting the location of debitage and other artefacts on an aerial photograph of the unit. The photo had each transect overlaid and broken into 100 m intervals. By this, surveyors could keep track of their location through pacing and physical landmarks. Flaked stone artefacts were collected, and ground stone artefacts recorded in the field. Finally, a 100 m x 100 m quad in the southwest corner was surveyed at 10 m transect intervals. Here, in addition to the standard survey methods, debitage was also collected. This sample was limited to 30 flakes in areas with dense accumulations.

Of the 40 units surveyed (6 freshwater, 15 brackish, 19 saline), only two were completely empty, 15 contained only lithic debitage, and one had a single millingstone. The remaining units contained combinations of flaked and ground stone tools as well as lithic debitage, with one quarter of the units surveyed (n = 10) containing debitage, formed flaked, and ground stone artefacts. No intact features such as rock rings were identified in the survey.

ANALYSIS

Initial predictions about the varied intensity of land use by wetland were supported with 20 tools per km² surveyed recovered in the freshwater habitat, yet only 11 and 7 tools per km² in the brackish and saline wetlands respectively. Eleven tool classes were identified, and due to the large geographic area covered, there is some variability in material distributions (Table 13.1). For example, the southwestern area is near a naturally occurring obsidian source. Some quadrats here contained obsidian raw material in the alluvium and are associated with dense distributions of obsidian debitage and assayed cobbles that were tested during obsidian procurement. Cores were also recovered in these areas of raw material acquisition and are absent from other contexts. Overlap with the residues of resource procurement, processing, and tool maintenance requires that these remain in the total sample, but one must keep in mind that some variation observed may be driven by these outliers.

Table 13. 1. Tool Distribution by Wetland Habitat.

	PPT	COR	BIF	FTL	HND	MIL	PST	MGS	BRM	ASC	CRTL	TOTAL
Fresh	0	5	2	14	2	1	1	0	4	5	0	34
Brackish	4	2	3	16	5	7	0	2	0	25	1	65
Saline	3	0	5	10	5	5	0	3	0	0	1	32
Total	7	7	10	40	12	13	1	5	4	30	2	131

	PPT	COR	BIF	FTL	HND	MIL	PST	MGS	BRM	ASC	CRTL
F.residual	−1.61	2.82	−0.45	1.57	−0.77	−1.58	1.70	−1.35	3.43	−1.32	−0.84
B.residual	0.41	−1.14	−1.29	−1.46	−0.58	0.32	−1.00	−0.44	−2.02	4.21	0.01
S.residual	1.17	−1.55	1.96	0.10	1.46	1.24	−0.57	1.89	−1.15	−3.55	0.85

PPT = projectile point; BIF = biface; FTL = flake tool; HND = handstone; MIL = millingstone; PST = pestle; MGS = miscellaneous ground stone; BRM = bedrock mortar; ASC = assayed cobble; CRTL = core tool.

Table 13.2. Tool Distribution (A) and Debitage Technological Distribution (B) by Wetland Class.

	OVER-REPRESENTED	NULL	UNDER-REPRESENTED	ABSENT
A. Tools by Wetland				
Freshwater	BRM, COR	BIF, FTL, HND, MIL, MGS, PST, ASC	–	PRJ, CRTL
Brackish	ASC	PRJ, COR, BIF, FTL, HND, MIL, MGS, CRTL	–	PSTL, BRM
Saline	BIF	PRJ, FTL, HND, MIL, MGS, CRTL	–	COR, PST, BRM, ASC
B. Debitage Technology by Wetland				
Freshwater	–	Core Reduc., Decort.	Bif. Reduc.	–
Brackish	–	Bif. Reduc., Core Reduc., Decort.	–	–
Saline	Bif. Reduc.	Decort.	Core Reduc.	–

PPT = projectile point; BIF = biface; FTL = flake tool; HND = handstone; MIL = millingstone; PST = pestle; MGS = miscellaneous ground stone; BRM = bedrock mortar; ASC = assayed cobble; CRTL = core tool.; Core Reduc. = core reduction; Bif. Reduc. = biface reduction; Decort. = decortication.

Using the tool distributions, a significant chi square statistic (X^2 = 52.50; df = 20; p < .001) along with adjusted residuals identifies sources of variation between the samples. Here, values greater than 1.96 or less than −1.96 highlight tool classes that are over- or under-represented (V = .05) relative to the overall sample, while those falling between those ranges are viewed as normally distributed or null (Table 13.1). As can be seen by Table 13.2A, there is much similarity in tool representation across wetland class with flake tools, handstones, millingstones, and miscellaneous ground stone distributed normally across the three wetland classes. Projectile points are absent from the freshwater area, implying an absence of hunting related activities.

One item that stands out as signifying a different strategy of land use is the over-representation of bifaces in saline habitats. While these are common in the other two regions, bifaces have been argued to signify a different mode of technological organization (Kelly 1988). Bifaces may be preferred items to bring to areas where toolstone availability is either unknown or lacking. These tools are argued to be easily transportable cores that can provide flakes for expedient cutting activities, in addition to being reliable tools used for a variety of cutting or scraping functions. Prevalence of bifaces in the saline habitats suggest a region of greater risk where people were travelling away from their residential bases and stores of toolstone but wanted to be sure to have enough material for necessary activities while on short-term forays.

Further support for the use of bifaces over other technologies in saline habitats comes from debitage analysis (Table 13.2B). Using only technologically identifiable debitage, there is a general distribution of flake types across the freshwater and brackish habitats with bifacial reduction debris being under-represented in the freshwater wetlands (X^2 = 13.70; df = 4; p < .01). In contrast, saline habitats have a prevalence of bifacial flaking debris, while core reduction flakes are uncommon, and decortication debris occurs at a null value. The abundance of bifacial reduction flakes and sparse amount of core reduction debris note greater use of bifaces in the saline habitats. These analyses suggest that there is some variability in land use strategy across wetland types, yet not much difference in the general activities conducted in the habitats.

If subsistence- and settlement-related activities occurred in relatively similar distributions across wetland types, how are these activities represented when considering general geographic areas within the basin? Similar to the previous examples, tools were grouped by class and location within the basin. A significant chi square value and adjusted residuals provide the information to study tool distributions by quadrant within the Basin (X^2 = 90.73; df = 30; p < .001). One pattern of note is the over-representation of flake tools and millingstones in the northwest, and handstones in the northeast (Table 13.3A). Prevalence of milling gear implies importance of plant-processing activities in the northern areas. That the two tool classes are in unequal distribution, one in the northwest, and the other in the northeast, may signify a pattern of mobility between patches, such as handstones being portable, with millingstones often left at processing areas. In fact, of the fifteen units that contained ground stone, nearly three-quarters (n = 11; 73.3%) of them included either handstones or

Table 13.3. Tool Distribution by Basin Quadrant (A) and Elevation (B).

	OVER-REPRESENTED	NULL	UNDER-REPRESENTED	ABSENT
A. Tools by Quadrant				
Southwest	BRM, COR, ASC	BIF, FTL, PST, CRTL	MIL, HND	PRJ, MGS
Northwest	FTL, MIL	PRJ, BIF, MGS, CRTL	–	COR, HND, PST, BRM, ASC
Northeast	HND	PRJ, BIF, FTL, MIL, MGS, CRTL	–	ASC, COR, PST, BRM
Southeast	–	FTL, HND, MIL, MGS	–	PRJ, COR, BIF, PST, BRM, CRTL, ASC
B. Tools by Elevation				
<1960	PRJ, BIF, FTL	HND, MST, COR	–	PST, MGS, BRM, CRTL, ASC
1960–1980	MGS, BRM	PRJ, COR, BIF, FTL, HND, MIL, PST, CRTL	ASC	–
1980–2000	ASC	PRJ, COR, BIF, HND, MIL	FTL	PSTL, MGS, BRM, CRTL
>2000	–	FTL, HND, ASC	–	PRJ, BIF, COR, MIL, PST, MGS, BRM, CRTL

PPT = projectile point; BIF = biface; FTL = flake tool; HND = handstone; MIL = millingstone; PST = pestle; MGS = miscellaneous ground stone; BRM = bedrock mortar; ASC = assayed cobble; CRTL = core tool.; Core Reduc. = core reduction; Bif. Reduc. = biface reduction; Decort. = decortication.

millingstones, but not both. Also of note is the paucity of these tools in the southwestern area, but rather a prominence of bedrock mortars, demonstrating a different technology used to process plants or other materials.

Ground stone distributions by quadrant demonstrate a degree of mobility in the north with seed-grinding activities generally occurring at disparate places, potentially away from the residential base. Some items were likely portable while others were cached. Additionally, the southwest area appears to have had a different technological focus with the presence of bedrock mortars. The variation likely represents the outcome of problem-solving strategies related to landscape topography and water flow.

The southwestern area contains two large streams that enter the lake through relatively steep topography. These do not create as much near-shore wet meadow or marsh habitat as there is in the northwest, where lower slope gradients slow stream flow, dispersing water across the alluvial fan. Additionally there are seasonal streams that flow to the lake from the north, creating diverse mosaics of resources that may have been best targeted at different times of the year. This affects the seasonality and residential stability afforded by each area.

One further question about the tool distributions is how are they arranged by elevation? Although Mono Lake undergoes natural fluctuations in elevation, this inquiry can still be informative about activities as they compare in general proximity to the lake. Tools were grouped into four elevation increments, and the distributions analyzed in the fashion as earlier examples (X^2 = 69.33; d.f. = 30; p < .001). Handstones appear at null frequencies in all four elevation classes, and millingstones are null in the lower three elevations (Table 13.2B). Also of note is the changing presence of projectile points, bifaces, and flake tools. These are all over-represented in the lowest stratum, then null in the next, and have a fluctuating presence in the final two strata. That ground and flaked stone tools have different patterns of abundance suggest that these two tool classes were used at different levels of intensity as the lake fluctuated or as diet breadth or settlement patterns changed.

CONCLUSIONS

Results of the current effort present important information regarding land use in an environment containing varied wetland habitats. Initially, these were segregated into three classes: freshwater, brackish, and saline. Although distributed across the wetland habitats, tool distributions did demonstrate varied use across wetland type and geographic area (Figure 13.2). There is an increased presence of bifaces and bifacial flaking debris in the saline habitat relative to the other wetlands, suggesting more short-term use of the wetland class.

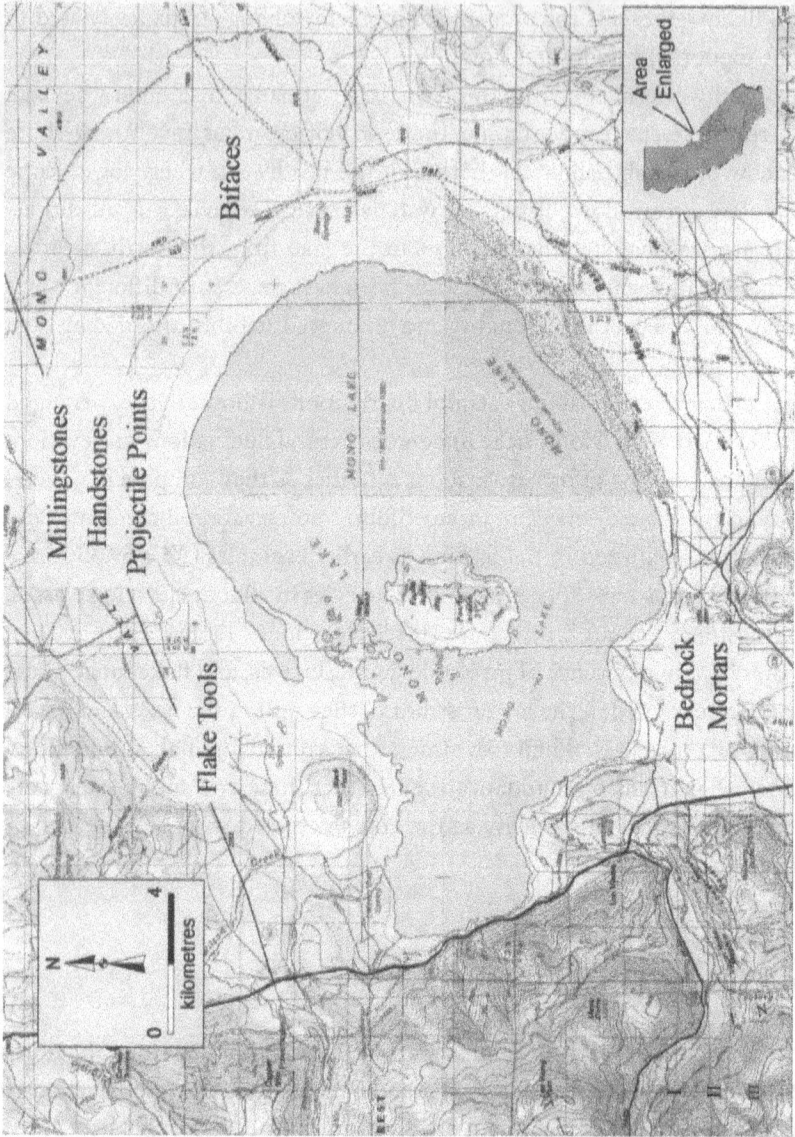

Figure 13.2. Important Artifact distributions in the Mono Lake basin.

RYAN T. BRADY

There is a different pattern of variability in artefact distributions when tools are grouped by basin quadrant. The northern half appears to have an important role for seed-grinding tools; however, handstones and millingstones do not often co-occur, implying mobility between resource patches and differential portability of the tools. These create discrepancies in tool discard and caching locations. In contrast, bedrock mortars are more prominent in the southwest, likely due to the exploitation of other resources and possibly more long-term habitation.

Finally, tool distributions relative to elevation demonstrate an over-representation of flaked stone tools in the lowest elevation strata, decreasing and fluctuating at higher elevations. In contrast, the distribution of milling gear is more evenly spread across elevation, suggesting stability in the use of these tools.

Relating these data to the discussion of whether Great Basin wetlands served as rich or poor resource patches, it is evident that one must consider, not just the intrinsic properties of the resource, but also the settlement and mobility patterns. By grouping use areas around Mono Lake by varied characteristics, it is apparent that the wetland habitats were used differently. The temporal extent or continuity of these patterns may be answered with other data.

Results of the present study indicate that the strategies in which Mono Lake's wetlands were used varied considerably. Their use must be viewed in the context of regional settlement and subsistence practices. Investigating tool distributions across a landscape is a powerful tool to identify varied settlement, subsistence, and mobility patterns.

Acknowledgments: Fieldwork was financially supported in part by the Archaeological Research Center at CSU Sacramento. CSUS graduate students and others generously volunteered their time for completion of the fieldwork. Any errors of logic or fact are, of course, my own.

REFERENCES CITED

Bettinger, Robert L.

1991   *Hunter-Gatherers: Archaeological and Anthropological Theory.* Plenum Press, New York.

1993   Doing Great Basin Archaeology Recently: Coping with Variability. *Journal of Archaeological Research* 1:43–66.

1999   From Traveler to Processor: Regional Trajectories of Hunter-Gatherer Sedentism in the Inyo-Mono Region, California. In *Fifty Years Since Viru: Theoretical Advances and Contributions of Settlement Pattern Studies in the Americas,* edited by B.R. Billman and G.M. Feinman, pp. 39–55. Smithsonian Institution, Washington, D.C.

Carpenter, Kimberley L.

2001   *Data Recovery Excavations at CA-MNO-891 and CA-MNO-2416/H.* Report submitted to the California Department of Transportation, District 9, Bishop.

Constantine, Helen

1993   *Plant Communities of the Mono Basin.* Kutsavi Press, Lee Vining.

Davis, Emma L.

1964   An Archaeological Survey of the Mono Lake Basin and Excavations of Two Rockshelters, Mono County, California. In *Annual Reports of the University of California Archaeological Survey for 1963–1964,* pp. 251–392. Los Angeles.

1965   An Ethnography of the Kuzedika Paiute of Mono Lake, Mono County, California. *University of Utah Anthropological Papers* 75. pp. 1–56. Salt Lake City.

Dunnell, Robert C.

1992   The Notion Site. In *Space, Time, and Archaeological Landscapes,* edited by J. Rossignol and L. Wandsnider, pp. 21–41. Plenum Press, New York.

Ebert, James I.

1992   *Distributional Archaeology.* University of Utah Press, Salt Lake City.

Foley, Robert

1981   Off-site Archaeology: An Alternative Approach for the Short-sited. In *Patterns of the Past: Studies on Honor of David Clark,* edited by I. Hodder, G. Isaac, and N. Hammond. pp. 157–183. Cambridge University Press, Cambridge.

Grayson , Donald K.

1993   *The Desert's Past: A Natural Prehistory of the Great Basin.* Smithsonian Institution Press, Washington.

Jones & Stokes Associates

1993   *Mono Basin Environmental Impact Report.* Report submitted to the California
        State Water Resources Control Board, Sacramento.

Kelly, Robert L.

1988   The Three Sides of a Biface. *American Antiquity* 53:717–734.

1995   *The Foraging Spectrum: Diversity in Hunter-Gatherer Lifeways.* Smithsonian
        Institution Press, Washington.

2001   Prehistory of the Carson Desert and Stillwater Mountains: Environment,
        Mobility, and Subsistence in a Great Basin Wetland. *University of Utah Anthro-
        pological Papers* 123. University of Utah Press, Salt Lake City.

Madsen, David B.

2002   Great Basin Peoples and Late Quaternary Aquatic History. In *Great Basin
        Aquatic Systems History,* edited by R. Hershler, D.B. Madsen, and D.R. Currey,
        pp. 387–405. Smithsonian Contributions to the Earth Sciences, no. 33. Smith-
        sonian Institution Press, Washington, D.C.

National Academy of Sciences (NAS)

1987   *The Mono Basin Ecosystem: Effects of Changing Lake Level.* National Academy
        Press, Washington, D.C.

Stine, Scott W.

1987   Mono Lake: The Past 4000 Years. PhD dissertation, University of California,
        Berkeley. University Microfilms, Ann Arbor.

1990   Late Holocene Fluctuations of Mono Lake, Eastern California. *Palaeogeography,
        Palaeoclimatology, Palaeoecology* 78:333–381.

1993   *Distribution of Substrate Types at Mono Lake, California.* Report submitted to the
        California State Water Resources Control Board, and Jones & Stokes Associ-
        ates, Sacramento.

Thomas, David H.

1975   Nonsite Sampling in Archaeology: Up the Creek Without a Site? In *Sampling
        in archaeology,* edited by G.W. Mueller, pp. 61–81. University of Arizona Press,
        Tucson.

1985   The Archaeology of Hidden Cave, Nevada. *Anthropological Papers of the American
        Museum of Natural History* 61:1. New York.

Zeanah, David W.

1996   Predicting Settlement Patterns and Mobility Strategies: An Optimal Foraging
        Analysis of Hunter-Gatherer Use of Mountain, Desert, and Wetland Habitats
        in the Carson Desert. PhD dissertation, Department of Anthropology, Univer-
        sity of Utah, Salt Lake City.

14

FILL IN THE GAP BETWEEN THEORY AND PRACTICE: MAKING A GIS-BASED DIGITAL MAP OF PACHACAMAC

Go Matsumoto

Abstract. As previous major studies have demonstrated, Geographic Information Systems provide archaeological research with powerful analytical capabilities as well as ease of data creation and management, nearly infinite scalability, and compatibility with various external data and modules. However, archaeological researches tend to occur in the regions that have not yet established an efficient (or reliable) geographical data management or related infrastructures and thus do not have enough data sources to achieve the research aims. Archaeologists are almost always required to produce their own maps within budgetary restrictions. Thus, in reality, even digital map making is not an easy task and does not make the desired progress, to say nothing of expected analytical endeavour. Through the digital mapping at the archaeological site of Pachacamac on the Peruvian Central Coast, I highlight a notable gap between theory and practice and urge the need of: (1) selection of the most efficient way to achieve immediate goals on the basis of a clear understanding of given resources and surrounding realities; (2) contribution to data accumulation based on a long-term plan for establishment of a more reliable site database; and (3) establishment of a collaborative work environment and active data sharing among archaeologists and/or projects.

INTRODUCTION

Since a handful of archaeologists began to employ Geographic Information Systems (GIS) for their analyses of spatial phenomena in the early 1980s, previous major studies on GIS (Aldenderfer and Maschner 1996; Allen et al. 1990; Conolly and Lake 2006; Forte and Williams 2003; Gaffney and Stančič 1991; Lock 2000; Maschner 1996; Robertson et al. 2006; Westcott and Brandon 2000; Wheatley and Gillings 2002) have put their primary focuses upon the analytical capabilities of the technology and attempted to improve the methods of conventional spatial archaeology originally borrowed from New Geography in the late 1960s and sophisticated by pioneering works such as Hodder and Orton (1976) and Clarke (1977). These earlier GIS studies were all premised on ready-made digital maps at hand and failed to discuss mapping procedures in detail. Coupled with practical problems discussed below, however, making digital maps is not an easy task. Although it is obvious that GIS hold some promise for archaeological research, I argue that its appropriateness and efficacy for our discipline needs to be more fully assessed. In so doing, digital site mapping, I believe, is worth focusing our attention on at this time.

Given ample funds, it would be feasible to map in great detail the whole area of interest using the most advanced digital survey equipment. However, in reality, this is not the case for most of us. Constraints such as tight budget and consequent limited resources will always complicate the situation and often lead our colleagues to suffer from "GIS-phobia." Furthermore, ethnographic and archaeological research tend to occur in the regions that have not yet established an efficient (or reliable) geographical data management or related infrastructures and thus do not have enough data sources to achieve our goals. It is not until we overcome a series of practical problems that the time efficiency and succinctness of GIS-based digital mapping and related data management will be gained.

The main objective of this paper is to highlight a notable gap between theory and reality and how such a gap may be filled in. As a case study, I will refer to my digital site mapping of Pachacamac, which is a part of the ongoing long-term archaeological project on the central coast of Peru, the Pachacamac Archaeological Project (PAP), directed by Izumi Shimada (Southern Illinois University at Carbondale). PAP has a clear vision for data creation and storage in both digital and analog formats. Following this vision, I worked during the spring of 2004 to create a digital map of the site and took part in the excavation in the subsequent summer to collect field data for the corrections and further refinements to the map.

SETTINGS

The site of Pachacamac is located approximately thirty kilometres southeast of Lima on a plateau on the north bank of the Lurín River and approximately one kilometre inland from its mouth. The plateau looks onto the river mouth, the Pacific Ocean, and a cluster of small islands offshore. While the full extent of the site still remains unknown, the site occupies an area of approximately 5.2 square kilometres (Matsumoto 2005). Three massive roughly concentric walls partition the area into four major sectors, I through IV, extending from southeast to northwest. The site is thought to have been one of the most powerful religious centres in pre-Hispanic Peru for over a thousand years or at least from the time of Late Lima occupation (Uhle 1991 [1903]).

MAPPING TECHNIQUES AND PROCEDURES

Currently available techniques of GIS-based site mapping can be broadly divided into two types: (1) small-scale mapping methods relying primarily on remote sensing data and techniques; and (2) large-scale mapping methods based on location surveys in the field.[1] Both require their own hardware and software, and the capability of the equipment and/or the reliability of data sources one selects will directly reflect the quality of final products. PAP adopted the former methods.

If one needs to cover a large area even at the expense of precision, the former approach would be recommended. Its relatively light workload does not cost too much to execute. The methods that we employed for our site mapping were relatively handy and thus may be more appropriate for preliminary survey or reconnaissance prior to the fieldwork. For the latter approach, on the other hand, there is no choice but to slowly build up the map by taking measurements in the field. You should choose this approach only in cases where you need a very precise map and are prepared to conduct location surveys with perseverance.

In Pachacamac, there is another ongoing archaeological project, the Ychsma Project, directed by Peter Eeckhout (Université Libre de Bruxelles). This project represents a notable contrast to our mapping and employs large-scale mapping techniques based on meticulous location surveys by means of a laser total station in order to represent the architectural features in three dimensions (Ychsma Project 2005). Their heavy workload would be fathomable from the fact that their mapping project inaugurated in 2002 was not expected to be completed until 2007.

As shown in this contrast, archaeologists in the United States tend to be compelled to individually and annually or biannually seek their research funds, whereas their colleagues in Europe and other regions of the world have relatively easier access to multi-year funding. Thus, many of the multidisciplinary research projects that implement digital site mapping and related technical examinations are based in European institutions with greater long-term stability and personnel support (cf. Bard et al. 2003; Campana and Francovich 2003; Cavalli et al. 2003; Johnson 2005; Lambers 2004). Given the difference, important future developments in the archaeological application of GIS are more likely to come out of major European projects.

Our digital mapping consists of three broad phases: (1) prototype map preparation based on the resources available prior to the fieldwork in the summer of 2004; (2) ground-truth checking of the archaeological structures and Ground Control Point measurements by means of Real-Time Kinematic Differential GPS[2] (RTK DGPS) of the highest accuracy; and (3) data post-processing and consummation of the map (Figures 14.1 and 14.2). This stepwise approach dovetails the basic design of GIS sub-systems, which allows separate data manipulation and display. Because any quest for perfection cannot be readily accomplished, we should make efforts to set up and achieve a sequence of midterm goals, depending upon the resources available.

With budgetary restrictions and an optimistic assumption that we could blend productively the conventional data sources and digital photogrammetry techniques, we chose to begin with a combination of traditional 1:5,000-scale topography maps and old film aerial photographs taken in 1957 (Figures 14.3a,b). Instead of conducting location survey on the ground, we planned to put those data in a GIS overlay and digitize archaeological structures and other topographic features on them. Because photographs in general suffer from various systematic and nonsystematic errors, to be used as planimetrically true

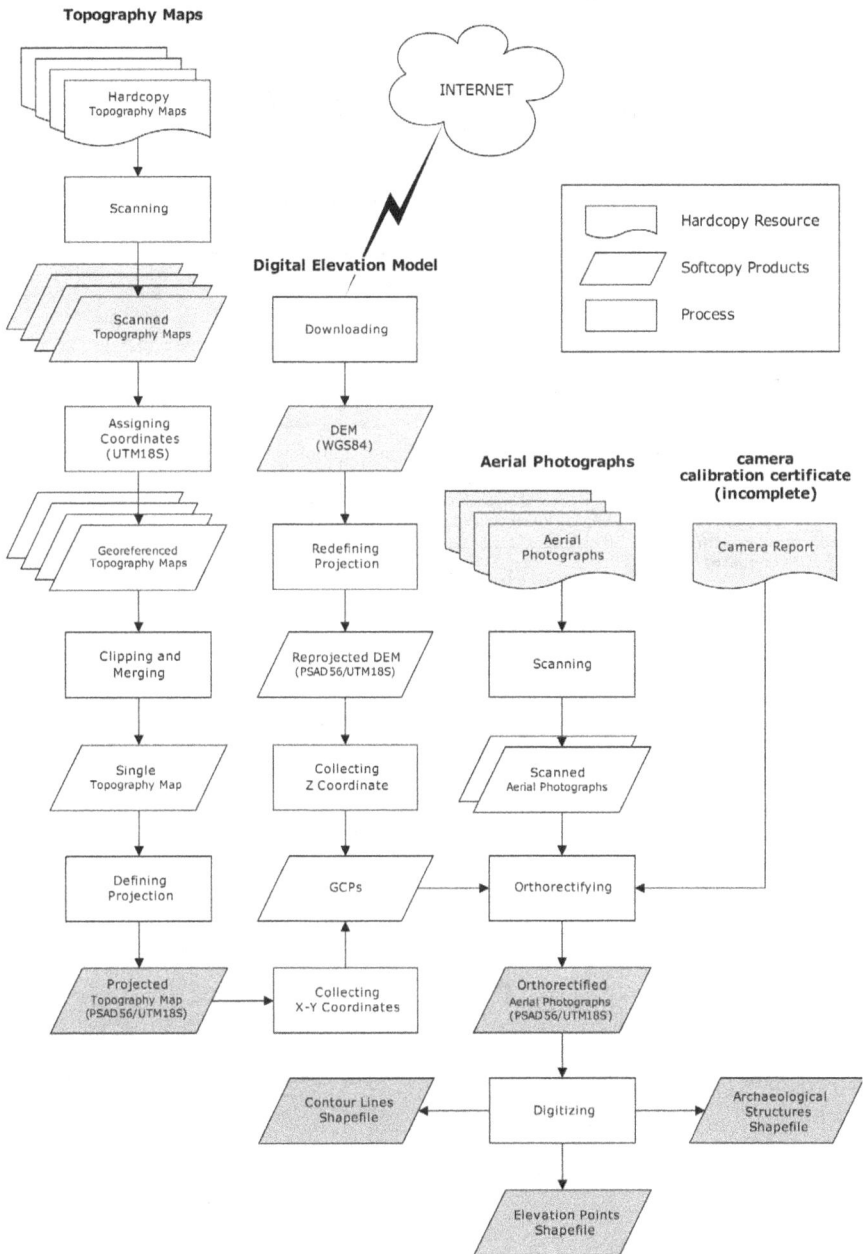

Figure 14.1. The workflow of prototype map creation (Phase I).

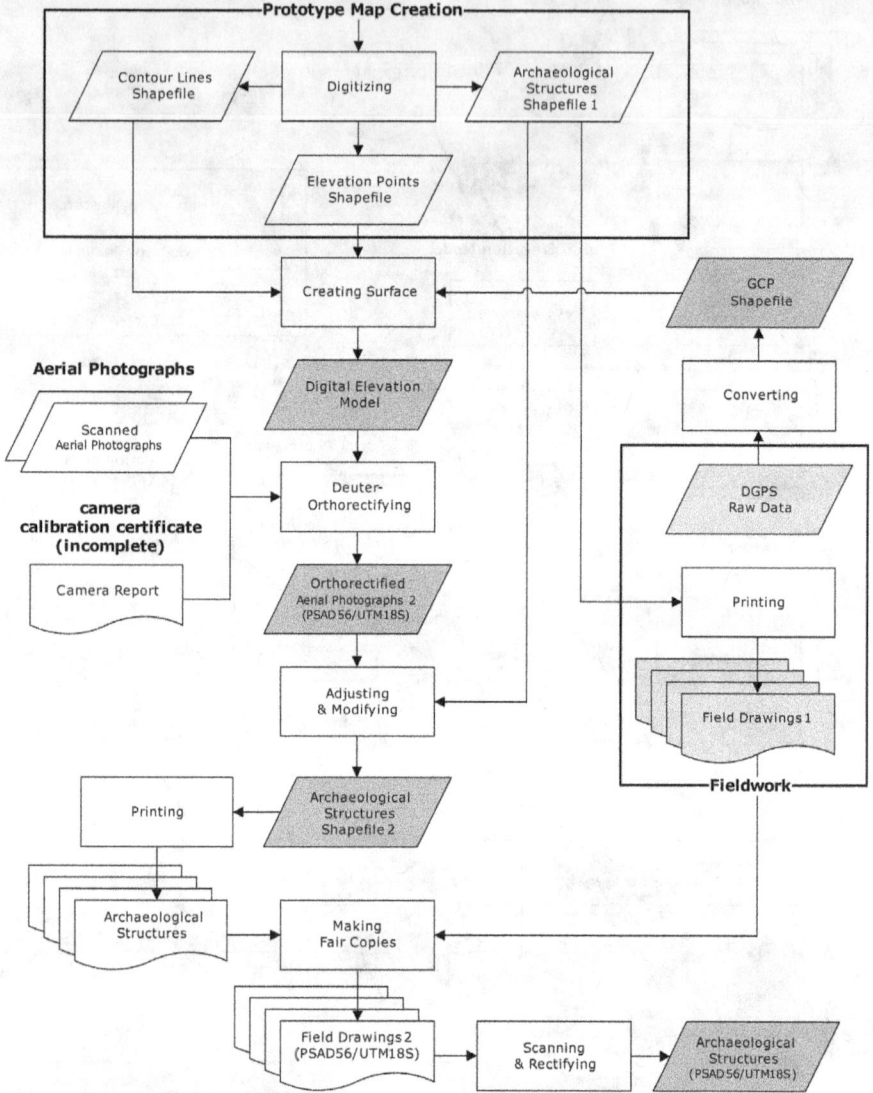

Figure 14.2. The workflow of post-fieldwork data processing (Phase III).

orthoimages, they need to be transformed from a perspective projection to a scaled orthographic projection in combination with the correction processes of various geometric errors. The success and failure of my site mapping primarily depended upon the success of this process. However, I confronted serious problems that defied a quick and simple solution. As a result, I had to be very inventive to resolve them. Below I discuss these problems.

PRACTICAL PROBLEMS

Most of the problems emerged in the forementioned transformation process that is called "block triangulation." The block triangulation basically requires four sets of data: (1) a stereopair of aerial photographs; (2) a minimum of three known Ground Control Points; (3) Digital Elevation Model (DEM) or Digital Terrain Model[3] (DTM); and (4) camera calibration report. Strictly speaking, however, none of them could be obtained in the form that we wished from the Servicio Aerofotográfico Nacional (SAN) or the Instituto Geomilitar. This difficulty stems mainly from the defectiveness and scarcity of data resources in Peru.

1: Pseudo-stereopair

The producer of the aerial photographs that I used confidently claimed that they were a stereopair (Figures 14.3a,b), but they were not. A stereoscopic parallax requires the photographs to be acquired at exposure stations from one or two flight lines at the same altitude on the same side of the terrain feature usually with 55 to 65 per cent overlap between them (Lillesand et al. 2004:131). The orientation of the images and states of exposure led me to conclude that our photographs were most likely taken from different sides and at different times. The overlap between them is no more than 51.3 per cent. The only solution to this problem is simply to process this pseudo-stereopair as a true stereopair since the processing software will not make any query about its validity. Of course, however, we should keep in mind that the resultant orthoimages may be problematic to some extent.

Figure 14.3. a. Aerial photograph 6512-57-5-626 taken on March 12th, 1957 by Servicio Aerofotográfico Nacional, Peru.

GO MATSUMOTO

Figure 14.3. b. Aerial photograph 6612-57-5-649 taken on March 12th, 1957 by Servicio Aerofotográfico Nacional, Peru.

2: Absence of Ground Control Points (GCPs)

Prior to the fieldwork, I had no coordinate information that I could use as GCPs. The GCPs should contain X, Y, and Z coordinates, and a minimum of three should be evenly distributed throughout the study area and clearly identifiable on the aerial photographs. Alternatively, I collected X and Y coordinates from the georeferenced topography map that I created by clicking the points at which I wished to place the GCPs. In the same manner, Z coordinates were extracted from a DEM of 90-by-90 m spatial resolution derived from Shuttle Radar Topography Mission[4] (SRTM) arc-3 interferometric radar data available on the web for free.

3: DEM of very low spatial resolution

In order to properly eliminate the spatial discrepancies caused by terrain relief, elevation information such as DTM, DEM, and Triangulated Irregular Network (TIN) is required to be integrated during the correction process. Because we could not afford to purchase expensive high-resolution DEM or DTM, the SRTM arc-3 DEM was again used for this purpose. However, as might be expected, topographic prominences within each 90-by-90 m cell cannot be depicted and rather are represented as a smooth surface, which means that it is not suitable for large-scale detailed contextual analysis.

4: Incomplete and/or incorrect camera report

A regular camera calibration certificate was not available for the aerial photos we purchased. A replacement document provided by the producer of the photographs contains only: (1) project number, (2) picture numbers, (3) date of shooting, (4) scale, (5) airplane altitude, and (6) focal length. It is lacking critical information for the triangulation process such as principal point, fiducial marks, and rotation angles. Furthermore, the document is not only incomplete, but also evidently inaccurate. The altitude of 50 m, for instance, is apparently hard to accept if you take into account that each photograph covers the ground area of about 2,300 x 2,300 m. Supposing the scale (1:10,000) and focal length (152.67 mm) stated in the document are true, the altitude should be about 465 m. The content of the document is internally inconsistent.

This problem was partially solved by consulting the data strip shown on the margin of the photograph. The data strip confirms that the focal length is

152.67 mm as stated in the document but concurrently indicates that the altitude at the time of exposure was 1,600 m rather than either 50 or 465 m. This value sounds quite reasonable for the forementioned ground area. According to the information of the data strip, the scale will be 1:10,480.

Without the film coordinates of the principal point of each photograph, I had no choice but to define them as (0, 0) assuming that the principal point was placed completely in the centre of the photo image with absolutely no displacement. The film coordinates of fiducial marks also had to be replaced with theoretical values. The producer's website states that they have been using 9-inch Wild-type film cameras such as Leica RC series. According to the FAQ of the Environmental Systems Research Institute Japan's website (ESRI Japan 2002), moreover, approximate values of 106 and –106 can be used for the film coordinates of fiducial marks in the photograph taken by 9-inch Wild-type camera. Although it goes without saying that I must be prepared to face substantial margins of error, as long as I use these theoretical values for interior orientation parameters during the error-correction processes, I had no choice.

Effective Solutions and Results

Effective solutions to the difficulties described above were offered by the ground-truth checking and GCP measurements in the field (Figure 14.2). This is obvious in a comparison of the qualities of pre-fieldwork prototype map and post-fieldwork counterpart (Matsumoto 2005:Figures 5–24 and 4–2). The extremely accurate GCPs of only several-millimetre difference derived from the RTK DGPS readings, in particular, allowed us to produce high-quality Digital Terrain Models for the overlap area of the aerial photographs and to minimize the margins of error in the subsequent triangulation process based on the DTM. The resultant orthoimages show that the new data reduced a substantial amount of horizontal displacements between DGPS readings and the corresponding points in the orthoimages. Archaeological features on the ground were again digitized on the orthoimages in reference to the field drawings. The subsequent shapefile[5] was finally superimposed over the other shapefiles of topographic and architectural features (e.g., contour lines, water bodies, and modern roads) in a single overlay and printed as the finalized site map (Figure 14.4). It is very important to note here that we have to pay attention to the fact

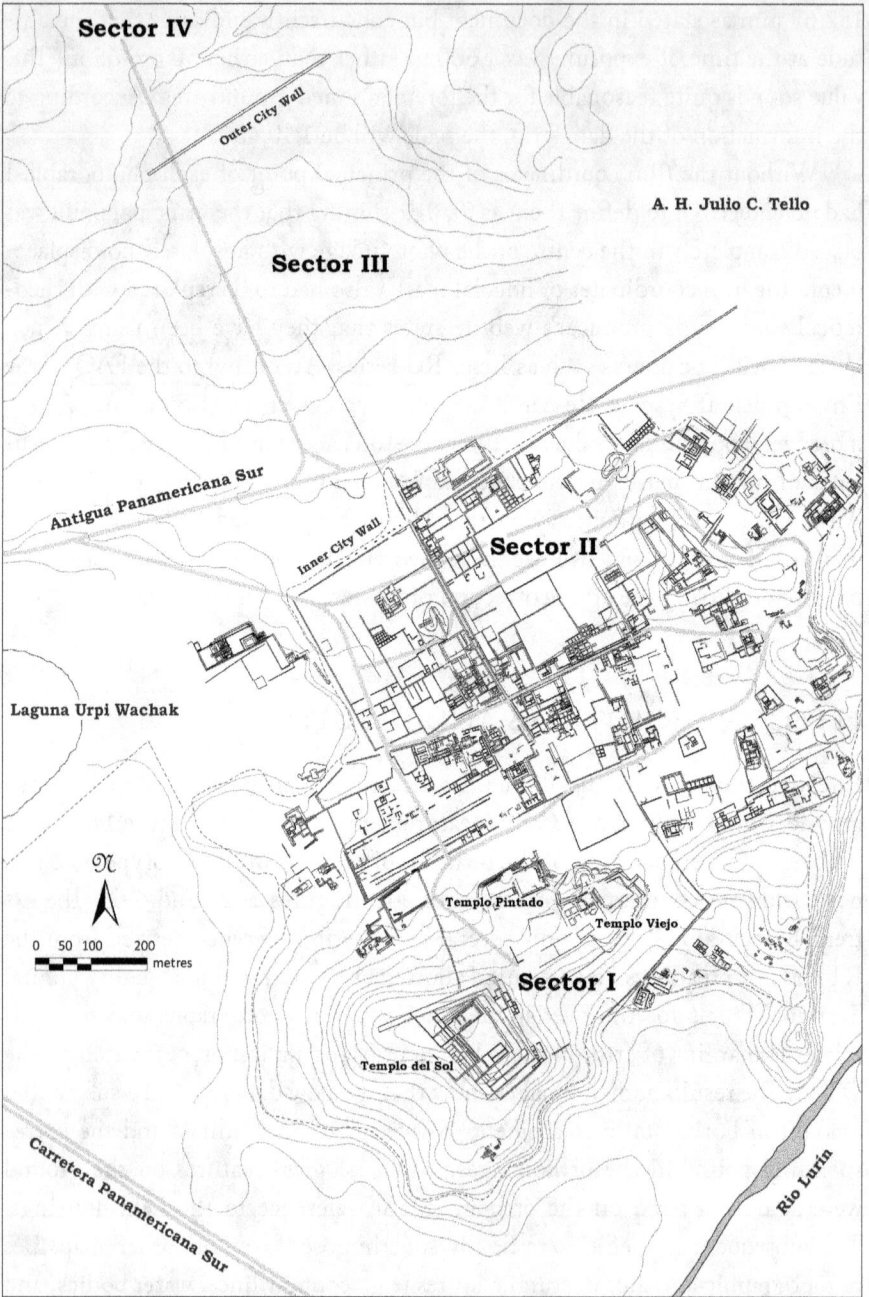

Figure 14.4. The resultant site map of Pachacamac (Scale = 1:10,000).

that the conversion process of the DGPS readings into a new shapefile induced a substantial amount of vertical displacements up to about 15 m in comparison with the conventional data sources. The discrepancy is probably due to the lack of a locally fitting geoid model for Peru.

Discussion

Over the last few years, we have obtained a growing number of external data sources inherently compatible with GIS; however, many old and new data available to us have considerable limitations in regard to precision, accuracy, and information density. Thus, as long as we have to use problematic data sources, both old and new, it would be virtually impossible for us to conduct site mapping and related data collections that are precise and accurate enough to undertake truly scalable analyses ranging from intra-feature to macro-regional levels. This implies that a full-scale application of GIS in archaeology is not yet practical or feasible in a true sense. Furthermore, even though one can obtain very precise and accurate data by means of the state-of-the-art equipment and techniques, they may not fit well into the conventional site data collected by old, planimetrically less accurate methods.

Since we inevitably face and have to accept substantial margins of error that stem from various practical details, it may not be worth pursuing the highest precision and accuracy at the expense of limited resources (Matsumoto 2005). Not only the selection of the most appropriate mapping techniques, but also the required level of precision and accuracy needs to be carefully considered according to our research interest, field conditions resulting from varied natural and cultural formation processes, expertise of field crew, and available data. Under no circumstances should we adopt any kind of technique without deliberate consideration. Inefficient applications will not only waste precious resources but also unnecessarily detach us away from our own duties such as explanatory explorations of material remains and, if temporarily, lead us to become absorbed merely in technology. We should keep in mind that GIS and other related techniques are nothing but research tools.

It is important to note here that I do not mean to be so realistic that I foreclose the prospect of future development of archaeological applications of GIS and surrounding technologies. It goes without saying that it is one of the critical issues for GIS-based archaeology to build and integrate more reliable site databases for subsequent archaeological analyses and discussions. However, the implementation of such an ambitious enterprise will require very careful planning based on a long-term perspective and a substantial amount of effort and perseverance to obtain and organize high-quality data. In order to maximize the efficiency with the minimum of exertion and expenditure, I argue that the establishment of collaborative work environment and active data sharing among archaeologists and/or projects would be most desirable.

In this regard, GLOBALBASE sets out architecture of great promise based on excellent philosophy (Mori 2005, n.d.). With its ultimate goals of storing every piece of existing spatial information within a single knowledge system and making it available free to the general public, this system enables us to share map information linked to each other through the World Wide Web (WWW) and to go freely back and forth between them, irrespective of the differences in coordinate system and whereabouts of map information. It no longer requires any resources except for a computer connected to the Internet. The only fear is that the system relies exclusively on the spirit of international volunteerism as with the case of WWW and open-source software. By improving its practicality and data quality, GLOBALBASE would not be impossible to get closer to the ideal in our mind.

Most of the serious problems that I have encountered in the course of map-making have not been explained elsewhere and thus can be resolved only through a continuing process of trial and error. A series of valuable know-how gained from such processes should be accumulated and made available freely to those interested. They are no less useful than what can be gained from formal in-class training, often complemented by laboratory exercises. Fully aware of this fact, a handful of graduate students of archaeology recently inaugurated an online study group in a Social Networking Site (SNS) and have organized offline workshops for active interaction and information sharing among the registered members (Archaeo-GIS Workshop 2007). I hope that such a grass-roots attempt, together with the data sharing scheme noted above, trigger macro-regional level cooperation among archaeologists.

Conclusion

In order to fundamentally resolve the aforementioned practical problems, as I noted above, there is no alternative but to sweep the slate clean and start over to slowly and meticulously build up the maps by taking measurements in the field by the use of state-of-the-art survey equipment. However, to aspire to perfection is virtually impossible, and there is little point in pursuing extreme precision and accuracy for archaeological problem-solving even though it is backed up by sufficient funds. What is most practical and sensible is to find the most efficient way to achieve immediate goals (e.g., rough mapping for preliminary research and precise large-scale mapping for detailed contextual analysis) on the basis of a clear understanding of given resources and surrounding realities, and concurrently to contribute to data accumulation based on a long-term plan for establishment of more reliable site database. Furthermore, the digitalization of archaeological resources for the years to come will also encourage active in-depth discussions concerning data acquisition and management at the stage of research design. Subsequently, I hope, many archaeologists will argue for the need to establish a collaborative work environment and active data-sharing networks among them. I believe that a critical key to filling the gap between theory and practice in GIS-based archaeology would be found in mutual collaboration and voluntarism of archaeologists.

Acknowledgments: First, I would like to thank Dr. Izumi Shimada (Southern Illinois University at Carbondale), who offered me a valuable opportunity to participate in his new project at the site of Pachacamac. I also thank Dr. Hartmut Tschauner (Binghamton University) who loaned me his own RTK DGPS. He devoted himself not only to giving me an on-site instruction as to how to operate the equipment, but also for helping me with GCP measurements and taking charge of attendant data post-processing. During the measurement processes, Dr. Ursel Wagner (Technische Universität München, Germany) assisted me as well. I appreciate her valuable advice.

Many procedures of map production could not have been accomplished without the understanding and cooperation of the Department of Geography, Earth Resources Project (ERP) program, and Library Affairs, SIUC. Topography maps were scanned utilizing the facilities in the ERP laboratory, and aerial photographs were processed using ERDAS IMAGINE 8.6 and ArcGIS 8.3 (ArcInfo License) in the Spatial Environmental Analysis Laboratory (SEAL). Plotting the prototype base map prior to the fieldwork in the summer of 2004 was completed using the plotter in the Graduate Assistant Laboratory of the Department of Geography. I thank for their generous support Dr. Wanxiao Sun, Dr. Xu Gang, Dr. Tony Oyana, Girmay Misgna, and Daniel K. Davie.

REFERENCES CITED

Aldenderfer, Mark, and Herbert D. G. Maschner (editors)

1996   *Anthropology, Space, and Geographic Information Systems.* Oxford University Press, New York.

Allen, Kathleen M. S., Stanton W. Green, and Ezra B. W. Zubrow (editors)

1990   *Interpreting Space: GIS and Archaeology.* Taylor & Francis, New York.

Archaeo-GIS Workshop

2007   archaeogis / Discussions. Retrieved February 23rd, 2007 from http://groups.google.co.jp/group/archaeogis/topics

Bard, Kathryn A., Michael C. DiBlasi, Magaly Koch, Livio Crescenzi, A. C. D'Andrea, Rodolfo Fattovich, Andrea Manzo, Cinzia Perlingieri, Maurizio Forte, M. Scott Harris, Gerald H. Johnson, Stefano Tilia, and Bartolomeo Trabassi

2003   The Joint Archaeological Project at Bieta Giyorgis (Aksum, Ethiopia) of the Istituto Universitario Orientale, Naples (Italy), and Boston University, Boston (USA): Results, Research Procedures and Preliminary Computer Applications. In *The Reconstruction of Archaeological Landscapes through Digital Technologies*, edited by M. Forte and P. R. Williams, pp. 1–13. BAR International Series 1151, 2003, Oxford.

Campana, Stefano, and Riccardo Francovich

2003   Landscape Archaeology in Tuscany: Cultural Resource Management, Remotely Sensed Techniques, GIS Based Data Integration and Interpretation. In *The Reconstruction of Archaeological Landscapes through Digital Technologies*, edited by M. Forte and P. R. Williams, pp. 15–27. BAR International Series 1151, 2003, Oxford.

Cavalli, Rosa M., Carlo M. Marino, and Stefano Pignatti

2003   Hyperspectral Airborne Remote Sensing as an Aid to a Better Understanding and Characterization of Buried Elements in Different Archaeological Sites. In *The Reconstruction of Archaeological Landscapes through Digital Technologies*, edited by M. Forte and P. R. Williams, pp. 29–32. BAR International Series 1151, 2003, Oxford.

Clarke, David L. (editor)

1977   *Spatial Archaeology.* Academic Press, London.

Conolly, James, and Mark Lake

2006   *Geographic Information Systems in Archaeology*. Cambridge University Press, Cambridge.

ESRI Japan

2002   Orthorectification of Aerial Photography. March 5th; retrieved March 24th, 2004, from http://www.esrij.com/support/erdas/faq/camera_model/camera-model.html

Forte, Maurizio, and P. Ryan Williams (editors)

2003   *The Reconstruction of Archaeological Landscapes through Digital Technologies*. BAR International Series 1151, 2003, Oxford.

Gaffney, Vincent, and Zoran Stančič

1991   *GIS Approaches to Regional Analysis: A Case Study of the Island of Hvar*. Filozofska Fakulteta, Ljubljana.

Hodder, Ian, and Clive Orton

1976   *Spatial Analysis in Archaeology*. Cambridge University Press, Cambridge.

Johnson, Ian

2005   Studying Angkor: Integration of GIS, GPS, Remote Sensing and Contemporary Observation. In *Reading Historical Spatial Information from around the World: Studies of Culture and Civilization Based on Geographic Information Systems Data*, The 24th International Research Symposium, pp. 188–205. International Research Center for Japanese Studies, Japan.

Lambers, Karsten

2004   The Geoglyphs of Palpa (Peru): Documentation, Analysis, and Interpretation. PhD dissertation, University of Zurich.

Lillesand, Thomas. M., Ralph W. Kiefer, and Jonathan W. Chipman

2004   *Remote Sensing and Image Interpretation. 5th ed*. John Wiley & Sons, New York.

Lock, Gary (editor)

2000   *Beyond the Map: Archaeology and Spatial Technologies*. IOS Press, Amsterdam.

Maschner, Herbert. D. G. (editor)

1996   *New Methods, Old Problems: Geographic Information Systems in Modern Archaeological Research, Occasional Paper No. 23*. Center for Archaeological Investigations, Southern Illinois University at Carbondale.

Matsumoto, Go

2005   *Pachacamac GIS Project: A Practical Application of Geographic Information Systems in Andean Archaeology*. M.A. thesis, Department of Anthropology, Southern Illinois University at Carbondale, IL.

Mori, Hirohisa

2005   Development of the Distributed GIS Architecture for Archaeology. In *Reading Historical Spatial Information from around the World: Studies of Culture and Civilization Based on Geographic Information Systems Data*, The 24th International Research Symposium, pp. 106–115. International Research Center for Japanese Studies, Japan.

n.d.   Globalbase Project. Retrieved April 8th, 2005, from http://globalbase.source-forge.jp/home/en/

Robertson, Elizabeth C., Jeff D. Seibert, Deepika C. Fernandez, and Mark Zender

2006   *Space and Spatial Analysis in Archaeology*. University of Calgary Press, Calgary.

Uhle, Max

1991   [1903] *Pachacamac: A Reprint of the 1903 Edition by Max Uhle, and Pachacamac Archaeology: Retrospect and Prospect; An Introduction by Izumi Shimada*. University of Pennsylvania Museum of Archaeology and Anthropology, Philadelphia.

Westcott, Konie L., and R. Joe Brandon (editors)

2000   *Practical Applications of GIS for Archaeologists: A Predictive Modeling Toolkit*. Taylor & Francis, London.

Wheatley, David, and Mark Gillings

2002   *Spatial Technology and Archaeology: The Archaeological Applications of GIS*. Taylor & Francis, New York.

Ychsma Project

2005   Topographic and Planimetric Survey: Project Description. Retrieved March 12th, 2005 from http://www.ulb.ac.be/philo/ychsma/en/topodescription.html

NOTES

1   It should be recalled that a small-scale map covers a large area, while a large-scale map covers a small area.

2   The difference between the known coordinates and the GPS-calculated coordinates is the error that needs to be corrected for the accuracy of survey or mapping grade GPS applications. The correction of this error can be done either by bringing the data from the Reference Station and Rover together in an asynchronous, post-processing mode after the field measurements are completed (Post Processed Kinematic or PPK) or by instantaneously broadcasting the error correction information produced by the Reference Station to the Rover for real-time corrections (Lillesand et al. 2004:34).

3   DEM and DTM are three-dimensional digital representations of the earth's surface or topography.

4   SRTM is a joint project of the National Imagery and Mapping Agency (NIMA) and NASA to map the world in three dimensions. During a single Space Shuttle mission on February 11 to 22, 2000, SRTM collected single-pass radar interferometry data covering 119.51 million square km of the earth's surface, including over 99.9 per cent of the land area between 60°N and 56°S latitude. This represents approximately 80 per cent of the total land surface worldwide and is home to nearly 95 per cent of the world's population (Lillesand et al. 2004:712).

5   Shapefile is a vector data format developed by Environmental Systems Research Institute (ESRI).

15

Economy in Ancient Egypt: The Use of GIS for Understanding Different Spheres of Exchange

José Roberto Pellini

Abstract. In the last few years, cost surface analysis has become part of exchange system studies. The basic problem with this GIS methodology is that the principles of analysis are based on modern economic theory and on the concept of economic rationality. This kind of analysis does not take into account the social aspects of landscape. In my PhD dissertation, I use a novel approach to cost surface analysis based on social and physical cost raster. This cultural cost surface map was added to archaeological distribution maps to create circulation maps.

Introduction

Geographic Information Systems have, for the past years, revolutionized the way in which disciplines such as geography, ecology, and archaeology handle and interpret spatial data. These information systems supply a way to manipulate varied complex data with much flexibility. One of the advantages of GIS is its ability to visualize data, either in two or three dimensions. Another advantage is the possibility to calculate distances and surfaces of spatial phenomena in relation to specific physical characteristics. Because there are numerous types of spatial analysis available to us through GIS software, this software is especially useful for studying exchange systems. In this context, cost surface analysis has emerged to model the movement of individuals through landscape. A cost surface is a computerized model of the landscape for which each part of the surface has a designated value or cost. This value or cost represents the effort or the energy required to reach a certain point after departing from another point. The total cost is determined by logarithms that incorporate not only the distances in relation to the final point, but also the incidental costs related to particular aspects of the landscape as well. The researcher determines these incidental costs as they derive from systems of classification in which, for each characteristic of the landscape, a certain value of cost is ascertained. For example, to find out the best route of access to a determined point within an area characterized as having savannas and dense forests, differentiated values of cost must be designated for each specific type of vegetation. When a model of cost surface analysis is constructed, the cost value of each area is established in relation to the area of lesser-cost value. Logarithms used for cost surface analysis can be classified in two large groups: *isotropic logarithms*, that is, those that consider the cost of moving in a surface without reckoning the direction of such movement, and *anisotropic logarithms*, in which the direction of the movement that affects the displacement cost is taken into account.

Generally in archaeology the expended energy is a function of differences in the elevation of the land. This is a simple idea, since other environmental characteristics may also influence energy expense. For instance, this is the case when one considers moving through dunes and areas of dense vegetation covering. One must also remember that going through landscapes is something conditioned not only by physical aspects but by symbolic ones as well. The existence of sacred areas, taboo areas, or the simple desire of passing through a specific village can have more influence upon the structure of displacement than the actual topography of the area. Nowadays the majority of cost surface analysis models follow an interpretative structure that derives from modern economic theory. That reduces the cost analysis to a question of distance rationalization.

Although cost surface analysis is in part related to theories of minimization of effort, cost is a relative measure that varies according to the specific society under analysis. In this perspective, cost surface analysis incorporates not only different physical factors such as declivity, soil types, and vegetation, but also cultural factors. This paper presents a new proposition for cost surface analysis, where cost is based in two differentiated groups of parameters: physical factors and cultural factors.

The Case Study

Until the beginning of the twentieth century, Nubia was a little-known and relatively unexplored region, at least from the archaeological point of view. With the gradual increase in lake level at the Aswan High Dam and the subsequent construction of Nasser Lake, the culturally rich area that lay underneath old Nubia was about to be completely flooded. Because of these factors, three campaigns of rescue took place in the Nubia region in order to salvage and to preserve the remaining archaeological portions of this area. UNESCO promoted the largest campaign in the 1960s.

For this research, an area was chosen between Qustul in Egypt and Gamai in Sudan, because this region has been one of the more intensively worked areas in the rescue projects. These regions have been excavated by different teams; the region between Qustul and Adindan was part of the portions attributed to the Oriental Institute of Chicago and the area between Faras and Gamai was excavated by the Scandinavian Joint Expedition. They have been chosen by us because they have also been the subject of more precise publications, especially regarding dated archaeological evidence of the New Empire.

In order to make the task somewhat easier, phases of occupation have been defined based on the chronology applied by Williams (1992) to the shafts excavated by the Oriental Institute. The chronology used by Säve-Söderbergh and Troy (1990) has also been applied to the shafts of the Scandinavian Joint Expedition.

These phases are:

I: Beginning of the eighteenth dynasty down to Hatshepesut (1550–1479 B.C.).

II: From Hatshepesut to Tutmosis III (1479–1427 B.C.).

III: From Amenophis II to Tutmosis IV (1427–1391 B.C.).

IV: Amenophis III and Amarna age (1391–1323 B.C.).

V: End of Amarna age to the beginning of the nineteenth dynasty (1323–1300 B.C.).

COST SURFACE ANALYSIS

Current models of cost surface analysis try to impose a Cartesian and abstract geometry on a reality that is basically subjective and contingent. Space in these cases is seen as a physical, purely separate entity of time and is expressed as an absolute value. Space is not a neutral Cartesian concept; it is socially constructed. Therefore, in cost surface analysis, it is necessary to map the environment in order to represent it in a contextual perspective.

Having this proposition in mind, in the cost surface analysis, cost was based on two different groups of parameters: physical factors and cultural factors, which are referred to as contextual factors. In the first group (the physical factors), characteristics such as topography, relief, vegetation, geological and palaeo-geological formation, etc., were used. The contextual factors group includes a series of historical data, like urban planning, the positioning of palaces and temples in relation to the urban architecture (O'Connor 1993), the number of villages around each city, the amount of grain consumption, and the demographic density (Hassan 1990).

The data was tabulated and entered into a database that was used to create three different layers: an administrative map with the location of the temples, centres, and villages of Nubia; a demographic density map; and a calories consumption map. These three layers have been united based on original raster of contextual cost.

The next step was to transform the raster of physical cost and the raster of contextual cost into a final raster that would include a representation of the general surface cost for the study area. The final result was a raster of contextual cost that united cultural and physical information.

With the creation of a contextual cost raster, the distribution maps of excavated archaeological materials were analyzed. For each object in each phase of occupation, a map of distribution was created. In this way, each archaeological object inside the study area was located using its original coordinates. Trend maps were then generated from this data. For the interpolation base, the method of Inverse Distance Weighted (IDW) was used. Finally, each map of distribution was recalculated in accordance with the contextual cost raster. The final result is a series of maps identified as circulation maps.

In the circulation maps, the blank spaces represent areas with little or no circulation of products, or areas where there are limited interaction links. The areas that present a gradation between black colour tones represent areas where the circulation of objects is intense, in such a way that the circulation intensity, or the interaction intensity, is demonstrated by the increase in colour variation. The larger the area covered with tones of black colour, the higher the interaction frequency will be, resulting in a greater circulation of products (a series of successive exchanges between one point and another). The isolated points in black colour represent areas where the circulation is centric. In these cases, the circulation is directed to a specific point. In this article, the analysis is limited to phases I, II, and V, as these phases are considered to be the most representative ones.

Beginning the analysis with the circulation maps of jars and bowls (Figures 15.1–6), items considered of ordinary domestic use, in phase I the vessels are circulated within a small area. The difference between the blank areas (areas with circulation absence) and areas with gradations of black colour (areas with circulation) are almost equal. In phase I, the circulation of these objects is limited and confined to few interaction links. On the other hand, in phase II there is a major diffusion of the circulation area. In this phase, jars and bowls are circulating intensely all over the area. This means that they take part in a greater number of interaction links. The absence of blank tones is an indication that these objects are circulating everywhere. In phase V, jars and bowls present a distinct circulation pattern. The jars lose popularity and, even though they still circulate, they seem to be restricted to a smaller area. As for bowls, they continue to circulate with some intensity, although in a more reduced way.

Regarding objects that are linked to importation (Figures 15.7–11), such as wine jars and amphorae, it is clear that they have a larger circulation pattern during phase II, much in the same way as the jars and earthen bowls. The difference is in the intensity of the circulation. While jars and bowls appear to be circulating all over the area, the imported objects, wine jars and amphorae, have a more centric distribution pattern.

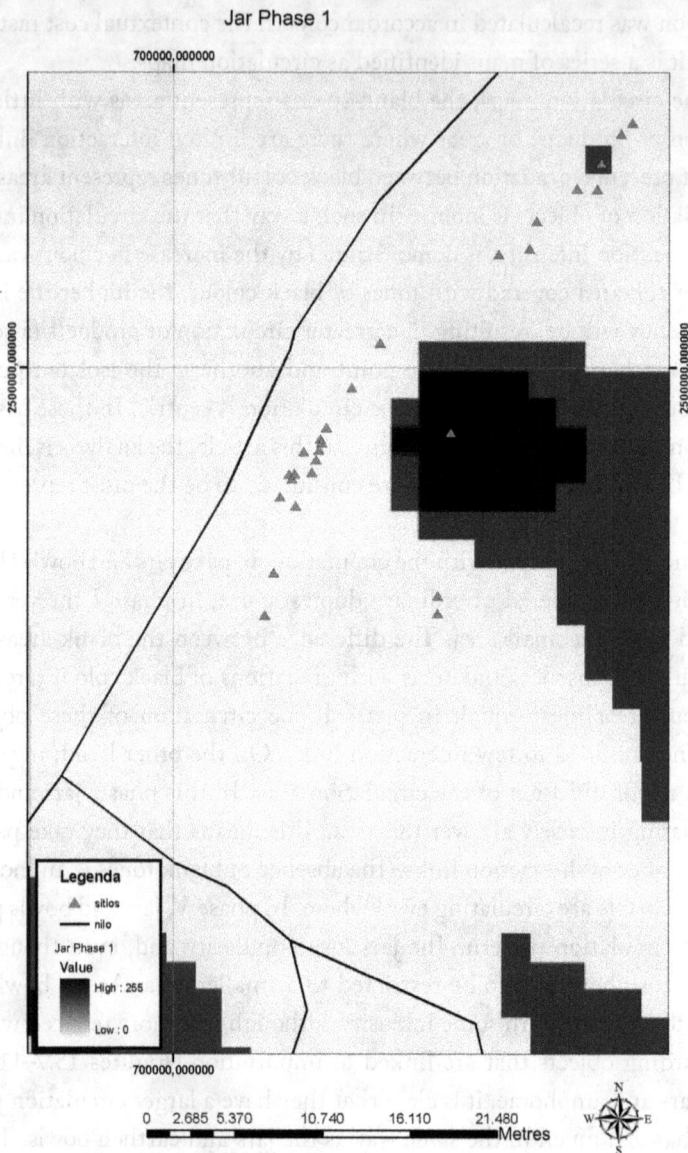

Figure 15.1. Jar Phase 1.

JOSÉ ROBERTO PELLINI

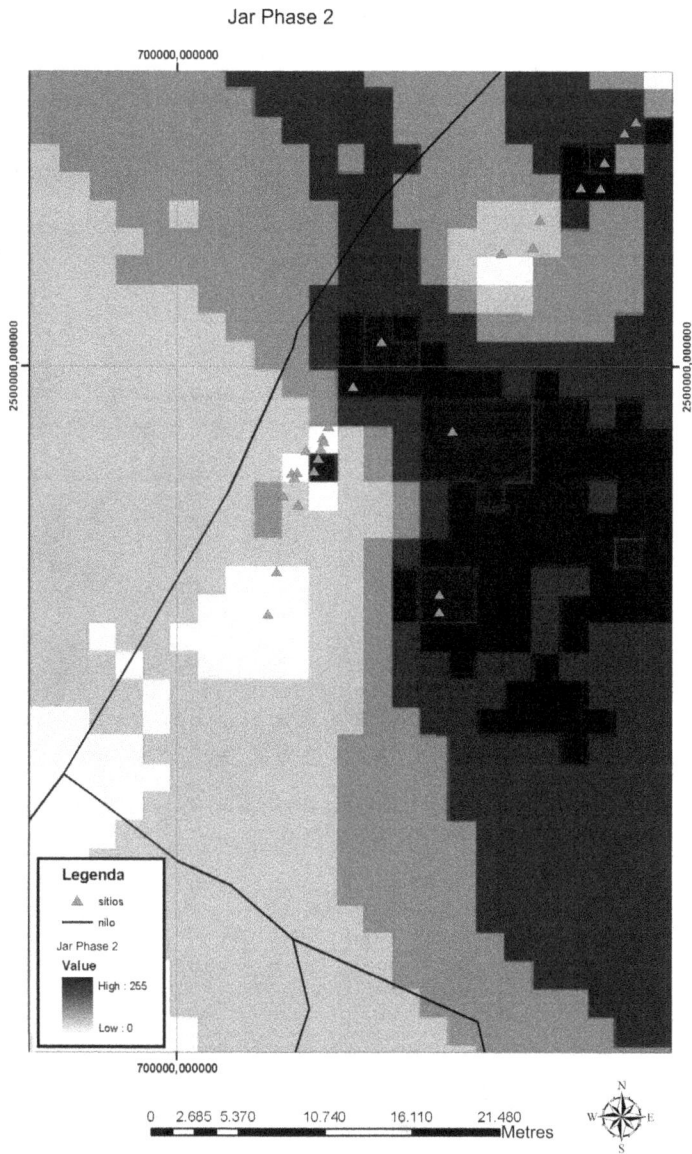

Jar Phase 2

Figure 15.2. Jar Phase 2.

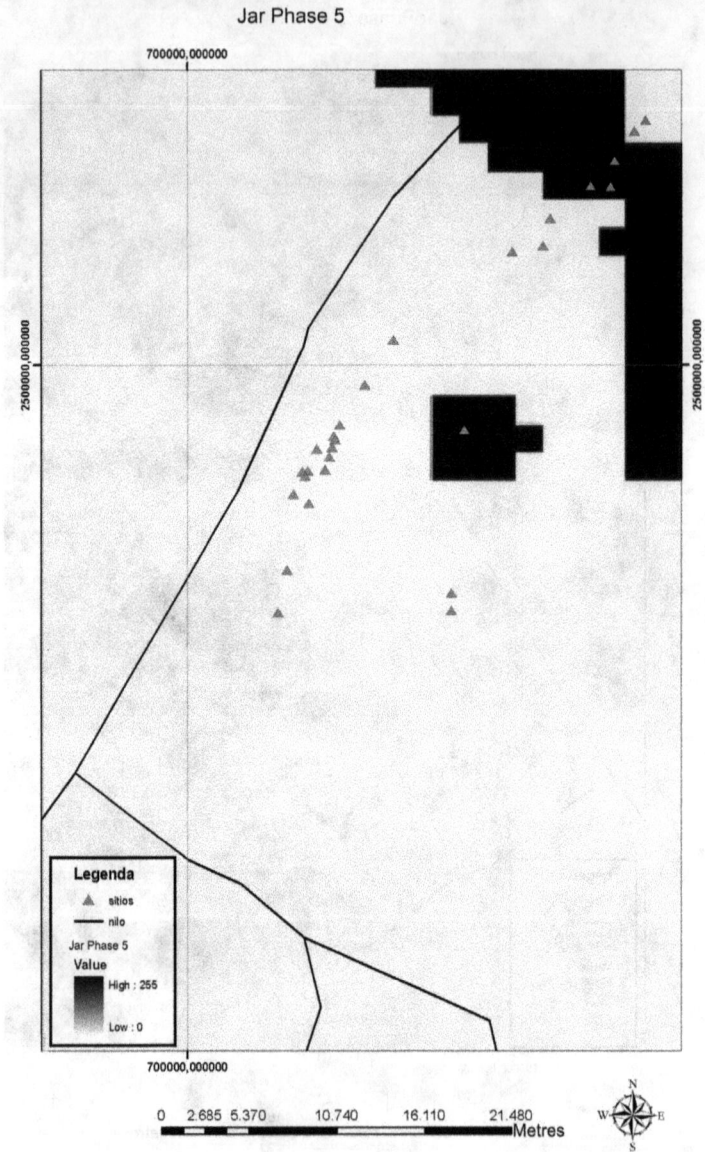

Figure 15.3. Jar Phase 5.

José Roberto Pellini

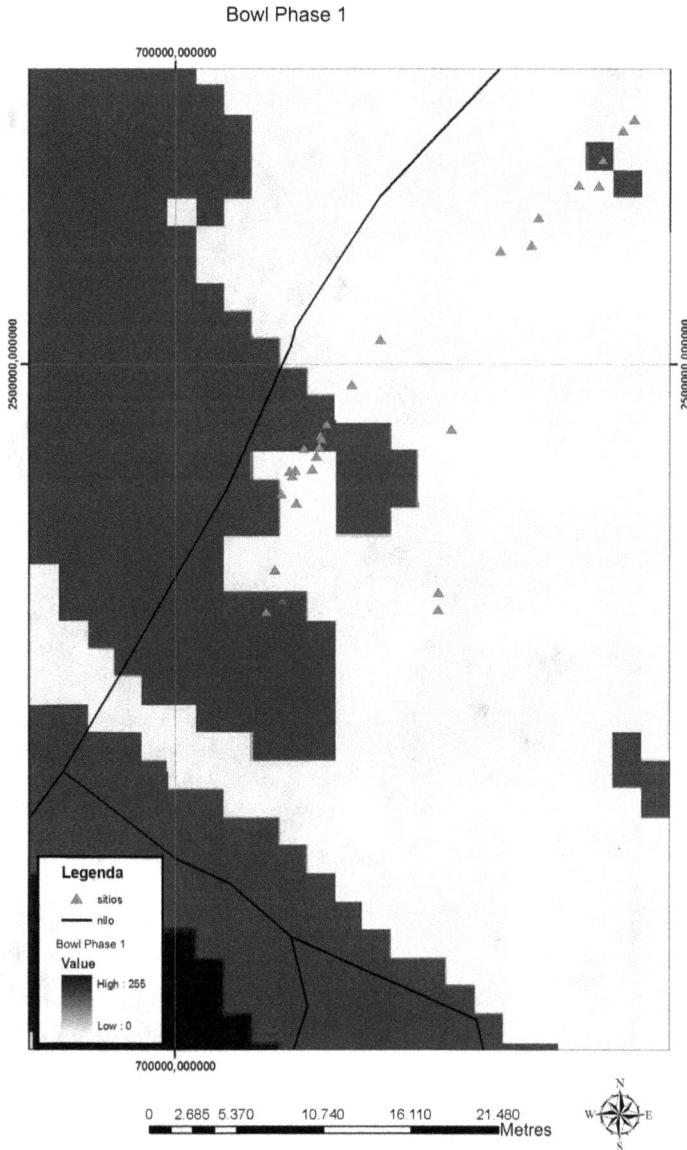

Bowl Phase 1

Legenda
sitios
nilo
Bowl Phase 1
Value
High : 255
Low : 0

0   2.685 5.370   10.740   16.110   21.480
                                                    Metres

Figure 15.4. Bowl Phase 1.

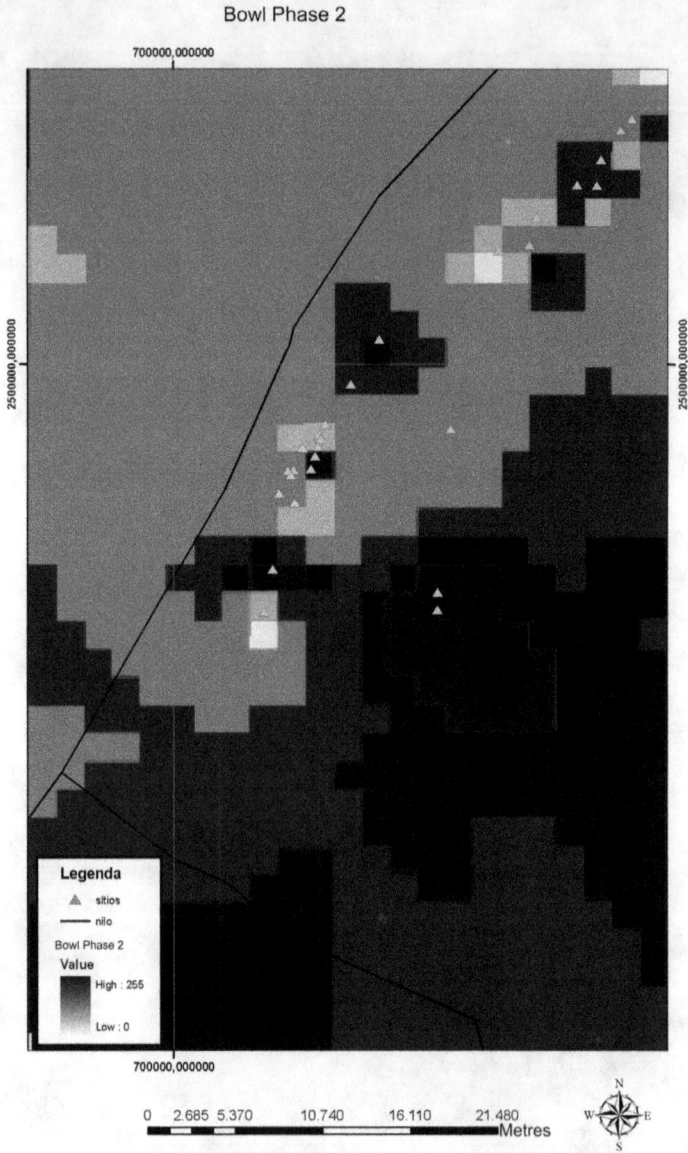

Bowl Phase 2

Figure 15.5. Bowl Phase 2.

José Roberto Pellini

Bowl Phase 5

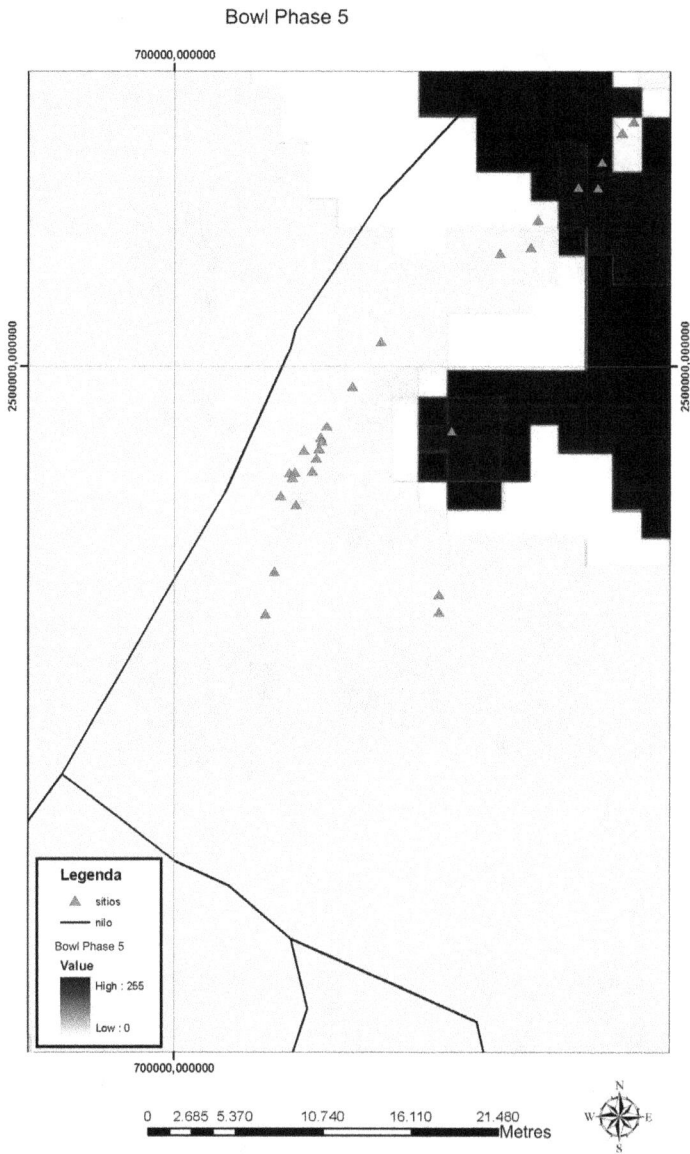

Figure 15.6. Bowl Phase 5.

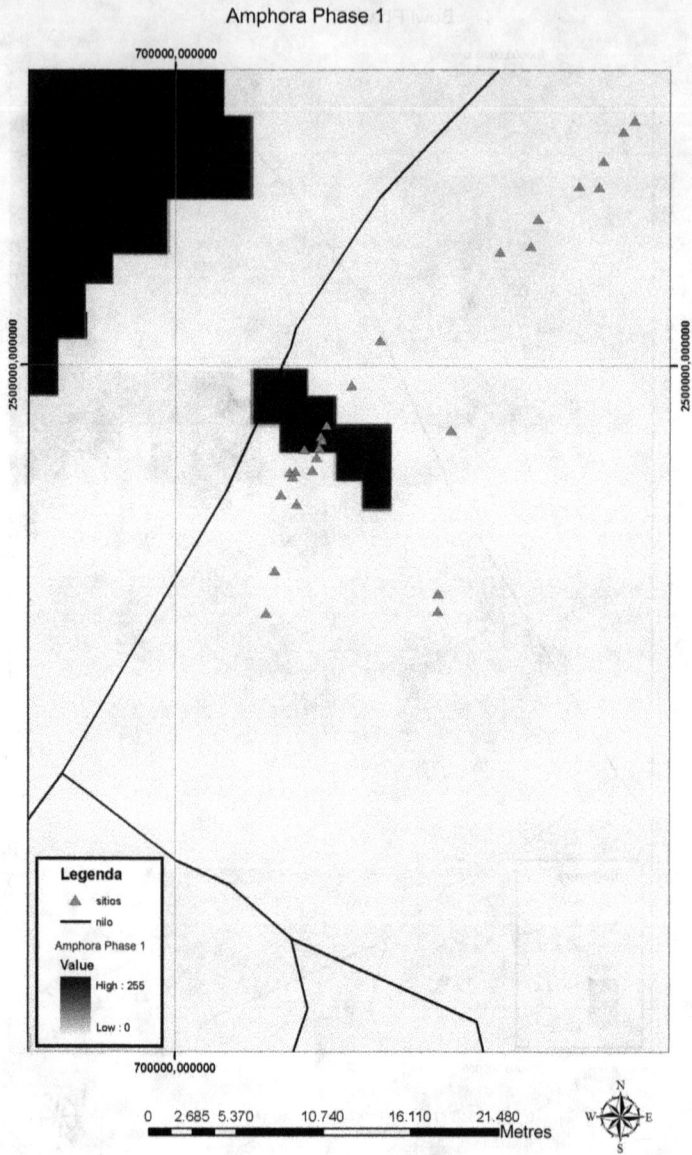

Amphora Phase 1

Figure 15.7. Amphora Phase 1.

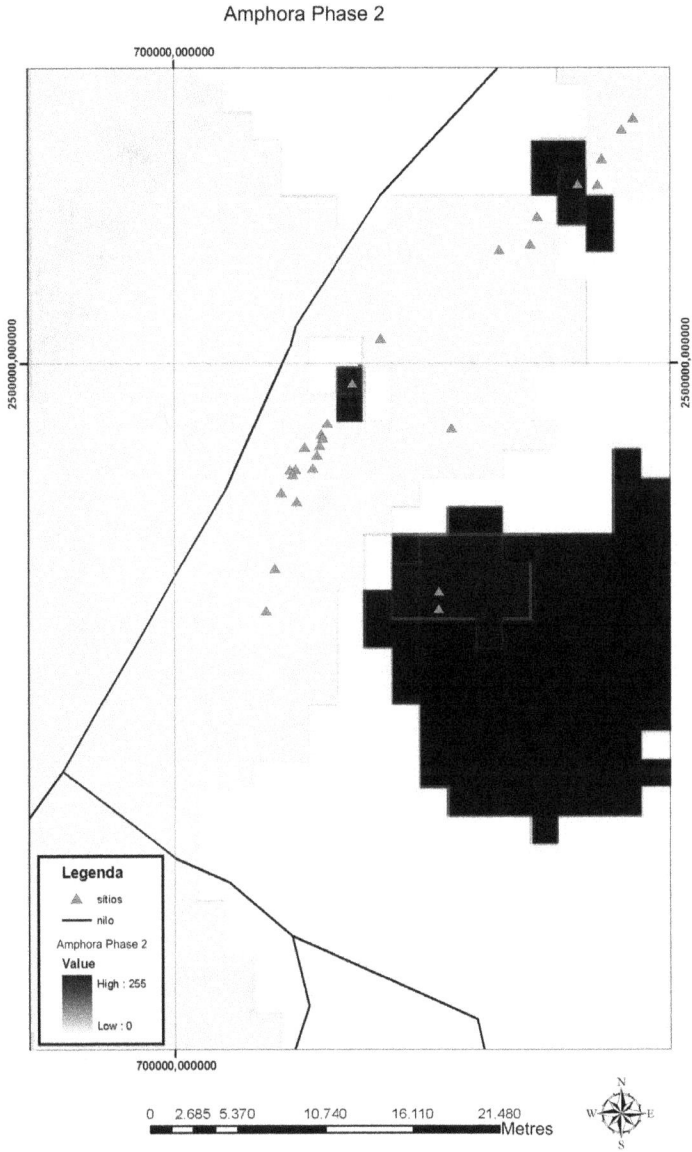

Figure 15.8. Amphora Phase 2.

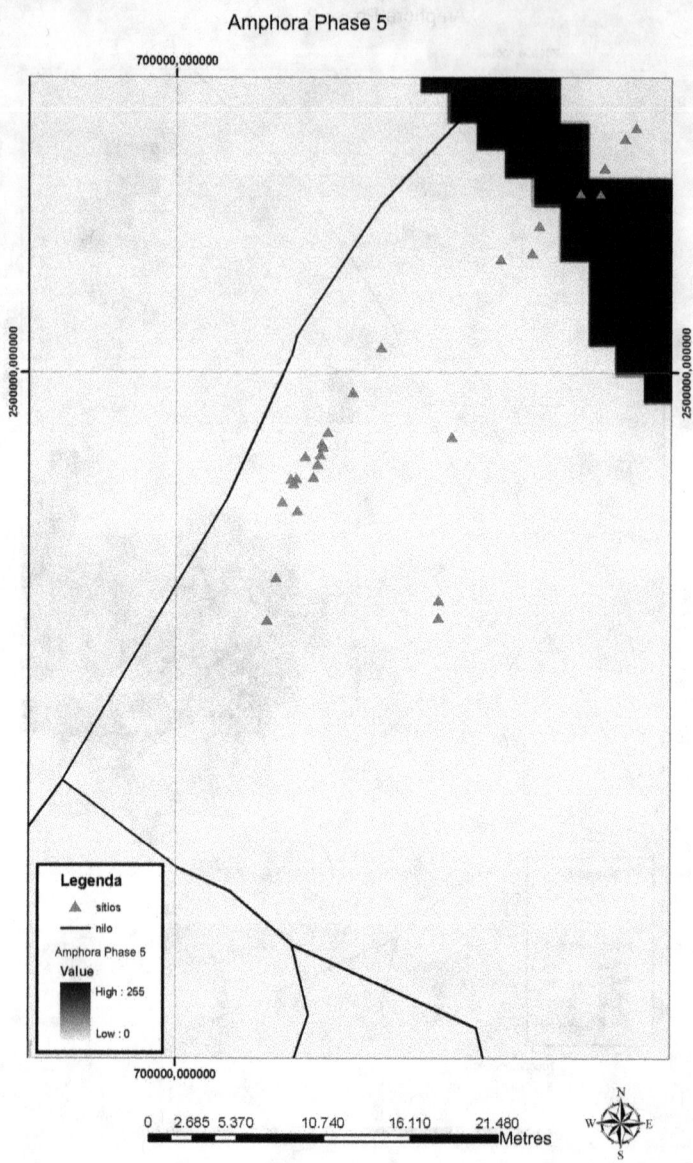

Figure 15.9. Amphora Phase 5.

JOSÉ ROBERTO PELLINI

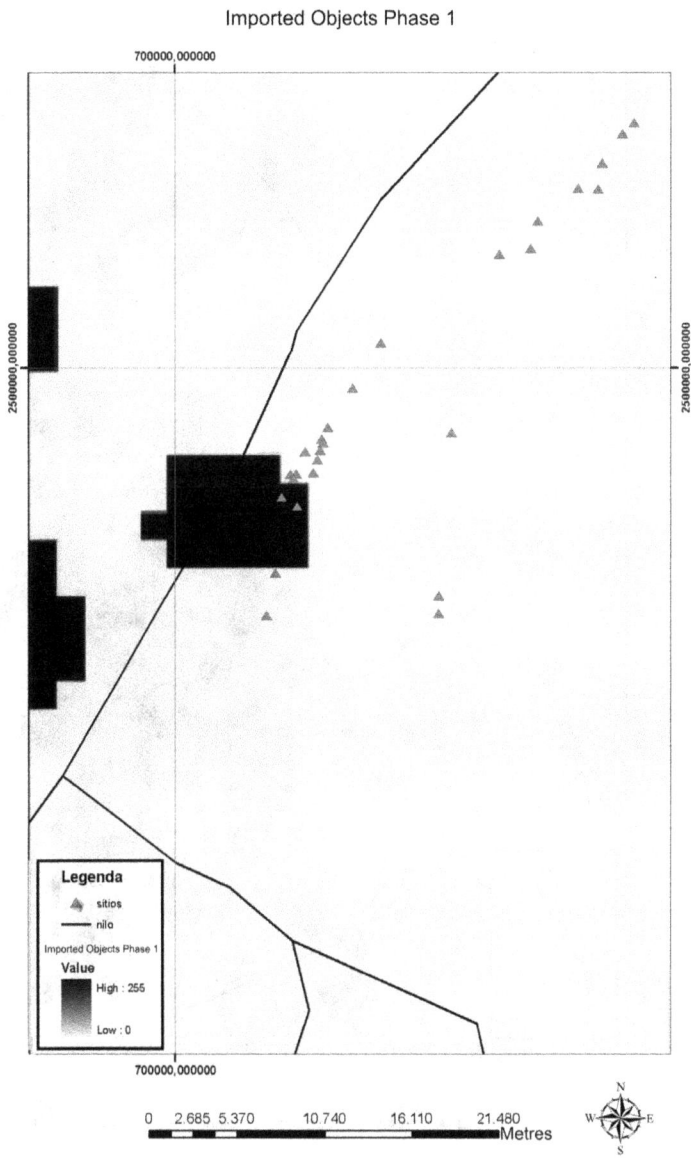

Imported Objects Phase 1

Figure 15.10. Imported Objects Phase 1.

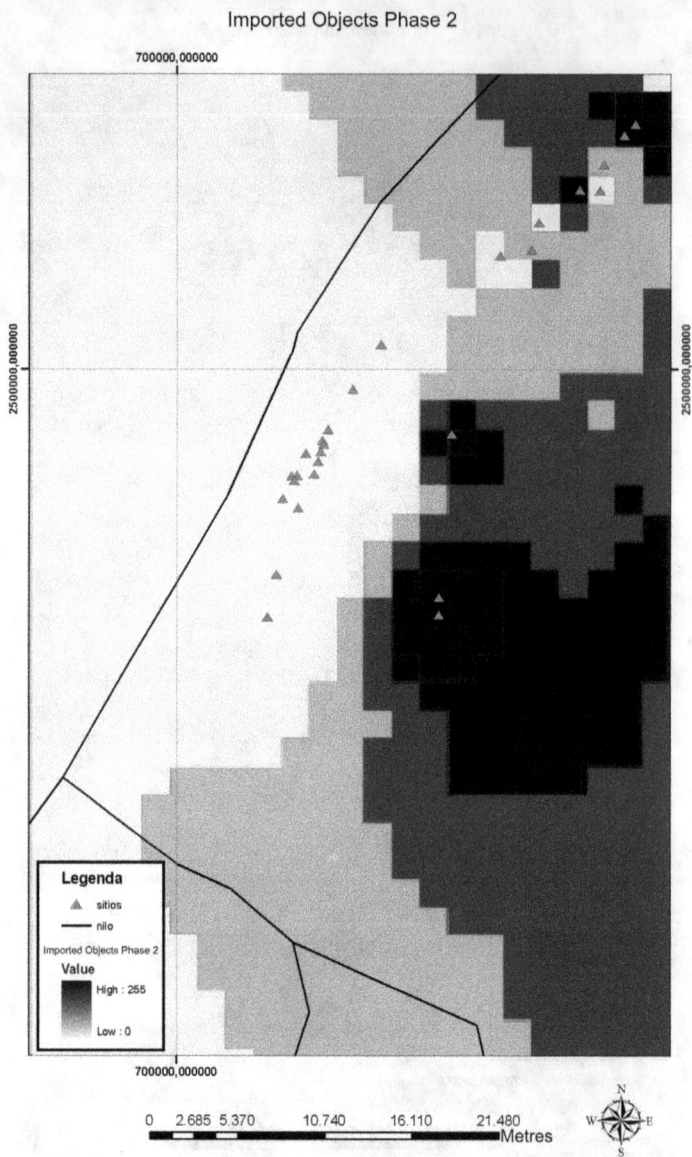

Figure 15.11. Imported Objects Phase 2.

JOSÉ ROBERTO PELLINI

Conclusion

After losing the political and economic control of Nubia during the Second Intermediate Period, the Egyptian state started a novel policy, that of reconquering Nubia in the beginning of the eighteenth dynasty. Old administrative centres were reconstructed and new forts were built. But what was the role of the Egyptians in Nubia? Was it settlement, exploration, reaffirmation of the real deity of the Egyptian government, or a policy of mutual benefit? Perhaps the answer can be found, at least in the initial phase of the eighteenth dynasty, in the great political and economic freedom enjoyed by the kingdom of Teh Khet, located between Debeira and Serra. According to Smith (1976), this little kingdom was left under the control of local princes, given that members of local families formed the majority of the bureaucratic sector. The Egyptian administration functioned in a higher sphere, mainly in matters related to the maintenance of local order.

The eventual freedom that the local government had made it possible for the people to have certain privileges, for example, access to imported products from Egypt. As it is affirmed by Säve-Söderbergh and Troy (1990), phase I of the Fadrus occupation is characterized by a generous and valuable distribution of goods, which made it possible for the high class and for part of the middle class to have direct access to goods of prestige and status. Therefore, the Egyptian policy in Nubia included a territorial dominance based on a balanced political relationship that aimed to generate mutual benefits for both sides.

During the middle part of the eighteenth dynasty (phases III and IV), Egyptian policy substitutes the old local high class for Egyptian bureaucrats. This act results in a significant reduction of the local high class. At the same time, there was a gradual shift of the administrative centres towards Dongola, in the south. This political shift leads to the weakness of the local economy at the old administrative centres. They lose their level of importance in the administration of the region. The consequence of this change can be observed in the burials that are analyzed below. In phases III, IV, and V of the occupation, there is a decline of the immobilized wealth in the tombs. At the same time, there is a significant increase in domestic items that are locally produced. This may be due to the disappearance of the old high class and to the increase in burials of members of the low class.

With these political and economic changes, the circulation patterns of products also change. In general, there is a drop in the intensity of circulation. In the beginning of the occupation (phase I), there was an increase in the circulation of ordinary and prestige objects. During the final phases of occupation (phases IV and V), the ordinary goods continued to circulate, but there was an almost complete reduction in the circulation of objects of value, such as metals, amphorae, imported wine jars, and other objects.

Based on the results of this analysis, two systems of exchange were in operation during the New Empire in Egypt and Nubia: a system that resulted in a diffuse and generalized circulation of goods and a system that resulted in a centric and directed circulation of goods. In the first system, ordinary objects and those in daily use circulated, and in the second system, prestige goods circulated.

In the areas where the presence of a diffuse circulation is observed, there is a system of direct circulation, that is, the members of each economic unit travel to other localities in order to acquire the products that they need. In this sense, the residents of each locality have to go to innumerable places to satisfy their needs, and this creates an increase in the distances covered, resulting in a similar increase of the transaction costs. In a direct system of distribution, for instance, as it occurs in the reciprocity case, in a set number of production points N, each producer would have the necessity to visit or to be visited by $N-1$ representatives of other localities so that there is a full distribution system operating, with one consequent express day for N of $(N-1)/2$. In systems like this there are increased interactions between individuals and so the objects leave their original point and travel, from one hand to another, until they reach their final destination.

As a greater number of people could be involved in these exchange systems, the maintenance of the social forces and good relations between neighbourhoods are some of the main factors sustaining the system. In this case, as is pointed out by Janssen (1994:135), everyone is a debtor and a creditor to someone else. Here the performance of the community is seen as proof of the willingness to participate with great generosity. The individuals that appear in this system are moral individuals. In the circulation maps (Figures 15.1–11), this system can be perceived where there is a predominance of areas with more gradations of black colour tones.

On the other hand, in the areas where focal and direct circulation is observed, the objects leave their original source and follow directly towards their destination without going through a great number of interactions. In this case there are probably movements of appropriation towards a centre and a subsequent distribution from this centre. This is an example of indirect circulation, where products and services of an economic unit are acquired in some central place; thus the individuals do not need to travel to different places to get the products that they desire. In indirect systems, such as redistribution or in market systems where a locality functions as a central place of distribution, the inhabitants of the nearby villages will have to travel only for a certain time, since the day can be expressed only for $N-1$. In the circulation maps, these systems can be perceived where there are concentration points. This happens because the products are being concentrated in local areas and being distributed around.

As was pointed out above, GIS has brought many advances in the study of ancient societies, mainly their exchange systems, but one must be careful when dealing with cultural data. This new model of cost surface analysis, a contextual cost surface analysis, is an attempt to adapt this new technology of GIS to the study of ancient societies. It is hoped that this research will contribute to a better understanding of past exchange systems.

References Cited

Hassan, Fekri

    1990   "Town and Village in Ancient Egypt: Ecology, Society and Urbanization." In *A History of African Archaeology*, edited by Peter Robertshaw, pp. 551–569. London, Portsmouth.

Janssen, Jack

    1994   "Debts and Credits in New Kingdom." In *Journal of Egyptian Archaeology* 80:129–136.

O'Connor, David

    1993   "Urbanism in bronze Age Egypt and Northeast Africa." In *A History of African Archaeology*, edited by Peter Robertshaw, pp. 570–586. London, Portsmouth.

Säve-Söderbergh, Torgny, and Lana Troy

    1990   *New Kingdom Pharaonic Sites: The Finds and the Sites.* The Scandinavian Joint Expedition to Sudanese Nubia, vol. 5:2. Scandinavian University Books, Copenhagen.

Smith, Henry S.

1976   *The Fortress of Buhen: The Inscriptions*. Egypt Exploration Society, Memoir 48. Egypt Exploration Society, London.

Williams, Bruce

1992   *New Kingdom Remains from Cemeteries R, V, S and W at Qustul and Cemetery K at Adindan*. Oriental Institute Nubian Expedition, vol. 6. Oriental Institute, Chicago.

16

A SPACE SYNTAX ANALYSIS OF DOHACK AND RANGE PHASE VILLAGES IN THE AMERICAN BOTTOM

Joshua J. Wells

Abstract. This paper describes methods and results of spatial analyses, based upon Space Syntax mathematics defined in Hillier and Hanson (1984). Base data came from maps of a set of eight Terminal Late Woodland (Emergent Mississippian) sites from the American Bottom of Illinois, built between AD 800 and 900, which belonged to the Dohack and Range phases. This study compared ratios of built space to open space in villages and made a metric comparison of the organization of open space in each site. Measurements were based upon the atomic organization of individual architectural components and their spatial relationships to one another. The data from this project suggest that, although the relative amounts of open space in the sites did not change, the organization of open space literally became more central through time. Sociocultural organizational implications are evaluated. Previous investigators did not note such patterns when they qualitatively described the built environment within these villages. The discrepancy suggests that Space Syntax methods may be useful for discerning archaeological trends in the built environment that are not otherwise readily apparent. Further testing in Mississippian and other archaeological contexts should be conducted to better determine the useful limits of Space Syntax as an analytical tool.

INTRODUCTION

This paper presents the results of spatial analyses made upon a set of Terminal Late Woodland (Emergent Mississippian) sites from American Bottom, using models and ideas based upon the techniques described in *The Social Logic of Space*, by Hillier and Hanson (1984). A number of authors were important in the development of this paper (Banning and Byrd 1989; Ferguson 1994; Foster 1989; Potter 1998; Van Dyke 1999). The intent was to test the utility of Space Syntax methodology as a tool to recognize spatial signatures among eight Emergent Mississippian communities in the American Bottom of Illinois, directly east of St. Louis, on the opposite side of the Mississippi River (Figure 16.1). These settlements are all components of the Range Site (11-S-47), five from the Dohack phase and three from the Range phase, which are adjacent in the American Bottom chronology at AD 800–850, and 850–900, respectively (Bareis and Porter 1984:129,134).

The general patterning of Mississippian architectural elements is well documented throughout the Midwest and Southeast of the United States. Mississippians arranged their towns around a central plaza. The organization of individual houses and group neighbourhoods served to accentuate this arrangement. The addition of palisade walls for controlling access to the towns added a further level of spatial definition, when present. The presence of mounds added another level of spatial definition, often providing a focal point for the plaza. These mounds were usually truncated pyramids, the tops of which were reserved for communal ceremonies, residences of important families, or charnel houses for honoured ancestors; however, many varieties of shapes have been recorded (Lewis et al. 1998). The Range site is about twenty kilometres from what would become the largest Mississippian site of Cahokia, which rapidly expanded about AD 1050 at the beginning of the early Mississippian period (Pauketat 2004). Many accomplished investigators have used the archaeological record of the Range site's earlier communities to trace the material remnants of later Mississippian culture in the American Bottom. Others have discussed the sociocultural implications of various Range site settlement plans in conjunction with changes in their artefact assemblages. Kelly (1990) and Fortier and McElrath (2002) have discussed the village plans of phases at the Range site, not included here, that preceded and succeeded those described in this paper.

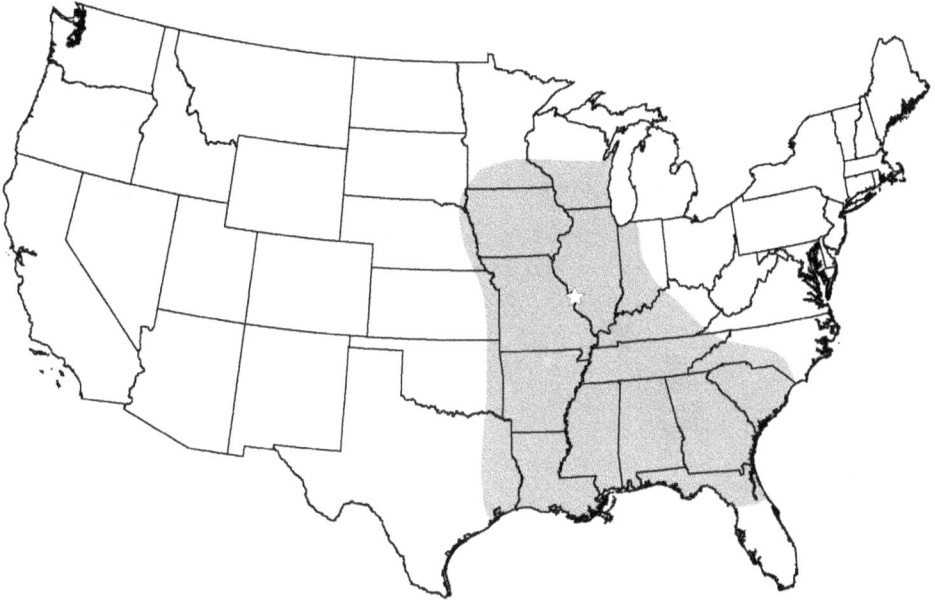

Figure 16.1. The extent of Mississippian influence in North America. The American Bottom is denoted by the star. Based upon maps in Hall (2000:12, 24) and Townsend (2004:13).

This paper tests a methodology which can mathematically describe some of these plans (these spatial syntaxes) and tests whether they may be differentiated in a quantitatively spatial manner, rather than in the illustrative, prosaic fashion that dominates the archaeological literature.

HOW SPACE SYNTAX WORKS

Put simply, Space Syntax is the study of open space that is bounded and divided by human construction (Figure 16.2). As people build the environment of their dwellings, hamlets, villages, and cities, subtle (and direct) manifestations of their perceptions towards order will begin to develop. In *The Social Logic of Space* (Hillier and Hanson 1984), its two authors studied, most notably, small villages in the French countryside, attempting to find patterns and meaning in the seemingly haphazard routines of their growth. Their notion of elementary formulae may be used to describe any arrangement of buildings based upon their most basic components (the common shape of a building and its orientation to others of this kind). When perceived in a recursive pattern, these elementary formulae will use their low-level attributes to form a more grandiose structure, analogous perhaps to atoms forming a molecule (Hillier and Hanson 1984:77–81).

The "*y* space," or open space, is the most important variable within the mechanisms of Space Syntax. The differences of how constructions relate to one another is immense; thus, Hillier and Hanson (1984) have developed several different ways of examining *y* space. These relationships are robustly quantitative and, as such, require well-made original maps in order to create new maps that interpret the *y* space as organized by the constructions, *X*. The basic elements of *y* space study are convex spaces and axial spaces. For brevity's sake, this paper only addresses the convex space of the Range and Dohack phase settlements.

X: human construction that occupies Y space and defines y space.

x: open spaces that are bound by human definition to X, such as courtyards and gardens. This space is binding towards y space.

y: open space within an area bounded by X and/or x.

Y: carrier space that contains X, x, and y; the whole of two-dimensional open space exterior to the boundaries of human construction.

Figure 16.2. Definitions of space by Hillier and Hanson (1984).

Convex spaces are entirely convex on the exterior of their boundary and entirely concave on the interior of their boundary (Figure 16.3). Their analytical definition was described by Ferguson (1994):

> The procedure for producing convex maps is essentially a visual one. First the boundary of the largest convex space in the settlement is delineated, then the next largest, and so on until all spaces have been sub-divided into convex spaces. The property of convexity translated into human behaviour means that in a flat convex space any two people that can be seen by a third person can also see each other. [Ferguson 1994:16]

To investigate the arrangement of convex space, we must first recognize the X and x constructions that bind and determine the organization of the y space. In this archaeological context, it means delineating the boundaries of a site and the position of each building within that site. This is necessary for any quantification involving the gross numbers of the constructions and convex spaces involved, and also for methods which need specific geographic measurements of perimeter and area. Secondly, the relationships between the buildings must be determined – taking specific notice of those buildings that conjoin or are built so closely to one another that they effectively leave no y space between them (this phenomenon is called an island, islands are the defining built feature that breaks up open space into convex pieces).

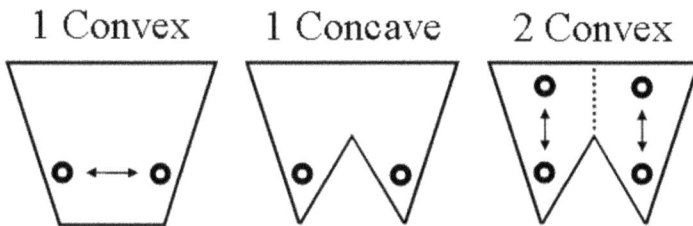

Figure 16.3. Examples of one convex space (l), one concave space (m), and one concave space divided into two convex spaces for analysis (r); based upon Ferguson (1994).

The first measurement of convex space is the *convex articulation* from Hillier and Hanson (1984). This is a measurement of the synchrony of a site, where synchrony is defined as the relative quantity of space invested in the set of syntactic relations at that site (Hillier and Hanson 1984:92). Convex articulation is defined as: (number of convex spaces) / (number of buildings). See Figure 16.4. The larger the quotient is, the greater the break-up of the *y* space is, yielding less synchrony. This can be easily conceived if you consider Figures 16.5a and 16.5b, where the more ordered graph has fewer convex spaces than the scattered one. The more ordered graph is also more synchronous, with a lower convex articulation value (Hillier and Hanson 1984:92–3, 98).

The second measurement of convex space is the *grid convexity score*, again from Hillier and Hanson (1984:99). This considers the layout of a site in relation to the most perfect orthogonal grid that might be formed using the built components of the site. Grid convexity uses the notion of islands, mentioned above, and is defined as: $\{[(\text{number of islands})^{0.5} + 1]^2\}$ / (number of convex spaces). The quotients given by this function will range between 0 and 1, where 1 is representative of a perfect grid. See Figures 16.4, 16.5a, and 16.5b.

James Potter (1998) expanded upon Hillier and Hanson's (1984) definitions and suggested his own *integration score* to study the organization of convex *y* space within an archaeological site. Potter (1998) found that he needed a way of overcoming spatial differences that were a product of scale but were not necessarily related to the recursion of atomic construction practices. By accounting for the size of the three largest convex polygons in a site, in relationship to the available amount of open area, he could better characterize the morphology of open space. He wrote:

> This method allows the efficient comparison of sites of radically different morphological configuration and scale. In addition, this method is sensitive along both spatial dimensions to changes in open space structure over time, and can thus help isolate the variable involved in the long term integrative strategies adopted by a particular settlement. (Potter 1998:143)

Integration is defined as: (a/b) / (b/c). In this formula, a = the sum of the areas of the three largest convex polygons, b = the total open area of the site (y space, or total site area minus the area occupied by houses), c = total site area (Potter 1998:140). See Figure 16.4.

JOSHUA J. WELLS

Convex Articulation:	$\dfrac{\text{(number of convex spaces)}}{\text{(number of buildings)}}$
(per Hillier and Hanson [1984])	

Grid Convexity:	$\dfrac{\{\{[(\text{number of islands})^{\wedge}0.5] + 1\}^{\wedge}2\}}{\text{(number of convex spaces)}}$
(per Hillier and Hanson [1984])	

Integration Score:	(a/b)
(per Potter [1998])	(b/c)

a = the sum of the areas of the three largest polygons
b = the total open area of the site (y space)
c = total site area

Figure 16.4. Ratio formulae for characterizing convex space.

THE RANGE SITE

The Range site was chosen because of the large number of sequential villages it contained. The investigated villages span a period of little more than a hundred years, perhaps five generations. During that century, material culture, domestic structures, and settlement patterns changed from earlier Woodland forms into a sequence closer to that of the early Mississippian period.

The Dohack phase (AD 800–850) is the first Emergent Mississippian culture recognized by the American Bottom excavators. It is represented in several other sites along the modern I–270 corridor, construction of which prompted the excavation. The Dohack phase is considered to exhibit a number of ancestral traits from the preceding Late Woodland Patrick phase (AD 600–800), most notably in the ceramic traditions, where jars dominate and most items

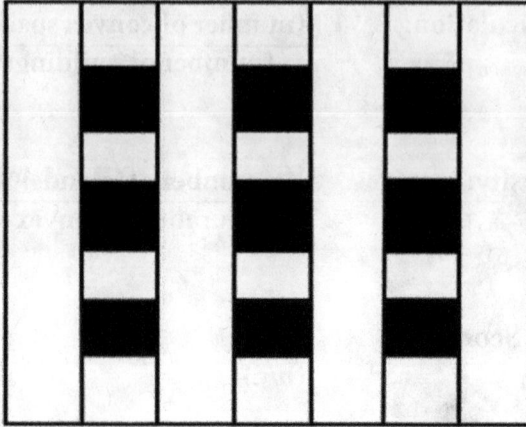

16 Convex Spaces / 9 Buildings = Convex Articulation 1.78

$((((9\ \text{Buildings})^{0.5}) + 1)^2)\ /\ 16\ \text{Convex Spaces} = \text{Grid Convexity } 1.0$

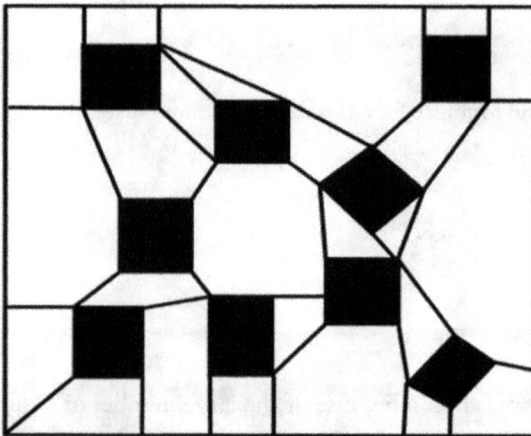

25 Convex Spaces / 9 Buildings = Convex Articulation 2.78

$((((9\ \text{Buildings})^{0.5}) + 1)^2)\ /\ 25\ \text{Convex Spaces} = \text{Grid Convexity } 0.64$

Figure 16.5. a. An ordered orthogonal grid. b. A deformed orthogonal grid.

are covered with cord-markings. Furthermore, people of the Dohack phase are considered to have been the first to produce maize in large quantities (Bareis and Porter 1984:129–134).

The structural features of the Dohack phase are considered to represent a social and spiritual model through their incorporation of a central square, with either a large, single structure, or four smaller ones contained within that space. John Kelly (1990) suggested that this was an early indication of the circle-and-cross theme associated with a fire and sun deity complex. He noted that in ethnohistoric accounts the four corners of this central space were marked by logs oriented to the cardinal directions. The central building or clump of four structures in each Dohack phase area does indeed appear to be representative of this sort of spatial structure. Often a sacred fire would burn in the centre of the square ground. Its flames were perhaps recognized as an agent of the sun, who was the people's source of food and religious knowledge. This central area might also be the location of the Green Corn Ceremony, a religious rite that incorporated the first ripening corn of the season and would have been of vital social importance (Kelly et al. 1990:289–96).

The Range phase (AD 850–900) ceramic assemblage is comprised by approximately 50 per cent jars, followed closely by bowls (41%). The jars and bowls are generally cord-marked (about the neck in jars), and the jars have squared lips, sometimes with lugs. Both are tempered mainly with limestone, though there is a minor use of grog and grit (28% total). Although pottery temper does not permit an easy differentiation from the preceding Dohack phase, the more elaborate Range phase design motifs are useful markers (Bareis and Porter 1984:134–40).

During the Range phase, some of the habitations contained interior courtyards, while in others the buildings were aligned to form rows. Clustering of buildings is not as prominent as in the preceding Dohack phase. Range phase habitations were generally smaller in size and contained fewer houses. Bareis and Porter (1984:140) wrote that Range phase habitations are considered to come in at least three different types of community pattern. One of these is analogous to the earlier Dohack formations, with a circular organization of structures surrounding a central area that contains a post pit in the centre. This is an example of a statement that can be re-evaluated, on the terms of Space Syntax, using the Range phase settlements' metric attributes.

Methodology

To produce the convex maps, I undertook a rubric similar to that of Ferguson (1994) in his volume *Historic Zuni Architecture and Society*. Ferguson (1994) noted that Hillier and Hanson (1984) neglected to supply mechanisms for demarcating boundaries on built areas that lack noticeable ending points (such as a road, wall, or natural object). To relieve this problem, Ferguson (1994) put an arbitrary ten-metre edge beyond all of the Zuni pueblos that he was going to study. In this vein, there is an arbitrary five-metre boundary beyond the farthest edges of the buildings under consideration.

The maps were overlaid with their individual convex attributes, then scanned in order to work with them in Erdas Imagine GIS software. Using the grid points on the Dohack and Range phase settlement maps, each settlement was spatially referenced. The distance and area measurement techniques of the software generated the data needed for the formulas important to this study (total area, largest three polygons' areas, and structural [house] area). See Figures 16.6a,b, 16.7a,b for examples of excavation and convex space maps.

Results

As can be seen in Table 16.1, along with Figures 16.8 and 16.9, the Dohack and Range phases at the Range site can at least be separated in their spatial typologies with the technique forwarded by Potter (1998), but not necessarily those directly from Hillier and Hanson (1984). The range of measures for grid convexity and convex articulation are overlapping between the two phases. However, there is a complete separation of the two groupings based upon integration scores and the percentage of areas contained within the three largest convex polygons.

Table 16.1. Summary Data for Convex Spaces in Range Site Settlements. Sites are listed chronologically from top to bottom per Kelly (1990). One Dohack phase settlement (D-6) and three Range phase settlements (R-3, R-4a/b, R-6) were inappropriate for this preliminary investigation.

SITE	H	I	CS	CART	GC	TA	HA	%O	C1	C2	C3	%A3P	IS
D2	35	32	62	1.77	0.71	3,778	188	0.95	508	335	239	0.30	0.32

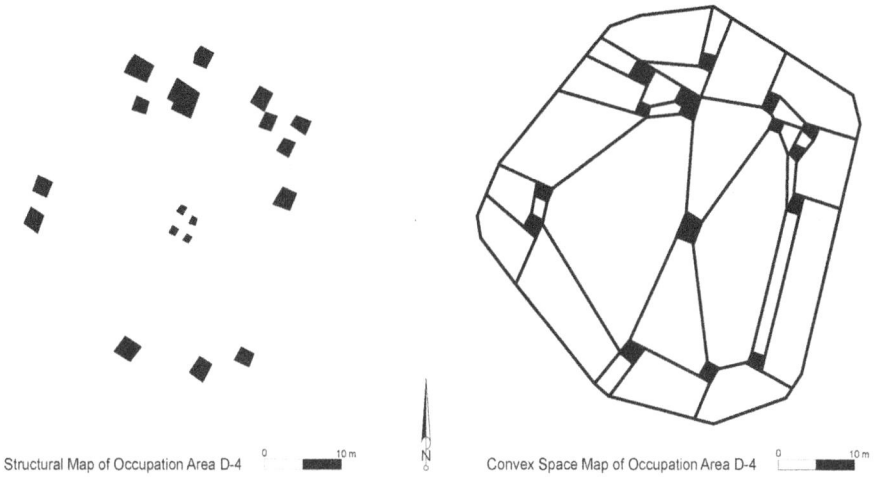

Figure 16.6. a. Excavation map of Occupation Area D-4, based upon Kelly et al. (1990). b. Convex space map of Occupation Area D-4, based upon Kelly et al. (1990).

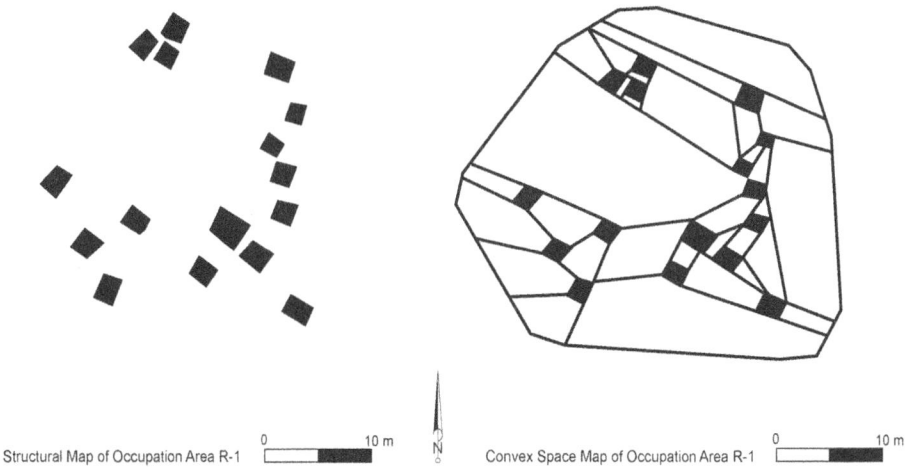

Figure 16.7. a. Excavation map of Occupation Area R-1, based upon Kelly et al. (1990). b. Convex space map of Occupation Area R-1, based upon Kelly et al. (1990).

	H	I	CS	CART	GC	TA	HA	%O	C1	C2	C3	%A3P	IS
D5	25	25	47	1.88	0.77	2,067	118	0.94	253	237	194	0.35	0.37
D4	16	13	31	1.94	0.68	1,994	65	0.97	369	243	135	0.39	0.40
D3	10	11	24	2.40	0.78	1,119	41	0.96	288	117	97	0.47	0.48
D1	19	16	35	1.84	0.71	1,583	76	0.95	217	166	160	0.36	0.38
R5	10	8	21	2.10	0.70	1,169	40	0.97	327	167	141	0.56	0.58
R2	22	18	41	1.86	0.67	1,877	94	0.95	628	164	141	0.52	0.55
R1	16	15	30	1.88	0.79	1,067	82	0.92	248	143	108	0.51	0.55
AVG D	21	19	40	1.97	0.73	2,108	98	0.96	327	220	165	0.37	0.39
AVG R	16	14	31	1.95	0.72	1,371	72	0.95	401	158	130	0.53	0.56

H: number of houses
I: number of islands
CS: number of convex spaces
CART: convex articulation
GC: grid convexity
TA: total area in square metres
HA: area of houses in square metres
%O: percentage of site open (%y)
C1, C2, C3: areas of three largest convex polygons in square metres
%A3P: percentage of y space covered by the three largest polygons
IS: integration score

The two phases may be described as follows: The Dohack phase, on average, contains more houses, islands, convex spaces, and sites than the Range phase – this was noted by the excavators in several studies in as far as they discussed size and spatial complexity. The two phases have very similar convex articulations, indicating that the break-up of their open y space among their X buildings, while slightly more in the Range phase, is not terribly divergent from

JOSHUA J. WELLS

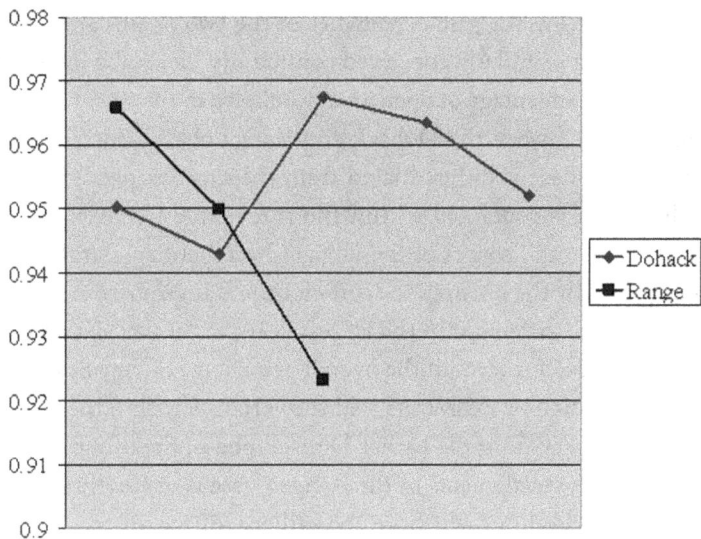

Figure 16.8. Percentage of open space (y) in Range site settlements. Sites for each phase are arranged chronologically from left to right per Kelly (1990) so that the rightmost Dohack settlement is D-1, and is followed in time by the leftmost Range settlement R-5.

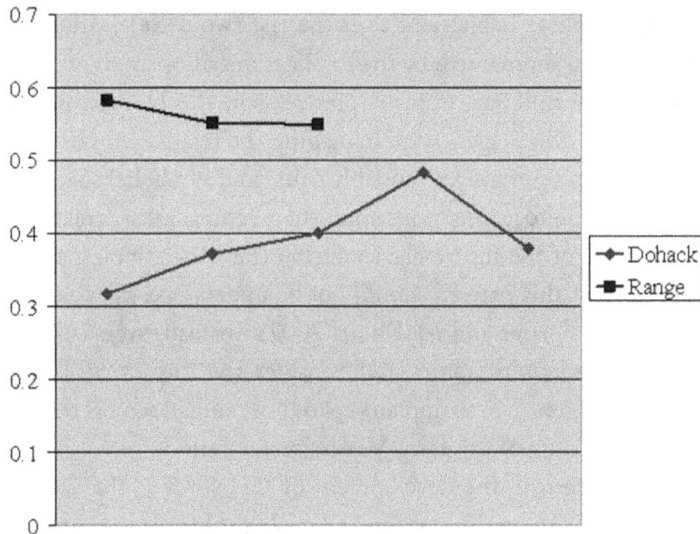

Figure 16.9. Integration scores for Range site settlements. Sites for each phase are arranged chronologically from left to right per Kelly (1990) so that the rightmost Dohack settlement is D-1, and is followed in time by the leftmost Range settlement R-5.

what it was previously. The grid convexities of the two phases are very similar, perhaps indicative of similarly conceived community ideals about spatial order.

Although the percentage of open area, y, relative to the site as a whole, does not change much between the Dohack and Range phases, the allocation of it does. The Range phase is differentiated from the Dohack phase in that much more of the y area is contained within the three largest convex polygons. In other words, the central spaces of the villages become much larger during the Range phase. Finally the integration scores for the Range phase are higher. This is mainly due to the difference in the largest polygons' y area since the integration score also takes into account the overall percentage of y space within a site. Despite the suggestion by excavators that the variation within the Range phase settlements is a legacy from the earlier Dohack phase, the overall morphology of y space within the settlements of the Range phase is distinctly separate from the y space morphology of those from the earlier Dohack phase.

SUMMARY

The observations of the researchers who have worked on the Range Site's Dohack and Range phase habitations over the last two decades are in some ways supported, but also augmented, by the implications of Space Syntax. The Range phase is distinctly different from its predecessor, the Dohack phase, regarding the way in which villagers were managing the relationship between private habitation areas and communal (possibly ritual and symbolic) space. The Range phase villagers were focusing more upon their central areas, creating a pattern more reminiscent of the future plazas during the Mississippian period proper. The recognition of this pattern should not be understood as evolutionary or as deterministic (cf. Fortier and McElrath 2002). Instead, archaeologists should vary their conceptions of space, and consider the impact of Terminal Late Woodland (Emergent Mississippian) spatial organizations on the milieu that sparked the beginning of the early Mississippian period.

A major concern in the development of this study is the accuracy of the maps used, and the limitations of the archaeological focus that produced them. I by no means fault the excavators but rather acknowledge the fact that as archaeologists we must work with what is left to us by all the ravages of time. It is likely that these maps do not represent the fine details within the various

JOSHUA J. WELLS

settlements during their occupations, where screens, pits, scaffolds, and other relatively ephemeral constructs would also break up the open y space. Also, even in the short life spans of these habitations, it is not possible to say what the exact pattern of building construction and demolition was, thus obscuring possible changes in the syntactic pattern. However, these limitations can be overcome, or at least mitigated through detailed consideration. The methodologies created by Hillier and Hanson (1984), and expanded by their readers, are robust and deserve a chance to perhaps blossom in a new archaeological environment.

For future investigations, it may be useful to study macro-blocks of buildings, rather than individual buildings, in sites where the number of X entities permits. This amalgamation might also permit the use of blocks of pits which suggest structures over them, or would in the very least restrict activity in their vicinities, although they must be separated from exterior storage and refuse pits that are scattered within the sites as X entities in their own right. Accounting for more facets in spatial reconstruction could provide a more realistic picture of the syntactic space in a Mississippian village, but it will take a great deal of concerted effort. If that is not possible, other methods should be devised and tested to attempt to gain more thorough understandings of site planning on the part of (pre)Mississippian peoples. Not least in importance are the villages and hamlets of the countryside, which, by the principles of elementary formulae, as described by Hillier and Hanson (1984), should reflect the notions of space that are writ large in Mississippian centres.

Although Hillier and Hanson (1984) have been critiqued for suggesting Durkheimian traits may be associated with various forms of space structure (Batty 1985; Lawrence 1986), and even though some employers of Space Syntax have attempted to create other proofs of cultural theory with graphs, the typological aspects of Space Syntax appeal to me the most. It may be possible, with enough information, to trace the development of Mississippian spatial organizational traits across time and geography throughout the extent of Mississippian influence. This could inform investigators testing for either the diffusion or the independent rise of Mississippian organizational values. Such a model would be useful, transferable, and testable; more so than a solely localized and subjective explanation of spatial patterning.

Acknowledgments: I thank Dr. P. Dawson for the opportunity to present this work to a group of interested peers and for inspiring broader anthropological interest in

Space Syntax. This work was made possible by the generous support of the Glenn A. Black Laboratory of Archaeology at Indiana University (IU), and its director, Dr. C. S. Peebles. Finally, I thank Dr. P. Munson, of IU, who allowed this unique experiment for a term paper and who provided useful guidance about where to find the best maps. All errors belong to the author.

REFERENCES CITED

Banning, Edward B., and Brian F. Byrd

1989 Alternative Approaches for Exploring Levantine Neolithic Architecture. *Paleorient* 15(1):154–60.

Bareis, Charles J., and James W. Porter (editors)

1984 *American Bottom Archaeology*. University of Illinois Press, Urbana.

Batty, Michael

1985 Review of *The Social Logic of Space*, by Bill Hillier and Julienne Hanson. *Sociology* 19(1):161–2.

Ferguson, Thomas J.

1994 *Historic Zuni Architecture and Society: An Archaeological Application of Space Syntax*. University of Arizona Press, Tucson.

Fortier, Andrew C., and Dale L. McElrath

2002 Deconstructing the Emergent Mississippian Concept: The Case for Terminal Late Woodland in the American Bottom. *Midcontinental Journal of Archaeology* 27(2):171–215.

Foster, Sally M.

1989 Analysis of Spatial Patterns in Buildings (Access Analysis) as an Insight Into Social Structure: Examples from the Scottish Atlantic Iron Age. *Antiquity* 63:40–50.

Hillier, Bill, and Julienne Hanson

1984 *Social Logic of Space*. Cambridge University Press, New York.

Kelly, John E.

1990 Range Site Community Patterns and Mississippian Emergence. In *The Mississippian Emergence*, edited by B.D. Smith, pp. 67–112. Smithsonian Institution Press, Washington, D.C.

Kelly, John E., Steven J. Ozuk, and Joyce A. Williams

1990   *The Range Site 2: The Emergent Mississippian Dohack and Range Phase Occupations (11-S-47).* American Bottom Archaeology, FAI-270 Site Reports, vol. 20. University of Illinois Press, Urbana.

Lawrence, Roderick J.

1986   Review of *The Social Logic of Space*, by Bill Hillier and Julienne Hanson. *Anthropos* 81:331.

Lewis, R. Barry, Charles Stout, and Cameron B. Wesson

1998   The Design of Mississippian Towns. In *Mississippian Towns and Sacred Spaces: Searching for an Architectural Grammar*, edited by R.B. Lewis and C. Stout, pp. 1–21. University of Alabama Press, Tuscaloosa.

Pauketat, Timothy R.

2004   *Ancient Cahokia and the Mississippians.* Cambridge University Press, New York.

Potter, James M.

1998   The Structure of Open Space in Late Prehistoric Settlements in the Southwest. In *Migration and Reorganization: The Pueblo IV Period in the American Southwest*, edited by K.A. Spielmann, pp. 137–163. Arizona State University Anthropological Research Papers, No. 51. Arizona State University Press, Phoenix.

Van Dyke, Ruth M.

1999   Space Syntax Analysis at the Chacoan Outlier of Guadalupe. *American Antiquity* 64(3):461–473.

17

THE SPATIAL MORPHOLOGY OF DEFICIENT SAMPLES: APPLYING 'SPATIAL STRING-MATCHING' METHODS TO AN INCOMPLETE DATA OF VERNACULAR HOUSES

Ciler Kirsan and Ruth Conroy Dalton

Abstract. Most of the architectural and archaeological studies that use space syntax methods to investigate the spatial morphology of houses employ cases that are perfectly recorded and exclude incomplete ones, as clearly labelled complete architectural plan layouts are usually considered for space syntax analysis. However, there are situations in which one would need to piece together the story from a series of clues present in an incomplete and imperfect data set as is usually found in vernacular and archaeological cases. This study, which is one of those, deals with one group of 'clear' and another of 'unclear' cases gathered retrospectively through first-hand observation and fieldwork from rural Cyprus and attempts to show how far it would be possible to make a prediction about unclear cases by extrapolating from analogous clear examples with the help of a recent technique known as 'spatial string-matching.' In order to be able to investigate the spatial morphology of 'deficient' samples and to predict unclear cases from analogous clear ones, certain analytical strategies have been developed that couple the well-documented and tested methods of space syntax with the technique of string-matching. String-matching evaluates how similar each individual case is to all the others in a sample with a value called 'similarity.' This method, together with the concept of the 'inequality genotype' in space syntax, has been employed in this paper for the syntactical analysis of an incomplete data of houses.

INTRODUCTION

Space syntax technique is a major tool in both architectural and archaeological studies, as a means for analyzing spatial morphology of built environments. Most of the architectural and archaeological studies which use space syntax methods to investigate the spatial morphology of houses, employ cases that are perfectly recorded and exclude incomplete ones, as clearly labelled, spatially accurate architectural plan layouts are essential in Space Syntax analysis (Chapman 1990; Cooper 1997; Dawson 2002; Gilchrist 1994; Kirsan 2005; Orhun 1997). However there are situations, which one would need to piece together the spatial history of a house from the series of clues present in an incomplete and/or imperfect data set as usually found in vernacular and archaeological cases (Bustard 1997; Düring 2001; Kirsan 2003; Shapiro 1997).

This study, which is one of those, deals with two groups of 'clear' and 'unclear' vernacular houses from rural Cyprus, gathered retrospectively through first-hand observations and fieldwork, and attempts to show how far it would be possible to reconstruct the unclear cases from the evidence of surviving remains, with the help of a recent technique of spatial analysis known as 'string-matching.' Unlike most of the archaeological studies of prehistoric buildings, which consist mainly of unclear cases, this study enjoys the privilege of dealing with some clear cases besides the unclear ones provided by standing architectural evidence. The clear cases are taken as a yardstick or base data, against which clues are investigated to predict the unclear ones. The prediction is based on the theory of genotypes first introduced by Hillier and Hanson (Hillier and Hanson 1984), and the use of Multimatch,[1] a tool to automate and apply the prediction in a systematic manner with the aid of an expert knowledge of vernacular architecture.

Space syntax theory and tools have been widely used in housing research for investigating their spatial morphology (Amorim 1999; Brown and Tahar 2001; Hanson 1998; Hillier et al. 1987; Kirsan 2003; Orhun et al. 1995, 1996;

CILER KIRSAN AND RUTH CONROY DALTON

Shoul 1993; Trigueiro 1994). The key methodological device for these studies has been the uncovering of spatial and spatio-functional consistencies or 'genotypes,' as Hillier names them (Hillier et al. 1987) that correspond to cultural or ethnic groups. The concept of the genotype, particularly with respect to domestic building, has been established in space syntax literature (Hanson 1998:32, 269–270; Hillier and Hanson 1984:12–13, 143, 154; Hillier et al. 1987; Hillier 1996:36, 83, 249–250, 429–431). In particular, Hanson provides the following, useful definition:

> Function thus acquired a spatial expression which could also be assigned a numerical value. Where these numerical differences were in a consistent order across a sample of plans from a region, society or ethnic grouping then we could say that a cultural pattern existed, one which could be detected in the configuration itself rather than in the way in which it was interpreted by minds. We called this particular type of numerical consistency in spatial patterning a housing 'genotype.' [Hanson 1998:32]

This body of research suggests that it is likely to expect a culture to manifest itself through one or two dominant syntactic 'genotypes' at any time and with variation associated with the passage of time.

The housing genotypes have been traditionally determined by the investigation of the way individual spaces have been configured within the house. For this reason, the spaces have been expressed as a numerical inequality, ordered from the most to the least integrated. This has been a key methodological device in space syntax studies to investigate the existence of a consistent order in the integration values of spaces across a sample. This type of consistency in spatial patterning points to the existence of a cultural pattern and is called the *inequality genotype* (Hillier et al. 1987:364).

The use of clearly labelled plan layouts with clearly identifiable rooms and entrances is fundamental to the very concept of building genotype. Hillier and Hanson argued in their earlier work, *The Social Logic of Space*, that labels are more significant in gamma[2] than in alpha and that, "a genotype in gamma can be identified in terms of associations between labels of spaces and differentiations in how those spaces relate to the complex as a whole, in terms of the syntactic dimensions"[3] (Hillier and Hanson 1984:154). On the other hand, as the integration values attached to each space are calculated on the basis of the relationship of that space to all the others within the configuration, all the spaces within a network of spaces contribute to the calculation. Thus, even if one of the relations between any pair of spaces is unclear, the results will be meaningless.

Given the ambiguous nature of so much archaeological material, archaeologists often experience difficulties when trying to use quantitative techniques (Brown 1990; Fairclough 1992; Leach 1978). The success of the application of space syntax analysis to archaeological material has been questioned in archaeological literature by Marion Cutting (Cutting 2003). The primary problem mentioned by the author has been the fact that, as a quantitative access analysis, space syntax requires full architectural plans where rooms and their entrances are clearly identified. In the absence of perfect data some researchers had to make assumptions when applying the technique, which made it a less convincing tool (Bustard 1997; Shapiro 1997). The question here is, *how can the concept of 'genotype' be utilized to investigate incomplete and imperfect data sets both in terms of labels of spaces and their permeability relations, as in archaeological cases where one would need to piece together the story form a series of clues present in the sample?*

In this paper, it is proposed that a technique known as 'string-matching' may be used together with the concept of building genotype to analyze deficient samples spatially and to make predictions about unclear cases based on a clear base data. It will include an empirical section examining a small sample of vernacular houses from Cyprus, which are close to extinction, in order to fully illustrate this method.

SPATIAL STRING-MATCHING

It was demonstrated in earlier work by Ruth Conroy Dalton (Conroy 2001) that a technique drawn from mathematics/information theory, known as 'string-matching,' could be brought to bear upon an architectural problem. This method of analysis is based upon the assignment of a unique, identifying label to specific, key spaces or locations in the environment. A string is simply a sequence of characters or symbols. In this particular case the characters represent the functional-spaces that constitute the house, and the ordering of the sequence (or string) is determined by the integration values of the spaces relative to each other, as calculated with customary space syntax methods. Therefore not only are labels fundamental to the very concept of the building genotype in space syntax but they are necessary for the string-matching method to be computable. Rooms, which make up the house, are assigned a label so that the house can then be represented as a character string constructed from the sequence of spaces according to their integration values. String-matching then measures how similar each individual inequality is to all the others in a sample of houses with a value called 'similarity.' The degree of similarity is equivalent to the average number of transformations required to fully transform one string into any other in the sample. The act of transformation is often considered to be a *cost*, and the purpose of all string distance algorithms is to calculate the *least cost* way of transforming one string into another. On a string, these acts consist of character deletion, character insertion, and occasionally (depending on the algorithm employed) character substitution, each with an associated cost.[4] See the example below.

STRING	ACTION
S-P-A-C-E	
S-P-A-C-E-D	The *insertion* of character D at the end of the string.
P-A-C-E-D	The *deletion* of character S from the start of the string.
P-A-V-E-D	The *substitution* of character C by V in the middle of the string.

Once the range of permissible acts has been determined, the weight or cost for each act must be established, and it should be noted that the application of cost may not be uniform.[5]

The measure of 'distance'[6] between any pair of sequences is determined by calculating the minimum number of transformations required to transform one string into another, and the value of 'similarity' is the average number of transformations required to transform a string into any other in the rest of the sample. Thus the technique is particularly useful for the identification of the most representative/popular or the most idiosyncratic house configuration in the whole sample. Low similarity values which point to low number of transformations indicate more popular or representative cases, and high values, more idiosyncratic ones. A string with the lowest similarity value is the most representative as it requires the fewest number of acts to be transformed into any other in the sample, whereas the one with highest value is the most idiosyncratic as it needs to be subjected to a greater number of transformations to be changed into any other. String-matching can also be used to evaluate the heterogeneity of the overall sample. This is simply the range between the similarity values of the most and the least popular cases in a given sample. The following section presents an example empirical application of this method, which attempts to show how far it could be possible to make a prediction about unclear cases with the available material, with special reference to the Island of Cyprus, where the vernacular houses are close to extinction and await urgent action.

APPLICATION OF THE METHOD TO A SAMPLE OF VERNACULAR CYPRIOT HOUSES

In order to illustrate how the feature of 'similarity' together with the concept of 'inequality genotype' can be employed to make a prediction about the original form of presently unclear houses, a sample of vernacular, rural houses from the Mesarion region in Cyprus has been analyzed. Figure 17.1 shows this study area within the island of Cyprus with specific locations of settlements from which the house samples have been selected. The sample of house plans analyzed date from the period before 1974, which marks the division of Cyprus into two ethnically diverse areas and the resultant exchange of populations and of their houses.

The vernacular rural houses of Cyprus are all 'courtyard houses,' essentially driven by a peasantry-based agricultural economy and way of life. Besides their main domestic functions, they serve as a 'workshop' or 'laboratory' due to their abundance of work-related functions (Christodoulou 1959). Regardless of their Greek or Turkish origins, both groups' houses are formed by similar spatial elements such as: 'courtyards,' multi-functional living spaces referred as 'rooms' and 'main rooms,' multi-functional transitional spaces as 'central hallways' and 'loggias,' secondary spaces as 'kitchens,' and storage facilities for animals and goods.[7] They follow a simple rectangular arrangement developed around inner courtyards and are one or two stories high.

Most of the traditional houses that exist today are either close to extinction due to the negligence induced by the ethnic conflict between the two native populations of the island, namely Turkish and Greek Cypriots, and the resultant

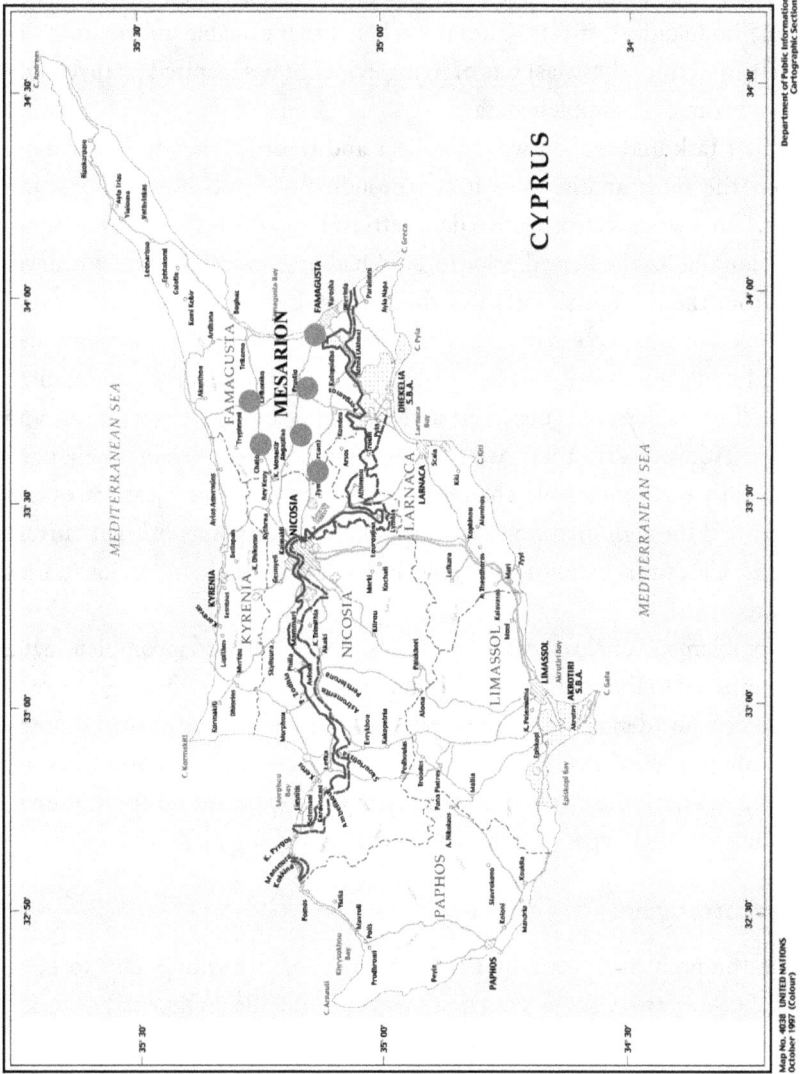

Figure 17.1. The study area within the island of Cyprus with specific locations of house samples.

economic difficulties; or were renewed, enlarged, and adapted to meet changing needs and ways of life. The scarcity of substantial records of architectural drawings of these houses and their vanishing originality meant that recording and understanding this housing stock was a task of high priority and would require special 'methodological' efforts. The strong belief that valuable information can still be retrieved from these last bits of living evidence has inspired an investigation into a realm of incomplete data.

The first task undertaken was to collect and record as much data as possible from the built architecture itself through first-hand observations and fieldwork.[8] This was a 'retrospective data retrieval' in which the original house layouts belonging to the period prior to 1974 had been reconstructed whenever possible from the present situation of the houses. In terms of original spatial layouts, together with access relations and functions, the processes mentioned above produced a number of 'unclear' cases, the identification of which required a special effort of personal judgment and reasoning besides observations and interviews. Additionally, there were cases that remained either unchanged or with readily distinguishable changes. These were noted as 'clear' cases and were identified through direct observations or clear statements of their current inhabitants. Cases that did not yield any clues at all about their previous forms were not recorded.

The problem of 'unclear' cases has resulted in a body of incomplete data, which, compared to the norm where "occupation" and "spatial form" go together, was necessarily 'deficient.' So the next task undertaken was to structure the sample through a set of 'detective' strategies and to attempt to uncover the story of unclear cases from the evidence and through the combinatorial application of the known methods of space syntax with string-matching methodology.

Analytical Strategies

To tackle the problems posed by the 'deficiency' of the sample and to piece together the story from a series of clues present in the incomplete data, certain 'analytical strategies' have been developed. It was evident that the plan layouts could be vague either in terms of permeability relations among the constituent spaces or of the functions of spaces. So, initially, the sample has been subdivided along this line as being 'clear' and 'unclear' either,

1. *syntactically*: in terms of syntactic layout, i.e., location of doors and partitions (permeability relations) (SC or SU); or,

2. *functionally*: in terms of labels, that is the functions of the spaces (FC or FU); or,

3. both *syntactically and functionally*: cases that are both 'syntactically' and 'functionally' 'clear' or 'unclear' (SC+FC or SU+FU).[9]

That is to say, in terms of uncertainties, 'syntactically unclear' (SU) cases are those whose plans are vague in terms of spatial relations (see houses in Figures 17.3a,b); 'functionally unclear' ones, those whose functions are vague (see Figures 17.2a,b), and the ones that are both syntactically and functionally unclear are the most complicated cases as they are vague both in terms of spatial relations and of their functions (SU+FU). This category has been excluded from the context of this study but will be addressed in future work.

Description of the sample

For the purposes of this study, forty-four houses which are both 'syntactically' and 'functionally' clear have been selected from a much wider database composed of both clear and unclear cases. This clear sub-sample is taken to behave as a 'base' data against which the unclear cases are to be compared and predicted. Then four unclear houses have been selected for the purpose of the study here, two of which are syntactically clear and functionally unclear (SC + FU), and two vice versa (SU + FC). Figures 17.2 and 17.3 display these unclear cases to be tested, respectively. In case of the first group (Figure 17.2a,b), the spatial layout and the permeability relations between the constituent spaces are clear; however, the functions of certain spaces are unclear. In the second group (Figure 17.3a,b), all the functions were identified; however, the permeability relations between some spaces are vague. Two houses have been selected for each category, one with only one unknown and one with more than one unknown variable. The house in Figure 17.2a is a typical, later period, courtyard house. It has a main living unit structured around a central closed hallway with two rooms opening off from it. It embodies several courtyard spaces as a kitchen, toilet, a stable, an independent room and a space whose function could not be identified, marked with the character '?'. This house is a simple case for SC + FU with single unknown function.

The house in Figure 17.2b is a more complicated case for the same category (SC + FU) with three unknown variables. The spatial layout is similar to the previous case, with a main living unit organized around a central hallway with all the secondary functions gathered around the courtyard. The main unit has an upper floor reached through a staircase located inside the central hallway. This house has an additional courtyard used exclusively by animals. The functions of the three spaces numbered as '4,' '5,' and '8' could not be identified.

Figure 17.3a and b, again, contains two houses which exemplify the SU + FC cases. House 3, in Figure 17.3a, has the main living unit on the upper floor and all the secondary functions are located on the ground floor dispersed around the courtyard. All the functions were clearly identified. However, it was not clear whether the second entrance that stands today used to exist in its original form or not. House 4 in Figure 17.3b is a more complicated case. It is a larger house with many courtyard spaces besides the main living unit, which was structured around a loggia running in front of the rooms. All the functions were identified with a high level of accuracy; however, it could not be identified with great confidence whether the courtyard formed by spaces '17' and '18' originally used to exist or not. This has accompanying changes with it, such as the presence of the toilet and the two entrances, one from kitchen and the other from the main living room (space 3). Thus this house had more than one uncertainty regarding the syntactic layout.

Procedure of Analysis

The key spaces of all the forty-four clear houses have been initially assigned a number for the space syntax analysis and a label for string-matching analysis. Then, the justified permeability graphs have been drawn and the houses have been subjected to standard space syntax analysis for the calculation of integration values. The labels representing individual spaces have then been expressed as an inequality, ordered from left (high) to right (low) according to their integration values. As a result, forty-four character-strings have been obtained. These character-strings, which form the 'base' data, have then been subjected to string-matching analysis with the help of Multimatch software.

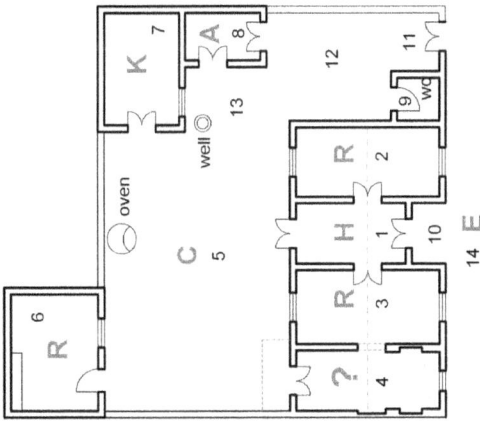

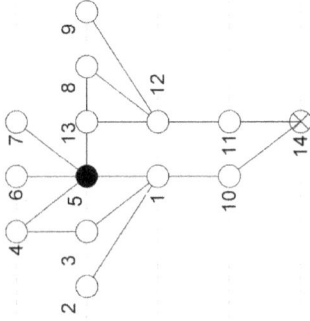

GROUND FLOOR PLAN   JUSTIFIED ACCESS GRAPH

C H ? A E R K R R

Figure 17.2. a. House 1: syntactically clear and functionally unclear case (SC+FU) with one unknown variable.

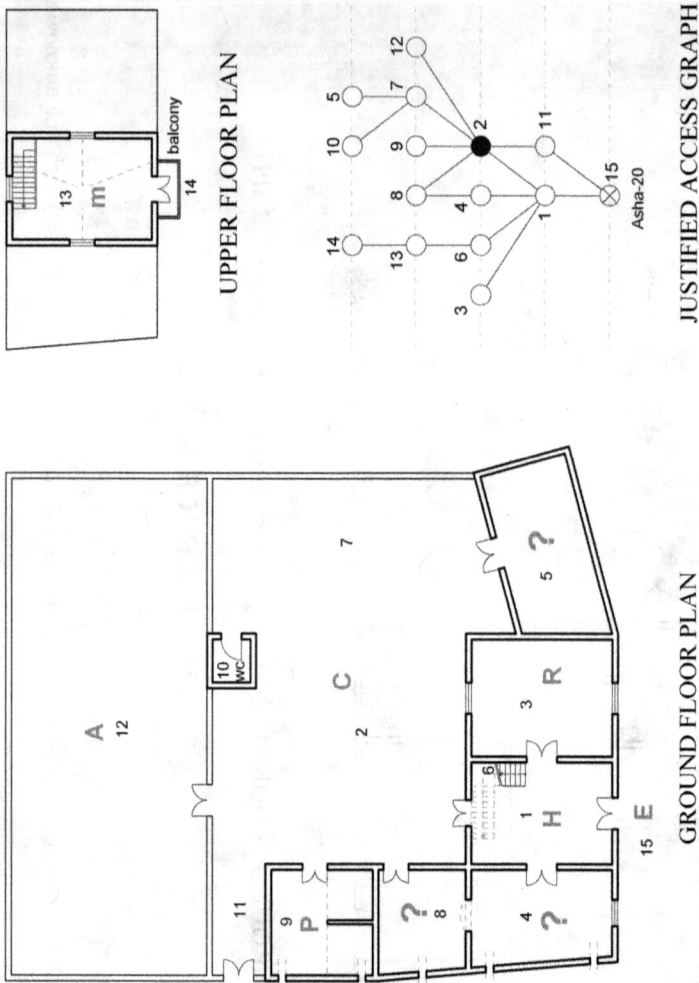

UPPER FLOOR PLAN

JUSTIFIED ACCESS GRAPH

GROUND FLOOR PLAN

C H ? ? E P A M m ?

Figure 17.2. b. House 2: syntactically clear and functionally unclear case (SC+FU) with three unknown variables.

15 E

5 A   3 S   4 P   2 T   ?

11

8 A

wc 9

10 C

6

1

oven

K 7

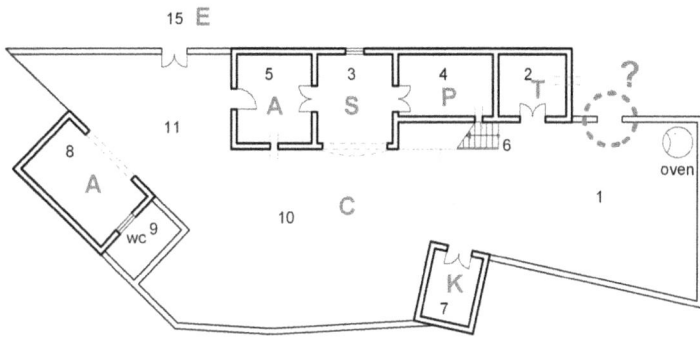

GROUND FLOOR PLAN

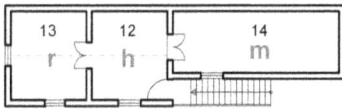

13 r   12 h   14 m

UPPER FLOOR PLAN

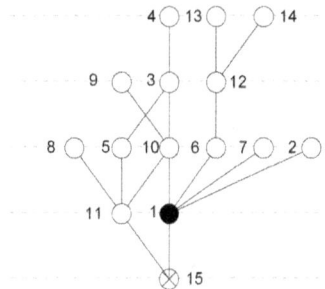

JUSTIFIED ACCESS GRAPH

C C E C S T K h A A P m r

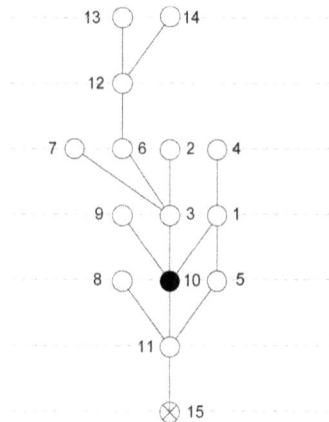

JUSTIFIED ACCESS GRAPH

C C C S T K A h A E P m r

Figure 17.3. a. House 3: syntactically unclear and functionally clear case (SU+FC) with one unknown variable.

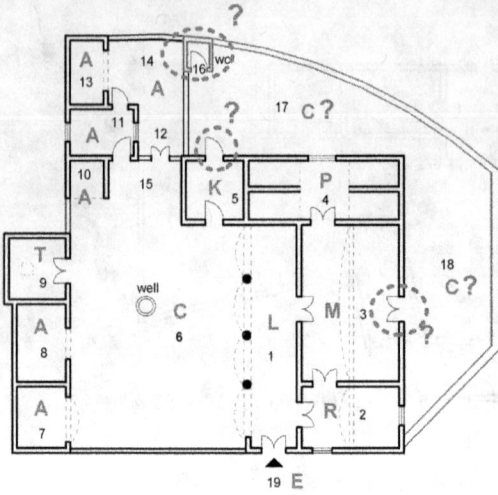

GROUND FLOOR PLAN

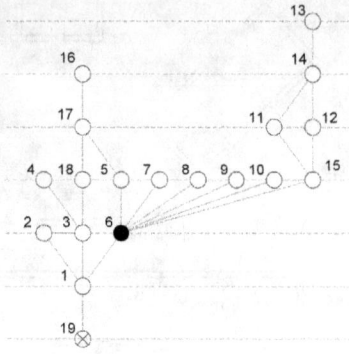

J. A. G. - Option 1

CLKMTAAARCAECPCAA

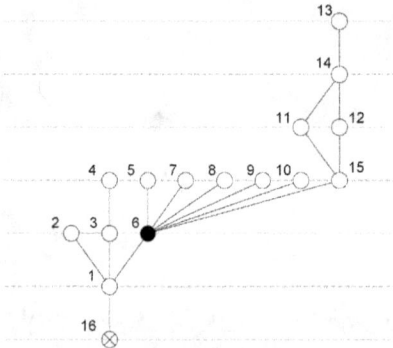

J. A. G. - Option 2

CLKTAAAAMREAPA

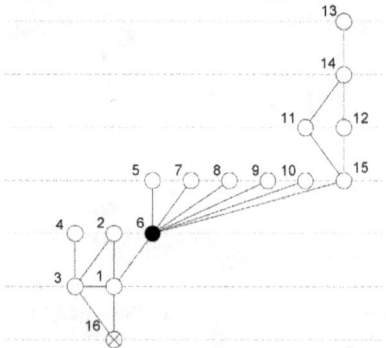

J. A. G. - Option 3

CLKTAAAMAERAPA

Figure 17.3. b. House 4: syntactically unclear and functionally clear case (SU+FC) with more than one unknown variables: a more complicated case.

Syntactically Clear and Functionally Unclear Examples (SC +F U)

House 1 – Single unknown variable:

House 1 has a clear spatial layout; however, the function of one of its spaces could not be identified. This space is represented by the character '?'. For the unknown space, the possibilities have been determined based on expert knowledge[10] and experience of the real world sample. Three possibilities have arisen: it could either be a 'produce store' (P), a 'straw store' (T), or an 'animal shed' (A). Then each label has been added one at a time to the string and three options of character strings have been obtained to represent the house:

Option 1: CHPAERKRR   **0.748**

Option 2: CHTAERKRR   0.761

Option 3: CHAAERKRR   0.756

Since the syntactic layout (spatial configuration) is clear, only the labels and not their position in the string are changed. Then, each of the possible strings has been individually subjected to string-matching analysis comparing it to the rest of the forty-four clear examples. Therefore, the analysis has been repeated three times for House 1. It was hypothesized that the option giving the lowest similarity value, when tested against the base data, is most likely to be the unknown function as it would be least idiosyncratic across the larger sample. In this case, Option 1 has the lowest similarity value, 0.748, as marked in bold. This implies that when the function of 'produce store' (P) is allocated to the queried space '4,' the resultant string is more similar to the rest of the clear cases: the 'base' data. Thus 'produce store' is conjectured to be the most likely function for unknown label '?'.

House 2 – More than one unknown label:

House 2 is another syntactically clear case – this time with three unidentified labels. These are spaces '4,' '5,' and '8,' as shown in the plan (Figure 17.3b). The inequality string of integration values is CH84EPAMm5. Since, once again, the relations among spaces are clearly identified, the order of the characters remains the same, and in this case there are three unknown characters within the string. From a purely mathematical standpoint, there could be many permutations (straightforward combinatorial mathematics). However, when expert knowledge is brought to bear on the problem, it can easily be seen that the enumerations are restricted to a great extent. Architecturally, and based on the real world examples in the clear data, it can be conjectured that, while space '5' could either be an 'animal shed' or a 'straw store,' space '4' can be either a 'kitchen' or a 'room,' and space '8' is either a 'kitchen' or a 'produce store,' but not an 'animal shed,' as it is directly connected to space '4,' which is part of the main living unit. In summary, space '8' could be a "K" (kitchen) or a "P" (produce store); '4' could be a "K" (kitchen) or a "R" (room); '5' could be an "A" (animal shed) or a "T" (straw store). If we start assigning labels from the first unknown label in the sequence and consider space '8' to be a kitchen, then space '4' cannot be another kitchen logically but a room, "R." Space '5,' which is the last label in the sequence could equally be an "A" or a "T." So we obtain two options here:

1. CHKREPAMmA

2. CHKREPAMmT

On the other hand, if space '8' is assigned the function "P" (produce store), then space '4' should definitely be a kitchen, "K," and similarly space '5' could be "A" or "T." So the other two options obtained are:

3. CHPKEPAMmA

4. CHPKEPAMmT

In total, four possibilities have been obtained to represent the original state of House 2. This means that four experiments have to be tested against the base data to determine which one is the closest to the real world examples or, in other words, is most likely to represent House 2.

Option 1: CHKREPAMmA	**0.743**
Option 2: CHKREPAMmT	**0.743**
Option 3: CHPKEPAMmA	0.744
Option 4: CHPKEPAMmT	0.746

The similarity values for the four options against the base data have shown that options 1 and 2 have the smallest similarity values, which are both equal. This implies that space '8' was a kitchen (K), '4,' a room (R), and '5' could equally be an animal shed (A) or a straw store (T). In most of the cases across the sample, these two functions are found to occur in the same space. It is a strong possibility that, in this case, space '5' was a multi-functional space with more than one usage – that of an animal shed and a straw store. It could be conjectured that this space used to serve mainly as a straw store (T), as animals had a separate courtyard in this particular house. However, when a more protective shed was required, some animals could be kept in the straw store.

Syntactically Unclear and Functionally Clear Examples (SU + FC)

House 3 – Single unknown:

The house in Figure 17.3a is a typical example of a syntactically unclear yet functionally clear case. All the functions have been identified; however, it is not clear whether a second courtyard entrance used to exist in the original situation. Two possible situations arise: one that allows for the existence of a door and one that does not. In this case, labels do not change between options; however, the configuration, that is to say the graph, does. The justified permeability graphs are drawn for the two possible scenarios, and each has been subjected to space-syntax analysis for the calculation of integration values separately. The character strings of integration values have been constructed in the next stage, which are both shown below the corresponding graphs in Figure 17.3a. The next step has been to test each option against the base data with the string-matching method. For this purpose, each string has been added one at a time to the base sample of forty-four clear houses and their similarity values have been calculated:

Option 1: CCECSTKhAAPmr   0.821   with door

Option 2: CCCSTKAhAEPmr   **0.782**   without door

Scenario 2 has a lower similarity value, which implies that it is unlikely that the house had another second courtyard entrance, as the string with single door is more similar to the rest of the sample.

House 4 – More than one unknown:

House 4 in Figure 17.3b is a case for multiple unclear situations in the syntactic layout. The original plan shown has been reconstructed from the current situation of the house (shown in Figure 17.4), which was modified to a great extent.

All the courtyard spaces, which were left unused (as shown in grey in Figure 17.4), have been kept and are all physically standing with clear implications of their original uses. On the other hand, the traces of original passageways and arcades were easily identified (as marked by blue dotted lines), just as the recently built additions and partitions. Thus, from the current situation of House 4 (shown in Figure 17.4), its original layout (in Figure 17.3b) has been easily retrieved. However, there were a few points that could not be identified with great confidence. The main factor which is unclear about this house is the availability of the second courtyard, which is formed from spaces '17' and '18' in Figure 17.3b. This means that if the courtyard did not exist, the space was a public or outside space and the toilet and the access from kitchen to this exterior space could not exist. However, even if it is a public space, there could be an access from the main living room (space 3) to this outside space. Thus three scenarios arise: One is the situation as shown in Figure 17.3b, which has the second courtyard, all of the connections to it, and the toilet. A second is the one without the courtyard, the toilet, and the connections from kitchen and main living space to the outside space. The third scenario is same as the second except for the access from space '3' (main living) to the outside. Justified permeability graphs have been drawn for each scenario and the character strings have been constructed based on the integration values as calculated by the customary methods of space syntax.

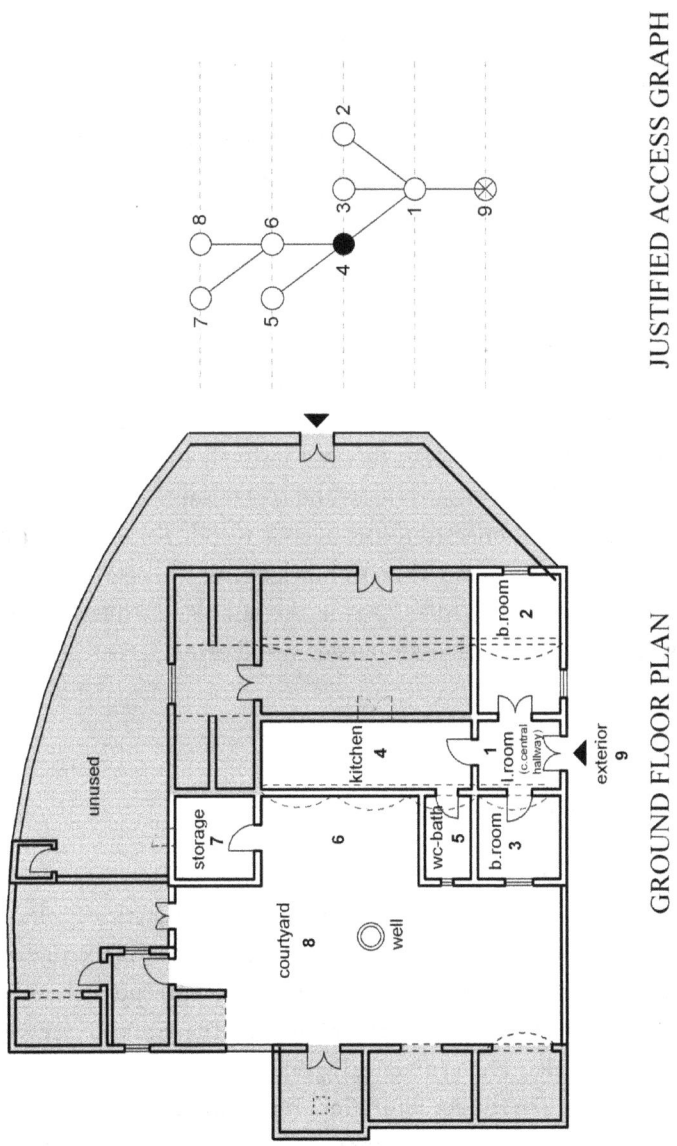

JUSTIFIED ACCESS GRAPH

GROUND FLOOR PLAN

Figure 17.4. Current modified situation of House 4 in Figure 17.3b.

Option 1: CLKMTAAARCAECPAA   0.973 with second courtyard
  + toilet + connections from kitchen and main living

Option 2: CLKTAAAAMREAPA   **0.901** without second courtyard + toilet + connections from kitchen and main living

Option 3: CLKTAAAMAERAPA   0.923 without second courtyard + toilet + connection from kitchen and with connection
  from main living to the outside

In general, this case is found to be the most idiosyncratic when compared to the other forty-four cases in terms of its number of constituent spaces. However, it is not the type but the number of similar spaces that matters. Among the three scenarios, scenario 2 has the lowest similarity value; thus it is the most similar to the rest of the sample. This implies that it is unlikely that the house used to have a second courtyard in its original form and that it is unlikely that the 'main living space' was directly connected to the outside world. This exactly matches our subjective intuition, given our expert knowledge of the data set, as houses like this one, which represent earlier cases in the sample, are interior-oriented and are rarely directly connected to the outside world through their 'main living units.'

DISCUSSION AND CONCLUSION

String-matching has been applied to a small sample of unclear, traditional Cypriot houses with apparent success. Cases that are 'syntactically clear' and 'functionally unclear' seem the easiest to analyze as the spatial configuration and the resultant inequality string remains the same with possible function insertions (labels) being tested in turn. However, the situation gets more complicated for cases that are 'syntactically unclear' and 'functionally clear.' As this implies a change in the configuration, it requires conducting the space syntax analysis for each scenario to obtain the inequality string and then comparing each string to the base data, in turn. This problem of complexity even further increases with cases that are 'unclear' both 'syntactically' and 'functionally.' These cases have been omitted from the present study. This would undoubtedly require constructing scenarios of strings for numerous permutations, which would dramatically increase the resultant test analysis as well. However, it should also be noted that the number of permutations generated mathematically for the unclear options could be reduced through the application of logic and expert knowledge.

As an automated methodology 'spatial string-matching' can easily and effectively be applied to large samples. Given the encouraging results of its application to unclear cases presented in this paper, it is suggested that string-matching can be applied, at least to an extent, with apparent success for the analysis of deficient samples and can be used by archaeologists to help them make valid inferences about any residual plans of their excavations. Considering the difficulties inherent in the application of syntactic analysis to imperfect and incomplete data sets, as already mentioned by most of the archaeologists, it is believed that the technique proposed here will provide a more reliable and convincing way to the application of quantitative access analysis of space syntax. In the absence of a well-recorded database, it is highly relevant to consider any kind of evidence present in a residual architecture. This paper has demonstrated the value of string-matching in interpreting and inferring the patterns in deficient, uncertain data in a detective manner through the combination of mathematical and expert knowledge.

Acknowledgments: The first author would like to express her gratitude to her PhD supervisor, Professor Bill Hillier at the Bartlett School of Graduate Studies, UCL, for his support and specifically for his invaluable contribution to the definition of incomplete data sets. The technical help of Myrto Zirini in creating the images of this paper is also greatly appreciated.

References

Amorim, Luiz M.E.

1999   The Sectors' Paradigm: A Study of the Spatial Function and Nature of Modernist Housing in Northeast Brazil. PhD dissertation, University College London, London.

Brown, Frank E.

1990   Comment on Chapman: Some Cautionary Notes on the Application of Spatial Measures to Prehistoric Settlements. In *The Social Archaeology of Houses*, edited by Ross Samson, pp. 93–110. Edinburgh University Press, Edinburgh.

Brown, Frank, and Bellal Tahar

2001   Comparative Analysis of M'zabite and Other Berber Domestic Spaces. *Proceedings of the Space Syntax 3rd International Symposium* 41.1–41.14. Georgia Institute of Technology, Atlanta.

Bustard, Wendy

1997   Space, Evolution and Function in the Houses of Chaco Canyon. *Proceedings of Space Syntax: First International Symposium* II:23.1–23.21. London.

Chapman, John

1990   Social Inequality on Bulgarian Tells and the Varna Problem. In *The Social Archaeology of Houses*, edited by Ross Samson, pp. 49–92. Edinburgh University Press, Edinburgh.

Christodoulou, Demetrios

1959   *The Evolution of the Rural Land Use Pattern in Cyprus.* Geographical Publications Limited, Bude, Cornwall, England.

Conroy, Ruth A.

2001   Spatial Navigation in Immersive Virtual Environments. PhD dissertation, University College London, London.

Cooper, Laurel M.

1997   Comparative Analysis of Chacoan Great Houses. *Proceedings of Space Syntax: First International Symposium* II:22.1–22.11. London.

Cutting, Marion

2003   The Use of Spatial Analysis to Study Prehistoric Settlement Architecture. *Oxford Journal of Archaeology* 22(1):1–21.

Dawson, Peter C.

2002 Space Syntax Analysis of Central Intuit Snow Houses. *Journal of Anthropological Archaeology* 21:464–480.

Düring, Bleda

2001 Social Dimensions in the Architecture of Neolithic Çatalhöyük. *Anatolian Studies* 51:1–18.

Fairclough, Graham

1992 Meaningful Constructions – Spatial and Functional Analysis of Medieval Buildings. *Antiquity* 66:348–66.

Gilchrist, Roberta

1994 *Gender and Material Culture: The Archaeology of Religious Women.* Routledge, London and New York.

Hanson, Julienne

1998 *Decoding Homes and Houses.* Cambridge University Press, Cambridge.

Hillier, Bill

1996 *Space is the Machine.* Cambridge University Press, Cambridge.

Hillier, Bill, and Julienne Hanson

1984 *The Social Logic of Space.* Cambridge University Press, Cambridge.

Hillier, Bill, Julienne Hanson, and Hilaire Graham

1987 Ideas Are in Things: An Application of the Space Syntax Method to Discovering House Genotypes. *Environment and Planning: Planning and Design* 14:363–385.

Kirsan, Ciler

2003 Detective Work with a Deficient Sample: Syntactic Analysis of the Houses of Conflict. *Proceedings of the 4th International Symposium Space Syntax Symposium* II:57.1–57.28. University College London, London.

2005 Is It a Greek or a Turkish House? A Comparative Morphological Enquiry into the Domestic Spaces of Coexistence in the Island of Cyprus. In *Designing Social Innovation: Planning, Building, Evaluating*, edited by Bob Martens and Alexander G. Keul, pp. 93–103. Hogrefe and Huber, Göttingen, Germany.

Leach, Edmund R.

1978 Does Space Syntax Really Constitute the Social? In *Social Organisation and Settlement: Contributions from Anthropology*, edited by David Green, Colin Haselgrove, and Matthew Spriggs, pp. 38–72. British Archaeological Reports, International [Supplementary] Series No. 47, Pt. 2, Oxford.

Orhun, Deniz

1997 Spatial Types in Traditional Houses of Turkey. PhD dissertation, University College London, London.

Orhun, Deniz, Bill Hillier, and Julienne Hanson

1995   Spatial Types in Traditional Turkish Houses. *Environment and Planning: Planning and Design B* 22:475–498.

1996   Socialising Spatial Types in Traditional Turkish Houses. *Environment and Planning: Planning and Design B* 23:329–351.

Shapiro, Jason

1997   Fingerprints in the Landscape. *Proceedings of Space Syntax: First International Symposium* II:21.1–21.21. London.

Shoul, Michael

1993   The Spatial Arrangements of Ordinary English Houses. *Environment and Behaviour* 25:22–69.

Trigueiro, Edja B.F.

1994   Change and Continuity in Domestic Space Design: A Comparative Study of Nineteenth and Early Twentieth Century Houses in Britain and Recife, Brazil. PhD dissertation, University College London, London.

NOTES

1   String-matching method is automated computationally by a software program called Multimatch developed by Ruth Conroy Dalton and is employed here to analyze the data. Multimatch is a small program written in C language to analyze data by Conroy Dalton for her PhD studies.

2   Gamma and alpha are the types of syntactical analyses provided for building interiors and settlements respectively which had been introduced in *The Social Logic of Space*.

3   It is clear from this statement that permeability relations between labelled spaces are essential in space syntax analysis.

4   Clearly a single act of substitution could be considered to be equivalent to an act of deletion followed by an act of insertion (or vice versa).

5   Detailed information on string matching algorithm can be found in Conroy (2001).

6   This is not metric distance.

7   The labelled spaces in the plans are represented as follows: C = courtyard; c = animal courtyard; L = loggia; R = room; M = main room; K = kitchen; A = animal shed; E = exterior; m = upper main room; S = semi-closed central space/hallway; H = closed central space/hallway; P = produce store; T = straw store; h = upper closed central space/hallway; s = upper semi-closed central space/hallway; r = upper room; F = front garden; G = garage.

8   Observations and fieldwork were all conducted by Ciler Kirsan between April 2000 and August 2000 as part of her PhD studies.

9   SC: Syntactically Clear; SU: Syntactically Unclear; FC: Functionally Clear; FU: Functionally Unclear

10 'Expert knowledge' refers to the knowledge of an expert who is an architect or architectural historian focusing on regional, vernacular types, in this case.

CONTRIBUTORS

KIRSTEN ANDERSON (University of Calgary) is a PhD candidate in the Department of Archaeology at the University of Calgary. Her research focuses on prehistoric hunter-gatherers of the Canadian Plains and the use of three-dimensional spatial analysis for the identification of hearth-related activities. Kirsten has spent the last five years working at the stampede site in the Cypress Hills, Alberta. This site has been excavated as part of the SCAPE project (Study of Cultural Adaptations to the Prairie Ecozone), a major collaborative research initiative project involving study areas in Alberta, Saskatchewan, and Manitoba

TOBIN C. BOTTMAN (University of Oregon) received both his BA (2002) and his MS (2006) in Anthropology from the University of Oregon. Mr. Bottman specializes in the precontact archaeology of Oregon with a focus on trade and interactions. He is an archaeologist with the Oregon Department of Transportation and lives in Portland.

RYAN T. BRADY (Albion Environmental, Inc.) received his BA in Anthropology from the University of California, Davis, in 1999 and his MA in Anthropology from California State University, Sacramento, in 2007. His research interests include ecological perspectives to hunter-gatherer adaptations, implications of technological organization, stone material provenience, and obsidian hydration studies for identifying changes in past hunter-gatherer life ways. This includes hunter-gatherer settlement studies in arid and coastal environments. Mr. Brady has collaborated with archaeologists working in western North American and Spanish researchers working in Tierra del Fuego. He currently works for Albion Environmental, Inc., in Santa Cruz, California.

SUSAN CACHEL (Rutgers University) is an Associate Professor of Physical Anthropology at Rutgers University, New Brunswick, New Jersey. She is a member of the Rutgers Center for Human Evolutionary Studies, the Rutgers interdisciplinary Quaternary Studies Program and has been an instructor with the Koobi For a Palaeoanthropological Field School in northern Kenya. Cachel does research on human and non-human primate evolution.

LESLIE G. CECIL (University of Missouri) is an Assistant Professor of Anthropology at Stephen F. Austin State University. Her research addresses issues of how the Postclassic Maya (ca. AD 900–1700), during times of social and political stress, used pottery to help identify themselves as part of a cohesive socio-political group. She gathers technological and stylistic data by employing an array of methods that include X-ray diffraction, scanning electron microscopy, inductively coupled plasma spectroscopy, and instrumental neutron activation analysis.

RUTH CONROY DALTON (University College London) is lecturer in architectural morphology and theory at the Bartlett School of Graduate Studies. She is director of UCL's MSc in Advanced Architectural Studies. She holds a BSc (Hons.) in Architecture, Building, Planning, and Environmental Studies, an MSc in Advanced Architectural Studies, and a PhD in Architecture. In addition to this, she is a Chartered Architect and member of the Royal Institute of British Architects. She is an expert in the architectural analysis theory of Space Syntax and has also authored over fifty peer-reviewed conference and journal papers.

EUGENE M. GRYBA (EMG Archaeological Services) obtained a BA (Hons.) in Anthropology from the University of Alberta in 1972 and an MA from the University of Manitoba in 1975. Since 1978 he has worked as a contract archaeologist primarily within Alberta. His interest in heat treatment of various lithic materials, and in prehistoric lithic technology, in general, commenced during the 1960s while he was growing up on his parents' farm by the Upper Campbell beach of Glacial Lake Agassiz near Swan River, Manitoba. His many publications include "A Stone Age Method of Folsom Fluting" (Plains Anthropologist 1988 33:53–66) and "An Assessment of the Free-Hand Pressure Flaking Technique of Precontact North America" (Lithic Technology 2006, 31 (1):57–77). A self-taught flintknapper, he has participated in lithic technology workshops in places as far off as Buffalo, New York, Austin, Texas, and Chatellerault, France.

LESLIE MAIN JOHNSON (Athabasca University) is an Associate Professor of Anthropology at Athabasca University, Alberta, Canada. She earned her MA and PhD in Anthropology at the University of Alberta in 1993 and 1997.

Her publications include *Landscape Ethnoecology: Concepts of Physical and Biotic Space* (co-edited with E. Hunn, Berghahn), and *Trails of Story: Traveller's Path – Reflections on Ethnoecology and Landscape* (Athabasca University Press), articles in *Human Ecology, Journal of Ethnobiology, Ecology of Food and Nutrition, Journal of Ethnobotany and Ethnomedicine*, and *Canadian Journal of Botany*, and a chapter in *Indians, Fire and the Land in the Pacific Northwest* (Oregon State University Press).

CILER KIRSAN (University College London, Gebze Institute of Technology) is doing a PhD in Architecture at the Bartlett School of Graduate Studies in UCL under the supervision of Professor Bill Hillier and is currently working as an instructor in Cyprus International University, Department of Architecture. In her thesis she analyses vernacular houses of Cyprus to see the effects of ethnic conflict on their spatial configurations by using the theory of Space Syntax. In CIU, she is giving Space Analysis Techniques course where she teaches Space Syntax tools for the analysis of houses, and Design Studio courses.

PURPLE KUMAI (Independent Researcher) has two Bachelor's degrees, a BA in Anthropology from the University of Saskatchewan, and a BA in Archaeology from the University of Calgary. She has conducted archaeological work in Japan, Russia, and the Canadian prairies. Her current research interests lie in the Japanese palaeolithic and the Ainu population of Japan's northern island, Hokkaido.

E. G. LANGEMANN (Parks Canada) has been working as a senior archaeologist with Parks Canada for nearly twenty years. Her primary responsibilities are in the Rocky Mountain national parks, particularly in Banff, Waterton Lakes, and Elk Island national parks. She has had the chance to undertake a wide variety of backcountry surveys, excavations, public education projects, and impact assessments, and to integrate these into a regional approach to understanding culture history and human participation in the mountain ecosystems.

AMBER E. MACKENZIE (University of Toronto) was attending the University of Alberta and working towards the completion of her undergraduate degree in Anthropology at the time of writing of the paper for this volume. She is currently a graduate student in the Department of Anthropology at the University of Toronto studying palaeoanthropology. Her research focus has since diverged, and she is now interested in the functional morphology of primates and reconstructing the positional behaviour of fossil apes to better understand the evolutionary past of modern apes and humans.

GO MATSUMOTO (Southern Illinois University) is a doctoral student of Southern Illinois University at Carbondale. With his primary interest in the roles of religion in social development, he has been working at two major ceremonial centres on the Peruvian Coast: Sicán and Pachacamac. His dissertation focuses on ritual sequences lasting over five hundred years from the Middle Sicán to the Colonial Periods at the site of Sicán. GIS and related techniques are important tools for his research and teaching. Recently, he has also been engaged in a project to promote professional training of GIS for anthropologists.

MARIA VICTORIA MONSALVE (University of British Columbia) holds a tenure-track position as an instructor in the University of British Columbia Faculty of Medicine. She previously spent two years (1995–97) as a Research Associate at the University of Cambridge, working with ancient human DNA. Her research history includes the study of human diversity and early migrations to the Americas using DNA extracted from ancient remains and contemporary peoples. Her research also includes DNA identification of faunal remains in archaeological sites. Her research findings have been published in the *Proceedings of the Royal Society*, *Annals of Human Genetics*, the *American Journal of Physical Anthropology* and as a chapter in the book *Biomolecular Archaeology*.

JOSÉ ROBERTO PELLINI (Universidade de São Paulo) is an archaeologist finishing his post-doctorate at the Museum of Arqueologia and Etnologia, University of São Paulo. He has worked with systems of exchange and interaction since 1992, mainly in ancient Egypt. Nowadays he works with the use and application of GIS in archaeology, mainly cost surface analysis, physiological movement, and network analysis to understand ancient exchange. He is the Scientific Director of Griphus Archaeological Consulting and Fieldwork Director of the Argentinean Mission at Luxor, Egypt.

MEAGHAN M. PEURAMAKI-BROWN (University of Calgary) is currently a PhD candidate in the Department of Archaeology at the University of Calgary. Her research interests include issues of Mesoamerican identity formation and manipulation, household archaeology, urbanization, and Maya socio-political organization. She is conducting her dissertation research at the site of Buenavista del Cayo, Belize, Central America.

JASON W. ROE (Lifeways of Canada Limited) works as an archaeologist for Lifeways of Canada Limited and is doing his master's degree at the University of Saskatchewan. His thesis examines the lithic technology of the Early Middle Period, more specifically the *chaîne opératoire* of Embarras Bipoints.

MICHAEL J. SHOTT (University of Akron) researches North American hunter-gatherers, lithic analysis, and how the archaeological record formed. He has more than twenty-five years of experience in the United States (the Great Lakes and Midwest, and the Great Basin) and has conducted ethnoarchaeological research in Mexico and archaeological survey in Argentina. He is a Professor of Archaeology at the University of Akron in Ohio.

NICHOLAS WABER (University of British Columbia) graduated from the University of British Columbia in 2006 with a BA in Anthropology, focusing in archaeology. He specializes in experimental archaeology pertaining to pre-historic tool use in western North America. Specifically, Nick focuses on lithic replication studies and microblade technology on the Northwest Coast. When he is not banging rocks together he travels throughout southwestern British Columbia looking at rock art sites. Nick commenced graduate studies at the University of Victoria in Fall 2008.

JOSHUA J. WELLS (Indiana University–Purdue University Fort Wayne Archaeological Survey) is a visiting Assistant Professor of Anthropology at Indiana University, South Bend, where he teaches anthropology, archaeology, and social informatics. His dissertation sheds light on pluralistic sociocultural dynamics within the Vincennes Mississippian culture in west-central Indiana and east-central Illinois. His research includes bioarchaeology, multiscalar geographic information system analyses, social network analyses, computational modelling, archaeological pedagogy, and human-technology interaction. He is currently investigating heuristics for integrating archaeological site and landscape data from numerous government, contract, and academic sources into digital atlas formats for research and management purposes.

JAYNE WILKINS (University of Toronto) received her MA in Archaeology at the University of Calgary and is currently completing her PhD at the University of Toronto. Her research interests include lithic analysis, hunter-gatherer archaeology, the African Stone Age, and modern human origins. She has participated in the excavation and analysis of archaeological sites in South Africa, Mozambique, and Alberta, Canada.

PAMELA R. WILLOUGHBY (University of Alberta) is a Professor of Anthropology at the University of Alberta. She specializes in palaeolithic archaeology and human palaeontology. She directs a SSHRC-supported archaeological project in the Iringa Region of south-central Tanzania, investigating the origins of our own species. Sites in Iringa contain a continuous record of human activity over the last 200,000 years, and so provide a laboratory for testing ideas about how our ancestors became both anatomically and behaviourally modern. Dr. Willoughby is the author of *The Evolution of Modern Humans in Africa: A Comprehensive Guide* (AltaMira Press, 2007).

D. Y. YANG (Simon Fraser University) is an Associate Professor in the Department of Archaeology, Simon Fraser University. He holds a BSc in Biology from Lanzhou University (Lanzhou, China), a MSc in Biological Anthropology from Chinese Academy of Sciences (Beijing) and a PhD in Physical Anthropology from McMaster University (Hamilton, Ontario). His current research interests include developing ancient DNA techniques for archaeological research and integrating ancient DNA into archaeological investigations of the past. He and his graduate students have been working on a variety of projects to retrieve and analyze ancient DNA from human, animal, and plant remains, as well as artefacts from many parts of the world.

INDEX

A

accuracy, xi
  atlatl, xvi, 51, 52, 55, 56, 57, 60, 61
  dating, 159
  maps, 220, 229, 231, 235, 270
  provenience, stable isotope analysis, 151
  space syntax, 284
Acheulean, 34, 40, 41, 44
aerial photography, 206, 220, 223, 224,
  225, 226, 227, 231, 233
  pseudo stereopair, 223
agency, xii, 82, 109
altruistic behaviour, 21, 22, 26
American Bottom (Illinois), 257–59, 263
anatomically modern humans, 13, 24, 40,
  41
anisotropic logarithms, 238
archaeobotanical methods (see also
  palaeoethnobotany), 184, 191,
  192, 194, 198, 199
archaeometry, vi, xiv, xviii, 74, 108, 125,
  126–35, 136, 137, 163, 164
  inductively coupled plasma spectroscopy
    (ICPS), 125, 126, 127, 130,
    302
  laser-ablation inductively coupled
    plasma spectroscopy (LA-
    ICP-MS), 130, 137, 138

neutron activation analysis (INAA),
  125, 126, 127, 302
petrography (thin-section), vi, xiv, xviii,
  xix, 107, 109, 112, 113, 121,
  122, 125, 126, 130, 136, 137
Athapaskan, xx, 183, 184, 185, 193
atlatl, v, xvi, xvii, 51–61, 62, 193
  accuracy, xvi, 51, 52, 55, 56, 57, 60, 61
  distance, xvi, 51, 52, 54, 55, 56, 58
  flexibility, 52, 53, 57, 58,
attribute (of artefacts), xii, 58, 60, 64, 77,
  79, 86, 91, 105, 265, 266

B

Banff National Park, vi, xix, 79, 167, 168,
  169, 172, 176, 178, 179, 180, 303
Barnes, 97, 98, 99, 101, 102. *See also*
  Parkhill phase
behavioural modernity, xvi, 8, 41, 42, 44.
  See also modern human behaviour
Belize, 11, 123, 135, 305,
  Tipuj, 128, 129, 132, 133, 134, 135
Bennyhoff, James, xix, xxiv, 140, 143, 145,
  146, 147, 148, 159, 161, 162,
biface, v, xviii, 81, 91, 93, 95–99, 101, 104,
  105, 207–11, 215
bifacial reduction, 209

palaeoenvironment, 194, 196

paleoethnobotany, 197. *See also* archaeobotanical methods

Palaeoindian, v, xviii, 91, 93, 95, 97, 99, 105

Palaeolithic, xvi, xxiv, xxv, 15, 18, 31–35, 40–44, 47, 49, 64, 73, 92, 93, 95, 104, 105, 303, 306

palaeontology, 32, 37, 38, 46–48, 162, 306

Pan paniscus, 2

Pan troglodytes, 2, 10

Parkhill Phase, 101

Perkins, Bob, 52, 57, 58, 61, 62

Petén Lakes Region, 128, 129, 133, 136
  Ch'ich', 128, 129, 132, 135
  Ixlú, 128, 129, 132, 135
  Mayapán, 129, 133, 138
  Postclassic Period, xviii, 125, 127–33, 135, 136, 138, 302
  Topoxté Island, 129, 133, 135
  Zacpetén, 129, 132–35, 138

petrofabric, 107, 112–21

petrographic analysis, xviii, 107, 109, 112, 113, 130, 136, 137

phyletic gradualism, 35, 46

planning, 15, 19, 24, 28, 230, 240, 271, 297, 298, 302

plant, vi, xv, xix, xx, 18, 44, 183, 184, 192–99, 203, 205, 209, 210, 214, 306
  bark, 183–86, 188–90, 195, 196, 198
  berries, 184, 190–92, 198, 199
  distribution (natural vs. artificial), 183, 191
  food, 183, 184, 188, 190, 192, 195–97
  medicinal uses, 183, 188
  visibility (archaeologically), 183–99

Pleistocene, xiv, xxv, 2, 19, 25, 31, 32, 33, 44, 45, 49

polish, use-wear, 69

Pongo pygmaeus, 2

potstands, xviii, 107, 111, 112, 118–20

pottery, xviii, 33, 44, 108, 111–13, 119–23, 125, 126, 129, 131, 133–38, 265, 302
  chemical composition, 126, 127, 130, 131
  clementia cream paste ware, 129, 130–33
  colour (core), 117, 118, 120, 122, 125–27, 129, 132,
  decoration, 33, 129–33
  firing temperature, 126, 129
  hardness, 126, 127, 129
  manufacturing patterns, 126, 127, 129, 132, 133
  measurement, 125–27, 129
  paste, 109, 111–13, 117, 120, 126, 127, 129–34
  slip, 126, 127, 129–32, 136
  snail inclusion paste, 129–33
  Vitzil orange-red, 129–33

pre-columbian Mesoamerica, xiv, xviii, 107–9, 111, 118

prediction, xxiii, 20, 22, 205, 207, 275, 276, 278, 280

pressure flaking, 65, 73, 302

primate, xiv, 1–3, 8, 11, 13–17, 19–27, 39, 301, 304

private space, xxii, 270

punctuated equilibria, xvi, 8, 38, 39, 46, 47

Q

qualitative approach, xiv, 83, 95, 103, 126, 257

quantitative approach, xiv, 83, 103, 104, 259, 260, 278, 295

quartzite, 79, 82–84

JAYNE WILKINS AND KIRSTEN ANDERSON

R

radio-carbon dating, 149, 151, 159, 167, 169

Rancho del Rio, Honduras, vi, xviii, 107, 109–13, 118–23

Range Phase, vii, xxii, 257, 258, 265, 266, 268, 270, 273

Range Site, 258, 263, 266, 269, 270, 272, 273

  Dohack Phase, vii, xxii, 257, 258, 260, 263, 265, 266, 268, 270

raw material, xvii, 2, 6, 7, 11, 15, 17, 18, 24, 35, 41, 45, 71, 79, 82, 84, 109, 111, 121, 147, 207

reduction distribution, 91, 97

remote sensing, xi, xiii, 219, 232, 233

replication, v, xvi, xvii, 63, 64, 70, 72, 73, 75, 81, 305

residue analysis, xiii, 108, 112, 119, 194, 207

Rocky Mountain Elk (*Cervus elapus nelsoni*), 168, 174, 175

Rocky Mountain House, National Historic Site, vi, xix, 167, 169, 170, 172, 175–77, 179, 180

S

Säve-Söderbergh, Torgny, 239, 253, 255

scavenging, 17, 24

schist, xviii, 111, 113–21

scraper, xviii, 91–93, 95–97, 99, 101–6111

Second Intermediate Period (Egypt), 253

settlement patterning, xii, xx-xxii, 42, 138, 143, 162, 201, 202, 203, 209, 211, 213–15, 258, 260–63, 265, 266, 269–71, 273, 296, 297, 299

  central place foraging, 202

  fission-fusion, 203

  foraging theory, 202, 205, 215

shell bead, xix, xxiv, 141, 143, 145–47, 151, 161

Simpson, George Gaylord, 32, 33, 37–39, 46–48

site, vi, xi, xii, xv, xviii-xxii, 2, 7, 9, 11, 15, 17, 18, 23–25, 27, 28, 33, 34, 38, 41–45, 47, 64, 65, 74–77, 86–89, 97, 102, 107–9, 111, 112, 118–21, 128, 129, 132, 133, 135, 139–43, 145, 146, 149, 152, 155, 159, 160, 162, 164, 167–72, 175–79, 183, 183, 188, 191–95, 198, 199, 201, 206, 214, 215, 217–20, 223, 227–32, 255, 257, 258, 261–63, 266, 268–73, 301, 304–6

sequence model, xvii, xviii. See also *chaînes opératoires*

social cognition, 14, 15, 20–23, 27, 29

social landscape, xxi, xxii, xxiv, 232, 237, 238, 298

Social Logic of Space, xxiv, 258, 259, 272, 273, 277, 297, 299

socio-political, 88, 125, 127–30, 132, 133, 135, 136, 302, 305

space, vii, xiii, xv, xvii, xxii-xxiv, 141, 214, 232, 234, 240, 241, 257–63, 265–73, 275–80, 282–84, 289–92, 294–99, 302, 303

  communal, xxii, 258, 270

  private, xxii, 270

Spanish contact, 125, 127–29, 137

spatial analysis, xii, xxi, xxii, 233, 234, 238, 276, 296, 301

spatial archaeology, 218, 232

spatial organization, xii, 24, 121, 270, 271

spatial string-matching, vii, xxiii, 275, 278, 295

  distance, 279, 299

  functionally clear (FC), 283, 287, 288, 291, 294, 299

  functionally unclear (FU), 283, 285, 286, 289, 294, 299

  integration value, 262, 263, 266, 268–70, 277, 291, 292

  Multimatch (software), 276, 284, 299

  permeability, 278, 282–84, 291, 292, 299

  prediction, xxiii, 275, 276, 278, 280

animal tool use, v, xiii, xiv, xv, xvi, 1,
    3–5, 9, 10, 12, 14, 16, 26, 28
function, xviii, 1, 16, 27, 51, 57, 61, 72,
    73, 79, 80, 85, 88, 92, 131,
    209, 304
manufacture, vi, xii, xiii, xvii, xviii,
    1–3, 7, 10, 12, 14, 15, 17, 18,
    35, 63, 64, 71–73, 75, 79, 84,
    85, 107–9, 111–13, 115, 117,
    119–22, 126, 127, 129, 132,
    133, 140, 143
primate tool use, v, xiv, xv, 1–12, 14
total station, xi, 220
trade, vi, xiii, xix, xxii, 41, 118, 121, 125,
    126, 130, 133, 136, 139–41, 143–
    47, 159–62, 64, 190, 193, 301
networks, xxiv, 41, 143, 159, 161, 231
patterns, 125, 126, 146, 147
routes, xix, 141, 144, 146, 147, 164
Trans-Sierran trail network, 145–47
Troy, Lana, 239, 253, 255
typology, 93, 95, 103, 104, 107, 148
ceramic, 107
lithic, 93, 95, 103, 104

Weibull, 91, 95, 97, 99, 101, 102, 105
wetland, vi, xx, 162, 163, 201–9, 211, 213,
    215
brackish, xx, 203, 205, 206–9, 211
freshwater, xx, 203, 205–9, 211
saline, xx, 203, 205–9, 211

Y

Yucatán, 121, 127, 128, 132
Chich'en Itzá, 128, 129, 138

Z

zooarchaeology, 168, 169
faunal assemblage, xix, 168, 176
preservation, xix, 169, 176

U

uniface, v, 79, 91, 97, 99, 100, 101
Upper Lovett Campsite, 77, 87
Upper Palaeolithic, xvi, xxiv, 15, 18, 40–43
use wear, v, xvii, 63–68, 72, 73
Uto-Aztecan interaction sphere, 145–47

V

vervet monkeys, 22
visual attentiveness, 19

W

Washington (state), 145, 146
weapon, xiii, 52, 54, 57, 60, 99

www.ingramcontent.com/pod-product-compliance
Lightning Source LLC
Chambersburg PA
CBHW050627280326
41932CB00015B/2551